GW01458674

"Through the decades with his work in astrology, Roy Gillett has been ahead of the curve, identifying critical milestones for humanity through the analysis of planetary cycles... that can inform, or inspire, those in position of influence, or us all, to make decisions that serve the greater good."   Maurice Fernandez

"'Astrological weather reports' are offered with his signature combination of practical wisdom, good suggestions, compassion, generosity of spirit and optimism. I always enjoy reading them."
                                                                        Melanie Reinhart

"... few astrologers can rival his mastery of the art. His virtuoso columns guide... into a larger understanding of collective events, a way of reading the sky that opens our awareness... precise insights that often have remarkable correlation with the events that follow, and yet never binds the reader with overly narrow predictions."
                                                                                Lynn Bell

"Roy has the ability to describe the astrology of current events in the light of a profound understanding of human nature. Experience in economics and Buddhism further enable him to integrate the mundane and spiritual sides of the science and art of astrology."
                                                                        Patricia Godden

"Having known and worked with Roy for nearly forty years, he is the nearest I have come to a master astrologer by his words and his actions."   Robert Currey

"For over twenty years, Roy Gillett has delighted astrologers with his insights on political affairs and current events... this beautifully presented compilation... would make a perfect keepsake for lovers of history and astrology."   Alex Trenoweth

"Roy's dedication to the art of mundane astrology is outstanding."
                                                                        Sharon Knight

"Whenever I'm not too sure about the astrological weather I know I can rely on Roy's *Working with the Planets* for some tips on navigation."   John Green

"Roy Gillett has been a mainstay of our UK astrological community for many years. It is a pleasure to follow his masterly 'take' on the ever-changing planetary picture during uniquely challenging times for us all in this long-awaited collection."   Anne Whitaker

Other books by Roy Gillett

Astrological Diaries 1978-1990
A Model of Health
Zen for Modern Living
The Essence of Buddhism
Astrology and Compassion the Convenient Truth
Economy Ecology and Kindness
The Secret Language of Astrology
Reversing the Race to Global Destruction
Winning Ways [with Carolyn Gillett]

To Stuart,
One Love,
Roy

Working with the Planets

Clearer Understanding   Better Decisions

Roy Gillett

Crucial Books

First published in 2021 by
Crucial Books,
Camberley GU15 1HU
http:/crucialbooks.co.uk/

A catalogue record for this book is available from the British Library.

ISBN 978-0-9956999-5-3

Printed and bound by Lightning Source

CONTENTS

Just as antidotes counteract poison, our destructive emotions can also be counteracted by constructive emotions like compassion. When you are warm-hearted everything else appears positive to you. In contrast, self-centeredness will only bring fear and negativities. Therefore, the practice of altruism is very necessary to retain warm-heartedness.

H H The Dalai Lama, speaking [11 November 2019] to Youth and community leaders from Washington State led by Cyrus Habib, the Lieutenant Governor of Washington.

Dedicated to our children, grandchildren and future generations that follow them. May they find wise and compassionate ways to heal and transform the exhausted, fractured world we generations of the twentieth century have bequeathed to them.

Author's Acknowledgements

This book is comprised of extracts from my 'Working with the Planets' column, written for the *Astrological Journal* between March 2002 and March 2021. Here they are linked with commentary and details of historical events at, and after, the time.

The copy submitted to the *Journals* was proofed, laid out and printed. The extracts in this book are drawn from the originally submitted copy. For this book, this has been re-proofed, with clarifying style/syntax improvements, and then laid out afresh. The full previously published versions can be obtained at https://www.astrologicalassociation.com/astrological-journal-shop/

I am most grateful to Chris Mitchell, whose forensic attention to detail has corrected, fine-tuned and encouraged improvement of my expression. This has put right quite a few of my 'Mars rushing away from Saturn in early Aries' oversights, that are always likely to undermine the Virgo Midheaven expression of an intelligent Aquarian stellium trined by the Moon in Gemini.[1]

The insights in this book are the product of incalculable hours, spent with fellow astrologers, for nearly fifty years now, sharing and deepening our knowledge and understanding of astro-cycles. The courage, persistence and integrity of this community of responsible astrologers offers wisdom, ready and willing to benefit the wider community, as it struggles to understand and master a rapidly changing future world.

As always, the profoundly kind and tireless persistence of Lama Thubten Zopa Rinpoche continues to generate hope. Without Rinpoche's example and my wife Carolyn's untiring support, my ability to offer these ideas would not have been possible and, in many other respects, any value of my life's endeavours would have been far less.

---

[1] I was born 10 February 1938 02:30 GMT, Tooting, London, UK (51N25, 0W10). Rodden rating a, from mother.

Images Acknowledgements

Charts and Other Astro-data

Generated by Solar Fire and AstroAnalyst software © Astrolabe Inc (https://alabe.com/)
Planetary Mandala Images in Chapter 3 created by Astrological Mandalas software © Astro Computing Services (https://astrocom.com/)

Pictures

Front Cover
Shutterstock – Abstract-space-stars-futuristic-new-age-135864119.
Back Cover:
Shutterstock – Patriotic-soldier-25221466, crisis-big-break-economic-financial-266278676, European Union and British Union Flag Flying against Big Ben in London 434358193, The City of Aleppo in Syria 1062013319.
Creative Commons Grenfell picture Natalie Oxford, CC BY 4.0, Brexit signpost: Christoph Scholz, CC BY-SA 2.0, Olympics in Tower Bridge Ivan Bandura, CC BY 2.0, Judgefloro, CC0, via Wikimedia Commons.

Inner Pages
Pages 23 & 33-34 images from the original *Astrological Journal* articles Astrological Association.
Shutterstock
Page 44 The City of Aleppo in Syria 1062013319, – Patriotic-soldier-25221466, **Page 85** Arrow_266278676.
Creative Commons
Page 35 "Nelson Mandela 1918-2013" Howdy, I'm H. Michael Karshis CC BY 2.0, **Page 44** Selected from UpstateNYer CC BY-SA 3.0. **Page 74** "Water Cycle" by Atmospheric Infrared Sounder, CC BY 2.0. **Page 88** Olympics in Tower Bridge, Ivan Bandura CC BY 2.0, Secret London 123 CC BY-SA 2.0. **Page 124** D. Trump Public Domain and Christoph Scholz, CC BY-SA 2.0. **Page 141** "Stay at Home text with marker" by focusonmore.com CC BY 2.0. **Page 156** "Catharsis" by jijake1977 CC BY 2.0. **Page 175** Labour Party Archives. **Page 176** Conversative and Labour Party Archives. **Page 177** votetoleavetheeu.co.uk. **Pages 183 & 243** "Seek Peace, And Pursue It " by takomabibelot CC0 1.0. **Page 187** "William Lilly, Astrologer and Occultist" by lisby1 CC PDM 1.0. **Page 191** Natalie Oxford, CC BY 4.0. **Page 221** "Beware" by plong is licensed under CC BY 2.0 **Page 234** Tim Dennell CC BY-NC 2.0. **Pages 239 & 278** From Kate Raworth Doughnut Economics (Endnote 224). **Page 254** "Peace, Love, Unity, and Respect Tattoo" by grantlairdjr CC BY 2.0. **Page 285** Bookplate The Royal Society (Great Britain), kladcat, CC 2.0 Generic.

Chapter 1
Understanding the Language of the Universe

Both astronomers and astrologers agree that the Universe is a vast complex mechanism of interdependently moving cycles that can be observed and predicted.

It is also agreed that the daily revolution of the Earth on its axis, the monthly cycle of the Moon around the Earth, the yearly elliptical path of the Earth around the Sun, all have clearly discernible effects on our life experience. They determine when it will be light or dark, hot or cold, high or low tide, measuring exactly in between extremes.

What we experience is the combined effect of our own position on the planet. We experience storms, droughts, heat waves. They happen due to the air's reaction to the Sun, Moon, the Earth itself, and indeed our own behaviour. We can see that each occurrence depends upon a unique set of circumstances, but none would occur that way without the exactly predictable terrestrial, lunar and solar cycles.

Is it just the Sun, Moon and Earth?
But that is not all! In our Solar System, there are seven (many still say eight) other planets, numerous dwarf planets, asteroids and comets, all drawn by our Sun's gravity, but also influenced by the gravitational attraction of each other. Withdraw any one of these bodies and the entire system will adjust. Take away Jupiter and it is unlikely that life on Earth would continue as it is, if at all. So, should we not consider the relationship, between all the Solar System and our life on Earth?

It is important to be clear what is meant by 'effect'. The Sun is a special source of light and heat, but the seasons of year depend on where you live on the Earth and the Earth's path around the Sun. The Moon's gravitational pull is close enough to draw and release liquids, such as the tides of water and sap in plants, but it requires water and plant life on Earth to do so.

However, we should not see planets as having a direct specific effect upon our life on Earth. Venus does not pour love and prosperity upon us. Indeed, we now know how poisonous and inhospitable life is there. It is the interactive path between the Earth and Venus, the pull and relaxation, as the two bodies move around the Sun that is the key. Through subtle changes in our pliable bodies and our general human activities, we experience love, harmony and create beauty. If conflicted by other planetary factors, there can also be the pain of losing these things.

All these points and planets are reference points. Astrologers use them, as does a surveyor with his theodolite looking to a stick placed at a crucial point in the distance. They focus on the position of a planet as it appears to move in front of a changing starry background. To measure, they divide this starry Celestial Sphere into twelve equal segments (named after, but not the same as actual constellations). From these measurements, they track cycles, to which they have allocated key words and concepts. These are combined into a complex descriptive interactive pattern of what pulls, pushes, traumatises, opens, closes, oppresses, releases the myriad experiences of our lives (fully explained in *Astrology and Compassion the Convenient Truth* [1]).

By juxtaposing the words and phrases, given to each point in the heavens, astrologers create a vast story of the nature and possible progress of people the unfolding situations they face

The ancient and modern understandings of life

Yes, for thousands of years humanity has looked to the heavens and compared these cycles to life on Earth. Why are people so excited and accident-prone, when the Moon's disc is largest? Why does love and generosity seem to grow when Venus and Jupiter are close and builds ever stronger as the Full Moon comes near?

Encouraged by such observations, astronomers/astrologers developed an interpretive language of living names and definitions that they applied strictly to their mechanical observations. Recent discoveries have uncovered their remarkably precise instruments, used with language focused on interpretation, not, as is today's astronomy, mere physical measuring divorced from any meaning.

Ancient astrologers (and those that continue their work today) may not have had the practical controls over the planet and space travel, as modern astronomers and their engineers do, but in very many ways, both had (and have) a better understanding of its nature. They integrated their observations of the changing patterns of human nature and life on Earth with their measurements of the moving cycles of the planets. All this they built into psychological insights combined into stories that explained the deep stresses, strains and resolution of Universal Understanding. By removing all this and relegating mythology to 'primitive', modern astronomers rip out the very soul of meaning from our lives.

Chasm of misunderstanding and mutual disrespect

Since the seventeenth century the chasm of misunderstanding between astronomy and astrology has widened. Now the latter is dismissed as outdated superstition, unworthy of consideration.

Tragically, this gap between ancient and modern ways of understanding the Universe leaves a key void in today's world, abandons us in a hyperactive wasteland of angst and facile distraction.

Humanity may have made unbelievable practical advances, but it remains as, if not more, ignorant of the differences between people and the world's cyclic changes. Crises come and go, seeming out of our control. We rely on mere whims, flirt with (are easily led along) fruitless, often highly wasteful paths, seduced by leaders we do not know and nearly always let us down.

Re-integrating astronomical and astrological understanding
The prosperity, precise focus and communication potential of the modern world has established a wonderful potential for greater tolerance and support between identities, groups and nations. Missing is an organically reliable language, with which to understand each other. What happens and might change, as we move into the future?

It is a grand paradox that we deny the very knowledge that would fill this void. We merely need to allow in and integrate the modern tools of astronomy with the ancient language of astrology. We need not go back to primitive superstition, but systematically to test the language in the modern world. Superstitious and corrupt distortions of the knowledge can be identified and dismissed. Others could prove to be just what we need. Blind faith is not required: rather open-minded respect.

André Barbault's *Planetary Cycles*[2] is a rigorously systematic study of mundane events alongside an uncompromisingly complete listing of outer-planetary angular relationships (aspects). It revealed clear and helpful indications that anticipated political and social developments in what could have been radically helpful ways.

This book consists of extracts from my 'Working with the Planets' column, written over twenty years in the bi-monthly *Astrological Journal*. They have a looser, more advisory approach, which the next chapter explains in more detail. They show that the expertise of the modern mind, together with the intelligent soul language of astrology, along with compassion, combine to make a reliable three-legged stool upon which we can base a much happier future.

Chapter 2
Universal Understanding Ourselves

Attachment is the driving force of creation. Intuitively the new-born baby is urged towards the mother's breast, finding comfort in this essential source of its growth. Months later, as the baby first senses its separate identity, it can cry in terror should the comforting parent leave the room. With a developing sense of time and space comes the ability to select, even to wait, but not for too long!

In adolescence, the parent – so prized, even faultless for all those childhood years – can become the obstacle, the barrier to the daring fun that those precious peer-group friends seem to be having. Someone close promises to be a friend for ever. Particular shared convictions, causes and interests seem super-alive. They must occupy the essential pattern of our lives. All those other things we 'have to do' are barely tolerated. They just get in the way.

So, we emerge into the adult world seeking support for the half-understood opinions and wishes that have sparkled our teenage years into purpose, loves that we were sure 'will last for ever'. Then can come marriage, children and the unexpected endless pressure of responsibility. This narrows the possibility of teenage idealism, as we struggle to find some space for its free-loving fun. Social life becomes a prized way to tolerate, even escape from, work and family responsibility. Many live for weekends and holidays, to get beyond themselves, through drink, sport, being spectators of other people's lives.

We are free to feed ourselves, to choose whom to love and what we love to do. Yet attachment remains in the fear we might lose that which we hold most dear. We need like-minded friends, a celebrity to look up to, something to believe in, a sporting team, a view of the way of the world, a political philosophy, a religion, or non-religion. Crucially we still need something that defines our world, underpins the decisions we have to make for ourselves, our family and friends. We feel more comfortable with those that share such views – awkward with those who do not seem to. Becoming trapped in such states of mind, are we all that much distant from dependence on our mother's breast?

Trapped in our own narrow world view
The world is formed into sub-groups, sharing common interests. Many of these at best tolerate each other with gentle, well-intentioned banter. Because their lives are based on partial understanding, each sub-group,

from the devoted sporting-team supporter through various forms of academic expertise to the fanatical racial supremacist, are ripe for exploitation. Rabble-rousers encourage us to argue, struggle, even fight for what we believe in. Family breakups, football hooliganism, institutional racialism and social unrest, financial and employment exploitation, refugees and war, all emanate from dependence, sometimes fierce – a limited understanding of the wider world. Have we really moved on from that baby-screaming-like attachment?

Universal understanding
Seeking to see beyond all this, our forebears looked up from the Earth, measured, and created a language to describe the patterns of our lives in relation to the light of the Sun, Moon, planets and stars that seemed to move around us. Most of today's astronomers claim that the language of astrology is primitive superstition. Yet their own astronomical terms, general European languages, and today's legal system, literary and psychological understanding, all remain based on a classical tradition, at the heart of which was this astrological understanding.

Instead, today's world makes its decisions upon a mechanical material and economic model that seeks and applies linear causes with the minimum of variables. When a variable undermines outcomes, research is undertaken to narrow down the outcome, until a result is entirely predictable in all, or nearly all, circumstances. Such mechanical rigour is invaluable in practical and specific action areas of life, but dangerously divisive in human understanding of relationships.

Here modern science leaves today's humanity out on a limb of uncertainty. How shall we use its wonderful discoveries? Exploit them to the maximum, even if this destroys life on the planet? Celebrate its brilliant creation of a vaccine that protects against Covid-19?

When, to what, and to whom we should turn? There seems to be nowhere to turn, but conflicting traditional religions, the impossible search for scientific perfection, personal prejudice, scapegoating of others, or pure and simple hedonism. Consume, enjoy yourself for as long as you can get away with it!

Astrological clarity helps fill crucial gaps in our lives
Quite simply, can astrology fill the gap between ourselves and the modern mechanical world? It can! By understanding ourselves and timing the way fashion and events will change, it explains not only what might happen; it also provides background to illuminate the best and worst possible ways to cope in a constantly changing world.

Astrology offers vital, deep understanding of underlying astro-cycles that drive personal and social trends and indicate how long they will last. By understanding the controls, we do not lose control. Its relieving clarity releases our subconscious memory from a screaming feeling that the whole world is coming to an end, when mummy withdraws the breast, or leaves the room.

Knowing other people, groups, and the times we are living through as they really are, we are no longer trapped, dependent on a partial view of reality. We can rise up much wiser from the desperate need to win, to conquer, to convert, to attack, to cheat for personal gain, to fear, to defend, to create a protective wall between ourselves and everything we do not understand.

By knowing the astro-cycles behind people and events, we begin to respect and appreciate others. We cease to base judgement in terms of ourselves, or the prejudices of our background. We begin to understand what it is like from the other person's side. We see what happens, not as conspiracy created by nasty opponents, but rather a circumstance we all face together in our different ways.

Now comes the next vital step. By taking this objective knowledge about each other and our groups sympathetically on board we are drawn to see the world through other people's eyes. We see their predicament. We can empathise, feel what happens to them – their disappointments, fears, joy, hopes – as though it were our experience. We can feel and act towards them with compassion. We can see the problems between us as something we can solve together.

The proof of the pudding is in the eating
Since March 2002, I have been writing a bi-monthly column for the *Astrological Journal* called 'Working with the Planets', focusing in detail on the astro-cycles of the next two months. It describes how life might be experienced and advises on the longer term. These explanations use the very language of astrology, key words attributed to astro-cycles, developed by our astrologer forebears over thousands of years.

Today, applying keywords to planets, other points and areas of the heavens (named after apparent star-groupings) might seem unscientific, arbitrary superstition. Yet this language was developed empirically from myriad observations of carefully measured planetary positions in relation to what the astrologers saw happening on Earth. Should we throw the language away, or seek ways to relate it to our modern astronomical understanding of the heavens?

Check it out for yourself.

❖ If you are a beginner, first learn a little of the language. My book *The Secret Language of Astrology* is carefully designed to be accessible to seriously interested beginners.[3] Spend as long as you can, ideally a year, in a part of the world with a clear sky. Watch the movement of the Sun, Moon and planets against the starry background. Compare this with the changing moods and events on Earth. See for yourself that it works. If you cannot travel now, just read and use *The Secret Language of Astrology*. Create birth charts for yourself and friends, using its online calculator.

❖ If experienced with astrology, you are ready to go.

See and judge for yourself
The key passages that follow are from more than a hundred articles originally published in the *Astrological Journal*, between March 2002 and March 2021. If you wish to read the original presentation with illustrations, all issues are available online at the Association's website.[4]

Chapters 3 to 8 present extracts of these articles. The extracts in Chapter 3 explain my ways of understanding and using astrology, as well as its shortcomings, with warnings about misuse. Chapters 4 to 7 examine specific themes, using the timing of events that were contemporary when the original articles were published.

Decide for yourself, not only the accuracy of the commentary and the understanding of the fundamental future issues, but also the quality of the advice. How different may the outcome of the years 2002-2021 have been if the information had been more widely understood and the advice taken?

See for yourself whether an understanding of astro-cycles offers wisdom. Does it stop desperate clinging to views that alienate us into fragmentary experience of our world? Astrology is not a religion. It should not and cannot replace the beliefs you hold most dear. On the contrary, it should help you understand and feel more comfortable with them and yourself. Astrology is not a belief system to fight for. It is a tool, an insightful language to use. It is available in the same way to everyone, as we go our separate ways; our universal holistic heart of understanding. Crucial question! If listened to at the time, would the advice have been useful? Could it have helped us make better decisions, live more happily together?

Read the extracts, alongside the events they refer to. Does astrology offer universal understanding? Decide for yourself.

This sixteenth-century engraving illustrates the two choices that face us. To be blindfolded following the ups and downs of chance, or to see ourselves as we are in the mirror of the zodiac and so direct our way clearly.

Five hundred years later, this indispensable wisdom is even more needed, as our domineering twenty-first-century power wrestles with the realities of our environment.

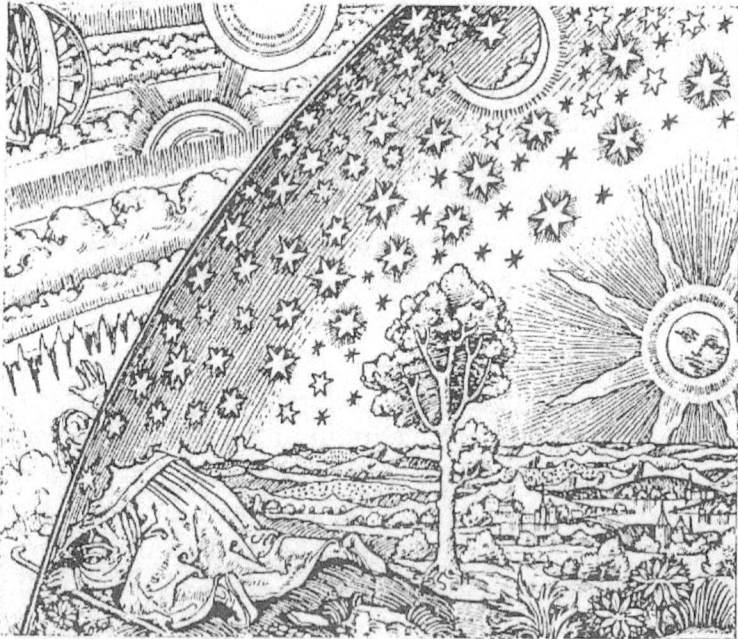

Heading the early pages in my 1979 first mundane astrology quarterly, and innumerable times before and after, these two Renaissance engravings clearly display the eternal role of astrological understanding in human existence.

Chapter 3
See Astrology Working

Rather than the systematic introduction to the concepts of astrology and their integration, outlined so beautifully in *The Secret Language of Astrology*, this chapter offers a first taste of the experience of using astrology – both in my own life and the way I observe the world in action.[5]

As well as showing how to use the mechanics, the selection reveals astrology working. It describes my personal experience, alongside insight into the neat ways astrology fits and reflects events exactly. So, it deepens our understanding of what is happening – even, maybe, what to do about it.

The very first 'Working with the Planets' column, published March 2002, introduced my approach to astrology, and so the foundation of the interpretations.

Astrology changed my life in the early 1970s. A major moment was when I started to track the transiting Moon around my natal chart. Oh, that burst of freedom, when the Moon crossed from the twelfth house on to my Sagittarian Ascendant! That grin of wry amusement, when month after month friends rarely called when the Moon was transiting my empty Capricorn second house, but crashed in on each other to be with me the next couple of days, when it was transiting my Mercury, Jupiter, Sun and Venus in Aquarius in the second and especially the third houses. It was all so right and predictable!

As months grew into years, I started to build up an understanding of the Sun's slower, but even stronger and longstanding indications. Then came the wonders of witnessing the effects of retrogression. How communications and commitments struggled to be clear and complete during Mercury's hanging back. How romance and business arrangements dallied and teased during the less frequent Venus retrogrades. How the focus of action seemed dominated in a particular way for some months during the Mars retrograde every other year. Then there were the annual breathings in and out of the outer-planetary retrogrades.

After several years of thumbing the ephemeris, then scanning my birth chart and those of friends in my spare time, it became clear I had hit on a system of analysis that was far more effective than anything I had learned in a four-year Bachelor of Education degree. So, in 1976 the real work began. I gave up teaching and started to travel the world with astrology as my guide. Every three months, I would create a diary with daily Sun and Moon positions, exact aspect and ingress times, plus lunar phenomena, including void of course and ingress timings. Each day, actions were guided by the planetary situation. Some days I would act appropriately – others inappropriately. Experiencing the difference between working with and against the planetary flow was indeed enlightening. Main events that happened were written in the diary. After two years and many thousands of miles, from 1978 three-monthly booklets were published. From 1984 until 1990 these became annual diaries.

Following daily astro events in this and far more advanced ways will be familiar, daily practice for many of you. Some may have done it for so long that now you only need to check up occasionally, when you are surprised by something very special. If you have never tried this, do give it a go. You can collect and write up the information from a printed ephemeris, as I did. Nowadays it is easier than this. You can just print out lists of transits and daily charts from a good computer program, or purchase an annual astrological diary. There are sites online that output reliable birth charts for free.[6] Never forget that the figures are the interpreter's friend. They tell you how the planets move and how they move is what they mean.

In this way we will learn astrology through our own experience, become aware of the challenges and opportunities we have to work with and how the world we are living in is likely to be. Working out what is happening and may come up for ourselves makes life as liberating as it can be. So, this column will not aim to give an exhaustive technical list of astro events, or daily descriptions and predictions. Instead, it leaves you to collect this information from your books and software and then helps you interpret for yourself. It will offer my own experience of how the planets work and some in-depth assessments of major events in the period immediately ahead.

Retrogression: There is no need to 'shut up shop' until the direct station – just the need to be careful. Retrogrades do not work like an on and off switch, but dynamically. Run your fingers down an ephemeris column. When the planet is farthest from its retrogression period it covers the greatest distance each day. From this it slows to the point it appears to stand still, then it eases backward and speeds up steadily and until it reaches its maximum retrograde speed, then it slows again to the direct station, then speeds to maximum forward speed and so on. Every part of this process is important in interpreting events. The retrograde station and subsequent speeding up times bring inattention and the discovery of pre-station errors. The slowing to direct period can be quite productive, if handled with patient careful attention to detail. From the direct station to maximum forward speed is the safest time to make decisions. From then until the retrograde station is a time to watch out for errors caused by rash decisions. Such errors may not be discovered until after the subsequent retrograde station.

Applying and separating astro events: Anyone who has stood on a railway platform, while an express train is passing will understand this already. As the train approaches, a sense of alarm, pressure, noise and anticipation grows. As it rushes through the station, we can do nothing but experience the event. Once it has passed and has faded into the distance, we are usually safe, but should be careful of delayed effects. Maybe something thrown from, or moved by, the train rushes towards us in the wind. Astrological aspects work very much in the same way. The anticipation of an applying difficult aspect can bring great fear that clouds decision-making and can actually make matters worse. This is one of the reasons why some priests counsel their 'innocent' flock against using astrology. We guard against this by putting our faith in being as honest, decent and careful as we can. Expectation can ruin a good aspect. It can create an air of greedy attachment, which blocks the benefit the aspect should bring. The moment of exactness is a time to act with great skill, or to do nothing more than observe and learn. We can get on with our lives in the light of the new experience during the separating phase, but do not take things for granted, especially while the aspect is within separating orb.

Retrogression and aspects: Retrogression can lead to aspects repeating themselves in a range of ways. Most frequently, it causes three rather than just the one exactness. The first event is usually the most powerful, because it brings real and often unexpected experiences for good or bad. The second, being the result of retrogression, brings a new perspective to the now familiar situation. The third tends to complete the process and leave us free to move on. Other moments to consider are when one or other of the planets crosses a point where the first astro event occurred, or when a third planet does this. The outer planets can make more than three aspect hits. There is much more to consider in future *Journals*.

-oOo-

The May 2002 column explained other key considerations that I take into account when interpreting.

Prophecy or social healing? We have all met those people, who 'in confidence' offer to share the secret of a crucial astrological detail they have 'discovered' and the deduced outcome that will make them 'famous'. Then there are those embarrassing newspaper predictions. 'A Uranus transit focused on Normalville will lead to a massive earthquake there'. Such actions trap astrology in an infertile double bind, where the only possible outcome is loss on all sides. To be famous as the predictor of massive death and destruction is hardly a cause for celebration. The expectation heaped upon astrologers in the massive glare of publicity afterwards would simply terrorise us and disappoint the public. Study Cassandra in the Greek tragedy *Agamemnon*, to know the fate of accurate prophets. More likely the prediction will not happen and so becomes recorded as another failure for astrology. Astrology is abused, when we seek to fix the future with our limited minds.

Astrology is much more useful as a diagnostic tool that measures pressures, possibilities and social trends. Understanding these guides our lives skilfully and can turn dire dangers into learning and positive transformation. Astrologer-prophets must put aside their egocentric need for recognition and develop skilfully beneficial ways to publicise likely dangers. They may help to 'save the world', but are unlikely to be recognised and thanked for it. Even if we do not have their self-consciously 'lofty' aims, astrology helps us know about and face negativity. The calmer and more aware we are when driving along the road, the less chance there is of an accident, however badly others are behaving.

Magical errors: Have you ever been progressing really well through a session with a client only to realise the time of birth is wrong? Then there are mistakes with time zones and all sorts of other embarrassingly silly errors that you kick yourself for. Take heart! If the motivation of the work was free of ego, then you can be sure the mistake was made for a very good reason. Such mistakes, I prefer to call 'magical errors'. Maybe the error in time describes a major distortion in the client's view of his or her self – especially likely, if it was twelve hours, changing AM to PM. The zone error in the March 'Working with the Planets' was like that. The energy of 26 May to 10 June 2002 is so intense that it needs a very special, three-step focus consisting of: a first statement, an error slip with charts and comments and now the deeper analysis that follows in this piece.

More about retrogression: It is a real insight to see the paths planets draw over time. Make a mark for each daily position. These form into a linear path. The mandalas below show these paths, which play on our consciousness. Their shapes are caused by the total and very physical force of gravity – the sum total of the whole mechanism of the Universe, as related to the Earth and that body. Below is the familiar annual geocentric pattern Mercury makes to the Earth, then what happens in six years. For comparison, the patterns of Venus and Mars over six years are also shown.[7]

A picture tells a thousand stories. Let your eyes rest on the diagrams, realising that every point in these cycles is relevant to the planets' 'influence' on events. Look for the moment of slowing and station in forward and retrograde. See how the loop completes, where the lines cross – possibly a crucial trigger point. Most of all look for the beauty and symmetry of how astrology works.

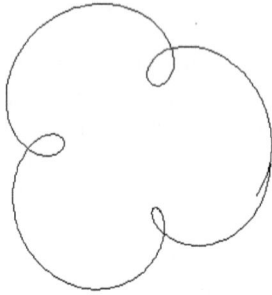

Mercury from Earth 1 year

Mercury from Earth 6 years

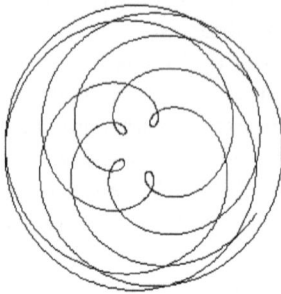

Venus from Earth 6 years

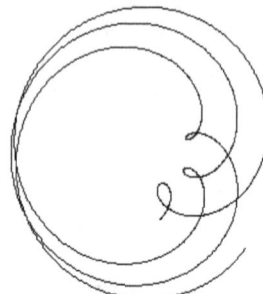

Mars from Earth 6 years

Jupiter is retrograde for around four months, Saturn five months and Uranus, Neptune and Pluto for nearly half the year. When they are, their individual energies turn inward, reflecting and readjusting upon us. As more and more of them 'gang up' to do this together, the overall development of projects 'breaths in' for long periods each year through the time of maximum retrogrades, then out as they go direct.

-o0o-

The September 2002 column contrasts the limited tools available to astrologers in the twentieth century, with what was not possible, following with the evolving potential of computer technology.

In the days before computers, Raphael's Ephemeris, or one of those 'new-fangled' 10-, 50-, or 100-year American ones, was all we had to support an instant reading. Unless we had an hour to sit down and write it all out, we would do it 'in our heads'. Firstly, look through the birth planets and make a rough calculation of the Ascendant/Midheaven and house allocations. Then, holding all that in mind, look for and interpret the progressions and transit hits. The pressure was a fertile force on our active young brains. Being so close to the columns of figures we became intimate with the minutiae of the planetary movements. Familiarity bred understanding and some remarkably accurate delineations and predictions emerged from this maelstrom of mental activity.

Today, it is not even necessary to know how to do the calculations before you interpret. Conscientious computer programming, guided by some of the most experienced minds in astrology, means that for a one-off payment of a few hundred pounds, you can have limitless astro information conveniently in front of you in no time at all. Great! But let us never forget that it is still as important to study the day-by-day movements and special features of the planets. Return to your printed ephemeris from time to time, or most astro-software will print one! Look down the columns. Study the latitude, or daily motion as well as longitude. If your software has animation features, set the tools to move backward and forward at varying speeds – watch and learn from the dynamics of the heavens.

-oOo-

The January 2003 column explained astrology's value in defining relationships between people and phenomena, free of cultural assumptions.

> As soon as we take refuge in something that is
> dependent on something else, we take a prejudiced
> view, and so do not see clearly. *The Essence of Buddhism*[8]

Do you remember that ground-breaking television series *The Ascent of Man*?[9] One programme showed how the instruments that we use for looking can have a radical effect on what we see. Similarly, rich, poor, black, white, Muslim, Jew, Christian and others make judgements by looking from their different perspectives. What they see is determined largely by what their culture holds to be true – not just the object itself. When people go further and assume their relative viewpoint is absolutely true, problems begin.

Although cultural assumptions can influence astrological method, astrology's big advantage in the main is that it looks at all cultures and people from the same perspective. No race, religion, or social position gives the person or event we study more importance. The transits of the time connect to different groups and individuals in different ways and lead to a variety of outcomes. The main thrust of the astrological thesis stays the same. Every person and moment of time is unique, but moments consist of cycles that have repeated countless times. So we can build up and combine past experiences to understand the present and be better prepared for the future.

People's unique astrological make-up indicates how they see phenomena and act. Knowing one's own make-up frees understanding from personal and cultural assumptions and opens the door to a clearer world. A paradox indeed! The main reason people who do not understand astrology reject it is that they do not wish their lives 'to be controlled'!

If they use astrology properly, it will not be! I have noticed three levels of use – each leading to a different outcome. If we ignore the astro-cycles, then things tend to happen automatically. In such circumstances, it is easier for astrologers to predict the future. If we use our understanding of the cycles to serve our egocentric greed and hatred, any short-term gains will turn to traumatically negative outcomes. If we use our astro-skills to step outside our personal and cultural viewpoint and see things from as many perspectives as possible, our understanding becomes more complete. We become more effective. For we avoid the counterproductive error of insisting that our way of seeing is respected and listened to, then using this platform of 'truth' to deny the same right to others.

Genuine truth does not exclude, but includes by understanding everyone and everything appropriately. It eases conflict by dissolving barriers of ignorance. The magic key is to find ways of giving permission, without encouraging exploitation. Then everyone learns.

-o0o-

The November 2004 column moves on from general approaches to astrology, to focus on a single concept – leaders with planets in the twelfth house. In doing so, it explains the root cause of the degenerate horror that then, and in the coming decades of the twenty-first century, would sour international relations.

Political Pointers
The Problems and Possibilities of Twelfth-House Rulers

Even before our Prime Minister [Tony Blair] was first elected in 1997 it was noted that he had five planets in his twelfth house.[10] Then we noticed Gordon Brown had six.[11] We wondered what to expect from this New Labour government. I wrote in the *Astrological Journal* at the time pointing out that twelfth-house people are so self-driven that you had to trust them, or lock them up! The piece then proceeded to focus on possible idealistic, almost saintly manifestations of the energy. Well, it did fit the mood of the time!

Seven years on, the more mundane expressions of the twelfth house can be seen in public life in all their discomfort: the tendency for the reins of power to be tightly controlled in fewer and fewer hands; the growth of spin and press briefing; more and more Labour Party members, who feel left out and not properly informed or consulted; a public that feels ignored and not sure if it wants to be served in that way at all. The Prime Minister's basic position over the War in Iraq – to control from behind the scenes, but generously accept that 'everyone should be respected for their opinion' is typically twelfth house. Most amusing is the long-standing claim of a rift between Tony Blair and his Piscean Chancellor [Gordon Brown]. The two hardly speak about it, but friends stir the pot. The struggle is reported to continue from a distance – 'Chinese whispers' at two hundred yards?

A whole article could be devoted to details of Britain's experience of twelfth-house rule and it does not stop there. George Bush has the Sun in Cancer in this house.[12] Using Placidus, Vladimir Putin's Sun is in Libra in the twelfth.[13] All in all, we have two Pisceans, a Cancerian and a Libran, all anxious signs with anxious twelfth-house Suns, making decisions that fundamentally affect the quality of life we are allowed to experience. Are they creating, or answering, the problems we face?

Essentially twelfth-house Suns do not trust others. So, their solution to most problems is greater control and inspection, to get into everyone else's twelfth house and find out what they are up to. We are told that the War on Terror justifies Homeland Security in the US and Identity Cards in Britain. It is interesting that the man in charge of this for us is Home Secretary David Blunkett, whose Sun applies to conjunct Uranus in Gemini in the twelfth house.[14] Also, his Ascendant-ruling Moon is in Capricorn in the seventh house!

As well as setting in place intrusive systems, which, even if not intended to be, are ready-made for future totalitarian rule, twelfth-house leaders can bring a deeper danger. The consequences of their reactions to threats and terrorist acts can be lethally uncompromising. It is so difficult for them to trust anything unfamiliar. They never ask whether they may be a partial cause of the problem. They rarely consider whether reaching out to bridge understanding might be the easiest way to remove the danger. Instead, they interpret the desperate acts of desperate people as proof of evil in others that must be rooted out. Could it be that the reactions of the dominant twelfth-house Sun world leaders (bear in mind we do not have reliable times of birth for the Muslim leaders) is creating a world culture where all of us are being forced to live unnatural, terrorised twelfth-house lives?

Conversely, it can be argued that all times throw up leaders ideally suited to those times. During the Pluto-in-Leo Second World War, we had larger-than-life leaders ready to deal with death on a large scale – Hitler, Stalin, Churchill, Roosevelt. Only Stalin remained in power after the war. In the frantically communicating, mutually receiving Aquarian/Piscean energy of the early twenty-first century years, we can live in each other's homes through travel, the media and the internet. So, we need to develop understanding and trust. We need to deal with secrets. We need to understand each other's deepest urges. We need to develop methods that prevent us treading brutally on feelings. Maybe the pain of misunderstanding that dominates right now is a first step in 'saying it as it is' and dealing with the outrage. Time will tell whether our present twelfth-house rulers have the spiritual depth and breadth to guide us from present defensive acrimony through to a positive experience of global intimacy.

-o0o-

The March 2005 column considered the astrology of the 2005 South-East Asia Tsunami.

> ...[we] shall know commonwealth again.
> From bitter searching of the heart,
> ...we rise to play a greater part.
>   Leonard Cohen *Villanelle for Our Time*
>   *'Dear Heather' Album* (2004)

In the previous issue, we looked ahead with some trepidation to the Saturn / Nodal axis T-square for the first half of 2005, with an ongoing cardinal grand cross for two to three months after the 2004 Winter Solstice.

Planets in cardinal signs suggest pressure that stirs - the stronger the change to cardinal the greater the stirring. Could the true Nodal axis, retrograding back across the Taurus-Aries/Scorpio-Libra axis (07:29 GMT) the day of the Cancer-Capricorn Full Moon (15:06 GMT) on 26 December 2004 and on its way to T-square Saturn in detriment in Cancer (with Mars just into Sagittarius) indicate the earth-changing pressure, activating a terrible tsunami?

Several colleagues have noticed the relationship between the Full Moon and the Indian and Indonesian Republic charts, others have looked at aspects to the 2002 eclipse. Most notable was N. Venkatanathan and his team, who presented a report about a possible Indonesian earthquake on 22 December to members of the Department of Science and Technology, New Delhi, that was within 157.11899 km and 28 minutes of the place and time of the actual event.[15] They were using their 'planetary angular momentum theory.' Is their work astronomy, geophysics, astrophysics, or astrology, or all four? Does it matter? When knowledge respects other knowledge, we will know more – maybe enough to save lives and alleviate suffering.

Atisha was a great Indian scholar, who is credited with bringing the systematic knowledge of Buddhism to Tibet in the first millennium CE. Before this, with firm kindness he mastered horrific storms during a thirteen-month voyage on his way to an island (claimed to be modern-day Sumatra) to visit a great teacher. Has the tragedy of our modern-day tsunami generated compassion that cuts through the labels of friend and enemy, good and evil, freedom and terrorism? Are we not all living beings, seeking happiness and wishing happiness for others?

It was interesting to note that one of the first consequences of the Tsunami disaster was (maybe unfairly) to put George Bush and Tony Blair on the defensive. At the same time this natural disaster did take the ongoing horror in Iraq off the front pages for a while.

The consequences of the Tsunami, Iraq and many other problems remain as cardinal tasks to be resolved during the first half of 2005. The problems will be solved when we remember what other people face is as traumatic, or worse, as what we are facing. Few solutions are found by pointing the finger and eradicating 'the accused' – that is how we created the problem in the first place. When situations seem absolutely impossible, we can only stop hating and fighting and open our hearts instead. It is amazing how many imagined 'enemies' turn to helpful friends when we do. If the world learns that lesson from the tsunami, then 220,000 people will not have died in vain.[16]

-o0o-

The July 2006 column offered a detailed understanding of the Jupiter/Saturn cycle and how we can understand and use this knowledge most beneficially.

'As you sow, so shall you reap'; St Paul's reminder to the Galatians (6:7) is often cited as the closest the Christian church comes to the law of karma. To astrologers it is a fascinating way to look at the cycles of the interactions of Jupiter and Saturn. To do so will especially help us understand the period from August to the end of October this year.

As is often the case with astrology, by focusing on the obvious, we come to realise something really profound – this is especially so with Jupiter and Saturn. The former moves nearly two and a half times faster than the latter. So, they are conjunct every twenty years and opposed at the ten years in between. Jupiter hurries from the conjunction, then ten years later starts to hurry back from the opposition to a new conjunction. It is when we consider the relationship of each of these planets to mundane, natal, progressed and directed planets that the implications become interesting. The further Jupiter is from the conjunction with Saturn, the longer it takes for Saturn to reach the point Jupiter was when it was conjunct, or otherwise aspected, to another planet. Hence, in the area of life represented by that connected planet, Jupiter's expansive over-optimism remains unchecked and not confronted by the reality and structural requirements of Saturn for longer and longer periods. In addition, looked at the other way, the nearer Jupiter is to a new conjunction, the shorter is the time between the experience of Saturn's frustration and difficulty being relieved by expansive opportunity. Hence the waning phase of Jupiter / Saturn is a time when we think we can 'get away with it' and probably actually can do so! We think we can sow opportunities, without reaping consequent responsibilities.

The first quarter of the cycle from a Jupiter/Saturn conjunction to the next one is very different – no sooner have we expanded into some exciting new possibilities than barriers and problems arise. This is our present situation. In 2003, with Saturn in Gemini and Jupiter in Leo, it was easy to put our intelligence to one side, take pride in our 'imperial ambitions' and have a good time. Now with Jupiter in Scorpio about to square Saturn in Leo, we are living to curse and be cursed for the consequences of our actions then. Having so recently sown the seeds of our egocentricity, we now find there is little to be proud of – just a passionate desire that cannot be satisfied and the brutality of blame just around the corner.

In the last issue, we saw the pressure of the eight-pointed star, formed by a double grand cross in the Summer Solstice chart, as an initiation gateway.[17] Whoever could dedicate the time to reconciliation would come through wiser and be a source for happiness. Whoever could only see black negativity and causes for conflict would be trapped and faced with just that bearing down and oppressing them. As you read this, many will be reeling with relief and / or helplessness from the experience. Perhaps you may feel it is too early to work out whether what has happened will be ultimately for the good, or something dark and impossible – maybe a bit of both for most of us.

-o0o-

The September 2006 column included a remarkable example of how pressure to the angles, especially the Ascendant of moment can graphically describe what actually happens.

Keep an Eye on Those Aspect Lines!

Drawing in aspect lines and making them thicker the tighter the orb may not always look elegant, but it can help us pick out the planetary pressures as they ebb and flow.

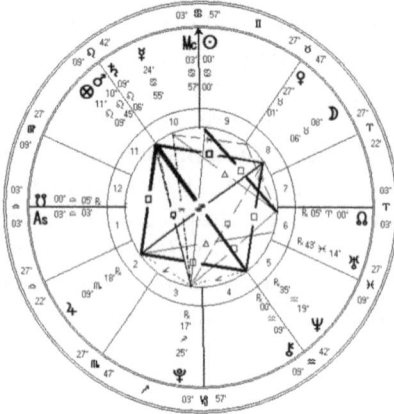

Summer Solstice 2006
21 Jun 2006 13:27 BST -1:00
Amesbury, UK 51°N10' 001°W45'
Geocentric Tropical Placidus True Node

This is important, because it advances our concepts of planets and derived planets in sign, house, rulership, strength, etc. beyond just expressing them as boxes of meaning. While these 'boxes' are vital tools of analysis, they are enhanced when viewed as a continuous dynamic flow of intensifying and relaxing planetary strengths, working just like the actual movement of planets in space. In predicting and measuring the increasing and decreasing strength of these pressures lies the science of astrology. In assessing and helping the free will within each of us to deep understanding of the archetypes and reacting in the happiest way to them, lies its art and potential for magic.

What happened during this year's Summer Solstice public access at Stonehenge provided a fascinating practical example of this , especially the importance of considering the transiting angles of the mundane chart. The access attracts a lively and varied range of people. We were building towards a double grand cross, but this year's preparations went surprisingly smoothly, as we gathered on site the night before the solstice day.

However, and perhaps instead, the weather that night seemed to be brewing up a storm. At 10 pm, as we entered the monument field, there were ominous spots of rain and a freshening wind in the darkening sky. We sensed the drama of being at sea on an approaching stormy night. 17,000 people were in the open air around the stones with little or no shelter. How would they 'ride the storm' of the coming night hours?

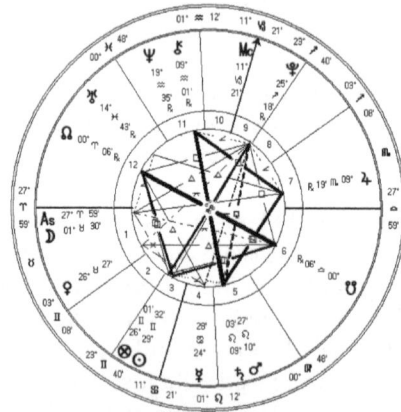

Kings Drummers
21 Jun 2006 02:00 BST -1:00
Amesbury, UK 51°N10' 001°W45'
Geocentric Tropical Placidus True Node

Every year a performing percussion orchestra with dancers and torch bearers' call up the Sun by processing around the field and then presenting an amazing standing set of synchronised drumming. They were to assemble at 2 am and to start not more than half an hour later. With the Moon having entered Taurus a few hours earlier, but the Ascendant not to enter Taurus until around 02:05, we were not surprised to see our earlier Arian enthusiasm blocked by practical problems. Someone had dipped some of the flares in the fire-safety water buckets, not in paraffin! Then the rain started in earnest! Having been delayed by a BBCE interview, I arrived at the venue around 02:20 BST to see the moving-rope crowd barrier established and the first torches about to be lit. What usually was a few-minutes process, this year was agonisingly slow. One torch lit reluctantly, was given to another, then both dwindled.

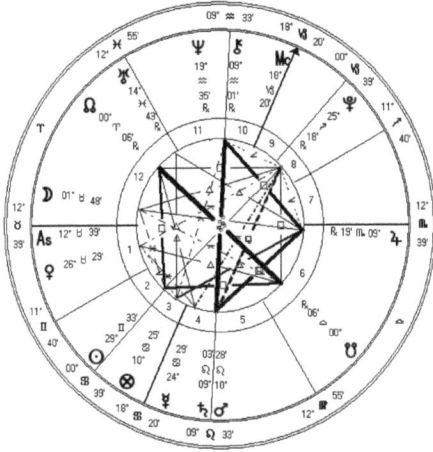

Kings Drummers 2
21 Jun 2006 02:30 BST -1:00
Amesbury, UK 51°N10' 001°W45'
Geocentric Tropical Placidus True Node

At 02:30 BST, with the Ascendant of the moment still separating from a grand cross and applying to square Neptune, the chief crowd-marshal's desperation grew. Thousands were becoming ever-closer packed and the procession should now be underway. Instead, as the drenching rain intensified, the dancers and drummers were pressed in a shrinking centre – a low and bent group. They had eight torches held close together, skilfully making the heat of all of them dry every flare sufficiently for each to stay alight when held high on its own. It was one of those Taurus experiences that seem to take forever!

Fortunately, as the Ascendant separated from its square to Neptune in Aquarius, the flares did hold their fire separately and the procession got under way. By 03:00, with the Ascendant now approaching the Taurus-ruling Venus to form a grand trine / kite with the MC and Nodal axis, the sound and light captivated the thousands that thronged around. The sheer audacity of the fire and force of the sound seemed to evaporate the rain and blow back the clouds. As the Ascendant entered Gemini thirteen minutes later, we reached the allocated performance place, from where all were both excited and enchanted by the wild (yet precisely controlled) timing, impact, pause and the texture of the playing.

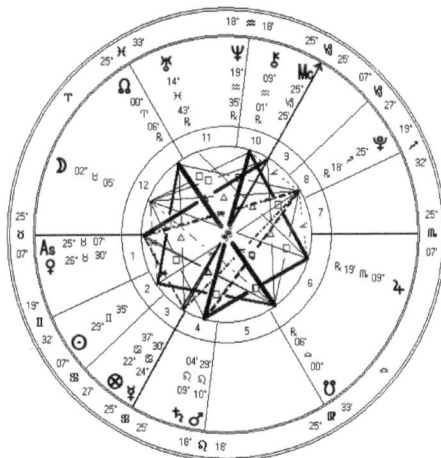

Kings Drummers
21 Jun 2006 03:00 BST -1:00
Amesbury, UK 51°N10' 001°W45'
Geocentric Tropical Placidus True Node

It was no longer raining at all and, looking over the heads of the performers to the north east, we could see the clouds parting to open up the first light of the day in preparation for the rising Sun. The eastern sky brightened gloriously, as the Ascendant trined Neptune!

-oOo-

The March 2007 column explored the astrology of the Christian date for the creation of the world and its possible connections with the birth and crucifixion of Jesus Christ.

The Creation of the World – a Really Great Idea!

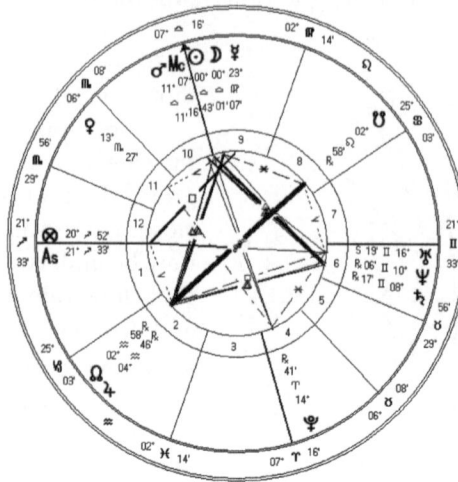

Creation of the World
23 Oct 4004 BCE 12:27 LMT -2:20:56
Jerusalem, Israel 31°N46' 035°E14'
Geocentric Tropical Placidus True Node

In Nicholas Campion's *Book of World Horoscopes,* he gives Maternus' data (18:00 on the evening of 22 October 4004 BCE in Jerusalem) for the creation of the world, according to the Christian tradition, suggesting that we should fine-tune the time to give an Aries Ascendant and Capricorn Midheaven.[18] I became even more excited, when I noticed that twenty-seven minutes after Noon LMT at the high point of first day the Moon entered Libra, and applied to the Sun, which is beside the MC.[19] Mars is at a key point in Libra, the scales that Milton referring to in his *Paradise Lost* as the Lord God's instrument of judgment.[20] Surely, this is a chart that we should take note of!

Drawing the chart with aspect lines in the modern fashion the picture becomes all the more exciting. Eight of the ten conventional planets and the North Node are in air signs – 'in the beginning was the word... and the word was made flesh' as the Apostle John tells us.[21] The coming together of such an appropriate number of air planets in such a formation must be indeed rare. That it was deduced by careful backward counting of events in the Bible, to become seminal to the Christian story, is significant for non-Christians as much as Christians. If you were to look for an election chart for the creation of the world, could you find a better one?

Alternatively, if you were to look for a date that would capture the imagination of the world for thousands of years as being the date for the *idea* of the creation of the world, could you ever find a better one? Were there ancient astrologers who understood the cycles of the planets so clearly that such a day was chosen and all the subsequent stories followed on from it? This does *not* seem likely.

More likely, this day is so special that it has formed an imprint on the consciousness of humanity for thousands of years – in short, astrology really does work! Two other details of the chart support this possibility. Mars in Libra opposing Pluto in Aries seems an ideal representation of Satan's temptation of Eve, the casting out from the garden and the Cain and Abel story. Venus, the ruler of the Sun, in fall in Scorpio in the eleventh house in a quincunx to Pluto in the fourth could help to explain the male chauvinism in the Judaeo-Christian tradition.

Maybe we should compare some transits and progressions for those biblical timing events that lead to this date being first decided. Is there an astrological explanation for Joseph being sold into slavery in Egypt, or his descendants escaping across the Red Sea? What transits describe the years wandering in the desert and the final coming to the Holy Land, or the exile into and return from Babylon?

Could such an approach make any contribution to the discussions about the birth of Christ? Several dates have been suggested. Among them are 20:06 LMT on 22 August 7 BCE[22], 20:05 on 2 March 5 BCE [23], and 08:07 LMT on 13 October 2 BCE (suggested by Wayne Turner), when a remarkable almost precise parallel and conjunction of Venus and Jupiter in Pisces' opposite sign of Virgo occurred.[24] As can be seen from the transits and the progressions of the Creation chart to the chart of the suggested day of Christ's birth (13 October 2 BCE), this third possibility seems especially interesting. Just over four thousand years after the supposed moment of creation, progressed Mercury is retrograding back to the same degree as its natal position. Also, that day transiting Mars and Pluto are conjunct near that same natal and progressed Mercury degree.

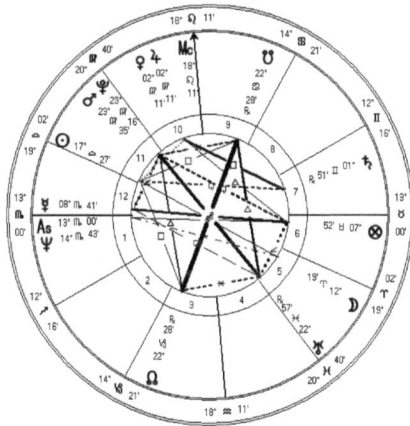

Jesus - Possible Birth
13 Oct 2 BCE 08:07 LMT -2:20:48
Bethlehem 31°N43' 035°E12'
Geocentric Tropical Placidus True Node

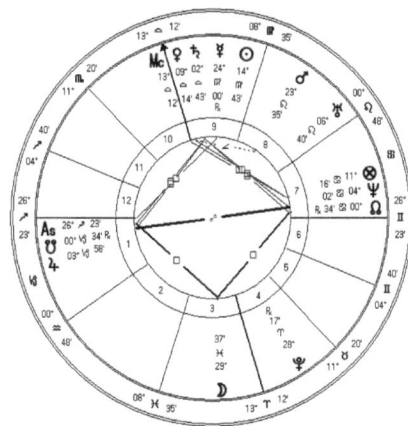

Creation of the World Sec. Prog. SA in Long
13 Oct 2 BCE 08:07 LMT -2:20:56
Jerusalem, Israel 31°N46' 035°E14'
Geocentric Tropical Placidus True Node

What better symbolism could there be for the communication of a virgin birth that is destined to lead to a religion that is based on the brutal crucifixion of the Son of God? Note also that the progressed Moon is about to enter zero degrees of Aries (the sign ruled by Mars) in an exact T-square to the progressed Nodal axis. This progressed Moon is in an opposition to the New Moon of the creation chart and within seven degrees of the IC of the creation chart.

-o0o-

The January 2009 column honoured the twentieth-century developers of mundane astrology.

Great Mundane Astrology Advances
(during the *Astrological Journal's* fifty years)

Barack Obama's Presidential victory marks another success for mundane astrology. A panel of seven astrologers at the 1200-delegate United Astrology Congress in Denver, Colorado in May 2008 all selected Obama as the next President of the USA (when he was yet to defeat Hilary Clinton). This follows on from Jim Shawvan's exact advance description of the many weeks of the long debacle surrounding the 2000 result, as well as his clear forecast of the US at war on the Afghanistan/Pakistan border, written ten months before 9/11.[25] Frequently since then, it has been possible to anticipate the direction of world affairs by studying outer-planetary transits and the horoscopes of the events and the leaders making the critical decisions.

That we can say such things is the result of intensive study and the development of skills by pioneers over many years. The *Astrological Journal* can be proud of its role in supporting great advances of Mundane Astrology for fifty of them. A failure to predict the First World War spurred on its development to a point where now just applying them to issues reveals deep insights.[26]

In 1951, Charles Carter's *Introduction to Political Astrology* pioneered its renaissance in Britain; while André Barbault in France was initiating a long lifetime of in-depth study.[27] Well into his eighties, André continues to write in the twenty-first century. American colleagues cite a late nineteenth-century astrologer William Chaney as their father of mundane, while noting the importance of Evangeline Adams' work in the first half of the twentieth century. Charles Jayne, Will Hand (father of Rob) and Hans Niggemann were in constant contact with each other in the fifties. Developing on from the example of such mentors and the discovery of what lay behind W. D. Gann's market forecasts, today's American financial astrologers have made brilliant advances that connect astro-cycles with movements in world markets.

As well as the study of events, finance, the fate of the leaders and their nations, interest in the newly discovered outer planets led to the mundane study of macro-cycles. These are especially relevant today, when economists are telling us it is unreasonable to expect them to have 'foreseen' the chaotic consequences of their decisions. A slow-moving planet's movement through the signs, or the interaction of two outer planets from conjunction through square to opposition and back again was found to point to generational and multi-generational changes of cultural assumption and fashion. Albert Ruperti's pioneering *Cycles of Becoming*[28] inspired studies that grew in such scholarly achievements as Richard Tarnas' *Cosmos and Psyche*.[29]

The advancement of computer technology since the 1980s revolutionised the possibilities for accurate mundane study. Before then, to find planetary positions for the time period around the birth of Christ it was necessary to consult inaccurate astronomical lists in large cumbersome books. Today, exact planetary data 5000 years into the past and forward to the future is there at the click of a mouse. Convenient software highlights the connections. Specialist astro mapping software places on geographical maps planetary, midpoint, house cusp, and paran lines. In a moment, we can display bar and polar-centric graphs, electional searches through time or batches of charts. As quickly, we can add depth and precision with dwads, sidereal and draconic zodiacs and asteroids. Relating historical patterns to astro-cycles has never been easier. So, most astrologers, whatever their main enthusiasm, dally a while with the charts of a country or leader in the news. Most have an opinion on how a change of outer-planetary sign or aspect will influence our lives and change the world.

The Association and its *Journal* pioneered such ground-breaking advances and scholarship. James Russell, our long-standing Vice President, wrote extensively on mundane astrology in the *Astrological Journal*. His early focus has occupied Association Presidents to this day.

In 1984, the ground-breaking *Mundane Astrology* was written by Nicholas Campion and Charles Harvey (with Michael Baigent).[30] In 1988 the first edition of Nicholas Campion's vital resource *The Book of World Horoscopes* was first published.[31] Its scholarship set a standard of accuracy and insight that has marked the astrological study of world affairs ever since. Charles Harvey read André Barbault in French as his preparation for writing *Mundane Astrology*.

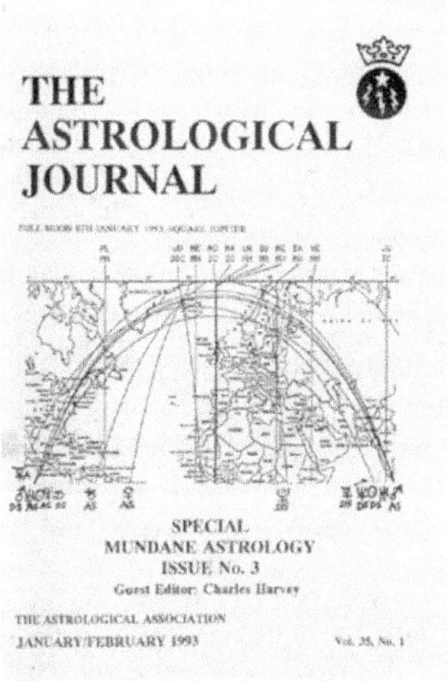

THE
ASTROLOGICAL
JOURNAL

SPECIAL
MUNDANE ASTROLOGY
ISSUE No. 3

Guest Editor: Charles Harvey

THE ASTROLOGICAL ASSOCIATION

JANUARY/FEBRUARY 1993   Vol. 35, No. 1

CONTENTS

Then President of the Astrological Lodge of London, Nick worked with the Association to organise annual mundane astrology days from 1985-1992. He also edited two special mundane editions of the *Astrological Journal* in January 1990 and March 1991. Charles edited a third in January 1993. The Contents, for the 1993 edition listed here, are a tribute to the vision and endeavour of writers working with limited tools available in those years. Their achievements encourage us to use today's advantages to bring more enlightened understanding to the world.

-o0o-

The May 2012 column suggested a link between Dr Rupert Sheldrake's concept of morphic resonance and astro-cycles.

Could Astrology's Workings Explain Morphic Resonance?

> It was six men of Indostan
> To learning much inclined,
> Who went to see the Elephant
> (Though all of them were blind),
> That each by observation
> Might satisfy his mind.
> **John Godfrey Saxe**

[The poem goes on to describe how, by touching different parts of the elephant, each blind man deduces radically different natures for it. Then they argue endlessly over whether the elephant is a wall, a spear, a rope, a snake, a fan, or a tree.]

The fundamental flaw in reductionist science

The poem illustrates the fundamental flaw in reductionist science. As well as encouraging narrow views, it takes disproportionate amounts of time and energy to defend partial truths. It insists the only reliable way to gain knowledge is to increase understanding piecemeal through rigid testing. Where aims are clearly defined, containable and mechanical, such a linear approach is vital and brilliantly successful. It is the basis of modern material advances. Where results may be within variable possibility, too fixed an approach is counter-productive. Reductionists should avoid arrogantly assuming that their success in mechanics means that everything is simply mechanical, and so they are the only adjudicators of all universal knowledge and experience. When they claim their way of working is the only science, they leave no room for a leap of faith and imagination that sees the whole 'elephant' as it actually is. Small wonder the prevailing ultimate destiny most Big Bang theorists visualise is absolute darkness! Is this where eighteenth-century 'Enlightenment' leads?

A bright and highly intelligent contrast

A bright and highly intelligent contrast to such defensive rigidity is Dr Rupert Sheldrake's new book, *The Science Delusion*.[32]

The book's aim is to cut through popular simplifications and put over-optimistic contemporary reductionist claims to the test; to 'free up the spirit of enquiry'. Packed with overviews of the history of scientific ideas and a wide range of experimental evidence, including serious reservations about the potential of genetics, this book offers a fine objective insight into modern science.

Sheldrake poses and examines ten questions for Reductionists to answer. His conclusions include the possibility of a living universe, consciousness existing beyond the brain, children inheriting characteristics their parents acquired, the brain being a mere receiver that tunes into the past, causation moving backwards and forwards in time, nature with evolving laws and an inherent purpose.

Reading this book restores to our minds the joy we felt for science in our younger years. A true scientist, he weighs evidence on all sides without fear or favour, leaving questions to be addressed and 'impossibilities' to be explained. It is in this spirit that I found myself relating his conclusions to the way I see astrology working. The brain tuning into past memories is like the intricate detail with which our birth charts relate to past astro-cycles. Could children appearing to inherit characteristics their parents have acquired be explained by progressions and transits to parental birth charts? Astrologers are comfortable with the intertwining of the past, present and future.

However, it was to morphic resonance, the key concept for which Sheldrake is known, that astrology seems to offer a crucial contribution. Experiments with apparently inanimate, as well as animate, objects seem to show that once a new idea or process and tendency starts to occur, then repetitions happen with ever-increasing ease. Once something is 'in the airwaves', it seems to be picked up all over the world, even though there are no contacts between occurrences. As we know only too well from this column, mundane astrology uses astro-cycles to explain and even predict developments and cycles of change. If such cycles mark moments in time that a new idea, process, or tendency will be attempted, it is not surprising this will also be a time, when otherwise unconnected phenomena all over the world will be increasingly attuned and ready for such developments.

With Neptune now in Pisces, it is not surprising that we seek both to know, and understand. Dr Sheldrake's book is a most timely step in the right direction.

-oOo-

For the January 2013 column, the *Journal* editor asked astrologers to describe their personal experience of outer-planetary transits – 'the planets working in us', as he called it.

Personal Experiences of Major Planetary Cycles

Our esteemed editor's theme for this edition of the Journal – 'astrologer's experiences of the big planetary cycles' – turns the thrust of this column around to 'The Planets Working with Us'! The narrative below looks at Uranus/Pluto and then Neptune through particularly dramatic years of my life before I knew astrology. Did that make any difference?

Preliminary considerations
To consider that a planet as small as Pluto can be the direct cause of anything is no dafter than saying the millimetre notches on a measure actually build a house. In both cases neither do anything directly mechanical, but without them as reference points nothing can be understood or properly performed. Whether dwarf or normal planet, Pluto's tropical sign position clearly describes the underlying social trauma of that time. So also, when its transits connect with the planets and angles of our personal charts, we notice predictable personal trauma. Uranus and Neptune as well, on their own or together with Pluto, bring change, new tastes and beliefs.

Talking about the minutiae of personal charts and their transits can be uneasy for both the subject and the listener. For the subject, describing how exactly a batch of transits fitted may necessitate a narrative that is far too real and intrusive to be revealed. If he/she does not mind, and especially is keen to describe 'everything', the outline may be far too full of self-indulgent detail for the listener to endure. Or is it just Aquarians that feel that way? May what follows demonstrate the first paragraph, but avoid the tedium of the second!

For the first 35 years of my life, I knew nothing of astrology and, if I had known, would have held the same outraged incredulity typical of today's Brian Cox devotees. I was a rational, humanitarian idealist, seeking fairness for all. I paid tireless attention to initiating actions to improve society, but (not realising then the dangers of having Saturn/Mars in Aries) was maybe not so good at anticipating the consequences! A decent idealist with left-of-centre reductionist attitudes, I believed in the reliability of modern knowledge and the professional expertise of those that administered it. As such, in the mid-1960s, I was well placed for a promising, high-flying career in education.

Remarkably and perhaps significantly, the events of my life before I knew about astrology show what happened, and my reactions to it, were even more predictable than the years after I did.

So it was that in September 1965 this ambitious young teacher began his career, just a month before the first Uranus/Pluto conjunction at 17Vi09, squared his natal Moon in Gemini! Two more conjunctions were to occur in that academic year. At the time I put the classroom experience down to first-year teaching always being a 'bloody' initiation. Full of energy I struggled on and gained respect and promotion in the years that followed, finally being seconded to complete a career-enhancing degree in the academic year 1970-71. Imagine and understand the above paragraph by tracing the numerous transits of Uranus and Pluto as they interweaved in direct and retrograde motion, firstly in square to natal Moon, then conjunct Neptune and quincunx Sun/Venus.

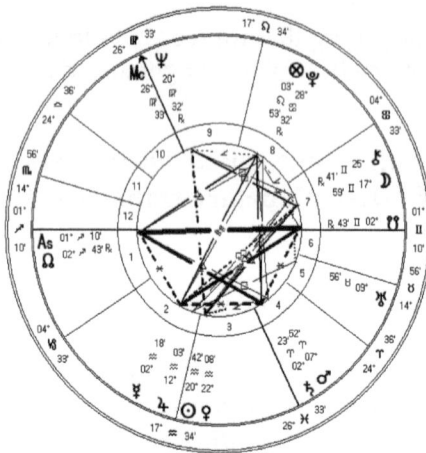

Roy Gillett
10 Feb 1938 02:30 UT +0:00
Tooting, UK 51°N26' 000°W10'
Geocentric Tropical Placidus True Node

Uranus/Pluto dancing on the Midheaven

From September 1967 Uranus commenced its conjunctions to the Midheaven. For quite a while, it was great to welcome exciting changes; a new house, helping to write and organise a school play, even a television debut.

Pluto transits, especially those across the angles, tend to reward the brave with power and standing, while undermining the very values and institutions, from whence the power emanates. My teaching and studies had offered ever-greater opportunities for personal advancement. Yet, the institutions, knowledge and world values, over which I was 'destined to preside', seemed to be failing me in my personal life. They were also losing their credibility all over the world through unjust wars and social unrest. My degree studies included the sociology of education. Studying the Berger and Luckmann writings that demonstrate 'knowledge' (even academic knowledge) is 'a social construction of reality' was both liberating and unnerving.[33] Liberating because it was no longer necessary to argue for and defend what my experience had told me was indefensible. Unnerving, because it left little or nothing of our Western material world picture that could be ultimately relied upon. The final year of the degree course that included this study started in September 1970, as retrograding Mercury conjuncted Pluto on my MC.   Ironically, obtaining it led to a major double promotion in my teaching career at the very time that the intrinsic nature of what I was teaching was being questioned by myself as well as many others. Such are the ways of Pluto!

Neptune on the Ascendant
In 1971, into this existential void, left by the Uranus/Pluto transit across my Neptune and Midheaven (1967-70), Neptune transited on to my Ascendant, soon to be joined by Jupiter. As both conjuncted the North Node on the Sagittarian rising sign in a trine to Saturn and Mars, I was stirred into exploring a wide range of exciting educational innovations that promised to 'answer' contemporary social problems. Many people felt then that education could make a major contribution to creating a better society, if only we could rid ourselves of what had been wrong with it in the past. A new open pupil-centred creative approach was the way to discover and build this better future. Can you hear transiting Jupiter/Neptune in Sagittarius trine natal Saturn/Mars in Aries talking?

Discovering astrology
All this was happening automatically. I still had not discovered astrology or anything like it during those early years of the 1970s. That watershed was not to happen until the late autumn of 1973, when Uranus trined my natal Sun/Venus, while at the same time they were being conjuncted by progressed and transiting Jupiter!

From this time, a very different, aware, mature and so fruitful relationship with the cosmos, world cultures and religion was to develop. Neptune in Sagittarius on another level is where the story really starts, but that will have to be left for another day.

Would it have been different if I had known astrology at the time? Certainly, these years would have been far less painful and lonely. Life is an experience of constant change, at some times more traumatic that at others. Yet it is not the change, but the lack of a pattern, meaning and purpose in that change that makes it unbearable. Understanding the astro-cycles certainly gives the pattern and time scale. Interpreting these reveals meaning from which we can often find purpose, even at the most difficult times. From this comes the strength to endure and move mountains.

-o0o-

The March 2013 issue included a detailed study of the astrology of Adam Lanza, the perpetrator of the December 2012 mass murders in Newtown, Connecticut. Not only was his capacity for such actions clear, but also the timing, when the killings occurred. 'For how much longer will the valuable workings of astrology be ignored,' is the cry!

Inside the Consciousness of a Killer

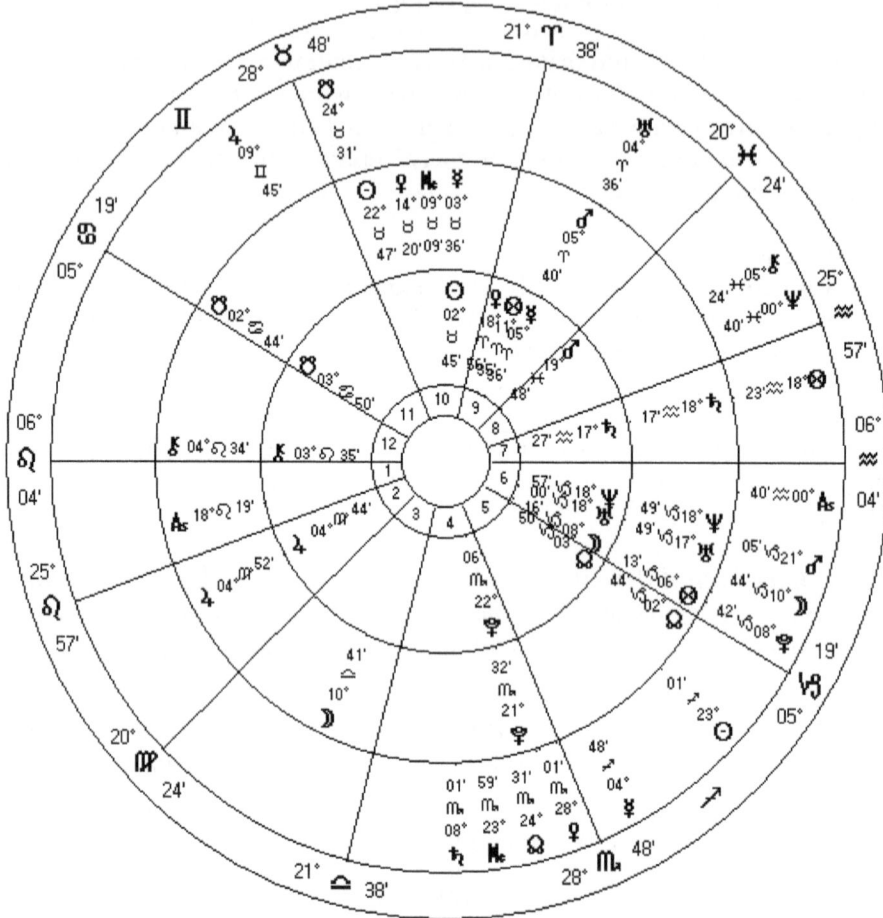

> Innermost wheel: **Adam Lanza** 22 April 1992 12:00 EDT Exeter New Hampshire USA
> **Middle wheel:** secondary progressed **to** 14 December 2012 09:45 EST Newtown Connecticut USA
> **Outer wheel: The Shooting** 14 December 2012 09:45 Newtown EST Connecticut USA
> Geocentric Placidus True Node

By the time you read this, events will have moved on from that terrible December 2012 day in Newtown, Connecticut. Hopefully, action will have been taken, as the US clarifies its understanding of the context and intentions behind the founding fathers' amendment on the ownership of arms.

If ever anything can be gained from such senseless loss of young life, it is the lessons learned that prevent similar tragedies happening in the future. While controlling the ownership and care of guns may be disputed in America, one area all can agree on is the need for advances in the treatment of mental health.

My book *Astrology and Compassion the Convenient Truth* makes a detailed study of the astrology of the perpetrators and timing of the 1980 assassination of John Lennon and also the massacre at Blacksburg, Virginia in April 2007.[34]   In both cases the astrology not only described the mentality that led to the terrible acts, but also the timing of their occurrences. It does again for the Newtown tragedy.

Even if we ignore the angles and house positions, Adam Lanza's birth chart suggests fixed, ruthless intransigence (Sun in Taurus, with ruling Venus in Aries, square Uranus/Neptune in Capricorn).[35] The natal Moon in detriment in Capricorn would have been a part of this square later in the day or squared his Mercury in Aries earlier around 6 am. The trine of the Aries and Scorpio ruler, Mars in Pisces, to Pluto in Scorpio suggests intense emotional need. These factors together, clearly point to self-righteous resentment. He will feel not understood, alone, with a deep need for emotional satisfaction that cannot be satisfied.[36] When Pisces is afflicted by other factors in the chart, its natural compassion can be turned around. Instead of feeling sorry for the pain of other, others can be blamed for being the causers of pain. It takes considerable compassionate spiritual maturity to sympathise with a world that does not seem to understand. Without this compassion a sense of isolation and rejection projects feeling as bitterness toward what seems like a separate, alien outside world. In such a state of mind, victims become objects and the consequences of actions are seen entirely from the perpetrator's side.

The tri-wheel places the progressions and transits around the natal chart, at the time of the atrocity. With his progressed Moon in Libra in a T-square to the natal Aries/Capricorn planets, 2012 will have been an emotionally disturbing year for Adam. Its opposition to progressed Mars (which is conjunct natal Mercury) suggests communication through violence. The transits clearly test the dangers intrinsic in the birth chart to bursting point. Pluto conjuncts Natal Moon and progressed Fortuna, while squaring progressed Moon. A few days earlier, transiting Mars would have conjuncted the natal and progressed Uranus/Neptune. This is compounded at the other end of the square by transiting Uranus conjuncting natal Mercury and progressed Mars in Aries. It being for Adam a most intolerable time of potential violence is strengthened by the Pluto and Uranus transits. Their square develops and is applying to his Uranus/Neptune in Capricorn and ruling Venus in Aries for some years to come. Here is a person trapped unrecognised, without respite in an alien world.

Most people experience difficult periods in their lives when hope and change seem impossibly distant. For most of us, handling the sense of isolation these bring requires (hopefully even creates) mental and emotional maturity. We may be wrong and, if not, we realise change takes time and work patiently with its process until all is ready.

Use your astrological knowledge to enter (without such maturity) the consciousness trapped in Adam Lanza's birth chart. Lacking meaningful explanation and guidance to channel the dark pent-up fury, he sees the negative way of Pluto, Uranus and Mars as the only escape. So at around 9:30 am as the local Midheaven conjuncts his Pluto and local Ascendant applies to square his natal Sun and progressed Mercury this way of horrific rampage begins.

In 2006, around the time that the innocent victims of the Newtown tragedy were being born, *Astrology and Compassion the Convenient Truth* suggested astrological information could have helped to anticipate, treat and prevent the slaughter perpetrated by Cho Seung-Hui in Blacksburg, Virginia.[37]

Like Cho Seung-Hui, Adam Lanza's birth chart has qualities that any enlightened society using astrology could and should have identified. They could have been channelled into positive expression, or at least contained carefully from quite early in his life. Especially, astrology could have provided authoritative support to his English teacher and also the judge he had been before on a lesser offence. In both cases, having the astrological information would have been a timely warning to anticipate and prevent the dangers.[38]

There are a range of opinions about whether we should encourage society to learn the benefits of working with the planets. One extreme opinion, held by reductionist scientists and associated comedian debunkers, rejects astrology entirely. With incredulity, they dismiss what they refuse to study – presumably, lest their 'pure' minds be tainted by its 'illogicality'. At the other extreme are colleagues, who understandably insist that using astrology in this full way cannot be promoted and will only be accepted by those who are ready.

With the astrology so clear and incidents such as Newtown and Blacksburg so tragic, it is difficult to forgive the arrogance of the first extreme view. It is also perhaps time to have more faith in the ability of the general public to learn new profound ways to understand and heal our challenging times.

What can be certain is that astro-events of the years to come suggest we will witness more individual tragedies, as well as world economic/ecological crises and misunderstandings between cultures, until we find ways to get inside the experience of others and make decisions in their interests as well as our own. Until everyone is 'on board', no one is entirely safe.

-o0o-

The opening of the September 2013 column gave systematic guidance for the proper way to practise mundane astrology.

The Best Way to Work with the Planets

> 'I had to rid myself of any illusions. My method was, if possible, to shut myself away in a remote faraway place where I couldn't guess at what was going on in the world, and depending only on the astronomical ephemerides, assign dates to history sometimes years and even decades in advance, the forecast thus becoming a gigantic leap in anticipating the future. It was the ultimate high-risk strategy!'
> André Barbault *The Value of Astrology* (trans. Kate Johnston)[39]

Those of you who have tried such an approach will resonate with André's words and know the amazing rewards such courage offers. Among André's notable successes was to look ahead from 1978 to the 1989 events that led to the disintegration of the Soviet system, and then from 1989 to predict a growing world economic crisis in 2010.

Background assumptions
Anyone shutting themselves away to project the future by astro-cycles alone will need a system. I use the time each planet takes to cycle the zodiac. Outer-planetary cycles for generational trends Their sign changes challenge our objectivity and attachment to the familiar by confronting us with new traumas (Pluto, every 11 to

20+ years), belief (Neptune, 14 years) and change (Uranus, 7 years). These sign changes rarely happen at the same time. So, keeping track of contemporary moods is really difficult without astrological knowledge.

Opportunity and Control

Upon this background, Jupiterian opportunity (expansion) interweaves against the controlling structural demands of Saturn. The interaction of their zodiacal cycles (12 and 29 years respectively) have been studied since ancient Babylonian times; especially their conjunctions then oppositions over a twenty-year period. When they are conjunct order and opportunity are attuned. As Jupiter rushes ahead for the next ten years, more and more seems possible. In the following ten-year waning phase, the wise do not seek expansion, but put their house in order. For, at the next conjunction, those that failed to will have a price to pay.

For this reason, today's world leaders' view that 'winning the global race' and 'growth' are panaceas to all our woes is both deluded and futile. For Jupiter and Saturn are in a waning phase; Pluto is in Saturn-ruled Capricorn and Neptune in Jupiter-ruled Pisces, while irresponsible Uranus in Aries is open to anything and no one is asking the key question: 'exactly to where are we running and why?' In the waxing cycle to 2010, it was claimed that economic innovation had 'defeated boom and bust for ever'. So, we failed to plan for the waning phase. Now economists advise our politicians to prop up a declining system with imaginary assets. Sovereign debt grows and resources are wasted, as we wait fruitlessly for boom times that are ten or many more years away!

Times and triggers

The speedy movements of the five inner personal bodies, Sun, Moon, Mercury, Venus and Mars make numerous aspect connections every year. The connections with the slower-moving planets indicate months, weeks, even days when pressures will intensify to make outcomes that have been building for some time to actually happen. Readers of André Barbault's book will marvel at his careful recording of the relationship between annual Sun/Jupiter conjunctions (strengthened with Venus sextiles) and armistice and international agreements that ended/suspended conflicts.

Finally, we can look to the exact day or even the time of particular events to find a trigger – a point in the monthly lunar cycle, the rising and culminating positions of planets caused by diurnal revolution. Some, but not all, minor events can grow into massive revolutionary change. A background of outer-planetary pressure needs to build with inner-planetary connections to it. Then an angular trigger releases the pressure. So, with strong underlying momentum a very small event can touch a nerve. At such times, understanding and a quick, wise and compassionate reaction is vital if disaster is to be avoided.

-o0o-

In December 2013, the column opened with detailed explanations of eminent people's lives. These showed astro-cycles informing and so leading to beneficial achievement for them and society, however difficult the circumstances they faced.

Inspirational Ways of Working with the Planets

We master the challenges of our charts and the times, by working selflessly with the planets to benefit the people we meet, the societies we live in and all they connect with. Selfless people do not seek happiness, but their nature ensures they experience it. We see this clearly, when we compare individuals' birth charts to their life's work, or contrast how different parts of the world react to the same transits.

Inspirational People

HH the Dalai Lama's birth chart shows the difficulties he faced and how well he mastered them to serve and benefit humanity.

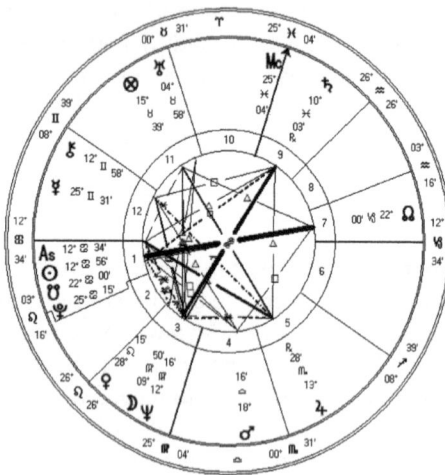

HH The Dalai Lama of Tibet
6 Jul 1935 04:50:02 LMT -6:44:48
Takster, Tibet 36°N32' 101°E12'
Geocentric Tropical Placidus True Node

The Moon in Virgo, the Sun and Ascendant ruler, applying to conjunct Neptune in the third house that is opposed to Saturn in Pisces in the ninth house, suggests someone born with a terrifying predicament. In a very public way, he has to find a way to communicate with spiritual perfection, while confronted by alien forces that have no sympathy with what he represents. Mars in Libra in the fourth house separating from a square to his Sun, applying to square the Nodal axis and Pluto suggests an unstable, restless, threatened home. The water grand trine between Jupiter in Scorpio in the fifth house, Saturn and Sun/Ascendant shows he has a grand capacity and responsibility to project sympathy and healing.

Martin Scorsese's film *Kundun* perfectly illustrates the birth chart. It depicts a small country boy taken from his family surroundings to a strange dark palace, where he is tutored by elderly magicians. Prepared for intensely responsible temporal and spiritual leadership; he was only fifteen years old, when threatened by an alien power, seeking to destroy all he had been prepared for. To save his people and culture, he was forced to flee to restore and rebuild it in foreign lands.

His reflective Cancer Sun/Ascendant, supported by that perfectionist ruling Moon in Virgo and the water grand trine makes his personality a perfect healing mirror; a compassionate mother figure to all. With Saturn in Pisces in the ninth house, he becomes internationally renowned. This also represents the coming to the West of the Mahayana Buddhist lineage that had been sustained in India, and then Tibet, for thousands of years. So, the difficult obstacles he was born with are turned around to inspire millions to work selflessly for the benefit of each other and the planet.

Charles Harvey was a tireless archetypal midwife, who brought into being many of the twentieth-century astrological institutions and developments in the UK that are now regenerating the understanding of astrology in the twenty-first century.

In his early life, Charles may well have found it difficult to come to terms with an intensely anxious need to do the right thing for other people. His packed Cancer stellium in the eleventh/twelfth houses, with ruling Moon in the sixth house is at the very cusp of Aquarius, applying to oppose Pluto in Leo in the twelfth house. Once he knew enough to understand the Cancer planets' symbolism, the message was simple and unavoidable – 'you were born to serve the development of knowledge in others, whatever the cost'. With Aquarius often seen as the sign associated with astrology, it was not surprising that its regeneration and recognition became the heart of his mission from a very young age. The Uranus/Pluto conjunction in Virgo was trining his Jupiter/Saturn conjunction in Taurus, when he joined the Astrological Association Council as Records Officer in 1965, soon combining this with the role of General Secretary. He became President as his progressed Sun entered Leo, opposing natal Moon and conjuncting the Pluto opposition. Also, the progressed Ascendant in Virgo trined his natal Taurean Jupiter/Saturn; his service in the role (1973-94) was regal and protective, and most kind in its generous attention to detail.

Charles Harvey
22 Jun 1940 09:16 BST -1:00
Bookham, Surrey, UK 51°N16' 000°W22'
Geocentric Tropical Placidus True Node

The *Astrological Journal* was expanded and *Correlation,* the only astrology research journal, was launched to coordinate major initiatives in the study of science and astrology. Annual Conference session recordings were instigated. Charles also supported the Faculty of Astrological Studies and College of Psychological Astrology, and developed the Urania Trust's astrology centre. Here a public astrological library was first housed. Charles' vision was often way ahead of the possibilities of his time. So much so, that many of these initiatives are only now coming to completion. Others will take some time yet!

Charles
Harvey

With such a strong focus in Cancer planets, Charles could be defensive, even over-anxious when his initiatives seemed threatened. At the same time, he was remembered by numerous people as an enabling 'mother', always there on the phone

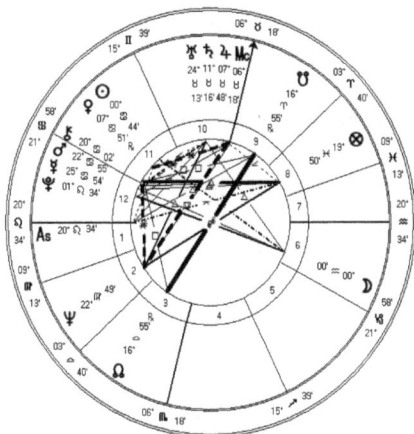

or in person to understand and support their endeavours. Could it be the deep sense of personal responsibility he felt for astrology, the ruling Moon opposition to Mercury conjunct Pluto in the twelfth house, feeling 'forced' to do so much himself, that took him away from us far too soon in the year 2000? Such incredible generosity, from which everyone who cares about astrology continues to benefit today, and which encourages ever more people to serve.

Nicholas Campion, Charles' successor as Astrological Association President, is a prolific writer and teacher, who works in mainstream academia, pioneering ground-breaking studies of those ancient and modern cultures that are founded upon understandings of astronomy and astrology.

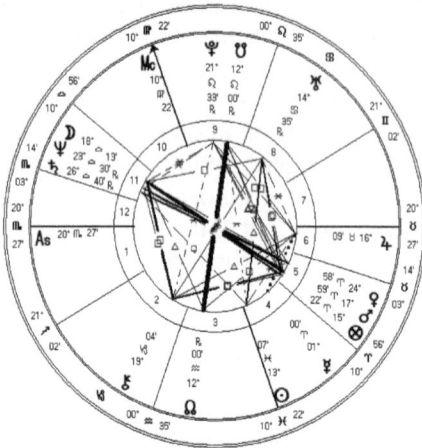

Nicholas Campion
4 Mar 1953 00:12 UT +0:00
Bristol, UK 51°N27' 002°W35'
Tropical Placidus True Node

Joseph Stalin, the USSR dictator, experienced incredible suffering until he died five days after his stroke on 1 March 1953. Nick was born on the fourth of these agonising days, when the Moon in Libra, just past its opposition to Mars, was applying to oppose Venus, and then conjunct Neptune and Saturn, as Mars applied to square Uranus. With Chiron included, the chart has a cardinal grand cross, which suggests pressured responsibility to initiate. This is focused on the eleventh-house Libra / fifth-house Aries axis indicating the service will be creatively pioneering. Jupiter in the sixth house reinforces an urge to work hard, the trine to Chiron and sextile to Uranus points to work for major healing change. The Sun is on the IC, in Pisces, the sign Jupiter rules. There will be a selfless, idealistic foundation to his life. Its powerful applying trine to Uranus in Cancer suggests a revolutionary social perspective. Whatever the cost, no stone will be left unturned or a detail overlooked in pursuit of

a great purpose. This determination to try to the limit is further emphasised by Mars applying to Pluto in the ninth house – philosophy, the knowledge of history, the scope and standards of scholarship will never be the same, when confronted by his rigour.

But what is the grand philosophical purpose behind all his capacity for determined endeavour? The answer was not clear for much of Nick's early life. To see why, we need to look closer at one more key planet; the all-important unaspected Mercury in early Aries. Not only is it in an immature sign, unaspected with little connection to the rest of the chart;

progressed Mercury moved into apparent retrograde motion around his sixth year and did not go direct until just before his Saturn return at 29 years. Yet all this time his ruling Jupiter in Taurus was progressing from the sixth house across his Descendant to the seventh house. He was fascinated with history, but deep-seated integrity made him question conventional approaches.

From 1982, with Mercury now direct, he was to apply great industry to astrology, especially how to chart its relationship to mundane events. A pinnacle of his achievement at this time was the *Book of World Horoscopes,* a scholarly study of the foundation of nations. He became a world authority in the history of Western astrology. Then, on his birthday in March 1999, both transiting and progressed Mercury came together to return at the planet's natal position - 1 degree of Aries. The threads of his life's work came together, as he worked toward creating and then teaching the Master's Degree in Cultural Astrology and Astronomy. Over the years since, Dr Nicholas Campion has published more than forty academic books and papers, including his authoritative two-volume *History of Western Astrology.*[40] Through these, his high standard of teaching and the consequent academic success of his students, the world is coming to see how the study of astrology, in all its culturally diverse forms, can further cultural understanding of the past, present and future.

People who know how to work with the planets
In 2012, the world rose to applaud the achievements of the Olympic athletes and the devotion of the organisers. This column remarked then how such selfless effort transformed the threatening T-square of the time in something truly wonderful for athletes and spectators worldwide, and indeed most people, who were living in the UK. You need to work under and master pressure to do great things. Those without will, who do not try, but instead whine for support, who give up on the way and complain that all is against them, will have difficult charts and may attract our sympathy. Yet, they will always be sad failures, unsatisfied and resentful. Those that persevere through equally difficult charts, create opportunity, seek new ways, rebuild what is destroyed, however unreasonably was its destruction, who face misunderstanding and condemnation and yet turn it to fresh resolve, these are the people who inspire us and change the world. These are the inspiring people who know how to work with the planets.

Nelson Mandela 1918-2013

-oOo-

Can understanding the individual astrology of mass murderers, along with the cycles of the times, help us understand, even anticipate and avoid, their mindless slaughter of ordinary people? The September 2015 column explores possibilities, first considered in Chapter 12 of my book *Astrology and Compassion the Convenient Truth.*[41]

Tunisia Massacre and Other Events:
Trines are Good News only with the Right State of Mind

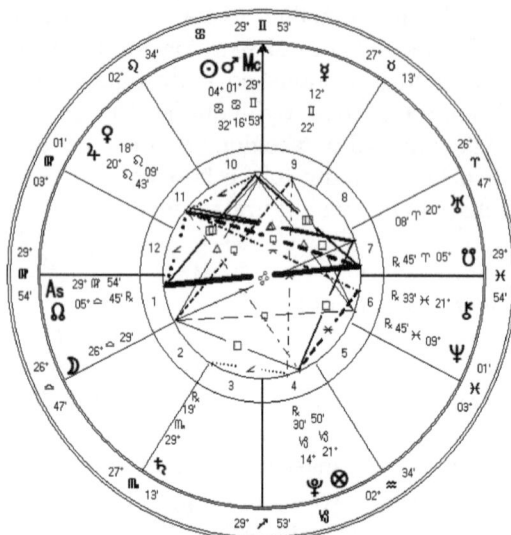

Bad News Day
26 Jun 2015 12:00 CET -1:00
Sousse, Tunisia 35°N49' 010°E38
Tropical Placidus True Node

Here is a chart that reminds us of what we should all know, but are always in danger of forgetting; not to see positive aspects as good and negative ones as bad. With Venus close to catching Jupiter in Leo (still less than a degree past its trine with Uranus in Aries), freedom and enthusiasm to act could not be greater. Two more trines stir the pot. Firstly, the Sun and Mars in early Cancer apply to trine Neptune in Pisces, intense emotional spiritual belief builds and seems unending. Secondly, that very day the Moon (void of course unless we count a semi-sextile to otherwise unaspected Saturn retrograding in Scorpio) ingresses into Scorpio and applies to make a grand trine with Neptune, Mars and the Sun. Except for that Moon, the only planet in air is Mercury in Gemini, just three degrees past a square to Neptune in Pisces. Was it a few days earlier that the wild decisions to attack was made? The only other (and crucial) stress connection is the T-square between Mars (on the Sousse MC) and the Nodal axis, which was the trigger for what happened.

So, this day, starting this moment on a beach in Tunisia, seventy-seven tourists were injured by a single religiously motivated gunman.[42] Thirty-eight of them were killed, of whom thirty were from the United Kingdom. Meanwhile in Kobane, Syria, 120 people were killed. There were more injuries and killings at a third attack on a mosque in Kuwait. In an unrelated incident, the over-excitement led to the throwing of life-threatening powder on a crowd in Taiwan.[43]

The unrestrained (unaspected Saturn) wild abandon symbolised by the day's free-flowing aspects show that the planets can work too easily together, leading to impulsive, destructive actions, especially when there is just enough negativity to trigger running riot and destruction.

In March 2015, the Germanwings disaster saw another individual action causing mass death, under even more sensational fire transits.[44] Again, Jupiter in Leo was close to its trine to Uranus and three other points in Aries, this time also near a trine with Saturn. Counter-balancing stress aspects were weak, except for Uranus completing its long-standing square with Pluto, and a tenth-house Venus in Taurus square Jupiter in Leo – determination to pay back the world for some unknown reason? With the Aries/Pisces stellium surrounding the local MC at the time, again we see that wild abandon to act recklessly, regardless, even perhaps because, of the consequences.

Such destruction is avoidable
Of course, this does not mean we should about-turn and assume that trine/sextile dominated charts are potentially malevolent; dangerously over-active if full of fire, resentful and emotionally self-destructive if water, possessive and greedy if earth, or neurotic and slanderous if airy. Strong negative stress energy can contain the excess, providing it counter-balances and does not reinforce the hyper-energy.

A far grander approach to all this is to learn how to combine astro-events, however unbalanced and difficult, for a beneficial outcome. It involves training ourselves, especially our leaders and therapists who care for those with troubled minds. All of us need to stand back, see and use the transits in the best way possible. Armed with astro-event insight, we can dig deeply into circumstances to find and correct root causes. We may even prevent problems in advance. However bad the action, it does not help to write it off as evil and seek extreme means to eradicate the perpetrator. Organising society to protect us against 'absolutely evil people' will keep us in constant fear and ignorance; far better to seek to understand why people do what they do.

Wikipedia outlined the people who influenced Abu Yahya al-Qayrawani, the Tunisian mass-murderer, suggesting his root inspiration was Abu Qatada.[45] It does not go on to explore how the conditions of Qatada's Palestinian upbringing in Bethlehem in the 1960s and 1970s might have led to him holding and preaching extreme views. We cannot excuse, but may be able to understand the mind of a growing boy, powerless to do more than throw stones at soldiers, who were well-armed by foreign friends.

Dominant forces may have the machines and methods of control to do as they will, but only at the risk of all their citizens and friends becoming 'fair game' for revenge. Having failed to seek and find genuine objective understanding that brings everyone together, when the astro-cycles indicate a window of opportunity for dramatic change, slaughter, not solutions, become the order of the day.

Even though we do not know the birth time, from the date of Andréas Lubitz's natal chart, we see a massive stellium of fiery Sagittarian planets, plus the Moon, Mars and Pluto together in Scorpio.[46] These show clearly a reckless death-defying character, who needs to be carefully watched, especially when his Sagittarian planets are making a grand trine with the crash day planets! A proper respect for and use of astrology with personnel engaged in aviation and other high-risk activities should have triggered a check on Andréas' state of mind, before he was allowed to fly on that day.[47]

Astrology helps us avoid being victims of circumstances. Whether they indicate stressful or easy flowing possibilities; by standing back and witnessing changing astro-events, we can see a time's best and worst possible outcomes. Then with clear minds we can see how to apply the transits beneficially. Developing such wisdom is astrology's finest function. It justifies a lifetime's devotion to its study.

-o0o-

Here is a helpful hint from the September 2018 column, on how to avoid the dangerous consequences of overconfidence.

The Astrology of Putting your Foot in It

We could all learn from the astrology of Donald Trump's Helsinki Press Conference

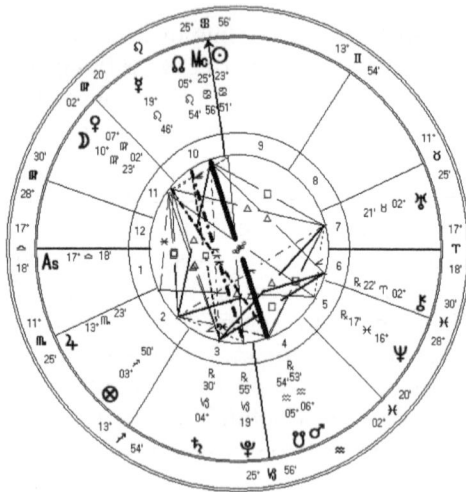

Helsinki Press Conference
16 Jul 2018 13:35 EEDT -3:00
Helsinki, Finland 60°N10' 024°E58'
Tropical Placidus True Node

problem. The clue is not only in particular planetary positions, but the close precision of their aspects.

Ascendant ruler Venus is six hours past being conjuncted by the Moon (the Sun and MC ruler), but also just two and a half hours past an exact quincunx to an exact Mars/South Node conjunction in Aquarius. He would have gone into the talks buoyed up by what he would have felt had been great success in NATO and the UK. The newly separating aspects would have relaxed and left him ill-prepared for the press conference; overconfident, feeling he could 'wing it' as he would a campaign rally before his unquestioning, adoring base.

The actual communication error is indicated by Mercury in Leo, a quarter of degree past an exact sesquiquadrate to Saturn in Capricorn and applying to a quincunx to Pluto in the same sign. The latter was to be exact as the chorus of criticism grew to a crescendo in the hours that followed.

The Icarian lesson! When feeling you have flown beyond many obstacles, it is time to redouble your focus, not just enjoy the ride. For this is the time when your shortcomings are most likely to be revealed and you lose your wings!

-o0o-

The September 2019 column included a snapshot of Boris Johnson, the new UK Prime Minister, and his early actions in office, all presented in astro-cycle clips.

Astro Moments with Boris Johnson

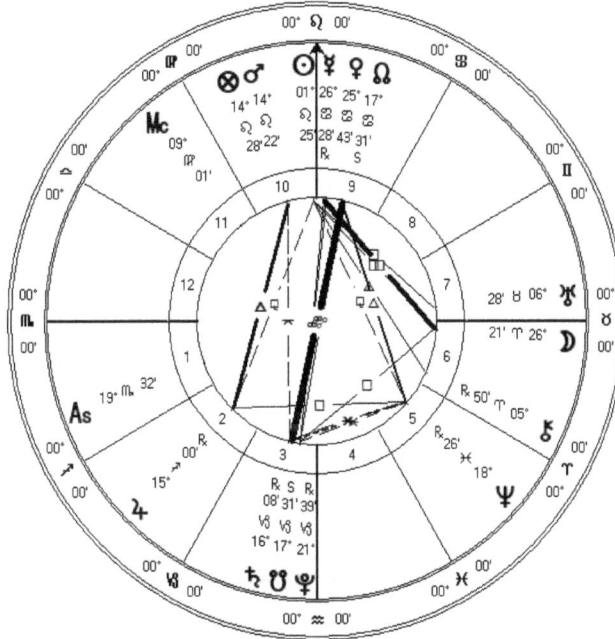

Boris Johnson
19 Jun 1964 14:00 EDT +4:00
New York, NY 40°N43' 74°W00'
Tropical Placidus True Node

There will be many full astro-analyses of the new UK Prime Minister's chart. Here are just a few of my own cameos, seeking to capture the essence of his fascinating character and show just how accurate astrology can be.

❖ *Mercury with Sun conjunct Venus all in Gemini in the ninth* clearly indicate a verbose scholar capable of commanding universal attention. Three oppositions show his combative nature.

❖ *Uranus conjunct Pluto in Virgo oppose Saturn in Pisces, with Mars, also in Gemini, applying to make a T-Square (eleventh, eighth and fifth houses).* His nature encapsulates the social revolution brewing at his birth time. His service will be disruptive, whatever the cost.

❖ *Jupiter in Taurus opposes Neptune in Pisces (eighth to second).* His expansive grasp of history will be confusingly based on desire, but not always reality – what he wants, not necessarily what is possible.

❖ *His Gemini Mercury, Sun and Venus approach North Node and oppose South Node (ninth and fourth).* His ideas and words aspire to great heights, but are they dangerously beyond possible reality?[48]

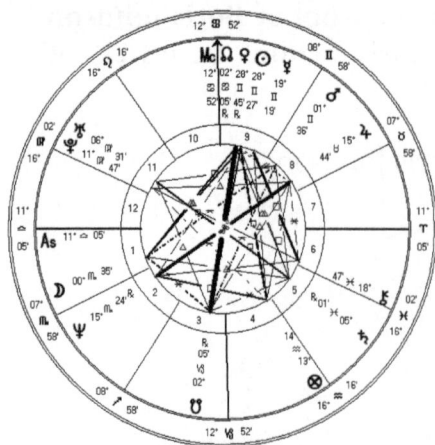

Boris Johnson Prime Minister
24 Jul 2019 15:35 BST -1:00
London, UK 51°N30' 000°W10'
Tropical Placidus True Node

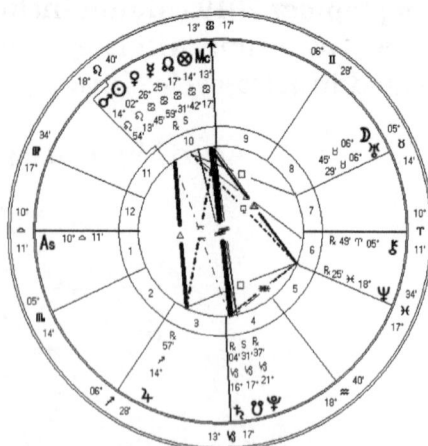

Boris Johnson First Speech to Parliament
25 Jul 2019 11:47 BST -1:00
London, UK 51°N30' 000°W10'
Tropical Placidus True Node

Whole Sign Chart of His Premiership

The moment of his photo with HM The Queen, the Ascendant rulers capture the premiership's essential nature with eminent simplicity.

- ❖ *Mars is in Leo in the tenth ruled by the Sun, also in the tenth.* This will be a premiership of imperial certainty that seeks to conquer and cast aside all opposition; to rule supreme.
- ❖ *Scorpio's modern ruler, Pluto, is in Capricorn in the third, ruled by Saturn, also in the third and conjunct the South Node.* He will find his immediate environment and fraternal relationships restrictive.
- ❖ *All third-house planets are opposed by sign to Mercury, Venus and the North Node in Cancer in the ninth, ruled by the Moon in Aries in the cadent sixth.* Outsiders are likely to fear his impact. They will be defensive and so put up barriers in the face of what seems unrealistic.
- ❖ *Jupiter in second in its ruling sign Sagittarius is square Neptune in the fifth in its ruling sign Pisces.* With eminent creative accounting the impossible may well seem within reach, but will it be no more than glorious dreams that fade when audited and faced with the test of time?

Unperturbed by any of the above obstacles, the UK's new Prime Minister lost no time in appointing twenty-five members of his cabinet (all committed to leaving the EU on 31 October 2019) and calling them together for a first meeting photo-call at 08:30 BST the following morning, announcing he would address Parliament at 11:30 BST.

Boris Johnson's First Speech to Parliament

Elegantly set up by Jacob Rees-Mogg, the new Leader of the House, Boris Johnson started at 11:47 BST with a wide-ranging idealistic outline of his administration's aims. Then he answered 129 members' questions. In all, this took two hours and twenty-eight minutes.

❖   The chart of the event is an exact example of astrology at work. *Midheaven two degrees applying to Fortuna, which is 23 minutes of arc from an exact conjunction to his natal Midheaven.* The right day and moment of day!

❖   *Mars in Leo at the other end of the Cancer/Leo tenth house stellium is well under a degree short of an exact T-square to his natal Jupiter in Taurus/Neptune in Scorpio opposition.* Was all this believable or what he and his supporters wanted to believe?

❖   *As nearly two and a half hours progressed the Midheaven crossed the North Node, Mercury and Venus in Cancer and then the Sun and Mars in Leo.* Still he continued, as the house emptied, but for his devoted team and those who still hoped to have their questions called, until *the Midheaven reached 27 degrees and 6 minutes of arc,* when the Speaker thanked the Prime Minister and wound up the session.

Concluding Comments

The contrast with the ponderous intransigence of his predecessor was absolute. Looking beyond the elephant in the room of his Brexit deadline vow, the new Prime Minster seemed to offer so much the nation desperately needed. He even reached into elements of the Labour Party's 2017 General Election Manifesto, albeit without the financial strategy needed to bring the kites he flew down to earth.

Time will tell whether the inertia of practical reality and events pull down and deflate his glorious vision. Will the incredible energy with which he started his Premiership be sustained? His detractors will be quick to dismiss his words as pie-in-the-sky bombast. His supporters will warm to his eloquent taste for struggle. They will see it as the sign of greatness that can indeed move mountains and achieve the world renown for Britain that he visualises. It is unlikely to be anything in between.

What can be certain is that the astrology of the man, and what he does, will always be a crucial guide to what can and cannot be achieved in the unbelievably challenging world we face this autumn through into 2020.

.-oOo-

As the UK moved towards a General Election the November 2019 column explored the astro-cycles driving the UK Prime Minister's key adviser, showing why he was the right man in the right place at the right time – for those wanting Brexit, that is!

Dominic Cummings - for How Long can Sagittarius Rule?

Even without a time, the birth chart of Boris Johnson's Chief of Staff certainly reflects his role in the intense Brexit debate that is building to fever pitch as I write.

His strong, behind the scenes, controlling energy suggests some twelfth-house focus and possibly a Capricorn Ascendant. So, I have guessed at around 11:00 GMT. In any event, there are five planets in Sagittarius. The Moon is either in, or about to enter, Pisces and then square the Sagittarian stellium, by progression, for the first few years of his life.

Just looking at the transits and progressions for 'Brexit Day', it is clear why he is the driving force in the centre of this time and issue. Transiting Jupiter had moved into direct motion and returned to its natal position just as Boris Johnson was elected leader of the Conservative Party. It is very nearly conjunct his progressed Jupiter on

'Brexit Day'. His progressed Moon has just conjuncted his natal Sun. The progressed Midheaven has been crossing his natal Ascendant and the Midheaven at the 23:00 UT time is just over two degrees past his progressed Ascendant. Transiting Mars will be in the middle of the two degrees between his natal and progressed Uranus.

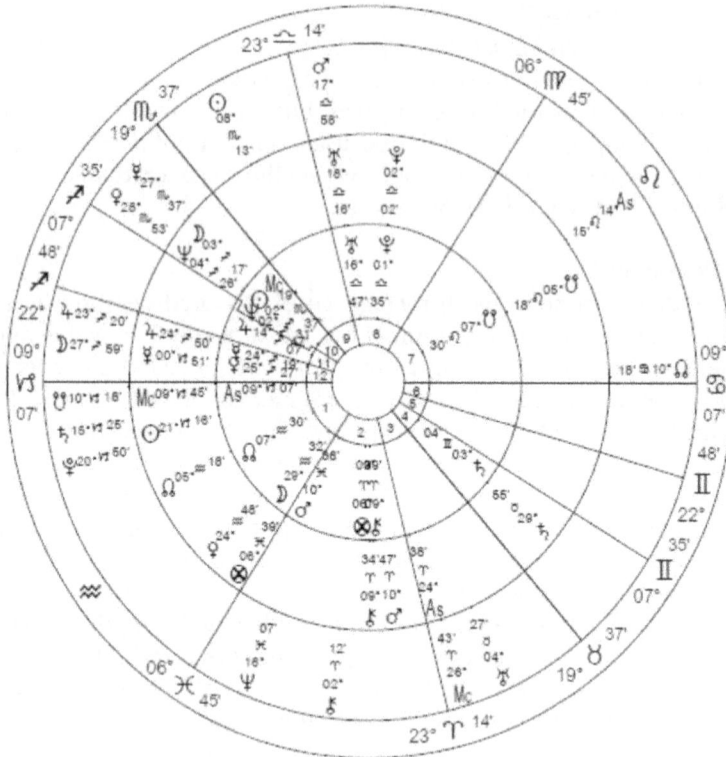

Innermost wheel: **Dominic Cummings Natal** 25 Nov 1971 11:00 UT +0:00 Durham, UK
Middle wheel: **secondary progressed** 31 Oct 2019 23:00 UT +0:00 London, UK
Outer wheel: **Transits** 31 Oct 2019 23:00 UT +0:00 London, UK
Geocentric Placidus True Node

However, transiting Pluto is twenty-one minutes of arc short of his progressed Sun and will conjunct it twenty-three days after the thirty-first. Also transiting Mercury makes a retrograde station just short of a conjunction to Venus, with both planets tantalisingly short of his progressed Moon/natal Sun conjunction in Sagittarius.

So crucial questions to ask as I write, but almost certainly will have been answered by the time you read this:

❖ Will his story be of the man who took hold of the nation and, against all odds and some of the best political brains in the country, took it over the edge to a no-deal Brexit?

❖ OR is this a man obsessed, who poured the heart and soul of himself, his leader and most of the Conservative Party into a constantly-repeated-slogan campaign, and came incredibly close, only to fail at the last hurdle?

What cannot be denied is that the transits describe either outcome really well.

-o0o-

The March 2020 column included an actual example of how understanding the astro-cycles alongside my natal chart made a very irritating day just about bearable.

Astrology Working Precisely

Visualise that traumatic moment, when your computer says you are password blocked! How irritating, so much to do, but now rejected as a dodgy stranger from your precious personal data.

If clicking the 'Forgot password' button in time does not restore access, security systems can be a nightmare. Can you access your email, mobile phone, do you have a signal? Can you remember that security question you set up years ago?

Financial sites ask for customer numbers you never otherwise use, phone numbers, other linked accounts, recent deposit information. Then temporary passwords only work once or twice, input fields only show dots in response to your keystrokes. Get it wrong and start again.

Finding the right phone help number may not be easy. After several tries at complex auto-menu systems and endless irritating music, finally you speak to a customer services employee, trained to be polite, patient and helpful, but rarely so well informed technically. The system seems designed to protect customers from the people who actually know how it works. So, I endured a whole day of music and three advisers with different incomplete answers.

Now to the astrology! For Aquarians, this year's many planets in Capricorn is difficult. Aquarians feel they know better and are frustrated by Capricorn insistence on another way. Making it worse, that day Mercury was void of course in Capricorn's last degree. Driving my determination to break through my frustration was transiting Mars in Sagittarius, trine to my natal Mars in Aries... an increasing struggle to restrain anger, when held back on all sides.

Now comes the reason for telling you all this. At 16:15, I made a fourth call to another number, tucked away in the very early setup papers. This was immediately answered by a man who understood my problem and patiently talked me through the solution step by step, teaching me so much about the back end of Google in the process. The call completed at 16:47 GMT. The bi-wheel of that time shows transiting MC exactly conjuncting my natal Mars and trining transiting Mars.

Always look to the angles to trigger the pressure of the day for good or ill!

-o0o-

Chapter 4
Towards and through the Iraq War
[Articles written March 2002 – May 2011]

Historical Background

Conflicts between predominantly Christian Western cultures and people in the Middle East go back to the Roman destruction of Jerusalem in 70 CE, through the Christian/Islamic Crusades, the Ottoman Empire's role in Eastern Europe, the First World War and the settlement that followed.

In modern times, relations have been profoundly affected by the discovery and exploitation of immense oil reserves in the region, described brilliantly by Daniel Yergin in his Pulitzer Prize winning book,[49] as well as the 1948 establishment of Israel as a Jewish State.

A perceived sense of injustice in decisions surrounding these issues have fuelled intolerable extremist action, and consequent counter-action. The astro-cycles of the twenty-first century noughties give incisive insight into this history. Understanding and applying them to the above history could have averted the horrific consequences of the 2010s.

Contemporary Background

11 September 2001 – Destruction of the World Trade Center in New York, USA.

7 October 2001 – US and allies invade Afghanistan in search of al-Qaeda.

11-12 September 2002 – President Bush visits site of World Trade Center and threatens Iraq at UN.

19-20 March 2003 – Invasion of Iraq by US and Allies.

1 May 2003 – President gives speech under a 'Mission Accomplished' banner.

30 January 2005 – First Iraqi post-war election.

4 June 2009 – Obama's speech to the Arab world at Cairo University, Egypt.

17 December 2010 – The beginning of the Arab Spring.

8 April 2013 – Abu Bakr al-Baghdadi declares a self-styled Islamic State Caliphate, which was to expand its control to vast areas of Syria and Iraq, only to lose the last of its conquests in 2019. Founded in 1999 to support al-Qaeda, ISIL [Daesh] developed its extreme philosophy in the vast prison camps, established by the United States, after its invasion of Iraq.

Introduction

Whether we see it as the last year of the twentieth century or the first of a new millennium, the spring of the year 2000 saw the bursting of the 1990s-generated dot.com bubble boom, followed by a very successful Australian Olympics.

Then from 7 November came the disputed result of the US Presidential Election, not to be resolved for over a month. Astrologically, everything was against a clear result. On the day of the vote, Mercury was building to a direct station, void of course at the last degree of Libra – neither one thing nor another. As the results were coming in overnight, the Scorpio ingress explained an eruption of passion that was to grip the nation. Results were disputed, with legal challenges going right up to the US Supreme Court.

The worst thing at such a time is a partisan dispute. The pressure was intolerable. Would delaying polling day for a week have allowed time for clearer minds to prevail? Would waiting that little bit longer for all the re-counting to be completed have led to another outcome?

Certainly, the situation harmed the apolitical image of the US Supreme Court, from which it still suffers. Events ahead were to change the world for decades, if not centuries. Would it have been different with Al Gore at the helm? The world continued to rest back through 2001, until the events of 9/11 shrieked deep long-unresolved issues between extreme Islamic and Western cultures into a rebellion that was to sour all our lives.

When relationships between people become violent, what happens next requires profound strength at the worst and best extremes of human behaviour.

- ❖ EITHER brutality and destruction pour out, accelerate and expand on all sides, ('Why should any human being conceive and celebrate such destruction of innocent human lives?')

- ❖ OR a courageous rising of objective selflessness seeks to understand and heal unacceptable hurt ('What have we, or our representatives, done to cause this?')

These vital questions were hardly explored at the time of the 9/11 atrocity. It seemed unacceptable to ask them. Only hard-hearted revenge would do. So, the carnage of death was to grow and grow to such an inconceivable extent, generated by multi-facetted injustice on every side.

What makes a young man or woman decide the best and most honourable thing to do is blow up themselves and an indiscriminate number of strangers? Such actions come from the notion of evil polarised at two opposite extremes. Each side, lacking the courage to seek for a cause within themselves, takes action that exacerbates the sense on the other side that it is justified to retaliate. This way the room for understanding is so narrow that resolution is impossible. Those we see and treat as our enemies are thrown into the arms of irreconcilable extremists. There is always one totally intolerant murderer in every ten thousand or so people. By not asking 'why' and addressing the response, we abandon naive young idealists and leave them at the mercy of fanatics.

Invading Afghanistan, to find and eradicate the source of the 9/11 attack, focused the world mind throughout 2001 into the New Year. Long before this was completed, troops were moved to a new campaign – the invasion of Iraq to complete the 1991 Gulf War!

-oOo-

The third 'Working with the Planets' column was written in May/June for the July 2002 magazine, when, we now know, CIA operatives infiltrated Iraq, through the Kurdish area, to find associates and targets to be used during the anticipated invasion. Movements for and against such an invasion were building.

What follows are the first two pages of that July 2002 article that urges a healing approach. If only something like this had been considered then, before it was too late!

> The spring is wound up tight. It will uncoil of itself.
> *Antigone* Jean Anouilh

Jean Anouilh was describing how the various elements of a tragic plot build and tighten up on each other like a spring wound to its maximum tension, from which point it can only unwind. As it does, various events dependent on the winding occur. In the case of a clock or watch spring the hands move, time advances. In the case of a tragedy like *Antigone*, the heroine buries her brother, suffers her fate and Creon, her judge and executioner, loses Haemon, his beloved son.

Both analogies are apt. The Greeks saw humankind at the mercy of the Gods and the planets as those Gods. Is this true? A clock or watch spring takes much longer to unwind than it does to wind up. So do the outcomes and consequences of planetary transits. *How the Planets Work* in this issue looks more deeply at both topics to help us understand and handle the *Major Astro Events* of the period ahead. For, while 'on paper' the coming months' transits are nowhere near as intense as those earlier in the year, we could still be confronted with some pretty dramatic situations.

At the Mercy of the Gods?
When Prince Oedipus was born, fearing the prediction that he would kill his father and marry his mother, his father ordered him killed, but a compassionate servant merely abandoned him in the desert, where he was found and cared for by a kindly

couple. In adulthood, he met and unknowingly killed his father, and then married his mother without realising his crimes until it was too late. Was this unavoidable – the result of 'fate' driven by the inevitability of planetary influence – or caused by his father's brutal attempt to circumvent the natural flow of the heavens?   A   modern psychological astrologer would note the 'Oedipus complex' and seek to work with the child and parents   to   recognise   and transcend it. Both men, by sharing a great love and admiration for the same woman, could bond and work closely together for the good of the kingdom. A generation later, Creon's fear of public disorder led him to command the live burial of his son's beloved Antigone. Yet their marriage could have unified a kingdom that was reeling from civil war. So it can be with planetary transits.   Specific   predictions create fears that fix outcomes by petrifying our power to act.

There is no difficulty that enough love will not conquer; no disease that enough love will not heal; no door that enough love will not open; no gulf that enough love will not bridge; no wall that enough love will not throw down; no sin that enough love will not redeem.

It makes no difference how deeply seated may be the trouble, How hopeless the outlook, How muddled the tangle, How great the mistake, a sufficient realisation of love will dissolve it all. If only you could love enough, you would be the happiest and most powerful being in the world.

Emmet Fox

The 'devil' lies in our attachment to outcomes – what we imagine will be the consequences of particular planetary events. How can we benefit from a generous-looking trine to our natal Venus? Is it possible to take advantage of an awkward Mercury retrograde transit to a business associate's chart? By thinking like this we abuse and lose the benefits astrology offers. We make ourselves even more the victims of fate than people who do not know astrology at all. Objective observation of such selfish use of astrology confirms the Greek view that we are at the mercy of the planets. Quite simply, selfish behaviour leads to predictable outcomes. If these people know about astrology, the predictable outcomes are indeed traumatic

'Godliness' comes from using an understanding of planetary events (be they easy or difficult) to ease pain and frustration and create a groundswell of happiness. Just as we try to organise our society to include disabled people, so we use astrological understanding to distribute benefits and avoid disasters. Such approaches create a groundswell of goodwill. This relaxes our vision, so we see well enough to avoid disaster. Whatever goes wrong, with positive support and friendship, the worst potential disasters the planets suggest may just be avoided. They were in 1999. In the build-up to the May/June, Saturn/ Pluto opposition; if by interfaith and cultural cooperation, we could come to forgive (even understand and care for) those who have harmed us, then 2002 could bring redemption, not war.

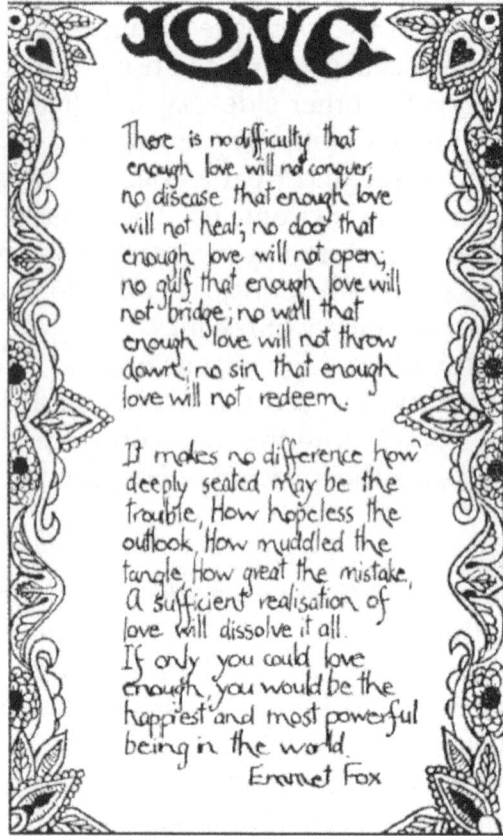

It will uncoil of itself.

The astrological basis for major events in world affairs and our lives is usually a complex build-up of outer-planetary pressure, activated by 'trigger' astro events, which on their own might be insignificant. The downturn in the Japanese Nikkei in 1989 was indicated exactly by a Capricorn stellium, triggered by the Capricorn New Moon; as was the bond market and equities correction in 1994. It took Jupiter having opposed Uranus, to be in exact opposition to Saturn and Neptune on the same days as Mercury and Sun squared the Nodal axis, to see the dismantling of the Berlin Wall and all it stood for in 1989. More recently the Taurus stellium, squared by Uranus in Aquarius, was triggered by New Moons in Aries and Taurus to burst the dot.com and technical stock bubble in 2000. My in-depth study of the Selby Train Crash in February 2001 outlines a complete pattern from the building pressure of outer-planetary transits to the triggering of exactly positioned angles at the moment of the crash.[50]

Another incredibly tight configuration will be just beginning to uncoil from its maximum intensity as this is published early July 2002. Retrograding Mars conjunct Pluto, opposed by Jupiter through the middle of 2001, symbolised the mass killing of animals in Britain's foot-and-mouth crisis, the growing suicide bombing threat in Palestine and the planning of the Twin Towers attack in New York. The serious consequences of these events have been working themselves out as Saturn replaced Jupiter to oppose Pluto – especially on the US chart close to 11 September 2001. In early May 2002, Venus and Mercury joined Mars, weak with Saturn, in the opposite sign Gemini. The declinations were almost close enough for Venus to occult Mars. Certainly, the Moon covered several planets. Saturn was joined by the eclipsed Sun on 10 June, two weeks after it completed its opposition to Pluto. These and other details were considered in the May 'Working with the Planets'. The effect is like a spring being double-wound-tightened so close in on itself that it will have been difficult to find room to act, despite an intense desire to do so.

As I write this (early May 2002) we are into the 'teeth' of the build-up to all that. Right now, it is easy to find many other astrological reasons to expect the worst in the period between my time now and when you read this in early July. As well as the obvious national and international conflicts, astro-consultant colleagues are reporting clients in trauma in their personal lives. A groundswell of change, broken promises and disappointment dominates our relationships. It would be easy to stand frozen in bitterness at the violation being perpetrated upon us personally, culturally, nationally and internationally.

-o0o-

Prophetically page three of the July 2002 article concluded with warnings of worse to come.

Nor is all this likely to clear with one or two trigger events. Mars is weak making us feel impotent to act for the time being. Venus is strong driving outrage at the 'ravishing of our values'. Saturn near the North Node in Gemini is opposed to Pluto making problems incomprehensible and ridden with death. For many it must feel very much like the end of days. 'Scores remain to be settled' and 'prices have to be paid'. With so much yet to be resolved, wise and inspired compassionate leadership in world affairs and patient understanding openheartedness in our personal lives is the only way to prevent problems erupting. If hearts have not opened, the world and our lives could be in pretty traumatic circumstances as you read this.

And there could be more to come as the consequences of the abuse of our values express themselves! This spring has been tightening for a long time. The uncoiling has just commenced. There is so much built-up resentment that, without patience and compassion, future minor astro-triggers, which at other times would be hardly noticed, could set off major events.

-oOo-

Inspired by Queen Elizabeth II's highly successful Golden Jubilee celebrations, the September 2002 column opened on a positive note.

> And in the end the love you take is equal to the love you make.
> The Beatles *Abbey Road*

The success of the Queen's Jubilee celebrations amidst difficult eclipses, the Saturn/Pluto opposition and other challenging astro events (outlined in the May's 'Working with the Planets'), shows just how much can be achieved with negative astro energy - providing there is respect for and cooperation between people and their sub-cultures. The processions and concerts did this great work really well. As a result, danger melted away. The forty-nine 'hells angel' motor-cyclists screeched to stop their speedy path along the Mall to salute and honour, not harm, the royal family, so vulnerably placed on a very low dais. Concord rose majestically up and away from the palace. The fire on Saturday night did not reach the masses of fireworks stored elsewhere in the building. What could have been disastrous was good, because our love and devotion made it so.

-oOo-

The November 2002 column was focused upon the dangers indicated by the applying Jupiter in Leo / Neptune in Aquarius opposition. It counselled against egocentric over-confidence, relating this specifically to the Middle East crisis and offering other ways of resolving it.

Written as the plan to invade Iraq was forming, the warning was to be ignored. With the Saturn/Uranus trine came the 'shock and awe' invasion of Iraq on the night of 19 March 2003.

Egocentricity - the Enemy of Astrological Understanding

The more we develop our esoteric and especially astrological insights and powers, the more dangerous a force the unfettered ego becomes. Pride, self-obsession and possessiveness about '*our* knowledge, discoveries and favoured techniques' is the harbinger at the gateway to delusion and conflict. For astrology is the study of all relationships. While such studies must be based on consistently definable criteria, to allow ego-driven motives to narrow down relationships and claim supremacy for one criterion, person, or opinion over others is to miss the point entirely. It misappropriates the authority of astrology, and uses it to harm others and misinterpret their behaviour. When, even for the best of reasons, individuals see themselves as vital custodians of 'the Truth', argument, resentment and loss of power inevitably follow.

Humility, respect for, willingness to learn from, others is the way to wisdom. To say we are right, more professional, qualified and informed may well indicate the exact opposite. A good code of ethics is rooted in the astrologer's care for the client and every person the client is likely to contact – including other experts and specialists they may need to contact. A good astrologer should liberate by opening doors, not trap people in rooms. Without a technique that tempers, it is malpractice to give astrological advice?

It would be an ideal world, if such standards of selflessness were those of our political leaders and all public debate. Posturing and position-taking are tedious to observe and doomed to failure. For the first step towards understanding is to open the mind to all possibilities – especially those one feels inclined to dismiss. However hard we argue our corner, no problem is solved until there is a cross-fertilising meeting of minds. Yet, in practice, the norm is the opposite. 'Public relations' experts are trained to push a line and make 'opponents' appear to be in the wrong. This separates the parties in a dispute even further, each desperately developing techniques to gather 'public support'. Imagine the joy of news analysis programmes, where people share their different views and genuinely seek, even find, resolution.

With Jupiter in Leo until August next year and not completing its opposition to Neptune in Aquarius until early June, egocentric posturing and illusions of grandeur are likely to bore, outrage, frustrate and confuse many people throughout the world. As I write this, the first hit of the opposition is due in fifteen days' time. Today's two news headlines are that 60,000 delegates are gathering in South Africa for a world summit and that the US government, whose President is expected to be a notable absentee, is focusing instead on the toppling of Saddam Hussein. The intensification and outcomes of both items are likely to continue to be dominating the news when you read this. Scientific 'discoveries' and the bureaucracy of its 'experts' may well be taking increasing control of our lives. Tighter control of vitamin sales is being considered by the European Union. There are moves to prevent countries from discriminating against GM products in the interest of 'free trade'. Generally, we are over-dependent on 'experts', who rely guardedly on statistical studies, whose findings frequently change. Expect attacks that seek to confuse the public mind about astrology. In our private lives, be prepared for egocentric posturing and especially a struggle over exactly who is motivated by self-interest and who by the greater good. Jupiter in Leo opposed to Neptune in Aquarius is the precise archetype of all these.

Clearing the Clouds of Confusion

With Jupiter retrograding back to its second opposition to Neptune mid-February, confused and misdirected egocentricity will certainly figure in these two months. A few days later, a second ongoing astro event makes a vital move. Saturn goes direct and begins to complete its trine to Uranus. Crucially this will occur in water, not air, signs. For the Uranus ingress on 10th March begins to explore the sensitivities of Pisces – the third and most important astro event of this period.

-o0o-

Written in March/April that year, the May 2003 column uses understanding of the astro-cycles to put the Iraq War in clear perspective, predicting exactly the likely consequences.

> So, first of all, let me assert my firm belief that the only thing we
> have to fear... is fear itself   Franklin D Roosevelt

The above oft-quoted words aptly describe the present astro energy. Jupiter in Leo opposes Neptune in Aquarius, while Saturn has been close again to its 2001/2 opposition to Pluto and now moves firmly forward towards Cancer. Well-intentioned over-confidence is driven by hysterical fear, caused by the traumas of the recent past. Once possessed by such energies, it is difficult to separate paranoiac fears from real concerns. Indeed, we may bring what we fear into actuality by focusing on the paranoia.

The build-up to another Gulf war (as I write) shows the astrology of the time perfectly. The stated war aim is to eradicate fear for the future, by disposing of weapons of mass destruction right now. People against the war say the consequent upheaval in the Middle East and resultant terrorism would create an even more fearful future. They remind us that every death leaves a family that may well seek revenge. Both views point self-righteously to the moral pre-eminence of their position. Both views are driven by Neptune in Aquarius (belief in the salvation of humanity), Jupiter in Leo (our imperial generosity) and their opposition (constantly expanding, by being at odds with each other). The result is a mass of contradictory terror scenarios – be they real, imagined, or even self-created by the anxious way we react to the astro energy. Of course, many of the problems are real, but, ask yourself, is now a clear time to know how to handle them? Solutions may emerge more easily, when the opposition has passed and the intensity of the anxiety calms down.

Are you noticing similar patterns and attitudes in your own mind, life and the lives of those around you? Much depends how exactly the Jupiter/Neptune opposition axis and other contemporary astro events connect with your natal chart. Avoid easy commitments – especially during May to July 2003. As the pressure releases, many will backtrack from what they rushed into earlier in the year. Learn from what happens to people in the news – 'as above, so below' at every level.

Where George W Bush and Tony Blair stand by the Autumn of 2003 will be especially interesting. They have been the 'men of the moment'. Their personal astrology explains why. The American President has Mercury, rising at 9Le50, two degrees below his Ascendant. It is followed by Pluto at 10Le35. The British Prime Minister has his natal Moon opposite at 11Aq30 close to his North Node in 6Aq54, both in the tenth house. George Bush is pushing the pace; Tony Blair is his most public supporter. They are linked by the Jupiter opposing Neptune transit, which occurred on 11 September 2002 at 8Le/Aq36, 16 February 2003 at 11Le/Aq16 and completes on 4 June 2003 at 13Le/Aq5. So, George W Bush hurries to act, as he dreams of the 'democratisation' of Iraq (even the entire Middle East), as crucial in easing his people's terror after 9/11. Maybe Tony Blair agrees, or feels his best way of serving the world at this time is to stay 'real close' to the main protagonist. Opponents of the war visualise innocent death, a quagmire of resentment and the consequent break up of multi-cultural tolerance between and within countries and communities. To a certain extent, all involved are driven and deceived by the astro-energy of the time. Whichever path dominates by the time you read this, read on (especially the *Major Astro Events* section) – there is still hope.[51]

Is political and military muscle the insurance policy to set minds at rest? Another aspect of the Jupiter opposed Neptune hysteria is the fear of homeland terrorism. Is the best future we can look forward to the constant threat of anthrax, smallpox, poison gas and explosion in our day-to-day lives? Is our best protection the spending of billions of pounds/dollars on expensive security operatives, regulations and hardware that increasingly regulate our every move? Without good will, are security teams likely to cap the 'erupting volcano', or just make our lives miserable while they try? Must we look suspiciously at whole groups, because a few of their number may threaten us? Is this the future world we wish to bequeath to our children? Or is there another way?

With Jupiter and Neptune at odds, working harder at religious understanding would seem to be more fruitful than political and disputed military action. When an alien culture attacks fanatics, it creates a cushion of partial sympathy for their idealism among those who share their beliefs, if not their methods. As well as speaking out against war, moderate religious opinion in the Christian, Jewish, Hindu and Muslim communities should meet, identify problems, admit errors and point to solutions. Each spiritual community could ease tension, by putting appropriate pressure on its own fanatics, making practical, political action easier.

The 6 pm BBC news broadcast on the day of the Pisces ingress this year gave hope. The Archbishop of Canterbury, with Britain's senior Roman Catholic cardinal, released a joint statement against military action in the Gulf. In the same bulletin was a news item describing a series of regular meetings between Jewish and Muslim clerics in London. Tension between those two communities had been reduced.

Hopefully, being in the midst of the 10 March to 15 September 2003 Uranus/Neptune mutual reception, we are beginning to see the end of an excessively Aquarian period of arrogant cerebral insensitivity.[52] It is not enough to know, think we understand and adopt suitable, scientifically-based altruistic procedures to improve the lot of humanity. To really understand, we have to *make contact* and go through 'our enemy's' experience just as deeply as he does. Pisces represents the eternal, universal sea, in which we are all linked together. What happens to one, happens to us all. When we have to struggle for the 'right to survive', we all drown.

Hope for Astrology

This is where astrology comes in. If material science rose ever higher during the Uranus/Neptune in Aquarius period, now, towards its end, the shortcomings of what technology can and cannot achieve can be seen clearly.[53] It will be even clearer in 2004. We need the contact of Piscean experience to give meat and life to the bones of well-intentioned Aquarian theories. May the mutual reception bring a whole that is far greater than the sum of its Aquarian and Piscean parts. Astrological explanations could enable such understanding, by informing and encouraging us to put ourselves in perspective. Rising above the distortions of cultural and socio-religious assumption, we seek solutions based on mutual respect.

-oOo-

Written the Autumn of 2003, the November column showed the West was in danger of repeating the errors made regarding the Middle East after First World War.

> So, I always say, if you wish to care for yourself, care for others. This
> is enlightened self-interest.   *HH The Dalai Lama of Tibet*

We come to a two-month count-down to 30 December 2003, when Uranus enters Pisces for a seven-year mutual reception with Neptune in Aquarius. As I write this, in early September, the Virgo/Pisces opposition and imminent return of Uranus to Aquarius is throwing up recrimination, accusation and misrepresentation in many vital areas. How 'hot these pots are boiling', when you read this will determine how low our society and our relationships with each other have sunk. For, however difficult the energy and however arrogant our adversary, problems can be solved and happiness achieved, if selfless patience and concern for others is applied.

The Astrological Association demonstrated this at their September 2003 Annual Conference. The many difficulties in the build-up were welcomed as opportunities to improve the event and its facilities. So, we adapted the programme, found a top-quality venue near water and enjoyed great success, in spite of a most difficult chart.

There are two vital areas in our world that would benefit from similar patience and compassion.

Resolving the World Crisis Rooted in the Middle East

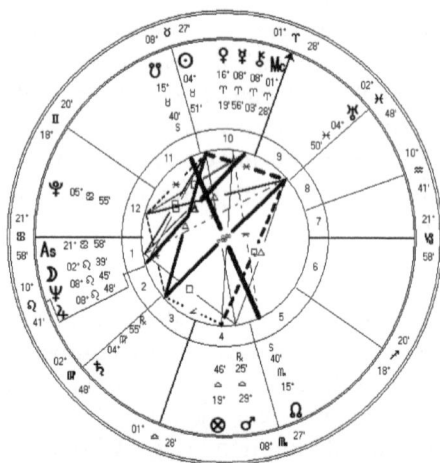

Middle East Mandate
25 Apr 1920 11:22 CEDT -2:00
San Remo, Italy 43°N49' 007°E46'
Geocentric Tropical Placidus True Node

Thanks to Nicholas Campion for reminding us of the chart for the moment that the League of Nations created the modern states of Palestine (with provision for a Jewish homeland, which became the modern state of Israel), Jordan and Iraq, under the stewardship of Britain, with Syria and Lebanon under France. These acts by the victors of the First World War are felt by many to be the root cause of the continuing crisis in the Middle East and consequent terrorism throughout our world. Uranus was in early Pisces then as well, but it was opposed to Saturn in Virgo (now it is trined). Crucially, Neptune was in Leo, opposite to its present position and conjunct, not opposed, to Jupiter at 8Le45. Both planets were about to be conjuncted by the Moon. With Mercury and Venus in mid-Aries, if ever there were a chart for ill-conceived impulsive, ego-driven decisions, this is it. The world and especially the people of the Middle East have suffered the consequences ever since.

The astrology of the implications for us today becomes clear when we remind ourselves that both the main Sibley US charts have 8 degrees Sagittarius/Gemini at the Ascendant/Descendant axis, almost exactly trine to the Jupiter/Neptune conjunction of the Mandate chart.[54]   Furthermore, the recent Jupiter/Neptune oppositions were at 8Le/Aq36 (11 September 2002, when all the world leaders gathered at Ground Zero), 11Le/Aq16 (16 February 2003, the anti-war peace marches) and 13Le/Aq6 (3 June 2003, world leaders meet in St. Petersburg and France). There are many cardinal tensions between the three charts as well. Clearly the US government was rushed by 9/11 into a war on terrorism, which is really about their karmic responsibility (with Britain and France) for the 1920 decision. It was the USA that pressed for the original League of Nations decision and especially for the United Nations one in 1948 that created the state of Israel.

The 'war on terrorism' cannot be won by force of arms, but only in the hearts and minds of everyone involved. For the problem is not, as it is being presented, a struggle between good and evil, between one religion (or culture) and another. What we have is an endless feud caused by action and reaction by both sides and their friends. The well-intentioned nation-creation of the 1920 decision, the billions of dollars of US aid to Israel, the secret support and arms smuggled to the Palestinians, the sacrificed young bodies of the beleaguered Palestinians all exacerbate the bitterness. Nor will tightly negotiated agreements bring lasting settlement. Without trust, the slightest hiccup can unravel years of careful work.

Feuds are not resolved by listing all the wrongs one party has done to the other, but by everyone involved admitting the wrongs they have done and offering genuine apology and redress. With Neptune now in Aquarius, opposed to its 1920 Leo position, and the egocentric idealism of the recent Jupiter in Leo opposition to Neptune in Aquarius having failed to force through a solution, we should look to the Uranus/Neptune mutual reception to initiate a process of healing. It will require modesty and compassion and grand offers of generosity from strong and weak alike. South Africa has shown the way.

Uranus in Pisces suggests dividing Palestine will not solve its problems. It would lead to further hurt, feelings of betrayal and endless struggles over land and resources – especially water. As in South Africa, what is needed is for both cultures to agree to live together, sharing the same land and capital city. Indeed, the old city of Jerusalem would be better internationally controlled – a symbol of peace for people of all faiths. Walls symbolise and create enmity, terror and counter-terror. Inflated egos created the Palestinian crisis and have perpetuated it ever since. The recent Jupiter/Neptune opposition has shown the futility of this egocentricity. May Uranus in Pisces bring the sensitivity and mutability to find another way, especially as Saturn opposed Chiron completes on 20 June 2006. Then Israeli Prime Minister Rabin will not have died in vain for 'The peace of the brave'.

With Uranus still in Aquarius, as you read this, you may find my efforts to be positive about situations and the people involved at best admirably unrealistic, at worst dangerous dreaming. Be heartened by the fact that when Neptune (after its time in Leo) and Uranus were in detriment and fall in the late 1930s/early 1940s, we had the worst of times. So why, with both planets mutually receiving rulership, cannot we now have the best of times and start putting right many of those past negativities?   This is what happened in 1507/8, 1670/75, 1835/43. Perhaps John Lennon was not 'the only one' after all.[55]

A future to prepare for and intelligently build through the two remaining Uranus-in-Aquarius months.

-o0o-

The January 2004 the column advised a positive healing way out.

It is Vital to Die with a Fortunate Mind

The above words are far more positive than they first seem. For, if we have a fortunate mind about death, we will live all the time with a clear mind, and so lead a happy life. Problems are caused because we are frightened of 'the consequences' – the 'death' of what we have. Fear of the consequences exposes us to all kinds of exploitation by those who manipulate, by offering protection from whom and what they claim 'is responsible' for our fears. Some advertisers, arms manufacturers, lawyers, insurers, politicians, priests, even astrologers grow rich by selling an empty pretence of salvation. It is far better to rely on compassion – a most powerful remedy, when we are confronted by difficult situations and people With it we ride problems, as does a sailor the dangerous currents and storms of the open ocean.

This is an appropriate image for the Uranus/Neptune mutual reception, now fully in place for the coming seven years. The boundless Piscean ocean of compassion reaches out in all directions to create the secure healing contact of understanding between all that is. Neptune in Aquarius – 'we believe in universal understanding'. Uranus in Pisces – 'we awaken to the experience of all existence'. Together 'we awaken to a belief based on the total experience of universal understanding'. Conscious and full of discriminating awareness, without fear or favour, we celebrate the many cycles of birth and rebirth, within and between lives.

Of course, Pisces is ambiguous and a lot can go wrong. Perhaps egos will surge and fuel fundamentalism in the storm winds just outside the still centre of the temple of ultimate truth. Being at the end of the zodiac cycle, Pisces can bring dissolution, decay and sacrifice. As all seems lost, 'death or glory' could well seem the way to 'heavenly redemption'. Also, the material pleasures of our permissive society could degenerate into decadent self-indulgence. Could it be that our high hopes for this long-awaited mutual reception will come to no more than an orgy of mutual destruction and/or a world that drinks and 'sexes' itself to death?

Far better to die and live with a fortunate mind! Such a mind realises nothing really begins, or ends. For every end clears the way for a new beginning. So, while we may be subject to change, we can never really lose anything. Indeed, within the fact of change lies hope for our salvation. Who knows what hidden benefits there may lay behind the 'loss' of something precious? Who knows what horror may turn into something wonderful? What friend is the source of all that harms us, what enemy the source of what is good, what stranger the bringer of everything that is missing in our lives? By realising this, we live happily and turn the poison of defensive suspicion into the nectar of hope.

Minds do change, even if this seems impossible in the darkest hour. In Auschwitz, who would have thought a State of Israel was possible? When Emily Davidson threw herself before King George V's horse at the 1913 Derby, would anyone have foreseen Prime Minister Margaret Thatcher just 66 years later? At Sharpeville, who would dare hope Nelson Mandela could become President of a black and white South Africa? Would the 1950s US southern states have accepted Colin Powell as Secretary of State for Foreign Affairs?

If these things can happen, then it is time to write our wish list. – especially now that Uranus is in Pisces! Looking at the main astro events of the coming two months suggested a strong process of healing is available to those of good heart.

-oOo-

The March 2004 column again focused on the meaning of Uranus in Pisces, showing how conflict could be changed through empathy.

Most of these extrinsic procedures to pick out and control others and so make our lives 'safer' and 'easier' are essentially flawed, simply because they are extrinsic. Using technology (Uranus) to get 'up close and personal' (Pisces) with those who seem to threaten us will have the reverse effect, because it does not break down barriers – it strengthens and/or merely shifts them elsewhere. However strong the physical or security barrier, its protection can only be short-term. In the end it merely moves the goal posts of the conflict.

We need to understand the intrinsic nature of Pisces. It is only by truly getting inside others, seeing what is happening through their eyes, feeling what it is like for them, taking on board their suffering and resolving to find ways of addressing and healing their *dis*-ease that we will ever be truly 'up close and personal' and feel safe. While a little regulation and technology is helpful to indicate boundaries and accepted behaviour, without consensus, regulations will never make us safe – only our recognition, faith and belief in each other will do this. That's Pisces for you!

As with all water signs, Pisces is reflective and when fuelled by anxiety, it projects its fears on others. This can lead to a horrendously impossible predicament. One group of people or an individual can become trapped in fear behind self-created protective barriers, or weapon systems. From this prison of paranoia their minds project every negative act they would like to perpetrate upon their enemies, imagining that this is exactly what these enemies are actually doing, or wish to do to them. So, our imagination creates and manifests our enemies, as the very worst in ourselves. That's Pisces for you as well!

How we stop such counter-productive rot in our personal, group, national and international lives is the crucial task of 2004. Recognising the astrological nature of Pisces may help stop our projections and clear the way to understanding, but how can we open a door and ease the minds of those who continue to project obsessively against us? The answer is not a soft giving-in, or teaching hard lessons, but by clean-clear truth that cuts through all complaints and makes recrimination irrelevant, plus kindness that seeks to put things right and start again. We begin all this when we recognise our own error and that this 'cuts both ways'. That really is Pisces for you!

Flexible willingness to push out boundaries, so that conflicts can be resolved will be vital. Fortunately, the charts drawn for key astro moments in the coming two months suggest there may well be some opportunities to start to make such progress.

-o0o-

Appropriately, the following first two pages of the September 2004 Libran column looked deeply into the nature of balance and the dangers faced by over-active action and reaction. It saw hope in how astrology had transformed the achievements of Ronald Reagan.

> 'The Eternal [God], to prevent such horrid fray,
> <u>Hung forth in Heaven his golden scales</u>, yet seen
> Betwixt Astrea and the Scorpion sign,
> Wherein all things created first he weighed,
> The pendulous round earth with balanced air
> In counterpoise, now ponders all events,
> Battles and realms: In these he put two weights,
> The sequel each of parting and of fight:
> The latter quick up flew, and kicked the beam,
> Which Gabriel spying, thus bespake the Fiend.
> Satan, I know thy strength, and thou knowest mine;
> Neither our own, but given: <u>What folly then</u>
> <u>To boast what arms can do?</u>'
>   John Milton *Paradise Lost*[56]

With this sensationally graphic image of divine justice, Milton depicts the judgement of God upon Satan at the conclusion of the battle in Heaven.[57] As in Egyptian mythology, the 'golden scales' at the Virgo/Libra cusp represent the notion of all actions and motivations being weighed and judged. In ancient Egypt, Osiris balances the weight of each soul's heart against a feather. In the Christian creation story, Satan's self-centred fight against the Lord God measured such extreme imbalance that it 'kicked the beam' of the scales.

The astrology of the coming months, when studied alongside the events of recent years, suggests that human affairs are approaching a time of great judgement and potential realignment. On the day of the always-balancing Autumn Equinox (this year on 22 September), the Sun conjuncts Jupiter and enters Libra. During the following seven days, Jupiter, then Mars, then Mercury cross the Libran cusp. All four bodies conjunct each other during the week.

Satan's error was to allow jealous ambition to arise and drive his struggle for personal power. He resented and battled against the Lord God, who cared for all. As a result, he burdened himself with a weighty force of arms that automatically bore him down from light, all-caring heaven to the isolation of deep, tortuous hells. As the scales showed it then, so will the transits around this year's Autumn equinox judge and redress the actions of all who rail against the common good.

Not that Libra brings automatic, pleasant peace! It is essentially about redressing the balance, creating order, putting things right – all fine, providing the judgement is accepted by the person receiving it. Like Satan, some recipients of justice may challenge the decision, project their blame on others, seek further retribution and so drive themselves and their associates deeper and deeper into suffering. To gain from this great Libran opportunity, we have to be ready to learn and adjust. For sure, the Solar and Lunar eclipses that follow in October will test whether we are.

Certainly, the Middle East and 'War on Terror' issues we have identified and discussed extensively in previous 'Working with the Planets' articles will be prominent. George Bush has the first hit of his second Saturn return on 9 October

2004. An entirely neutral computer-generated interpretation tells us 'During this time your past comes under close scrutiny. You are being forced, whether you like it or not, to face life with a new maturity.'[58] On such occasions the record is put straight, whether we, she, or he like it or not!

This urge to restore balance and put the record straight will extend into many other areas of our lives, where premature and over-simplistic assumptions have undermined understanding and so caused confusion and suffering. Some of these 'other areas' will be personal to each individual. So, be open to new insights about your life. They may lead to possibilities that previously seemed impossible. Approach every person and situation with an open mind. Let go of past baggage. You may see things in an entirely new light.

Some of these 'other areas' will be more public examples. The Aquarian Uranus and now Neptune period have seen quite a few people in power arrogant and over-certain of what they think they know and others should be allowed to do. We live in a society, where experts are academically initiated into bureaucracies that claim the right of judgement over some of our most personal decisions. In recent extreme examples grieving parents have been falsely accused and jailed for murdering their children, by 'expertise', based on deeply flawed statistical probability. So, the various parts of this 'Working with the Planets' seek to restore balance, where it is sorely needed.

-o0o-

In November 2004, the Venus and Mars interaction, combined with the ending words of Romeo and Juliet, highlight the tragic consequences of feudal conflicts in a most timely way.

> A glooming peace this morning with it brings;
> The sun, for sorrow, will not show his head:
> Go hence, to have more talk of these sad things:
> Some shall be pardon'd, and some punished:
> For never was a story of more woe
> Than this of Juliet and her Romeo.
> Closing lines, Shakespeare *Romeo & Juliet*

Romeo and Juliet ends with the Montagues and Capulets learning how much is lost, when budding youthful potential and the melting sensitivity of human contact is ignored. The feud between the two families led each to seeing, then projecting, only 'evil' upon each other. From each family's vision of 'evil', grows paranoia that everything it stands for is being threatened. Each attacks the other to protect itself and its way of life. Each act of self-assertion is seen as 'evil' by the other side. The feud grows by justifying itself, until there is such enmity that love, which could reunite the two families, can only be expressed in a dangerous and secret world. The consequent misunderstandings cause the death of each family's most tender youthful promise.

Of course, it is so easy for us to see how silly the behaviour of these renaissance Italian families was. *We know* that love conquers all and would not let our parents put us through what Romeo and Juliet experienced. Or would we? The play cuts to the very essential root cause and tragedy of ongoing feuds. For them to continue, the behaviour of the other has to become more and more 'unforgivable'.

Each side seems to be 'slaughtering the innocents' – be it through the bombardment of Chechnya's capital in the early 1990s, or the hostage-taking of Russian theatre goers and school children in 2003/4. Retribution breeds retribution and it is always that very act that is 'entirely unacceptable' that drives and perpetuates the feud, until only those who fuel it are listened to. Terrorised into impotence, we are at the mercy of the mayhem of manipulators, who grow fat on the simple phrase 'nothing justifies behaviour like that'.

Having come agonisingly close to conjuncting in May this year, Venus finally catches Mars late on 5 December 2004. Do you remember those balmy June days of the Venus transit, when Mars was rushing through Gemini with lots of promising ideas and Venus lingered so pleasantly with the Sun? Finally, the long-awaited conjunction completes in mid-Scorpio, where incisive and effective action is strong and jealousy and resentment dangerously close by. Will it all end in desperate, bitter tears? Not necessarily, there is hope. While Venus is in detriment in Scorpio, it does have the sign it rules, Libra, expanded by the justice of Jupiter. Fair play for all could indeed move mountains.

What we mean by justice will be the key question to ask and answer through the coming two months. Are our minds set on creating the cause for the destruction of what was wonderful between Romeo and Juliet over and over again? Or are we ready really to 'balance the books' and see what has happened through the eyes of those we have always labelled as the 'evil doers'? Yes, it is true, what we have done has looked just as bad to them. When both sides realise this, then the 'War on Terror' can start to be won.

-o0o-

The horror of the Iraq War brought death to thousands and degenerated the credibility of world leaders. Sensing no end from this ever-worsening situation for many years to come, the January 2005 column explained, to deaf ears, that the simple way out was to satisfy everyone.

> Who's sorry now, who's sorry now
> Whose heart is achin' for breakin' each vow…
> Right to the end, just like a friend
> I tried to warn you somehow
> You had your way, now you must pay
> I'm glad that you're sorry now
> *1950s pop song by Bert Kalmar, Ted Snyder, and Harry Ruby*[59]

Just about every conflict and resentment is resolvable by a, *heartfelt* apology.

Instead, we prefer to brood and plot revenge in defeat and to glory, when triumphant. As a result, the offence and consequent need for an apology becomes ever greater, but the possibility of receiving one ever less. Osama's experience of the 'destroyed towers in Lebanon' leads to the destruction of New York's twin towers, which leads to the Taliban losing control of Afghanistan. Then comes the war in Iraq. George Bush's 'mission accomplished' becomes the prelude to the deaths of hundreds American soldiers and thousands of Iraqis.

In October 2004, the BBC2 television channel presented a three-part documentary entitled *The Power of Nightmares*. In what could be described as a negative expression of Uranus in Pisces (laced by a degenerate manifestation of mutually received Neptune in Aquarius), the series suggested that the way politicians controlled their populations had gone through a radical change in recent years. Since the Second World War, populations had been offered optimistic visions of hope, happiness and prosperity, provided they supported particular political/economic beliefs. The liberal permissiveness this created led to corrupt and degenerate societies. To correct this decline in moral values, fundamentalist/neo-conservative politicians felt it necessary for populations to be controlled (and so purified) by images of fear. It does not matter whether these images of fear are real, or distortions created by those in power, providing they marshal the population in a particular idealised direction. This approach of controlling populations through fear lies at the heart of both the Christian and Islamic charismatic movements. It explains the development and events of terrorism and counterterrorism over the past fifty to sixty years and current strategy in particular.

If this thesis is the case, then it brings a further dense layer of difficulty in healing our problems with each other. We were brought up to feel a little guilty if we found ourselves gloating, when someone who had harmed us 'got what was coming to them'. While it was widely held that we had to stand up for ourselves in the 'real world', the religious view was that we were all 'God's children' and capable of redemption. Now it seems there are evil people, who do not deserve to live, or have rights, or even have the truth spoken about them. We should fear those people, as we would fear the 'undead' and every other negative creature depicted in the most terrifying horror movie. The last thing to do is to say 'sorry' to such people!

If we cannot say sorry, or, even worse, do not need to say sorry, how can there ever be forgiveness? If there is no forgiveness, how can there be resolution? If there is no resolution, like birds and wild animals, we must be continually vigilant against the enemy. We become suspicious of strangers, blindly loyal to our friends, however wrong they may be. Unable to learn, how can we put right misunderstandings? With such minds, how can we end, let alone win, the 'War on Terror'?

To be aware of and cleanse our minds of such simplistic delusions of absolute good and evil is very relevant as we reach 2005. Fortunately, we have astrology to help us. Astrology does not seek to label, condemn and frighten, but to understand. Through understanding, psychosis can be eased and transformed. We become able to live with situations. Often, we can find ways of including and accommodating people in circumstances that would be impossible if we did not use astrology to 'see through their eyes'.

The charts and commentaries that follow suggest that 2005 will start with many people feeling obliged to defend their positions and/or seeking to force others in to new ones. We face a cardinal intensity that could be productive and bring change for the good, as did the massive Capricorn/Cancer opposition in 1990. The liberation of Eastern Europe occurred, because the authorities gave into the cardinal intensity, rather than use it. People to force control were allowed their freedom and found their long-held fears need be no longer.

-o0o-

The consequences of the Iraq War were to expand to encompass the entire Middle East in the 2010s. The March 2009 column gave a little background to the Palestinian/Israel conflict.

The sign Leo dominates the creation of the modern Middle East and especially the foundation of the state of Israel and its consequences. Study the table alongside, create the full charts for yourself and let the symbolism speak for itself. Hope that out of the horror might come some real resolution this time lies in Jupiter's transit through Aquarius until 14 June 2009. The 1973 Yon Kippur War, while largely confirming Israel's US-financed dominance in the region, did return some standing to Egypt. This made its 1979 Camp David peace treaty possible and paved the way for peace with Jordan. Bill Clinton came close to sustaining the momentum and clinching the ultimate peace prize just before he left office in 2000. With Barack Obama in power and Bill's wife Hillary to be Secretary of Defence, perhaps the Clinton family has more worthwhile Middle East business to complete than the Bushes had! For sure, Jupiter will transit the fourth house of the Israel chart and oppose its tenth-house Leo planets. If these troubled nations seek a peaceful and successful future, they must find ways to bridge the gap, by bringing freedom and prosperity to their Israeli and Palestinian citizens. With Leo so dominant, it can be overlooked that many people in the world feel compensation from the United States and Israel remains outstanding. Were this to be recognised and paid in ways the dispossessed can accept, they and the world could find peace.

Transits - Foundation and Some Conflicts in the Modern Middle East

1. Middle East Mandate 11:22 CEDT 25 Apr 1920 San Remo, Italy. [Moon 2° 39', Neptune 8° 45', Jupiter 8° 48' all in Leo]
2. Israel Foundation 16:32 EET 14 May 1948 Tel Aviv, Israel. [MC 2° 39', Moon 4° 40', Pluto 12° 38', Saturn 16° 25', Mars 28° 18' all in Leo]
3. Palestine Autonomy 11:55 EEDT 4 May 1994 Cairo Egypt. [No Leo, Taurus/Scorpio seesaw, sad Pisces Moon/Saturn and impulsive Mars in Aries]
4. Six Day War Starts 07:45 EET 5 June 1967 Jerusalem, Israel. [Jupiter 2° 13', Fortuna 18° 21', both in Leo – Israel expanded its control three-fold.]
5. Yom Kippur War 14:05 6 October 1973 Cairo, Egypt. [Jupiter 2° 23', Moon 4° 36' both in Aquarius – improvement in Egyptian position]
6. Iraq invades and annexes Kuwait [2 to 8 August 1990] Noon Chart 6 August 1990 Kuwait City, Kuwait. [Grand Cross 13/16 degrees, Sun Leo, Moon Aquarius, Pluto Scorpio, Mars Taurus]
7. First Gulf Ground War *Desert Storm* announced, Noon Chart 15 February 1991 Kuwait City, Kuwait. [Solar Eclipse 26° Aquarius, Jupiter 6° 30' Leo] First infantry combat the next day.
8. Second Gulf War US Pre-emptive strike 20:00 BAT 20 March 2003 Baghdad, Iraq. [Jupiter 8° 23' Leo, Neptune 12° 21' Aquarius]
9. Israeli Air Strikes on Gaza Noon chart 27 December 2008 Jerusalem, Israel. [Jupiter 27° 38' Capricorn will transit to its 27° 01' Aquarius Rx station on 15 June 2009]

-oOo-

The May 2011 column showed clearly the astro-cycle thread of the history of Israel since the destruction of the Temple by the Romans in 70 CE. The birth charts of George Bush and Tony Blair show the astro-cycle link that seduced them into making matters in the Middle East far worse. See page 64 overleaf for charts.

Read in its entirety the chart for the Destruction of the Jewish Temple (4 August 70 CE) is monumentally tragic. The central theme highlighted on the first chart shows Sun and Jupiter (with Mercury nearby) in Leo opposed to Pluto and Uranus in Aquarius. It suggests an act of outrage attempting to obliterate the cultural identity of an entire race that will be remembered for all time. The second chart is for the key moment in the creation of the map of the Middle East as it is today; an agreement finalised by the First World War victors in 1920. On 8 March 1920, Jupiter and Neptune had made an exact retrograde conjunction at 9Le12 (two minutes of arc from the Destruction of the Temple Sun position). The belief in returning to a Jewish national home encouraged here became a reality in May 1948, when, as the third chart shows, Pluto (in the tenth house) was to the minute opposed to its 70 CE position (in the fourth house).

For many Palestinians and Israel's new neighbours, the new state was as egocentrically oppressive as the Roman action in 70 CE. Many charts could be included to illustrate the Leo and fixed sign theme running through their reactions, the discovery and production of petroleum, and consequent social revolutions. This short introduction just fast-forwards to show this ancient astrological pattern still there describing the delusory nature of the 2003 Iraq War.

The fourth chart is drawn for the first return of the Sun to its position at the 11 September 2001 atrocity. One year on, President George W Bush gathered together the world's leaders at Ground Zero (the next day he was to address the United Nations warning of Saddam Hussein's Iraq). Jupiter in Leo was exactly opposed to Neptune in Aquarius. As well as being close to the Destruction of Temple and Israel State Leo and Aquarius positions, the 11 September 2002 Jupiter/Neptune opposition is within seven minutes of arc of the 1920 Jupiter/Neptune conjunction. President Bush's chart has a Leo focus below his Ascendant and especially Mercury within fifteen minutes of arc of the Destruction of Temple Sun and just over a degree from the 1920 Jupiter/Neptune conjunctions and 2002 opposition. Near to his Moon/North Node midpoint in Tony Blair's Aquarian tenth house is the other end of the Jupiter/Neptune opposition at the time of the war. His decision on the war was to tarnish his public standing irrevocably.

If astrological advice had been sought in 1920, 1948 and 2002, with a genuine intention to find the best outcome for everyone, the destructive arrogance of the 1920 decisions, and certainly the dangerous lack of realism in 2003, could have been avoided. Even now, using the astrology to understand what is needed to redress the extreme brutality of past errors might be of considerable benefit, as it was when Ronald Reagan used astrology to help him agree peace with the Soviet Union.

Destruction Jewish Temple — Jerusalem, Israel — Natal Chart — 31°N46' 035°E14' — 4 Aug 0070, Sat — Placidus — Geocentric, Tropical — 12:00 EET −2:00 — True Node

Middle East Mandate — San Remo, Italy — Natal Chart — 43°N49' 007°E46' — 25 Apr 1920, Sun — Placidus — Geocentric, Tropical — 11:22 CEDT −2:00 — True Node

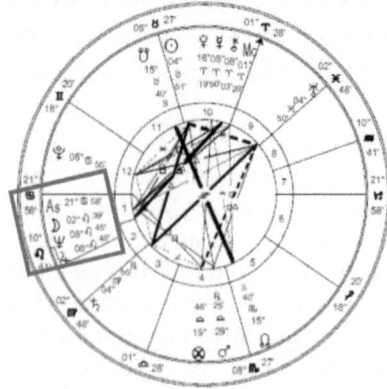

Israel — Tel Aviv, Israel — Natal Chart — 32°N04' 034°E46' — 14 May 1948, Fri — Placidus — Geocentric, Tropical — 16:00 EET −2:00 — True Node

World Leaders at Ground Zero — New York, NY — Natal Chart — 40°N42'51" 074°W00'23" — 11 Sep 2002, Wed — Placidus — Geocentric, Tropical — 14:30:43 EDT +4:00 — True Node

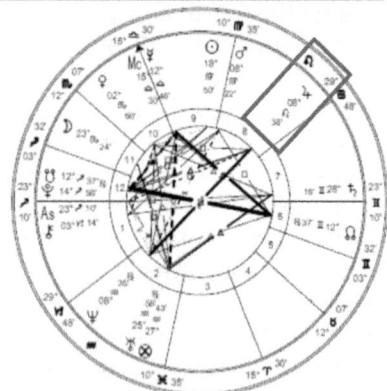

George W. Bush — New Haven, CT — Male Chart — 41°N18'29" 072°W55'43" — 6 Jul 1946, Sat — Placidus — Geocentric, Tropical — 07:26 EDT +4:00 — True Node

Tony Blair — Edinburgh, Scotland — Natal Chart — 55°N57' 003°W13' — 6 May 1953, Wed — Placidus — Geocentric, Tropical — 06:10 −1:00 — True Node

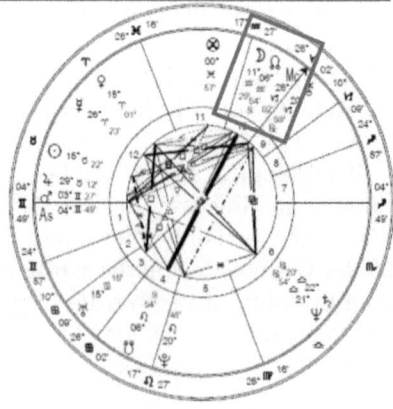

-o0o-

Chapter 5
Twenty-First-Century Radical Change before 2009
[Articles written March 2003 – September 2008]

Contemporary Background

Increasing problems in Iraq, Afghanistan and consequent international terrorism cast shadows through these years and far beyond. Recovery at all costs from the year 2000 dot.com financial collapse dominated the first decade of the new millennium.

Relaxation of financial regulation at the turn of the century allowed dramatic expansions of credit, especially in the mortgage market. This created liquidity that encouraged return to equity investment, which boomed until end of 2008.

In the UK, the decade was dominated by Tony Blair and Gordon Brown and their ongoing top-dog struggle.

19 July 2000	*Big Brother* first aired – accelerated growth of reality TV.
March 2003	Major equity indices bottom and start to recover
24 April 2004	Abu Ghraib atrocities revealed
7 July 2005	Terrorist bombing of London transport
23 August 2005	Hurricane Katrina in New Orleans
25 May 2006	Enron trial commences
August 2006	Pluto downgraded to dwarf planet – at IAU Conference
12 September 2007	Run on Northern Rock bank – nationalised February 2008
11 July 2008	In the US Indy/Mac fails – sub-prime mortgage problems
8 August 2008	Olympics open in Beijing
15 September 2008	Lehman Brothers bankruptcy – global banking collapse

-o0o-

Already in the March 2003 column, present and upcoming astro-cycles were beginning to reveal the historical perspective of the powerful changes due in first two decades of the twenty-first century.

The extent to which we will be happy this year will be determined
by how much we understand diversity and act sympathetically on
the implications of this understanding.

Have you noticed how naturalistic game systems are becoming? Adventures over incredibly varied landscapes, football and other sports competitions are peopled by virtual characters that are realistically human in appearance. Very soon actors could become redundant, as it becomes possible to people feature films in the same way. Already, a dinosaur series on television computer-generates virtual creatures in credible settings. We do not realise we are watching very clever computer programming, based on the study of fossilised bones, intelligent deduction and guesswork. These reconstructions are so real that they could be taken as proven fact. The media can create new 'realities', using these moving pictures to tell a far better story than thousands of 'boring' words. Then there are the propaganda possibilities. What would Hitler, Stalin, even many less brutal, but just as unscrupulous, leaders have done with such facilities? For, with Uranus in Pisces in mutual reception to Neptune in Aquarius, all realities can become possible and what you believe will drive what you do.

Look at these ideas alongside those outlined in January's 'How the Planets Work' column and recent claims regarding human cloning.[60] Clearly, we need pure and compassionate beliefs, with a strong and ethical foundation more than ever. Only then can we cut through myriad delusions and manipulations by people who wish to use us for their own purposes. Present attempts to 'identify and eradicate terrorism' are a rather crude effort to establish some rules. 'Of course, we have different beliefs and approaches, but there are standards of behaviour, such as mass killing and intimidation, that are unacceptable'. 'Quite so, but who is really doing what and where do you draw the line?' 'How do ordinary people fight against despots?' 'Who says who is a despot?' 'Some of the most admired people in history have been imprisoned terrorists at some time in their lives.' Such arguments could go on all through a long-suffering Piscean period, if we cannot look for deeper principles. Could the key to it all be for us to focus on solving problems and creating happiness? Quite simply as long as cruelty and misery do not decrease as a result of our actions, we are not seeing, or understanding, the truth. This lies at the very heart of making the most of Uranus's transit through Pisces.

How the Planets Work
Uranus enters Pisces every 84 years. At its previous entrance [1919], Neptune was in Leo and Pluto in 'family-shattering' Cancer. The roaring twenties were the natural consequence, as was the Wall Street crash, soon after Neptune reached Virgo. The mutual reception to Neptune in Aquarius makes the 2003 ingress rather different.

To investigate previous occurrences, we used a computer program to create and scan a 20,000-year chart database.[61] This combination has occurred at intervals between 163 and 169 years since 1507. Interestingly, there was a gap of no mutual receptions for 2,900 years before this. Also, after 2339 there will be no mutual receptions again until 5108 CE. The upcoming mutual reception of these two planets is at the midpoint of a series of six such periods. These were 1507/8, then 163 years to 1670/5, then 165 years to 1835/43, then 169 years until 2003-4/11, followed by 166 years to 2170/75 and finally 168 years to 2338/9. Clearly the nineteenth and twenty-first century periods are the longest and most significant.

These dates seem to mark important stages in the development of individual power and responsibility. 1507/8 was at the beginning of global discovery and the rounded human-centred view of reality. This led to the modern scientific view of nature. Man became the focus and power behind what happens. 1670/5 brought the development of this process, with the foundation of the Royal Society and the beginning of the so called 'Age of Enlightenment'. 1835/43 marks the end of slavery and spread of democracy. It was the development of methods to generate electricity from this time that made our modern world possible. For 2004 to 2011, we must use our sensitivity to define and master electronically generated 'reality'. By the end of the period, anyone who wishes may well be able to offer a fully operating television channel on the web, as easily as word and still picture sites are today. Holographic projection may replace flat screens. Will this bring a nightmare of manipulation and exposure to the worst excesses and abuses, or will it free us from lonely isolation, with a chance to express, understand and heal our confusion about each other?

The cynicism and scandal-mongering prominent in today's media is a part of a process that is moving social organisation away from 'the ignorant masses' being dependent on 'benevolent decision-making by revered leaders.' We are at an awkward interim stage of the process. The media seem to expose the limitations, methods and people that control us. It can pick out and 'destroy them publicly', but these are just selective reactions to specific events, often based on prejudice. The media does not give us the understanding and influence to create meaningful alternatives. The technology of the Uranus in Pisces period will offer us the capacity to feel, understand and contact people, ideas, societies and situations that are very different to us. With kindness as our heart goal, we could move our world away from impeding disaster towards a sharing and celebration of individual self-expression. Without it, we will degenerate into maelstrom of accusation, unnecessary self-sacrifice and martyrdom.

What happens in 2003 will go a long way towards determining which way it will be.

-o0o-

Re-read pages 14-15, where the November 2004 column considers whether the twelfth-house planet focus of contemporary leaders was the root cause of the degenerate horror that was to sour international relations increasingly in the coming decades.

-o0o-

By May 2005, with Saturn in Cancer preparing the ground for Pluto's Capricorn ingress in 2008-09, the column identified seismic social change of historic proportions. Could the people trust authority and social institutions in an age of advanced technology?

The price of freedom is eternal vigilance
Thomas Jefferson

The defining moment in a March edition of the BBC's *Any Questions*, was when the Home Secretary sought to use Jefferson's words to justify restricting human rights, because of the danger of terrorism. Shami Chakrabarti, the director of Liberty, was there to remind Charles Clarke that Jefferson sought to urge vigilance against abuse of our liberties by our *own* governments, not the actions of foreign groups and powers.

10 May 2005 marks the final precise T-square between Saturn and the Nodal axis. Over the rest of May and June the aspect moves steadily out of orb. For six months it has linked with various inner planets moving through Capricorn to form a series of grand crosses. This cardinal stirring was referred to in January and March 2005's 'Working with the Planets'. It indicates a constant need to marshal all our formative energies and advance effectively. The Cancer/Capricorn axis drives a struggle between those who are in power, or subject to it. The Aries/Libra Nodal axis suggests the struggle will only be resolved by means of new beginnings of justice.

As well as security and individual human rights issues, this cardinal struggle urges wider structural change, both globally and locally. As I write (12 March), we have already seen dramatic elections in Ukraine, Palestine and Iraq, then demonstrations and counter- demonstrations in Lebanon. Third world needs in trade, debt burdens and AIDS confront us. China has just overtaken Britain as the world's fourth largest economy. In Britain we are building to a General Election that no one should take for granted.

Indeed, nothing should be assumed to be as it seems. The classic analogy of peeling the layers of an onion applies, as issues take on deeper and deeper significance. In Iraq, was the election a success, or is it more important to consider the significance of the Shia victory? After the pro-Western protests, it was the Shias in Lebanon that staged much larger demonstrations in *support* of Syria. In contrast to the late 1980s, when Saddam's war acted as a buffer on the Iran border. The Shia branch of Islam is strong from India in the East to the Mediterranean.[62] In the past, Shias were disempowered as significant minorities, or even persecuted majorities; now democracy, 'the way to peace and freedom', offers them more power that they have held for decades.

In every walk and detail of *our* lives, the same Saturn-in-Cancer cardinal process can empower the disempowered and prevent people's rights being taken from them by those 'in power'. More groups and minorities are likely to insist they be understood and respected. Selection processes at all levels of society will be pressured to abolish preconceptions and privilege, and then focus fearlessly on finding the 'right person for the job'. Social values and assumptions will be more easily accepted, if they emerge from deep searching of our hearts and minds, not bullied into us by special interest groups, their bureaucracies and financial 'incentives'. If we cannot address and gentle the outrage that stems from disempowered injustice, the 'war on terrorism' will never end.

The battle between the empowered and disempowered could well become the central world struggle that replaces the Cold War between Western capitalism and the Soviet state system. George Bush giving the lives of US citizens to support a freely elected Shia majority government in Iraq is an inevitable part of the process. The more examples there are 'across the divide' like this, the more chance there is for us to enjoy the victorious, lasting peace that comes from recognising the genuine rights of all.

In Britain, was the Government's Bill on Terrorism to protect us from danger, to assume dangerous and ill-thought-out new powers, a political manoeuvre to outflank the opposition just before an election? To what extent did the ghost of his 2003 WMD claims undermine the Prime Minister's credibility?

How have these issues developed, as the cardinal intensity has grown between my writing this and your reading it?

As the T-square builds, an increasing number of people will feel that they have been literally fighting for the essential nature of the planet's future. We are 'casting the die' of the kind of world we and our descendants will live in. So, keep on looking deeper for the fundamental issue that lies beneath and drives the surface arguments. Seek truth that 'explodes' deception. Is this *really* what we want and do we *really* have to pay this price?

It is a good time to consider the question carefully. Pluto enters Capricorn in 2008/9. The last two times it was there saw fundamental social upheaval. 1762/78 brought enclosure, the industrial revolution, the struggle for the rights of man, leading to the foundation of the USA (it has its second-house Pluto return in 2022!), and the French revolution. 1515/32 saw Martin Luther's protests (and excommunication in 1521). In 1533 Henry VIII divorced Catherine of Aragon, the Church of England was born and the monasteries fell. What we aspire towards now, or even what we fail to aspire towards or to protect, will bear its fruit for good or ill during and immediately after Pluto's sojourn in Capricorn.

In addition, in 2010/11 Jupiter and Uranus enter Aries together and Neptune and Chiron conjunct in Pisces. We will find ourselves projected into new situations and sufferings. These will be the consequences for what we started, or forced ourselves and others upon, between Winter Solstice 2004 and June 2005.

With decisions that can lead to such long-term consequences, we have to be especially careful. However much we trust those making present decisions, these people will change, as will their supporters. Just a decade or so later, new leaders and followers may see and use the structures we are creating very differently. Adolf Hitler was one of many leaders, who used the existence of democracy (that idealists from the eighteenth century had worked and died for) to gain power, and then abolished it. Procedures introduced to catch and control just a handful of dangerous people once established can easily be extended to whole populations. Innocent identification techniques can be expanded to give centralised control over every action of each ordinary citizen. Why should they mind, if they have nothing to hide? Well, it depends what those in control want to know and why. Computer systems make little or no allowance for human frailties and variables – maybe it is time to watch the beginning (at least) of the film *Brazil* again.

--o0o-

The September 2005 column explored the social obsessions of the Saturn-in-Cancer transit, including the birth of reality television, and anticipated the increasing threat to personal freedom and cultural disputes.

As we look back over the more recent Saturn-in-Cancer days since June 2003, again kindness and caring for others have been the dominant themes. However, this time, the better-behaved element of that 'hippie generation' has been in power. Protection has become institutionalised. 'Nanny state', fear of terror, obsessive systems of security have grown in strength. Immense spending on health systems and campaigns against smoking and obesity have been launched. The movement to end world poverty can be seen as a late-in-the-day attempt to observe our responsibilities to be a mother to all. Dangers to children, exposure of abusers and compensation for past misdemeanours have dominated the news.

During the 1975/8 Saturn transit through Leo, Uranus was in Scorpio with its ruler Pluto in Libra. Intimidation, destabilisation and desecration of the ego became the 'heart theme' of the culture. Between 2005 and 2007, Uranus is in Pisces and its ruler Neptune is in Aquarius opposed to Saturn in Leo. While Saturn has been in Cancer, it has trined Uranus, which is mutually receiving Neptune. This explains why new regulations to protect citizens, children and our health have been proposed and many have passed into law and practice so easily. At the cruder end of culture, we have seen the dominance of reality television – looking through the keyhole to ordinary people's Cancer private places. With Saturn in Leo, opposing Neptune and quincunx Uranus, the intrusiveness of so much video surveillance and regulation may start to grate and be challenged. Will the bombings[63] help us to accept identity cards, or will we heed an older generation's reminder that when we defeated Hitler, we threw away identity cards, as something *he* not *we* stood for? The punk generation born with Uranus in Leo will be coming into power. This will no longer be the 1975/8 battle over style and how to challenge the system between young adults and their adolescent siblings, but rather a wrestling for power between grown up and well-equipped adults. Great tolerance will be needed, if we are to avoid cultural conflict and religious wars.

-o0o-

The Saturn in Leo, Neptune in Aquarius and Jupiter in Scorpio T-square building through November/December 2005 meant that issue's column focused on the karmic consequences of the actions of recent years – as things turned out unerringly prophetic!

'Karma - the only thing certain is that it will ripen.'
The eastern notion of karmic consequences does not accept that 'negative' and 'positive' actions cancel each other out. It says all karma has to be experienced and worked through. For it is not so much the act itself that is the problem, but the state of mind that leads to the act and is reinforced by it. It is our state of mind that causes constant suffering to ourselves and others. A thief fears for his property. The trickster sees no-one as reliable. The hunter is always hunted. As long as the mind remains trapped in such patterns of thought, then it confirms the behaviour, repeats similar acts and reinforces that unclear view of the world. So, our deluded minds force us into those very situations that will perpetuate our negative actions. Unless the mind changes, nothing changes.

The more positive our actions, the easier it is to see our negative mental attitudes for what they are and change our behaviour. Yet, however positive our behaviour, the consequences of past negative actions ripen and return to haunt and test us again and again, until all negativity is exhausted.[64]

Astrology is a vital help in training the mind to understand and monitor the process of karma exactly. Planetary combinations at birth reveal the challenges of this life. Progressions and transits show when opportunities to address and purify past negativity will ripen. Knowing this helps us develop clear states of mind that can cope beneficially with anything that happens.

The same applies to the karmic consequences of group, social, national and international actions. November to December 2005 is a trigger time for the multi-level global karmic purification that will continue until the autumn of 2006.

From the true beginning of the twenty-first century in early 2001, the challenges of the Saturn/Pluto opposition led to automatic, brutal reactions to events. Be it the money-motivated slaughter of hundreds of thousands of animals in Britain, the Intifada in Israel, 9/11, its world-shattering aftermath and the resentments these and personal issues wreaked upon our lives; we were brutalised and reacted with brutality.

The Jupiter/Neptune opposition, precise from September 2002 until mid-2003, deluded our minds into over-simplified and essentially flawed 'solutions' to the problems left over by the Saturn/Pluto opposition. As well as imbalance and the ill-considered invasion in the Middle East, we were ignoring warning signs within our own society; so building up resentment and alienation. The consequences are becoming dire. The Uranus/Neptune mutual reception in Aquarius/Pisces that so many hoped would marshal in a 'golden Aquarian age' has spawned vast computer technology that it is said will 'contain terrorism' by keeping electronic 'tabs' on world citizens! The Aquarian idealistic view that society is the sum total of its people's deeply held thoughts and feelings has been turned on its head. Instead of inspiring a climate of charity and clarity that lightens people's lives, our governments encourage commercial and state institutions that aim to confuse, manipulate and exploit our basest instincts. So, what else can our children do, but grow up to be binge drinkers, in all they think and do?

Of course, we have thought, written and said maybe too much about this already. We remind ourselves about it now, because in November/December 2005 much of its consequent karma will ripen. Unless there is a profound and self-effacing change of heart, the consequences of our failure to understand and behave properly through those Saturn/Pluto, Jupiter/Neptune times will return to haunt us. It will become our nemesis.

-oOo-

The January 2006 column explained how our unprincipled mechanistic insensitivity to the planet and its reactions causes and accelerates the problems we and the world face.

Can We Turn Doom Prophecies on their Head?

Since writing November's 'Working with the Planets', a sense of doom about 'inevitable consequences' seems to dominate, as I compare notes and generally converse with colleagues.[65] Whatever the astro-method used, it seems that difficult times lie ahead.

Our world is in the grip of a desperately dangerous mix. The tight mechanistic contemporary view of 'reality' is driven by the spin of narrow self-interest. There is no ethical discipline, except disputed religious beliefs developed in times when the world was less of a global village. While intrinsic kindness, goodwill and the wish for happiness for everyone remains at the heart of

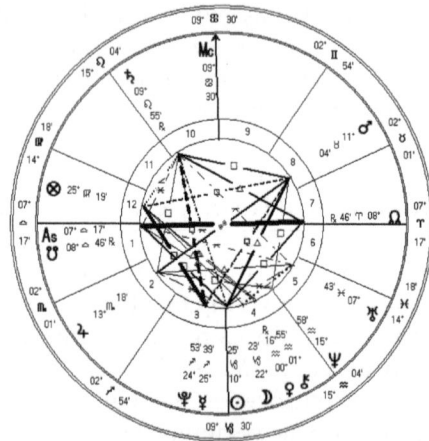

New Year 2006
1 Jan 2006 00:00 UT +0:00
London 51°N30' 000°W10'
Geocentric Tropical Placidus True Node

human nature, the way to provide it has been hijacked by the self-interested fanaticism and ignorance of those who lead us. Manipulating the facts to win the short-term argument and survive seems to be all that matters – the long-term consequences are 'beyond our control'; 'the fault of those who oppose us'. Not so! Without wisdom, we blame others and despair with outrage at their behaviour. The wise change and realise that anger is the only real enemy.

What can be done? International affairs, be it in trade, man-made famine, war, or economic short-sightedness, could be addressed. We just need to turn away from visions of victory toward solutions that seem fair to all sides involved. Yet, the increasing incidence of natural disasters remain – cyclones, earthquakes, floods and the imminent threat of 'bird flu', or other worldwide epidemics.

We will begin to find a positive answer, if we see what we call 'natural disasters' not so much as 'acts of God', but the consequences of the view of reality we have embraced and the way we treat our planet. There have been twenty major world earthquakes since 1960.[66] Fourteen of these have been since 1990 and seven in the last four years! The number of cyclones and typhoons has also increased. Could our actions be the cause? Is our error to see the planet as a passive and non-reactive resource for us to harvest as we wish?

In fact, the planet not only reacts to what we do to it, but also offers traumas to release the pressure of our counter-productive behaviour. Hurricane Katrina raised issues of administrative imbalance and insensitivity in the USA. The South Asian earthquake came at time when extra co-operation between India and Pakistan might further resolve the Kashmir conflict. Closer to home, flooding and terrorist attacks have encouraged us to care for and understand each other's cultures. The immense force of the planet's reactions puts humanity's pathetic disputes into perspective. When we give our hearts and support to those in desperate need, sub-group conflicts and even wars pale into insignificance.

The chart for midnight in London on 1 January 2006 shows this challenge for the year in stark focus. It also shows the value of drawing aspects in our charts! Two grand crosses combine close to creating an exact eight-pointed star. A similar pattern of aspects occurs at midnight LMT all over the world.[67] Even if we take away the MC as a point of aspect focus, a fixed grand cross between Saturn, Mars, Neptune and Jupiter, plus a T-square between the Nodal axis and the Sun remain strong. The grand cross continues to apply through the months ahead. So, we have the astrological explanation for the difficulties we already know and are yet to know as 'the chickens come home to roost'.

In recent years, there has been a 'slack' that allowed choices of behaviour, the consequences of which were not bad enough to be entirely unmanageable. Now we have to react to events with perfect appropriateness, or the outcome will be beyond anything humanity can bear. International openness and co-operation about bird flu, making available expertise and medicines that prevent and cure are essential. We face dangers to which the most stringent immigration controls offer no protection. The needs and motivations of humanity as a whole are far more the same than anything that separates us.

This is the only way to see the difficulties of 2005 to 2006 in a positive way. Easy flowing astro-events, although pleasant at the time, lead to slackness of thought, opinion and action that build up dangers for the future. Far more beneficial in the long run are the confrontations with reality and experience of immediate consequences those stressful squares, conjunctions and oppositions bring. These sharpen our actions and focus our understanding. Harsh judgements and dire consequences are likely, if we get things wrong in the coming months. The New Year midnight chart symbolises that humanity is on trial and 2006 will be a seminal year in this process.

In a very fundamental way, this is good news. Because the outcome or error is likely to be traumatic, only an extreme fanatic will allow prejudice to drive actions that fly in the face of reason. Indeed, we may find ourselves doing the right thing almost automatically. The trick is to act intuitively and stop the mischief-making mind getting in the way. When children are trapped suffering underneath a building, only the most heartless would ask their religion before acting. So, enmity diminishes and friends are made.

Great sporting champions will confirm that, although a little luck is always a blessing, the hard slog of careful and rigorous training is the sure heart foundation of all great achievements. 2006 will be like that. If we lose our determination and willingness to learn (however surprising and unacceptable the lesson), we could become trapped in the grips of one difficulty, danger and frustration after another.

But, if we take the immediate and natural course of action, we may well find ourselves resolving far larger problems than we ever felt would be possible.

To achieve this positive outcome, the relationship of the people to their leaders will be crucial. The nature of this has turned completely upside-down, even in the partial democracies that go by that name in our G8 cultures. Strategists use focus groups to discover approaches that will appeal to 'swing voters', then design their propaganda accordingly. When elected, politicians use all their skill to select 'facts' that make it appear they are implementing what they promised. In a genuine democracy, the experience and wisdom of leaders recommends foresighted solutions for the people's approval, by giving full details that inform and change minds. True leaders hold their ground and inform public opinion. Bereft of this, people become trapped and impotent in this politics of deception. It leads to popular frustration and tighter and tighter controls to discipline the resultant excesses. The intolerable heightening of this frustration in 2006 may well lead to the emergence of conviction politicians, who break through the taboos.

Even deeper and more vital questions likely to be asked in the coming year will concern the very basis of the reality paradigm we take to be absolute truth. Mechanistic materialism is both illogical and inadequate for our times, when feelings, beliefs and opinions exploit science with *laissez-faire* selfishness. Indeed, it could be argued that insensitive self-interest is an inevitable product of basing our social institutions on mechanical 'reality'. In contrast, understanding the nature and timing of the cyclic pressures that lay behind our mental and emotional motivations will discipline the decision-making process, before it gets out of control. Knowing the astrological factors that drive our feelings and explain our prejudices can put the events of 2006 in perspective. Understanding this cyclic model leads to natural balance in actions, based on concern for others. Deciding this way will be good for astrology and ever better for the world.

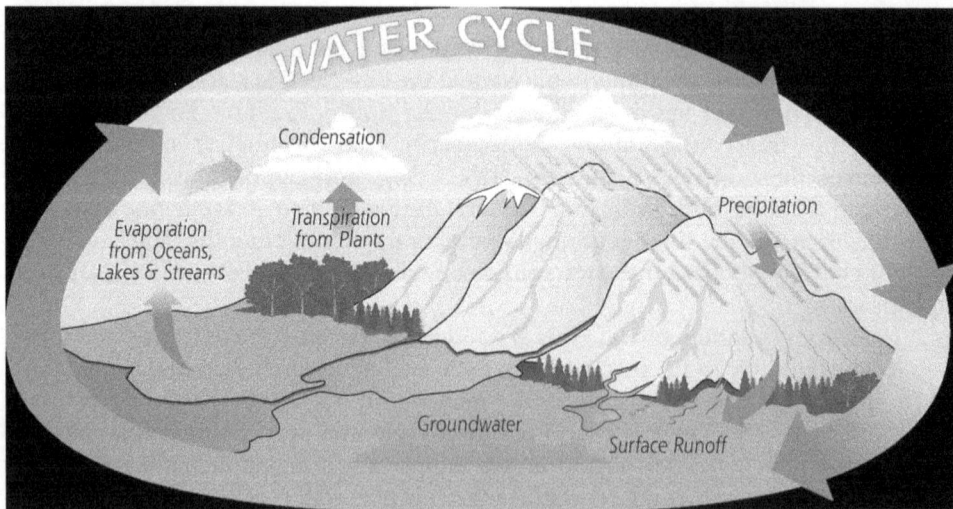

-o0o-

The March 2006 column took stock of the social consequences of Neptune's ongoing Aquarian transit.

> Things fall apart; the centre cannot hold;
> Mere anarchy is loosed upon the world,
> The blood-dimmed tide is loosed, and everywhere
> The ceremony of innocence is drowned;
> The best lack all conviction, while the worst
> Are full of passionate intensity.
> > *The Second Coming* W. B. Yeats

> Today we can dispose of vast material resources, but the men and women in our technological age risk becoming victims of their own intellectual and technical achievements, ending up in spiritual barrenness and emptiness of heart…
> A united humanity will be able to confront the many troubling problems of the present time: from the menace of terrorism to the humiliating poverty in which millions of human beings live, from the proliferation of weapons to the pandemics and the environmental destruction which threatens the future of our planet. *The First Christmas Address* of HH Pope Benedict XVI

The transit of Neptune through Aquarius has symbolised global obsession with rapid advances in communications technology and, since 9/11, the ability to track and control individual actions. At the end of 2005, the first satellite in the European Galileo positional locality technology was launched; when all thirty satellites are in place, this system will locate cars and anything else on Earth to the nearest metre. The *Google Earth* internet system is a compilation of satellite and aerial photographs that enable anyone with broadband internet access to look into back gardens from anywhere in the world and to link into strategically placed web cams. Advanced identity and shopping loyalty cards will enable personal information about individual behaviour to be available to anyone, who those in control of the system allow. Cable and satellite television channels and mobile phone systems already make a mass of entertainment and personal visual contacts available for international transmission. Once all the links are in place, anyone could theoretically know anything about anyone else. Appropriately, such rapid developments have occurred when the world was ruled by leaders with strong twelfth-house planetary positions. Do they know what these new systems could lead to? A pre-computer punched card system was a sufficient organisational base to find and efficiently transport millions to their death in Nazi Europe.

At the same time, Aquarius is the sign of individual human freedom and invention. Indeed, much of the motivation for the technical advances outlined in the previous paragraph is to bring greater individual comfort and 'opportunity with responsibility' for all. The justification for the 'War on Terror' and surveillance is to protect us from intimidation and crime. The internet gives ever more people access to information and the power this brings. The Aquarian belief in humanity makes us care for other people's predicaments and tragedies. A tsunami, or earthquake on the other side of the world touches hearts thousands of miles away. With Neptune and Chiron transiting this sign, then moving into Pisces for quite a few years to come, sympathy and a determined need to go through suffering to cure the 'world's ills' will be our constant wish.

All these Aquarian advances and inclinations are at odds with Jupiter in Scorpio and Saturn in Leo. So, because 'the road to hell is paved with good intentions', we must be careful that our actions do not intensify rather than resolve conflicts. The recent history of Iraq remains a central example of this. Occurring as the Winter Solstice Grand Cross was building; the recent elections there may well bring very different outcomes than the optimism first expressed at the high voting turn out. There can be no peace, only civil war, as long as each group insist that 'my' solution is better for you than 'yours'. Wherever you live in the world, the power of governments, global capitalism and commercial promotion is more likely to manipulate individual 'need' to suit their own corporate growth; usually by appealing to the lowest common denominator, rather than individual enlightenment.

So, will we be better off in a world where information is available and linked? Will just one global control process, caring for individuals as it thinks best and repressing those that do not conform, be better than living in a world of unconnected information, divided by two misguided communist/capitalist methods of social control? Where in the future world will individuals, or misunderstood groups turn to for support? Under what banner of freedom will the future of human individuality gather and protect itself from centralised oppression? It is in the environment of the major transits of 2006 that these key questions will be faced and addressed. Will it be individual access to an increasingly wide range of information that liberates, or enslavement by government and commercial interests, who know all there is to know about us?

Will the fear of those that order our destiny dominate their desperate attempts to contain the self-obsessed anarchy Yeats so clearly describes? Instead, can the heart idealism of the Pope's message become a liberating banner inspiring us to care for others by setting them free?

-o0o-

The November 2006 column suggested that astronomers downgrading Pluto to a dwarf planet was a conspiracy to close the world's eyes to the terrible events its upcoming Capricorn transit indicated. Interesting to look back on from the 2020s!

Can Death Die?

Pluto was discovered and first researched when it was transiting Cancer. So, it is interesting that, with it about to enter the opposite sign Capricorn, astronomers should strip it of full planetary status!

Of course, none of this diminishes the existing excellent research into cycles based on the movement of Pluto through the zodiac. Whatever astronomers' improved instruments decide to classify it as, Pluto has not changed and is still there!

In saying this to wider society, it gives us another chance to explain that astrology seeks to understand the relationship between ourselves and the whole solar system, indeed the whole Universe. Astrology can use anything in the heavens as a point of reference, around which to focus and study the effects of a cycle. Such a reference point (be it a planet or not) does not have to cause directly any of the effects we seem to attribute to it. The validity of a cycle depends upon what we observe, not its point of reference, which merely disciplines the space and time of the cycle. It is the same as finding out that an object we had used as a reference point to measure distances from was not a tree, but a mildewed telegraph pole.

Discovered the same time that humanity learned to split the atom, Pluto's cycle through the signs has been found to indicate how particular generations will experience death and regeneration. For example:

❖ 1912 to 1939 in Cancer – the death and transformation of ruling dynasties and the individual family structure

❖ 1939 to 1957/8 in Leo – death and transformation through individual courage, megalomania, 'schoolboy heroes' in war.

❖ 1958 to 1971/2 in Virgo – death and transformation through criticism, the anti-hero, finding fault in the leaders of previous generations.

❖ 1971/2 to 1983/4 in Libra – death and transformation of relationship conventions, unstable nuclear arms race.

❖ 1983/ to 1995 in Scorpio – death and transformation of sexuality, especially AIDS, advances in genetics.

❖ 1995 to 2008 in Sagittarius – death and transformation through travel and religion, by budget airline (but with terrorist threats), virtual 'travel' through the internet (with support of Uranus and Neptune mutually receiving each other in Aquarius).

❖ 2008 to 2023/4 in Capricorn – death and transformation of government and authority, the struggle for a new order.

Perhaps, with 2008 approaching, the downgrading of Pluto is a cunning plot by governments to avoid being transformed!

Whilst these observations may be nothing to do with Pluto itself, they are real and may be explained by the effect on our dispositions of other factors in the mechanics of the solar system. Rather than messing around with classifications, it would help if astronomers paid more attention to today's ongoing studies of all traditional and more recently discovered planets, built on the observations of ancient astrologers. Then we may learn the reason for the correspondences between patterns of life experience and the geocentrically observed cycles of the heavens.

-oOo-

Then, January 2007 developed the theme, by relating it to the North Korean first nuclear test.

Pluto and Astrology – 'Alive and Kicking' in North Korean affairs!

With Pluto applying to T-square the Nodal axis, it was not surprising that the karmic consequences of nuclear activity were in the news when Korea decided to announce its intention and then claim to have tested its first nuclear bomb. Predictably for an event that was generally condemned by just about every nation in the world (and claimed to be a non-event by some!), the MC of the event[68] applies to conjunct the South Node, which is itself squared by 'nuclear' Pluto.[69]

The charts on the next page show there are many interesting comparisons between the event and the natal and progressed charts.[70] The event's Midheaven is four minutes of time before a conjunction to the natal Sun. The test was generally accepted as a publicity-seeking answer to rejection by the US (in recent years the progressed MC has been passing over North Korea's progressed South Node). Transiting Venus conjuncted progressed Venus a few days before the impending test, and was a day past a conjunction to natal Mercury when it occurred. It was conjuncting natal Neptune the day immediately afterwards, when the world community agonised over what to do next. Transiting Mercury conjuncted natal Mars and South Node during the week leading to the announcement of the explosion. The day before the explosion, transiting Moon was in Aries trining natal Saturn in Leo in the natal ninth – challenge in foreign affairs. Natal Pluto is very near to being exactly trined by the progressed Mars – trauma to the world community. Progressed Sun is less than a year from squaring that Pluto. Clearly in the arena where events live and breathe, Pluto and astrology are very much 'alive and kicking'!

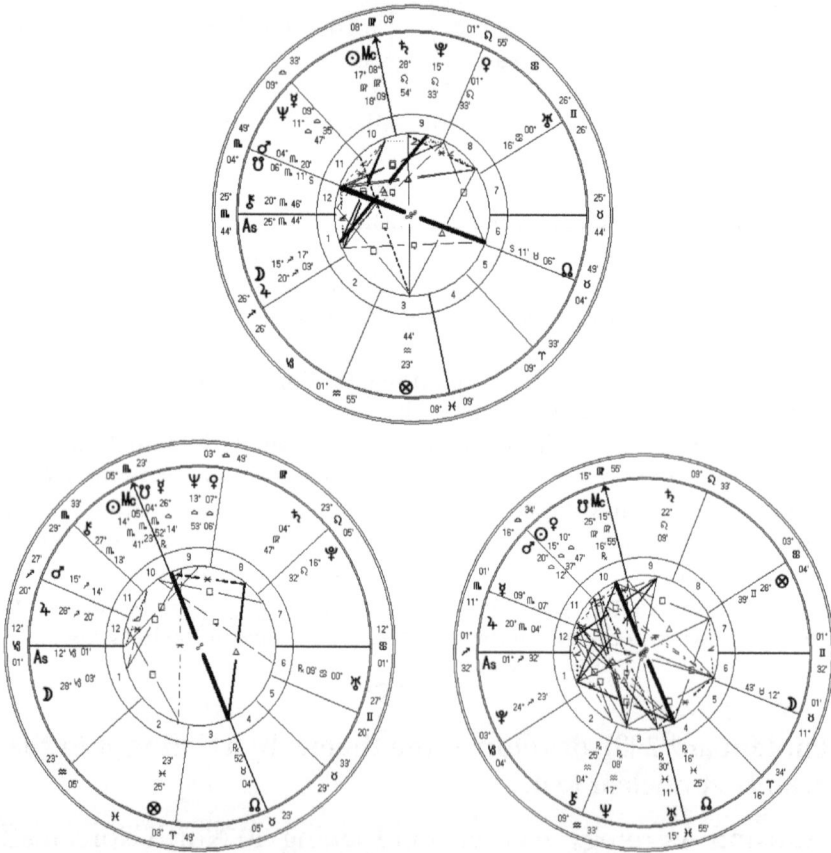

Top: North Korea **Founded** 10 Sep 1948 12:00 JST -9:00 Pyongyang, N Korea, 39°N01' 125°E45"
Left: Secondary Progressed 9 Oct 2006 10:36 JST -9:00 Pyongyang, N Korea,
Right: North Korea Nuclear Test 9 Oct 2006 10:36 JST -10:36 Place Est. 41°N00' 128°E00'

-o0o-

The May 2007 column looked at the January 2009 US Presidential Inauguration Day chart to consider which of the then three contenders fitted it best.

US Presidential Election 2008

Political astrology enthusiasts! Now is the time to join colleagues in what will undoubtedly be a most intricate and multi-faceted astrological study. Who will be the next President of the USA? There are many methods and possible charts that can be studied. In addition to those of the candidates and parties. As Jim Shawvan showed at the 2000 election, the transits on Election Day can be critical.[71] However, for the 2008 election, I intend to focus on the 2009 Inauguration Chart.

It seems to make sense. The exact time, date and place is always in Washington, DC Noon on 20 January every fourth year. The Presidential swearing-in is a most public and sacred ceremonial world moment. If astrology works, this moment will not only define the nature of Presidency, but also relate very specially to the person who will be taking office.

The 2001 Inauguration of George W Bush certainly had key links to the man.[72] Transiting Mercury was in an exact trine to his Moon and nearby Jupiter. Transiting Moon was applying to trine his Venus in the coming five hours. The transiting Nodal axis was applying back to his Sun and the Ascendant of the moment was just over four degrees past a trine to his Mars. Here was the man of the moment. Unfortunately, the Inauguration Chart of that moment had Mars squaring Mercury/Uranus and clearly indicated the violent upheaval we have suffered as a result. Did the US have to elect George W Bush to fit such a destiny? Many would argue that with wise astrological advice this difficult energy could have changed the world for the better. Astrology could have helped us understand well enough to reorientate economic and ecological priorities, to educate and so resolve international misunderstandings – rather than taking knee-jerk actions based on blind 'cowboy' ignorance.

The 2009 chart has Venus/Uranus opposing Saturn, suggesting upheaval based on kind, realistic service in difficult financial circumstances is likely. With ninth-house Mars trine Sun – both in earth signs – expect a philosophy of practical realism. The conservative overtones of Capricorn/Virgo may indicate a return to the more conventional tolerant middle ground of American politics after the 'oddball' extremism of recent years. What stands out however is the Cazimi Sun/Mercury applying to Jupiter less than three degrees away – all are culminating in Aquarius. Of course by definition of the event, every Inauguration has the Sun

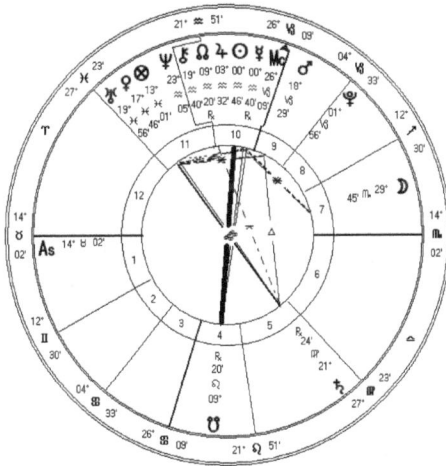

US President Inaugurated
20 Jan 2009 12:00 EST +5:00
Washington, DC 38°N53'42" 077°W02'12"
Geocentric Tropical Placidus True Node

near the MC, but the other two planets joining it suggests a great heightened moment of public understanding.

Interestingly, John McCain's Mercury at 2Li15 is trine these early Aquarian degrees.[73] Even more interestingly, Barack Obama's Jupiter is 00Aq53 (at noon) well under a degree from an exact conjunction to the Sun/Mercury Cazimi, whatever time of day he was born.[74] In contrast and not so easy is that, if he were born at 12:36 AHST that day, his Moon would be in an exact opposition to the 2009 Inauguration Moon. Hillary Clinton's Venus trines the Inauguration one and her Jupiter is within a few minutes of a sextile to the Inauguration Cazimi.[75] Taking no chances of another charismatic Leo getting in the way of her political destiny, she decided to announce her intention to stand exactly two years ahead on 20 January 2007. With Mars exact the MC at the 10:20 EST time of that announcement, battle can indeed commence!

UK fans of Channel 4 television's *West Wing* (and its viewers in other parts of the world) will remember the mock presidential campaign of its very last series. Could McCain and Obama bring the Alan Alda/Jimmy Smits battle to real life? Or will Hillary or someone else bring an entirely different dimension to the American Presidency? Time for more study!

-o0o-

Written in July, the September 2007 column included a major analysis of the upcoming Pluto in Capricorn period, putting it in the context of what had happened in the twenty-first century to date and giving clear warnings of the changes ahead.

Great Changes Ahoy!

Looking back, the past six years have been desperately frustrating for those of us who saw what was coming and how it could have been avoided from the very beginning. Perhaps we should have shouted louder, but who would have listened? Who in power would have understood the lethal Saturn-opposite-Pluto symbolism of the Taliban's destruction of the Bamian Buddhas in 2000 and acted wisely in good time to marginalise the danger? When Mars joined Pluto in the spring of 2001, without a thought for the karmic consequences, we acquiesced in the indiscriminate slaughter and burning of hundreds of thousands of Britain's animals as a response to the outbreak of foot-and-mouth disease. After the aspect's effect reached New York on 11 September 2001, who would have listened to pleas for discriminating awareness and kindness to understand the cause? With Jupiter in Leo applying to oppose Neptune in Aquarius for two years after, knee-jerk reactions and delusions of grandeur were so much more satisfying.

The astrology of Tony Blair's karma could not be starker. His last full day in office, 26 June 2007, saw the completion of the Saturn/Neptune opposition that frequently we have shown to represent the karmic consequences of his Jupiter-opposed-Neptune Iraq flirtation with George Bush. Not only was it appropriate that he could not hold on to his job beyond that date, but also that immediately he left it, he accepted the Middle East Envoy role. If Iraq is not to be Tony Blair's legacy in history then perhaps, he is destined to be a key force in the resolution of this central world problem. One is reminded that Ronald Reagan made peace with the USSR, the very country he labelled in his election campaign as 'the evil empire'. In 2007, with

Saturn's time opposed to Neptune a thing of the past, the dust is settling on the consequences of all that.

Looking forward to the coming six years, the outer-planetary transits suggest even more radical changes. To react as automatically and mindlessly to these transits as we have to those of the last six years will compound the errors of the past into global disaster. To serve and enable a better future, we can expect astrologers to examine, talk and write about the upcoming transits with some rigour. Here we shall consider the most imminent – Pluto's transit through Capricorn. The months before its first ingress on 26 January 2008 offer space to consider and prepare for what this change might suggest. Firstly, let us remind ourselves by quoting below the key clarification paragraph in November 2006's 'Working with the Planets' column. This answered any suggestion that Pluto is too small to be significant (especially in view of the then recent demotion by the IAU).

> Astrology can use anything in the heavens as a point of reference around which to focus and study the effects of a cycle. Such a reference point (be it a planet or not) does not have to cause directly any of the effects we seem to attribute to it. The validity of a cycle depends upon what we observe, not its point of reference, which merely disciplines the space and time of the cycle. If we discover that an object we have used as a reference point from which to measure distances is not a tree but a mildewed telegraph pole, we are still the same distance from it!

Pluto is a most incisive reference point that helps us describe fundamental culture shifts in history, even if they occurred before its discovery. Its apt opposition to Uranus during the American and French revolutions is well known. Pluto in Gemini brought the radical ideas of Jules Verne, H G. Wells, George Bernard Shaw, Oscar Wilde and Albert Einstein that revolutionised society. It also brought major changes in Western artistic convention. With Pluto in Cancer came changes in family values, social welfare, the class struggle and the disintegration of Europe's royal ruling family. Pluto in Leo saw megalomaniac leaders and proud heroism. The Virgo period was one of intense criticism that saw traditional values being questioned and swept away. The Libran period brought radical tolerance that liberalised what was acceptable in relationships. Pluto in Scorpio saw AIDS and sexual explicitness. We are still experiencing Pluto's movement through Sagittarius. The growth in cheap air and road travel threatens our environment. Yet, the internet enables us to be in many places without moving at all. Hanging over us all is the spectre of fundamentalist religious conflict.

So, what will happen with Pluto in Capricorn? The literal keyword interpretation is 'the death and transformation of organisational and political control'. Capricorn controls by establishing vital structures. The body needs a skeleton; a business needs executive and management structure; a society is based upon its body politic and civil service. The effect on a structure when Pluto is in Capricorn is to contain and focus behaviour along certain lines, but in doing so to create the need for a liberating counter movement. To succeed, such a movement must see beyond the constraints of Capricorn structure to a higher, less didactic one. Here comes Pluto in Aquarius. As we get nearer that time, astrologers will study society morphing into a time when that transit will dominate.

For the moment, it is important to understand Pluto in Capricorn. We can do this by considering key developments when this transit occurred before. As a result of Marco Polo's journeys during the 1272-95 transit of Pluto through Capricorn, trade with the East expanded, power was given to the merchant middle classes, and this led to the growth of towns. In time, it was to spur on more voyages of discovery and questions about the absolute truth of the European view of reality. The 1517 to 1533 transit saw the reformation. Martin Luther nailed his thesis to the door of Wittenberg Cathedral on 31 October 1517. The transit reinforced and accelerated the process of effective challenge to central Church control, already building from the stellium of outer planets a few decades earlier. Church wealth in England was redistributed. Through the 1763 to 1779 transit, the mapping of land led to enclosure and colonialism. Captain Cook travelled to the east and west coasts of America and around Australasia. The counter to this was rebellion of the masses, anti-imperialism, popular culture, and increasing cynicism about the right to lead.

When combined with the recent technological revolution indicated by Uranus and Neptune in Aquarius, we can anticipate that the upcoming Pluto in Capricorn period will see authorities turning their capacity to map into the very privacy of each individual's outer and inner life. Those in power will have the technology to track and trace all we do. One central database: our shopping decisions, our unique identity patterns, memberships of organisations, health, genetic structure, and psychological characteristics. Anyone who can gain access to the 'machine' will have all they need to decide how we shall live our lives and to find and deal with us if we 'rebel'. It is often said that George Orwell got everything right in his book *1984*, except the date!

There is another side of the coin – the Uranus/Neptune Aquarian period that is soon to end also developed advanced methods for individuals to discover and distribute information. Governments and multinational companies may have much power, but to date this depends on satisfying the very consumers created by these political developments. So, in the coming years, it will be difficult for a global economy dependent on mass consumption to contain the growth of human understanding. The media, and the advertisers that finance it, may be powerful and pervasively manipulative, but the availability of information and global communication will make it difficult to control the populace and make it pliant in the way that Orwell visualised. The more we know, understand, and work with each other on the human level, the more we develop the wisdom to ignore and reject the propaganda that will otherwise enslave us.

It is important that we do. For, even well before Pluto enters Capricorn, powerful forces are influencing governments and the workplace. Their methods pin down and isolate workers by means of increasingly detailed targets and systems of supervision. We are seeing methods of bringing 'efficiency' to the British National Health Service, education, policing and the civil service. Results are often unreliable and counter-productive. Minor operations are cleared to reduce waiting lists. Police charge insignificant offences to meet targets. In response, targets are made more sophisticated and detailed. Forms become longer and more numerous; ever more people are employed to check them. The room for initiative and creative innovation in the workplace is ever more restricted.

While some will take advantage of loopholes in a loose and incompetent system, subjecting the vast majority to ever-intensifying scrutiny compromises such workers' kindness and decency. They feel forced to cheat and trick what they see as petty bureaucracy. Many will reluctantly decide to give just the minimum they can get away with. As we lose personal commitment in a free and professional work environment, there will no longer be space for ever-flowering goodwill to emerge. When we genuinely and deeply believe in what we are doing, we do our best. It is a fundamental error to fear and mistrust a workforce. Goodwill can indeed move mountains. Rigid, bullying regimes harden and build ever higher barriers to progress and efficiency.

So, will Pluto's transit through Capricorn lead to 'colonial rule' of our very souls, or an inner struggle for personal independence by an increasingly enlightened population? It will be both. For Capricorn indicates those that govern and their institutions on the one hand, and the reaction of the governed on the other. Pluto in Sagittarius brought a kind of 'death' through travel by an expansion of air travel that threatened both the planet's ecology and industrial stability. Now Pluto in Capricorn will bring an expansion in the government's power to see and control, but also an expansion in the citizen's ability to see and challenge those that govern. To be safe, we have to keep it that way. Provided that citizens remain wise and independent, by the time Pluto enters Aquarius, we may yet achieve a Star Trek openness, rather than a lying and oppressive *1984* society.

Al Gore's film *An Inconvenient Truth* has already activated the starting gun of what will be another dominant theme of the Pluto in Capricorn transit – the ecological survival of humanity on the planet. Many leading players in international politics, business and media seem eager to leap on his bandwagon. Changes in energy creation methods to reduce global warming are the subject of national and international policies, discussions and hoped-for agreements.

As would be expected when dealing with such issues, with Neptune still transiting Aquarius and Pluto and Jupiter in Sagittarius squared to Uranus in Pisces, everyone assumes the solution will be found. It is just a matter of agreeing to make technological adjustments. Most confine themselves to urgent statements that have little to do with urgent action. The transits encourage the feeling that the answer will be simple. Maybe just switch to that 'cuddly pollution-free' nuclear power that generates the energy for the new Wembley football stadium and supports all those exciting cricket matches! We could build more windmills and wave generators, change the light bulbs we use, find a way of persuading the Chinese and Indians... At this point, the sentence seems to stop midstream!

As Pluto establishes itself in Capricorn, the other outer planets change sign and we build toward the 2010-11 major cardinal T-square between Pluto in Capricorn, Jupiter/Uranus in Aries, and Saturn in Libra, something much more real and effective than anything mentioned above will need to be done. This will not just be with regard to ecology. Whether the current world economy is sustainable as it is will also be questioned. With fire, air and mutability having been dominant for so long, we have become convinced we can 'get away with it' for ever. With cardinal earth and fire mixing with the fixed water of Saturn in Scorpio in the last quarter of 2012, reality will be with us indeed.

For now, just relax and seek to see clearly. Let those dusty clouds of confusion settle. This is the best way to prepare for those great changes ahead.

-oOo-

The November 2007 column emphasised the urgent need for the growth of wisdom within ourselves, to control the incessant development of technology and hyperactivity outside. It is our thieving inner desires and fears that need taming, if we are to create a happier world around us.

> Your real enemy, the thief who steals your happiness, is the inner thief, the one inside your mind – the one you have cherished since beginningless time. Therefore, make the strong determination to throw him out and never let him back in.
>
> *Ego, Attachment and Liberation* Lama Thubten Yeshe

Astrologers know more than anyone that the outer planets moving on from their longstanding Aquarius/Sagittarius focus will lead to radical changes in public perception, taste and experience over the coming four years. Two months ago, this column prepared for the first of these changes with an advance in-depth study of the implications of Pluto's ingress into Capricorn.

The last two months of 2007 until late 2008 will be transitional. With Pluto hovering across the Capricorn cusp, Neptune remaining in Aquarius and continuing to mutually received Uranus, many will still seek solutions by means of familiar technological adjustments and refuse to accept just how radical necessary changes will have to be. Forests destroyed to produce ethanol make it far from carbon neutral. Nuclear power may bring even more lethal pollutions and dangers.

At the other extreme, with Jupiter in Capricorn from 18 December 2007, immediate badly thought-out authoritarian 'solutions' may suddenly gain favour, however counter-productive they may be in practice. As I write, the media is reporting a sudden turnaround from Pluto-in-Sagittarius *laissez-faire* indulgence in alcohol at 'happy hour' prices, to raising the drinking age to twenty-one and taking some under-age drinkers into care. In other areas of public life, it may seem much easier to pour resources into pursuing apparent scapegoats, rather than looking deeper and financing genuine solutions. Our private relationships may be soured by chattering minds that blame others for all our disappointments. We may seek allies to bring down those 'responsible' and refuse to accept our own part in what happened.

Scientists and engineers may find it difficult to accept the slowing down of the immense technological advances of recent years and the need to take time to integrate them efficiently into the world economy. It has been such a wild and amazing ride of ever-expanding possibility. In a hundred years, nuclear physics and astronomy have advanced from seeing the atom as the smallest unit of matter to activating chain reactions that split one element into many others and could destroy the planet. They claim to be able to explain all the basic stages of the creation of the Universe from a fourteen-billion-year-old Big Bang and its immense heat that formed the core elements of hydrogen and helium. In the past ten years, we have developed global face-to-face communication, with its truly international economic market place and general information resources.

Yet amidst all these wonders, we can see that mechanical science is close to reaching the very limits of what it can discover from its three-dimensional perspective. It can calculate the precise value of pi to billions of places, but never to its final place. It can trace creation back to the Big Bang, but not explain or even conceive of what came before that. It can freeze matter from a state of gas, to liquid, to solid, to Bose-Einstein condensate, yet never reach more than incredibly close to absolute zero degrees.

Similarly, in our private lives, we can spend all the time and resources we have to make ourselves famous and successful, or to protect ourselves against fears of competitors and enemies. We can cover all likely eventualities ever more carefully, give people everything we think they want, or put-up defensive walls if they will not give in. Yet, whatever we do and however much we spend, only another's willingness to care for us from their side will make us safe and loved by them. This is something money cannot buy.

Whether in the immense macrocosm of space, or the minutiae of our personal private needs, paranoiac resentments and fears, true understanding and happiness come from openness and trust. We need to love the unknown and be ready to see beyond separation into another dimension. Quite simply, as mystics of all religions have always taught, to be safe and clear we have to let go of the ego and express compassion.

The last twenty years have seen amazing advances in our electronic power to link information. This follows two hundred years of sensational industrial growth. So much more seems possible, but Pluto moving into Capricorn with Jupiter in a trine to Saturn, plus Mars retrograding back from Cancer into Gemini, could be a shocking confrontation with reality.

It does not have to be, if with wise foresight we develop a genuine understanding of the Capricorn archetype. Jupiter applying to trine Saturn in Virgo early 2008 will help us avoid 'jumping in', but rather encourage the examination of 'solutions' in careful detail. Capricorn is the tenth-house archetype and the 'managing director' of earthly affairs, because it is strong and realistic. The Pluto-in-Sagittarius years could be seen as irresponsibly over-expansive. We have accepted what our scientists, economists and leaders have offered and told us far too easily. Now, as they feel defensive regarding us, we need to be defensive about them. We need to contain their power, as they seek to contain ours. Keep options open. Be less easily convinced. Stop jumping on bandwagons. Let the best answers emerge by their sheer strength, effectiveness and the sense of longstanding well-being they bring. If we cannot welcome and approach change in such sensible ways, we will develop resentments and prejudices that could tear us apart.

-oOo-

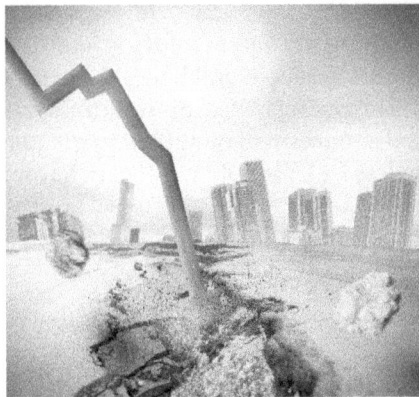

The New Year message in the January 2008 column was remarkably accurate.

> Above all 2008 is a year for each person and group to recognise what they owe, not demand what they are owed. Before things become ever more didactic, it is a time to look at all sides…[then] decide the best way to proceed. 'Working with the Planets' November 2007.[76]

The dominant aspect for January is, of course, the Jupiter trine to Saturn on the day of the Aquarian Solar ingress, combined with Pluto entering Capricorn just five days later. With the Sun tightening toward an Aquarian stellium comprising Chiron, Mercury, Neptune and North Node, Capricorn taking ordered control of Aquarian innovation will not be without paradox. That Venus will have opposed Mars a few days earlier and now be applying to conjunct Pluto less than two days before that planet (dwarf or otherwise) enters Capricorn suggests the nemesis of over-optimism. Now is the time to be realistic and truly scientific.

Before mechanists become beside themselves with ecstasy however, we should ask radical questions about the nature of realism and genuine science. Throughout the Sagittarius/Aquarius dominated period 1995 to 2007, it could be argued that we have witnessed a science that was out of control, even in terms of its own criteria. Every day a fresh statistical study told us a new fragment of 'scientific' information, always incomplete and impossible for lay people to assess fully, often contradictory. Vast sums were spent to explore, even 'prove' the commercial interests of those investing the money. Even in theoretical science, conclusions such as the Big Bang theory have been too easily extrapolated from very limited information. In genetics one system to analyse the workings of nature has been assumed to be the only system and reality re-ordered accordingly. How much of all this will stand up to the harsh rigour of Capricorn/Virgo examination?

Of course, the times are degenerate and Jupiter is not at its most comfortable or beneficial in Capricorn. So, authority could be 'up for grabs' in these early January days. Realism and economy will be the key. Keep on demanding deeper, long-term solutions. Remind decision makers that for scientific enquiry to be worthwhile it needs to be wide-ranging, fully explained, and open to development through further learning. Genuine science seeks to evolve truth, by scrutinising with unshaken questions. It broadens understanding by including and giving a proper respectful place to all human experience. The limited range we are used to today is a shambolic mass of incomplete precise details.[77]

What is true of the limitations of contemporary scientific assumptions of reality will also show itself in economics, business and hence the everyday experience of our lives. Unwise investments, borrowings, use of resources and dependence upon unnecessary consumption and services will be subject to greater scrutiny. Authorities and regulations may become less flexible. Life may seem harder, less fun.

-o0o-

Written in late July, the September 2008 column clearly anticipated the major structural changes that the years 2008-10 were to bring, as irresponsible global expansion 'hit the buffers'.

The Regeneration of Authority

Key themes in recent 'Working with the Planets' columns have outlined the unsustainable nature of a world society that takes blind refuge in mechanical scientism and with the right technology and economic manipulation, our 'experts' can change the universe to fulfil all our desires. The world approaches the nemesis of such dreams.

As well as Pluto's ingress into Capricorn, with other outer-planetary changes due until 2012, the astrology of this nemesis is focused upon five Saturn/Uranus oppositions. The first occurs on 4 November 2008 at 18° Virgo/Pisces. Retrogression keeps it in orb for the two subsequent years, with exact hits on 5 February 2009 (20° Virgo/Pisces), 15 September 2009 (24° Virgo/Pisces) and 27 April 2010 (28° Virgo/Pisces) to complete at 0° Libra/Aries on 26 July 2010. These astro events will dominate a major period of economic and social adjustment, not dissimilar to reversing the direction of an ocean liner when it is travelling 'full speed ahead'.

Engineering brilliance and the consequent technological achievements of mechanical scientism have been the driving force behind two centuries of economic and social expansion. Base Aquarian values and a permissive Pluto in Sagittarius (1994 to 2008) have encouraged dramatic electronic innovations and so accelerated this process exponentially and irresponsibly. So, the past two decades have brought unsustainable excess. Having based financial policy on the economics of failing to rein in a runaway horse, we now face commodity price inflation and a desperately over-exposed credit crisis.[78] Pluto moving into Capricorn[79] and an opposition between the traditional and modern rulers of Aquarius will not only call a halt, but also mark out a process of 'cosmic rationalisation'.

Students of astrology soon learn that the 'water' poured down in the image of Aquarius is not liquid, but the wisdom that pervades, refreshes, and so enables every aspect of universal understanding. The degenerate base manifestation of this core image is the arrogant assumption of total authority, based on partial understanding. At the exalted, opposite extreme is the realisation that wisdom includes every person and possible aspect of knowledge. Only with the latter, comes the humility that enables true understanding. Without trust and respect for every person and element of nature we know very little, however clever we think we are. Having a scientific method that enables us to 'pick and mix' arbitrary collections of mechanical relationships is dangerously incomplete.

So, how do Saturn and Uranus fit into all this? Clearly, to be viable and stable, a genuine Saturnine structure needs to take account of everything. Yet, modern society's scientist model is far from such absolute truth. For it bases all decisions and actions on research that is constantly open to challenge. In medicine, a cure is tested, and then used until further research finds a danger or a better method. In economic infrastructures, systems of transport, mining and industrial processes are assumed to be beneficial, until sufficient alternative research shows this to be otherwise – recent ecological concerns dramatically display the dangers. With economic self-interest so dominating our material society such counter-research may not be undertaken. In any event it takes time. While it is good to explore and discover new information and methods, to give such a piecemeal model absolute authority to rule our lives is proving to be lethal. Its effect has been the very opposite of the stable reliability we would expect from reliable science. For all its claims to be the foundation of a stable process of discovery, scientism has created chaotic *laissez-faire* societies.

If it is not truly Saturnine is our modern scientific method Uranian then? Uranus urges change, turns assumptions upside down, considers people and ideas that may have been ignored, innovates and is revolutionary. In many ways modern mechanical science does do that, yet it also insists on the opposite – that it is the sole authority. Individual ingenuity, inspirations and decisions must submit to its rigid systems and time scale for testing. In short, its notion is that Saturnine authority should control all Uranian activity. Progress can only emanate from current assumptions. Although our schools are called 'secular', they focus upon and teach 'scientism' as the only acceptable view of reality – just as fundamentalists teach a religious faith. Modern society would not have developed as it is has, should such a prejudiced and selective notion been allowed to prevail unchallenged in the seventeenth century.

The need to survive five Saturn/Uranus oppositions will see reassessment on a range of fronts; all of them about the nature and status of authority and innovation in our lives. On the political level, do we wish to live with confrontation, terror, suspicion and surveillance, or turn to trust, reconciliation and friendship? On the ecological level, do we project and impose one invention after another upon nature, or cooperate with its cycles? On the economic level, we can fight over resources, or use cyclic insight to satisfy our needs sustainably. On the level of 'truth', do we calcify progress in eighteenth century assumptions, or ask whether the 'enlightenment' and subsequent scientistic revolution were adolescently over-simplified? Did we 'throw out the baby with the bathwater'? Can the great achievements of our modern world only be understood, put into perspective and enjoyed, if integrated with considerable amounts of ancient cyclic wisdom?

-o0o-

Chapter 6
Twenty-First Century Radical Change 2009-14
[Articles written November 2008 – September 2014]

Contemporary Background
Underlying the whole period was the world struggle to recover from the effects of the 2008 economic collapse. Government bailouts of the banking system led to financial crisis in many countries. Greece was especially badly hit, needing bailouts in 2010, 2012, 2015, as well as a reduction in the debt repayable in 2011.

Ordinary citizens experienced austerity measures, tax increases, cuts in welfare benefits and public services, removal of rights at work, and zero-hours contracts. Such increasingly flexible work place regulation, alongside deregulation of international trade, disproportionately benefitted the wealthy, leading to a growing core of popular unrest.

The Middle East saw a struggle between popular rebellion and increasingly brutal responses by governments. Destabilisation allowed extreme fundamentalist forces to occupy large areas of Syria and Iraq.

20 January 2009	Barack Obama inaugurated as President of USA.
4 June 2009	Obama's Cairo speech on democracy.
6 May 2010	UK General Election – the Labour Party loses power.
25 January 2011	Egyptian Rebellion.
29 July 2011	After unrest the Free Syrian Army is formed.
27 July 2012	London Olympics open.
24 February 2013	Raul Castro fully replaces his brother Fidel.
5 March 2013	Hugo Chavez dies.
13 March 2013	Papacy of HH Pope Francis begins.
14 March 2013	Xi Jinping becomes Chinese President.
8 April 2013	Margaret Thatcher dies.
5 December 2013	Nelson Mandela dies.
21 March 2014	Crimea reintegrated into Russia.
12 May 2014	Narendra Modi wins absolute majority in India.
8 June 2014	Sisi becomes Egyptian leader.
30 June 2014	ISIL declares Caliphate in Iraq and Levant.
7 August 2014	First US-led airstrike against ISIL.
18 September 2014	Scottish Referendum votes to stay in the UK.

-o0o-

Introduction

The economic collapse in the autumn of 2008, just as Pluto was poised to enter Capricorn, commenced a radical confrontation with reality. The twelve years that followed were to see a reluctant world system being dragged, kicking and screaming back to the hard limitations allowed to beings that live on planet Earth.

Ironically, 2008 had seen a ground swell of optimistic hope for the future. Just as the US prepared to elect and celebrate a young, idealistic, charismatic new President, the simplistic economic gospel of Thatcherite Reaganomics was to collapse the global economy into horrendous debt.

-o0o-

The keynote 'Working with the Planets' column, written in October for this November 2008 column considered and advised on both trends. Not for the first, or last, time astro-advice was to be ignored.

Economic Change – Nemesis or Opportunity?

At Neptune's direct station on 2 November anxious clouds of uncertainty will clear to reveal dramatic and difficult-to-accept choices. On 3 November, Venus T-squares both Saturn and Uranus that are in exact opposition the next day. Six hours before the opposition Mars squares Neptune, less than three hours after Mercury enters Scorpio. For many different reasons, these days will be a struggle to decide what is real and believable. Caught at the apex will be the electorate of the United States of America.

Early November brings decisive pressure for change. Do we understand, face and master it or will we ignore, be driven and defeated by it? The answer will determine the fate of civilisation and the planet we live upon for decades, even centuries, to come. The early November 2008 days will trigger ongoing realignments up to July 2010, as we seek to adapt to change using the mutable opposition between Saturn and Uranus. Then that T-square becomes cardinal and ongoing transits will show if we have learned to cooperate and use sustainable methods; or have just marked time and are at the mercy of forces well beyond our control.

Before and especially since September 2007 this column has been anticipating and preparing our minds for the issues we now face.[80] We have considered Pluto's movement across the cusp and into Capricorn, the Uranus return of the 1923 German hyperinflation, a series of five Saturn/Uranus oppositions from now until July 2010, plus many other outer-planetary sign changes – all adding up to the unrealistic expectations and authoritarianism of those that guide our lives. Astrologers may understand the issues better those who have the biggest buildings and greatest resources. Certainly, the optimism of many people in power is proving misguided. Can the symbolism of astrology suggest some key principles that explain and help us use change for the good?

Astrology can predict exactly if the pattern is powerful enough, but it is best used to describe the range within which a number of possibilities will manifest. It tells us how changing planetary patterns relate to changing assumptions and opportunities. Farmers use the relationship of the Earth to the Sun to determine the seasons of the year. They sow, nurture and harvest their crops, and then regenerate and rotate the land to keep it constantly productive. So, we should use our more intricate knowledge of the cycles of the Moon and planets to decide times of opportunity, consolidation and change. These helps us distinguish between genuine achievement and fortunate opportunity. We should use astrological symbolism to make the most of our chances and preserve resources for more difficult times. In contrast, our current short-term, linear-looking, decision-making methods erroneously assume that the time of maximum understanding is right now – the past 'got it wrong'. Every piece of new natural scientific knowledge is presented as progress. 'We are wiser than our forebears.' Studying the cycles of astrology shows us, however much we knew or now know, we can always get it terribly wrong.

Where are we going economically?

The March/April 2008 'Working with the Planets', noting that Uranus direct station in Pisces on 24 November 2007 had been just a few days and minutes of arc after the direct station at the climax of the 1923 German hyperinflation, I wrote:

> Indeed, it could be argued that for the 21 years or more since the London *Big Bang* introduction of electronic trading, it is the new money and new derivative instruments that have kept the financial markets not just afloat, but expanding rapidly.
>
> Big question, can this introduction of new money or ways of hedging and offsetting continue indefinitely? Big problem, Pluto is leaving Sagittarius and, through 2008, establishing itself with Jupiter in Capricorn. The over-optimism that has encouraged us to use our Aquarian technological brilliance to find ways to expand, consume and speculate to death is in its very end days. Quite simply, we cannot go on as we are. The financial ingenuity will have to give way to realism, especially with Saturn now in Virgo. The consequences of our consumption of raw materials and energy will have to be faced – with or without nuclear power.[81]

By August 2008, reports of the credit default swap and other debt exposure of financial institutions confirmed February's astrology-based anxiety.[82] 84 years on, financial institutions have found a new, ingenious way of 'printing money' that has now become a problem for us all.

With Pluto in Cancer and Neptune in Leo the mood of the 1920s was a questioning of all family values and the celebration of self-pleasure – the F Scott Fitzgerald Roaring Twenties. Boom time was still to come building to the 1929 crash and 1930s depression. Today, with Pluto in Capricorn (after Sagittarius) and Neptune in Aquarius/Pisces, we have had the boom. Furthermore, the boom has extended to far more of the planet and its ecosystem. Seeking a quick fix through a return to nuclear, developing ethanol, new oil drilling, or awaiting a change in cycle to get back to business may put off the day of reckoning a little, but will be even more disastrous.

Relating the coming years' transits to key financial market charts (see and study the table) gives credibility to such anxiety. Strong pressure in earth signs (especially Capricorn) for some years to come suggests that the times of easy credit and unrealistic 'passing the parcel' of debt are over. Rationalisation of the markets based only on tangible assets is imminent.

Financial markets chart data with selected transit connections
1. NYSE Constitution 00:00 LMT 8 March 1817, New York City, USA
2. Dow Jones 10:00 LMT 3 July 1884, New York City, USA
3. US Federal Reserve 18:02 EST 23 December 1913, Washington DC USA
4. NASDAQ (Index) 10:00 EST 8 February 1971, New York City, USA[83]
5. FTSE 100 08:30 3 January 1984, London Stock Exchange, UK
6. Nikkei 08:30 4 January 1984, Tokyo, Japan[84]
7. Shanghai SE Time unknown 19 December 1990, Shanghai, China[85]

Connections to 4 November 2008 Saturn/Uranus opposition at 18Pi/Vi57
  ❖ NYSE Constitution Sun just over 1 degree before
  ❖ DJ First Index chart Ascendant and Mars 3 degrees before
  ❖ Node of Federal Reserve Chart in Pisces 7 minutes of arc from exact
  ❖ Second-house Moon NASDAQ chart 3 degrees from exact T-square
  ❖ Nodes on both the FTSE 100 and Nikkei charts just over 3 degrees before

Connections to the transit of Pluto into and through early Capricorn
  ❖ Federal Reserve Sun 1Cp33 separating opposition to Pluto at 0Cn05,
  ❖ NYSE Constitution Asc/Dsc at 7Cp/Cn07
  ❖ DJ First Index Mercury 0Cn47 and Sun 12Cn00
  ❖ NASDAQ Venus (rules second) at 0Cp00, Uranus 13Li21 and MC 17Cp35
  ❖ FTSE 100 opened 2 degrees after a New Moon, Sun 12Cp12
  ❖ The Japanese Nikkei opened one day later.
  ❖ Shanghai SE six planets and North Node 8 to 28 degrees Capricorn

Of course, the financial market charts alone do not give the full story. Even though the FTSE and Nikkei started trading a day apart and their regular ups and downs do respond similarly to planetary cycles, their major trend reaction to the Capricorn stellium in 1990 was dramatically different. This is because the place and economic health of the country as a whole has to be considered alongside.

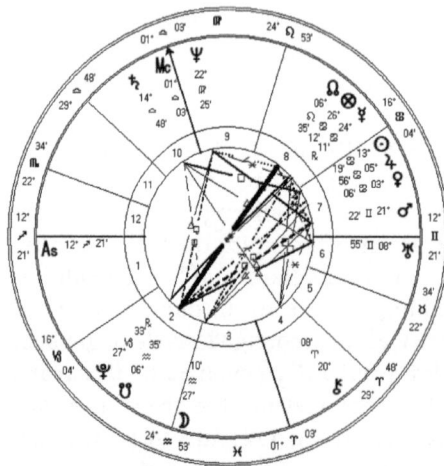

USA Sibley Chart
4 Jul 1776 NS 17:10 LMT +5:00:40
Philadelphia PA 39°N57' 075°W10'
Geocentric Tropical Placidus True Node

Since 9/11, the Sibley chart has been widely accepted for the USA. Jupiter's transit through the seventh and eighth houses that followed brought extravagance. The Saturn transit that came next was misused. Financial discipline and legitimate authority were disregarded. As a result, the country's popularity diminished and it was left deeply in debt. In the winter and early spring of 2009, Pluto commences an opposition to the Cancer stellium that will last into the early 2020s. The inability of the US economy to pay its way could present radical challenges to the entire world marketplace.

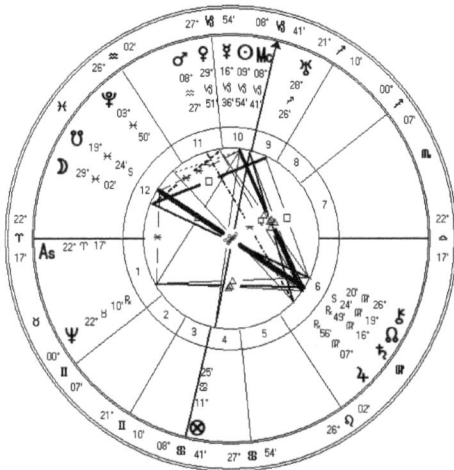

England Coronation William I
25 Dec 1066 12:00 LMT +0:00:40
London, England 51°N30' 000°W10'
Geocentric Tropical Placidus True Node

The 1066 England chart has Sun at 9Cp54 nearly a degree past the Capricorn MC. The 1801 Union Chart Sun is at 10Cp10, just under a degree after its IC. Both will be conjuncted by Pluto from the end of this decade and squared by transiting Uranus and Saturn the following years. The Nodal axis and sixth-house Saturn of the 1066 chart are near the 4 November Saturn/Uranus opposition, which squares the Mercury of the 1801 chart. City of London market manipulation may become a less key factor in the world economy. If so, the UK could face longstanding employment issues. This could lead to the completion of the UK's industrial realignment that has been on artificial hold since the changes of the 1980s.

. Until the 2020s transiting Pluto makes an ongoing conjunction to the fourth and fifth-house stellium of the chart for the Flag Raising of the new Russian State. The stellium opposition to the US chart's Cancer stellium suggests that the Pluto transit could fuel ruthless conflict between the two nations. Alternatively, recognition and respect of opposites could bring fertile understanding and efficiency. The best Cancer/Capricorn marriages carry all before them. The special relationship between Capricorn Britain and the Cancer US has blossomed since their 1776 'divorce'!

China's eighth-house Libran stellium (see chart next page) suggests the gentle but

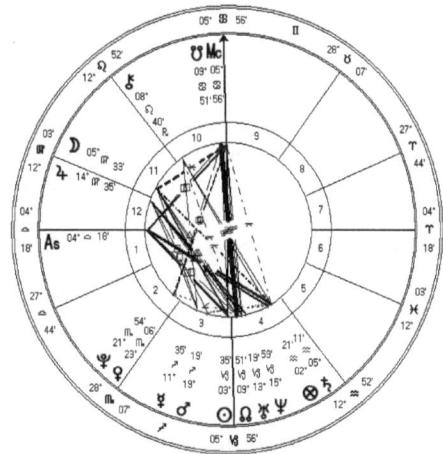

Russian Flag Raised
25 Dec 1991 23:40 EET -2:00
Moscow, Russia 55°N45' 037°E35'
Geocentric Tropical Placidus True Node

sternly unyielding politeness of a debt collector, applied with the strain of hard-headed realism. [How powerfully did China exploit their seventh-house Saturn at those 8 pm opening 8 August 2008 Olympics!] Key planets in the Russia, USA, China and United Kingdom charts make a grand cross with the 2010 cardinal T-square.

We are faced with several years when tension and its causes have to be addressed and resolved. A radical change in the basic assumptions that rule both our personal and international expectations is unavoidable. We may try to duck and weave to avoid 'the inevitable' while the Saturn/Uranus opposition is in Virgo/Pisces. When, in July 2010, Jupiter and Uranus oppose Mars and Saturn and square Pluto across the early degrees of Aries, Libra and Capricorn, the cardinal

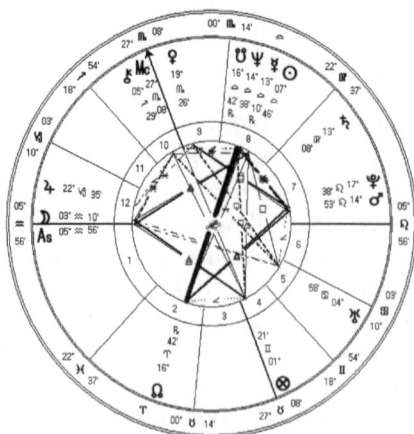

China Communist
1 Oct 1949 15:15 AWST -8:00
Beijing, China 39°N55' 116°E25'
Geocentric Tropical Placidus True Node

pressure of 90 degree multiple connections will be irresistible. The more we
have used the mutable energy to prepare
ourselves between now and then, the
better it will be.

Such change has to be based on
sustainable efficiency. With few ways of
finding new money, energy and other
resources, prizing economic growth as the
basis of all success and happiness is
clearly wrong. If we and the planet are to
be well and happy, the god of 'economic
expansion' will have to be replaced by a
new focus of devotion – 'sustainability'.
In the interests of everyone and
everything, we have to be realistic, to sow
and reap in proportion to planetary
ecological realities. We have to put our
needs in perspective. Consumption
without concern for future consequences leads to degenerate stumbling
incompetence, constant irritation and dull-minded conflict, as the clock of disastrous
global bankruptcy ticks ever faster.

Moving from growth to sustainability does not have to be bad for us, providing
we welcome and learn from the cardinal grand cross pressure. Everyone's life could
be much easier; we could find hope in what first seemed to be unavoidable disaster.
By scaling down our expectations, we avoid the struggle over resources, can have all
that we really need without threatening the planet.

The key to establishing sustainability instead of growth at the heart of our
endeavours is to base our values on genuine understanding and appreciation of each
other. This involves moving away from seeing success in terms of things, delivered
by brutal market forces, driven on by the 'get rich quick' tricks of mechanistic
ingenuity. The crisis we face today will be with us without end, until we see the error
of making competition the basis of our economy, culture and leisure life in sport and
celebrity entertainment.

Instead, we should prize the quality of life and help as many people as possible
to enjoy it. Science should serve by enhancing our judgement of others' needs; not
arrogantly dictating what we must think and do. Understanding how the planets
incline our lives and mould the fashion of our times can make such distinctions clear.
If we can achieve this, then the Saturn, Uranus and Pluto transits helped us
understand and remove the counter-productive. Far from taking away what we want,
they will allow us to have exactly what we need.

Who are we going with?
This brings us back to the day of the US Presidential Election. Should a positive vision
be possible, who would lead or symbolise the way? In such monumental
circumstances, anyone elected is unlikely to grasp what is happening fully. He may
well be at the mercy of and reacting to events. Governments may struggle to control
what happens, as they did in the 1970s. Now the difficulties promise to go far deeper!

The candidate chosen will indicate readiness of America and the World for a
positive way ahead. Refer again to the 20 January 2009 Inauguration Chart and

comments in September's 'Working with the Planets' column. John McCain's Moon is at 27Cp02, less than a degree past the MC of ceremony's start.[86] He could be many people's choice, but with transiting Saturn conjunct his natal Venus will the choice be for the right reasons? Would he bring anything new or just be a more measured and workmanlike version of what has gone before? Selecting him could suggest a pessimism that seems safer in the short-term, but avoids key changes and so leads to American down-sizing and being defeated in world affairs.

Barack Obama's Jupiter/Saturn conjunction straddles the Inauguration MC.[87] His Jupiter conjuncts its Sun/Moon Cazimi and his Moon is only 11 minutes short of an exact trine to that Inauguration Jupiter. Does this suggest he understands the new Aquarian paradigm vision outlined above, or is he just a bundle of carefully chosen words? We have been so disappointed before. In democracies based on self-indulgence, a candidate with a realistic vision of the future may only succeed by avoiding saying what really needs to be done until elected. How then do we tell the 'real deal' from the trickster politician, who uses words that seem to match the personal aspirations of many people, but in the end delivers to no one?

-o0o-

Written just after President Obama's November election, the January 2009 column expressed hope for a brighter future.

Can We?

What's that coming over the hill? Is it a monster?
Monster song by The Automatic

Yes We Can   Barack Obama Presidential Campaign Slogan

These two quotations offer diametrically opposed insights into our hope for the future and especially the predicament of today's generations under forty.

Firstly, the monster
Since Neptune with Jupiter entered Capricorn on 19/20 January 1984, we have found increasingly deceptive ways to appear to balance the books of the world economy. As we move on from the Saturn return of Margaret Thatcher's 4 May 1979 election towards that of Ronald Regan's victory in November 1980, we are suffering the consequences of the role these two 'political lovers' played in the financial challenges we are facing today. Mrs Thatcher sold off Britain's public assets and both leaders encouraged market deregulation and the development of ingenious ways to hedge debt.

With the nation's assets spent, Tony Blair and Gordon Brown embarked upon mortgaging our future. Public-private partnerships and index-linked student loans are two examples that will haunt us for years to come. As the future was mortgaged and markets over-heated with unrealistically cheap credit, we joined George W Bush in enterprises that alienated potential friends and emboldened our enemies.

Such policies were based upon key delusions. Constant success and happiness are possible for ever more people, if they are left free to compete in an unregulated market place. The basis of all happiness was to do as you wish and encourage others to do the same. Anyone who felt differently was an enemy of freedom.

Pluto's Capricorn ingress reminds us that it will soon return to its position during the eighteenth-century Industrial Revolution and the time of the American Declaration of Independence. These and the Thatcher/Reagan Saturn returns being opposed to Uranus suggest the consequences for the young may be far darker – very much like the morning after a party. They have been educated with amoral tools to survive in an unfriendly competitive market place. Yet, that 'world of plenty', in which they were to compete, is fading into a past memory, leaving ecological bankruptcy. Hope degenerates into the facile world of government emergency remedies. These seek to repeat the failure of the last thirty years by encouraging more debt to spend our way out of recession, 'kick start the cycle', restore assumed assets values, so as to support more debt. This is the solution of economists, whose theories encouraged us into our present problems and are still our business and political leaders. Powerless in the face of such intransigent intellectual bankruptcy, teenagers and young adults in Britain see alcohol and violent defence of sub-group loyalties as the way to survive, while they wait for the 'monster' to come over the hill.

Now the hope
After a party, the better course is to put aside the alcohol for a while and focus upon repairing the damage, get back to a more balanced way of life? The way Barack Obama achieved the US Presidency offers hope, because his success is very much driven by the ways and enthusiasm of ordinary under-forty Americans. Refusing to accept the brute ignorance of old-style leaders, they believed in and worked for new ways.

As well as the great racial symbolism, Barack Obama's victory represents something as important for many who lived through the decades from the 1950s – the regeneration of the family. The process started with the clean pre rock 'n roll nuclear family, so well depicted in the film *Pleasantville*.[88] This family was fatally flawed because its ignorance of the world permitted the McCarthy hearings and Vietnam War. So, the Pluto/Uranus conjunction in Virgo led to excessive critical questioning of everything the nuclear family stood for. The consequent break-up of many family structures is clearly illustrated by the circumstances of Barack Obama's birth and upbringing. Yet, as a result of this upbringing, in his blood is the heritage of both pre-slavery Africa and traditional white American. In his experience are white, Hawaiian, Indonesian Asian, Christian, Polynesian and Islamic cultures; two generations of mothers, but, lacking a father, a heightened sense of paternal responsibility. Within this one man is crystallised the journey of American society's discovery of world culture and how to care for it. In his election is the symbol of a new generation's willingness to stand up without prejudice to accept worldly wisdom. When the Obama family walked on the stage to accept the Presidential victory, we saw the healing had come full circle. We saw an ideal 1950s loving nuclear family, now armed with an understanding of the world and its cultures in their very blood, ready to dedicate itself to healing the world.

Genuine lasting and effective change does not come by violent revolution, but by starting a process of discovery and then leaning in the right direction. It needs to be more deep-seated than the Clinton-style boom that was doomed to flounder against the Taurus stellium in the last year of his second term. Far better would be a Roosevelt-style 'New Deal' that invests in projects of lasting value and encourages people to lead meaningful interactive lives, not indulge aimlessly. The world's ecological and monetary balance sheets need to be based on real, sustainable value. With a Capricorn and Saturn focus on the future, we must look calmly at every issue.

By putting aside preconceived assumptions and creating a momentum to deal with each issue on its merit, perhaps new young approaches will be more than a match for the monster their forebears have encouraged. If so, the endurance and courage of that minority of their elders, who have struggled to keep hope alive over the past sixty years will also have been rewarded.

Does the astrology confirm such optimism?

Regular readers will remember, this column in the spring of 2007 identified John McCain, Barack Obama and Hillary Clinton as the key contestants for the Presidency and wrote the following interpretation of the Inauguration Chart:

> The 2009 chart has Venus/Uranus opposing Saturn, upheaval based on kind, realistic service in difficult financial circumstances is likely. With ninth house Mars trine Sun – both in earth signs – expect a philosophy of practical realism. The conservative overtones of Capricorn/Virgo may indicate a return to the more conventional tolerant middle ground of American politics after the 'oddball' extremism of recent years. What stands out however is the Cazimi Sun/Mercury applying to Jupiter less than three degrees away – all are culminating in Aquarius. Of course, by definition of the event, every Inauguration has the Sun near the MC, but the other two planets joining it suggest a great heightened moment of public understanding.

It was noted that 'Barack Obama's Jupiter is 00Aq53 (at noon) well under a degree from an exact conjunction to the Sun/Mercury Cazimi.'[89] In fact, with the subsequent release of his birth certificate[90], we were to learn that the Jupiter position was 00Aq51 – just 4 minutes of arc past the Sun and that his natal Moon was at 3Ge21 just 11 minutes of arc applying exact trine the Inauguration Jupiter in the tenth. It is difficult to get more astrologically the man of the moment than that!

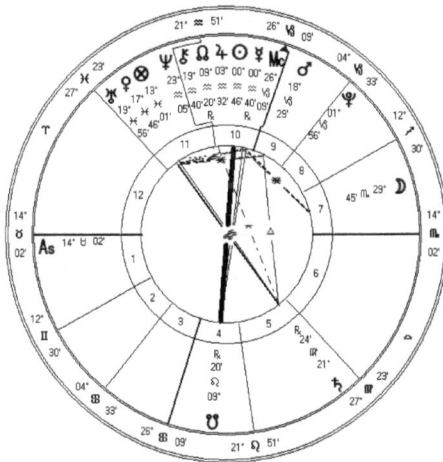

US President Inaugurated
20 Jan 2009 12:00 EST +5:00
Washington, DC 38°N53'42" 077°W02'12"
Geocentric Tropical Placidus True Node

The Moon is void, but enters Sagittarius just fifteen minutes of time into the ceremony; possibly when the oath is taken. It will apply to oppose the new President's natal Moon in mutable Gemini suggesting everyone has ideas and wants a relationship. The packed Aquarian tenth house and Pisces conjunct Venus in the eleventh will focus him upon great work larger than any one person or cause. Being an Aquarian mission while Pluto is in Capricorn suggests a more mature and systematic approach toward knowledge and method – common sense, not mechanical systems and boyish experiments. Pluto virtually unaspected in the eighth suggests danger in shared experiences and resources; a desperate need for compassionate and objective regeneration.

Many people have expressed anxiety that he may not survive, but the opportunity that the Obama election represents cannot be taken from the world. It is too late for that. From the moment that America's new 'first family' strode out into Grant Park, the power to bully and gag the wisdom of ordinary people was lost. The genie of people-power was out of the bottle. We have seen his cool, friendly, considered, compassionate, Aquarian common sense.[91] We know how to approach our challenges.

In the midst of the Beijing Olympics and at regular intervals since, the CNN Channel has been broadcasting a *Foundation for a Better Life* sponsored advertisement. It depicts seven children with Downs syndrome in a race. One boy pulls ahead, much to the excitement of his parents in the crowd, and then he trips. All the children run past him, except one girl who stops and offers him a helping hand. Then we see that all the children have returned to link arms and, to even greater applause from the crowd, cross the finishing line together. The words 'True victory – pass it on' appear on the screen.

To develop efficient methods, we need the intelligence of such mutual support. At the height of the October Libran banking crisis, it was the resources of the ordinary people and the co-operation of other nations that the destitute financial institutions turned to. Every person, whatever their political leanings, learned from this. We may be persuaded it is in everyone's best interests to prop up the existing system, but for how long? How well will decisions made in October and November 2008, when Pluto was void in Sagittarius, last? Pluto does not fully leave Capricorn until the end of 2024. The transits will demand we solve the global crisis in the radical way, with give and take at every level of our personal and global lives. We will need friendship and decency toward each other, the planet we live on and in the way we consume. Brilliant science must be focus upon improving our environment, not searching for ways to take from it. Capricorn and Saturn demand such efficiency. Enterprises so engaged, will run with consummate ease and be rewarded by these symbolic planetary managers of the cosmos.

By learning from recent trauma, the coming years could see great advances in human relationships and plenty for all.

-o0o-

The March 2009 column identifies the lessons the Pluto-in-Capricorn transit could teach us, but we are yet to learn in the 2020s. Having ignored the column's advice for eleven years, the world economy entered the 2020 Covid-19 crisis in the midst of a wasteful boom. In 2021, we take on even more debt to try to bounce out of the crisis.

Doomed? Surely Not!

I believe that unarmed truth and unconditional love will have the
final word in reality. Dr Martin Luther King Jnr.

Had the retailers in London's famous West End shops consulted astrologers or were they responding to the astro-cycles automatically? Whatever the explanation, they choose highly-appropriate black, white and purple for the Christmas 2008 theme in their famous seasonal window displays. These colours almost exclusively dominated high fashion clothing and many other stores. Even the Christmas lights were confined to darkening purple. It was pouring with rain too when we were there!

Christmas shopping 2008 was very much a joyless experience of going through the motions – the sense that we had not earned or even needed the celebration. We had been undeservedly (and temporarily!) 'let off the hook' of facing the consequences of years of self-indulgence.

Astrologers will be both frustrated and amused by the Governor of the Bank of England's insistence that he could not be expected to plan 'with the benefit of hindsight'! They can only look with amazement at the inept and automatic way those arrogant and dismissive economists, politicians and other 'experts' responded to the Saturn opposition to Uranus; especially Alistair Darling[92] squeezing that last drop of Sagittarian flexibility in his misdirected giveaway budget – just four days before the Pluto Capricorn ingress. If a doctor, teacher, train driver or even an astrologer had been so cavalier and foolhardy with other people would they have been allowed to practise again?

Previously confident experts of boom optimism now suggested we may be doomed. What to do but accept an unavoidable crisis and wait, spend and hope it will not be for too long? Good astrologers see it differently! They know there is no such thing as good and bad news – just easy and difficult or stressfully flowing planetary combinations. We need the pressure to build the strength and cut out counter-productive slack. Constant expansion can only lead to jaded exhaustion. A pause to reconsider can bring far better decisions, relationships and lives.

Pluto in Capricorn comes just in time to save the eco-system of the planet and ourselves from hyperactive psychosis, driven on by our boom-crazed political tempters. Is 'doom' the only way to see less work, less consumption, less aimless running about? Is spending more time with our loved ones learning how to 'tighten our belts', having less, but enjoying it more such a tragedy? Maybe the problem is more for those who seek to develop, and then manipulate our greed and misuse the fruits of our endeavours.

During the Uranus and Neptune Aquarius/Pisces transit and mutual reception, the humanitarian expression of Aquarius was sidelined by technological and scientific developments. Of course, the internet, mobile phones, digital technology, international travel, GM foods and medical research are endeavours intended to benefit us all, but have they done this yet? Has the focus been too much on the needs of these *things* rather than the *people* using them? The heart-crisis the Pluto-in-Capricorn period has to correct is the very depersonalisation that occurs when Aquarian energy becomes too linear and mechanical.

--o0o-

As the 2008-10 economic meltdown was dominating the world economy, the May 2009 column noted the crisis coincided with the Saturn return of Margaret Thatcher coming to power as UK Prime Minister. Simplistic monetarism, sired by her and Ronald Reagan, now faced its nemesis. The column warns against attempts to avoid radical change by throwing money at the problem. Also to be ignored!

> The meaning of the word 'credit' is trust. And yet over the years, as commercial banking has become institutionalised, it has built its entire edifice on the basis of mutual mistrust.   Muhammad Yunus
>
> Money is a good servant, but a poor master   *Traditional saying*
>   Both quoted in *16 Guidelines to a Happy Life*[93]

As I write, it is one crisis after another, yet social activities continue ('Crisis – What Crisis?') amidst ever increasingly outrageous revelations about irresponsible banking ('The Crime of the Century'). We 'old fogies' could be forgiven for thinking we are at a 1970s *Supertramp* concert.

The Emperor's new clothes
The vision is pertinent. It feels like we are experiencing the 1970s in reverse and face the consequences of failing to resolve the problems of that disturbed decade. For all the triumphalist 'free market knows best' hype since the mid-1980s, we can now see that the pain of job losses and commercial reorganisation was in vain. Little of lasting fundamental value was learned or achieved. The economic powerbase merely shifted from one dysfunctional group to another.[94] A spending spree following a one-off sale of public assets and irresponsible banking deregulation created a false 'prosperity' that made it *appear* 'the market knew best'. A notion that ever-expanding consumption was the source of all happiness perpetuated though the 1990s up to 2008. As 'sell off' funds ran out, it was perpetuated by reducing interest rates to encourage unnecessary spending. As electronic trading attracted more funds into financial markets, amoral financiers risked everything. They exposed vast resources they held in trust on crass schemes. These sought to perpetuate credit, by creating illusory assets no more substantial than the emperor's new clothes[95].

Saturn return shows economic problems of the 1970s were never solved
September to November 2008 was when we learned it had ended in tears, because that was when Saturn returned to its 'UK Winter of Discontent' position; just over two months before Pluto fully entered Capricorn. At Saturn returns karmic consequences of the previous 29+ year cycle have to be faced. In direct contrast to the view of most established opinion leaders at the time, having failed to follow well balanced and structured reality, we were to reap the consequences.

The iconic 1978/9 'Winter of Discontent' cross-roads in Britain's industrial relations intensified through the winter to a climax on 22 January 1979. By 21 February most workers had accepted substantial wage increases and started to return to work. Through these weeks Saturn retrograded between 12 and 11-degrees of Virgo. The exact return of the 22 January 1979 Saturn occurred on 14 September 2008. At that time Saturn was moving forwards quickly. On 17 May 2009, it directly stations at 14Vi54, not quite making the second and third hits.

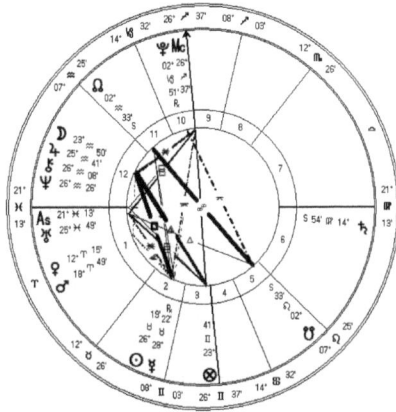

Saturn Direct Station
17 May 2009 02:06:15 UT +0:00
London, UK 51°N30' 000°W10'
Geocentric Tropical Placidus True Node

In 1979 Jupiter was in early Leo and Pluto in late Libra. Waiting in the wings was Margaret Thatcher with Saturn in Scorpio on her Ascendant! In 2008/9, Jupiter has been moving from Capricorn to Aquarius and Pluto is newly in Capricorn. Also, the returning Saturn is opposed to Uranus, not sextile as it was thirty years earlier. Barack Obama may do his utmost to make the experience as bearable as possible, but radical pragmatism will be needed as he learns on the job. This Saturn return brings the lessons of a tragically missed opportunity. Britain, with the help of Ronald Reagan's America, exported a degenerate, self-deceivingly simplistic economic model. It seduced nearly all world economies and shades of political opinion – even 'communist China!' If we fail to find the right answers on its solar return, expect far worse than a winter of discontent. This time it is global!

Changing attitudes to technology
With Saturn in mutable Virgo opposed Uranus in mutable Pisces, many attempts are being made to avoid or divert the consequences and deny what the planets suggest is coming. Billions are being spent or risked by governments. Quantitative easing will buy worthless assets, so lending can recommence and increase the money supply. All will dissolve into mutable nothingness and make the long term worse. Pluto is in Saturn's earthy sign. On the direct station chart, the remnants of the Aquarius stellium are squared to Sun and Mercury. The cosmic response will be uncompromising. 'Get it right or suffer!' Seeking to avoid will only make things worse. Pluto offers fifteen years to face the truth, or to suffer the consequences.

-o0o-

The paragraphs below from the July 2009 column were written in the midst of the British Members of Parliament's expenses scandal, in a world still rocked by the 2008 banking crisis. They showed the astro-cycles were giving early warning of the consequences of continuing unprincipled behaviour towards each other and the planet.

Astro-cycles Insist the Principled Way is the Most Efficient

Many people see Capricorn as focused upon harsh realism. Yet this realism only appears harsh to those seeking unrealistic, Sagittarian lack of control – the story of the years since 1994 when Pluto entered that sign. Many people see Saturn as restrictive to invention. In fact, it seeks to sustain viable invention by insisting upon purposeful and directed structures. So, with Pluto in Capricorn and Saturn opposing Uranus, we are forced to ask what growth and production is sustainable? We are also asked to question the use of rules that we know others will seek to avoid and whether we really want to live in a world without principles. Can ever more laws and rules, police and armies to enforce them, surveillance to observe us, and prisons to confine us ever make us happy?

One of the few benefits of the rise of twentieth-century fascism was the stark choice it gave reasonable and humane people. By what principles and in what world did they wish to live? They fought the bloodiest world war in human history for human freedom and against corrupt state control. Today, Uranus is about to re-enter Aries. This time Neptune and Pluto transit in opposite signs – Pisces and Capricorn. Events are again forcing us to question the social values and the behaviour of those that lead us. Boom times will not return, however much we borrow and gamble with our financial future. Politicians guided by focus groups will deceive our fundamental self-interests. We have to turn away from growth-based material self-indulgence to realistic give-and-take economics. We must do less, need less and so consume less and care for the planet and each other much more. Then everyone will be a lot happier.

Looked at in this joined up thinking way, Pluto in Capricorn and Uranus opposed by Saturn seem like pretty fortunate astro-cycles for today and the Jupiter/Neptune conjunction a wonderful energy to help regenerate our principles.

-o0o-

The September 2009 column headlined the cause of mistrust and reliance on rules and surveillance that sadly had become the main product of the Uranus/Neptune in Aquarius/Pisces and mutual reception period. It hoped, perhaps futilely, that Saturn's exalted ingress into Libra might restore healthy tolerance.

Restoring Trust

The Eternal [God] …
Hung forth in Heaven his gold scales, yet seen
Betwixt Astrea and the Scorpion sign,
Where in all things created first he weighed.
John Milton *Paradise Lost* Book IV

It is five years since this column first referred to John Milton's epic symbolism of the constellation of Libra as a focus of divine judgment. Between 2003 and 2005, when Saturn was detrimental in Cancer and squared to Libra, we ignored the need for balance. Closing our eyes to reality, we anxiously accepted that to 'be safe' we needed ever more debt responsibilities, rules, surveillance and control. The consequence has been the economic, social and political downturn we have been experiencing since the final months of 2008, when Pluto entered Capricorn and Saturn first opposed Uranus.

Approaching the 2009 autumn equinox, profound re-balancing is needed. With Saturn's exalted ingress into Libra, we stand at the cusp of a transitional year that will initiate a new phase of radical change and new understanding.

Three key astro themes in the Autumn Equinox chart reveal the root of our past problems and the heart of the understanding needed to be free of them.

Self-imprisonment

The mutability of opposition between responsible Saturn in anxiously dutiful Virgo and innovative Uranus in intimately caring Pisces has been unhelpful. With so much residual paranoia due to past blunders, dishonesty and the bad blood of dirty tricks; the mutability has been focused upon avoiding the consequences. We have used it to do little more than persuade ourselves and everyone else that whatever has happened was not our fault. Even more lethal has been a willingness to use the mutability to persuade ourselves that real change is not needed. With a few adjustments to the rules and safeguards, upset will go away. The cycle will turn and all will be 'back to normal'. In our hearts we do not believe this, but the feared 'reality' is too horrific to allow in the truth.

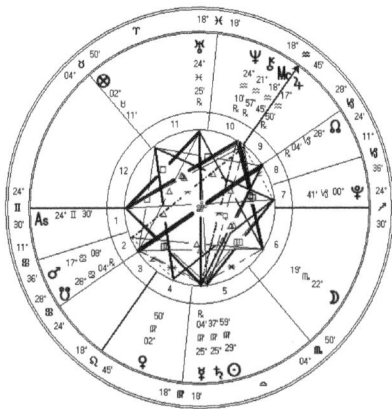

Autumn Equinox
22 Sep 2009 21:18:36 UT +0:00
London, UK 51°N30' 000°W10'
Geocentric Tropical Placidus True Node

Now Saturn is moving quickly through the last degrees of Virgo to its third opposition to Uranus on 15 September 2009 and enter Libra on 29 October, avoidance just will not do any longer. We have to face up to our fears and work out ways out of them. To do this, identify the root cause of the problems.

It is no accident that the present and previous British Prime Ministers and previous US President all had key planets in the twelfth house. Whether synchronistic or deterministic this helps us to understand why the world society has become so self-serving, enslaved, lonely and terrifying under their watch.

The twelfth house can be saintly, devotional, holy, even enlightened but, because it is so private, there is no way of knowing whether its dire and degenerate contrary negative expression is dominant. Worse still, when self-serving and negative, the way of a twelfth-house person is projected on everyone else, believing they too avoid, scheme and machinate. Assuming this, they create around them a world of constant suspicion. They, and everyone populating it, need to control and wrong-foot an increasing number of enemies. When such people have massive political control, their nation or the entire planet becomes like the darkest reaches of their sad and frightened minds.

As Saturn moves toward Libra, an important part of this new balance is to see a way out of such a self-perpetuating trap. Trust needs to be restored. For it is the abuse and lack of trust that is the root reason we live in a rule-obsessed, unprincipled, uncaring, irresponsibly broken society.

To be liberated from the unnecessary anxiety this brings, each of us needs to develop confidence in our own inner wisdom, the courage to trust and support others to do the same and to rejoice in their achievements.

Loyalty enables freedom

Because he cannot be everywhere and supervise everyone, the absolute monarch relies upon courtiers he can trust. With wise discriminating awareness, he distributes his largesse to enable the person chosen to achieve the stated aim in any effective way he chooses. Should so blessed a courtier abuse this trust, he faces the monarch's God-given divine right to impose severe arbitrary punishment. It he acts honourably, there are immense benefits to enjoying a monarch's patronage. It opens opportunities to go freely; to do and create as one wishes. The opportunity that comes from such generous trust enables the creativity of the Leo archetype.

In 2009, the lack of Leo planets and dominance of the opposing Saturn-ruled Capricorn and Aquarius ones leads to a denial of such trust. Instead, we feel obliged to create more and more structures to protect ourselves. To solve our present-day problems, the irresponsible freedom of action symbolised by Pluto in Sagittarius (1995-2008) is replaced by creating more and more rules and systems of checks.

Such a mindset squashes the freedom of the individual and diminishes creativity, risk-taking and fun. It produces a rule-obsessed world without creative opportunity that makes life worth living. Yet it still fails to make our lives safe; rather it identifies an ever-growing range of 'enemies' that, for our own good, we have to be protected against. Paranoia intensifies, as trust and friendship diminish.

Universal acceptance

Libra is the air sign that stands and adjudicates between Leo and Aquarius. Saturn is exalted in Libra. Its transit through the sign, if used with positive confidence, can symbolise the bringing of balanced order out of chaos, providing reasonable tolerance and forgiveness prevails.

-o0o-

The November 2009 column, warning against inappropriate use of the rare coming together of Jupiter, Chiron and Neptune in Aquarius, was to be largely ignored. Instead, it formed the negative core of the coming 2010 decade's destructiveness

Idealistic Belief
the Jupiter, Chiron and Neptune conjunction in Aquarius

In the 3,000 years between 500 BCE and 2500 CE, only in 1179/80, 2009/10 and 2495/6 are these three together in Aquarius and only on the last two occasions are they in a tight conjunction [96] Of these two the present time is by far the strongest, because it is the only one when Jupiter and Neptune are mutually receiving Uranus in Pisces. If ever there were a time for radical transformation of belief systems, the months ahead are this time.

To take full advantage, it is vital to understand the archetypal nature of each astro ingredient, and then synthesise their unique combined meaning. Chiron invokes the wounded healer. By understanding and mastering our own suffering we learn not only how to heal ourselves, but also to heal everyone and everything with which we make contact. With Neptune involved, be particularly careful. If handled with selfless objectivity Neptune brings inspired insight. When used to cloud the truth, deceive and abuse others' and their beliefs, the deception and abuse aimed against them bounces back appallingly on the perpetrators. To be the victim of a confidence trick, you have to have been seeking to be a confidence trickster yourself. Jupiter will expand both. All three together create the dangerously vulnerable notion of embracing suffering for idealistic reasons.

So, careful now! How do we avoid being 'taken for a ride' at such times? By being clear not only about what, but *how* we believe. We need to seek guidelines that go deep and cut through all illusions, be they deluded 'self-interest' or even 'selfless righteousness'. When Neptune is strong sacrificial religious and political beliefs can cloud and deceive. Masses can be manipulated into behaving with blind aggression by being made to believe that their way of life, the very stability of their family and home, are threatened.

Avoiding obvious religious fundamentalist manipulation, while desirable, is not enough. Through the current transit, assumptions will threaten that are far more dangerous, because they are disguised as helpful common sense. With the conjunction occurring in Aquarius, we should avoid being unquestioningly over-dependent upon reductionist scientism, its piecemeal statistical research 'experts' and the politicians they serve. Practical facts have an important part to play, but not if they are implemented piecemeal, but seen as an absolute belief system.

It is equally dangerous to be seduced by the sensual bombardment of pleasing media promotion. The commercial press, television and web are not free. We pay by sacrificing discriminating awareness, even our very souls!

Economic exploitation by an unholy political alliance of the forces of 'rational' scientistic expertise and seductively populist emotional marketing disempower. It prevents us from seeing how to relate to and care for the planet. The 'truths' forced upon us at school, in the press, on television and in political campaigns trap us in a destructively self-indulgent world picture. They make us continually dissatisfied, wanting more, insecure – never happy.

-o0o-

As the Barack Obama US Presidency got under way and David Cameron and Nick Clegg, summer-of-love-born leaders, came to power in Britain, the September 2010 column explored the astro-cycles relationships between generations. What effect might the history at the time a person was born have on their opinions and adult decisions, when they came into power? Was society ready to implement the idealism of the 1960s, rather than just indulge itself in its licence?

Goodbye and Hallo to 'Rocking n' Rolling'

The cycle of Uranus has especial relevance to the so called 'generation gap' in relationships between parents and their offspring. On average marriage and the bearing of children dominates most people's twenties – the period when Uranus' position is squared between the parent's and child's birth charts.[97] Hence, the two generations' views of change and innovation are naturally at odds with each other.

For the best of reasons and not realising they are doing it, the tendency is for parents' particular tastes for innovation, even rebellion, to be the root cause of the problems their children will grow up to face. Parents with Uranus in Aries indulged their baby boomer Uranus-in-Cancer generation, seeking to give them the perfect freedom they themselves had been denied through the Saturn-in-Aries/Taurus war years. As this boomer generation grew up to and through Uranus in Libra, they made radical changes to family and social relationships, to which their children (born with Uranus in Capricorn) must develop proper social structures to order and contain. The Uranus in Gemini generation developed the electronic revolution, which grew into obsessive computer games as Uranus reached Virgo, to be introduced via the personal computer to our commercial world with Uranus in Sagittarius and entirely dominate the way we do business and relate to the World Wide Web by the time Uranus was in Pisces; more problems for these generations to resolve.

Now broaden out from this view of one underlying cycle to look at the whole chart of a time in history from two dramatically different generational perspectives; the parents' and the children's. By the very nature of their relationship, the two must approach the same astro cycle situation from radically different perspectives. The parents have both enjoyed and struggled with the astro-cycles to come to a point where they have conceived their children, and then created the environment to bear and care for them. To sustain all this effort, they have developed opinions and practices that work for them. In direct contrast, the offspring have been presented cold with a set of astro-cycles they are expected at least to cope with, and hopefully master.[98] As children mature and become independent, they see their parents' attitudes with fresh eyes. Often ignorant or indifferent to the cycles and circumstances that formed their parents' decisions, they may well feel the reverse of what their parents did is a better way. If parents appear over-disciplined and hypocritical, the children may be undisciplined and naive – the way of many post-Second World War baby boomers. If parents appear to have been over-permissive and prone to risk taking, their children may develop a 'health and safety' culture – the Uranus-in-Libra way of the baby-boomers' own children!

It is helpful to immerse ourselves in these considerations, because in the past two years radical changes have started to take place in the age and hence generational experience and consequent policy perspective of world leaders. We are moving on from early 1950s baby-boomer leaders, epitomised by the self-indulgent 'party time' plus twelfth-house paranoia of the Bush, Blair, Brown years, to the 1960s generation. To understand the mindset of this new generation of leaders, it is helpful to look at what was happening when they were born.

The 1961 world Barack Obama entered was full of the naive 'we can change the world for the better' peace core idealism of the early Kennedy years.[99] Unfortunately, although Jupiter had just conjuncted Saturn in late Capricorn with both planets then moving to Aquarius, in 1962 it was to square Neptune and then oppose both Uranus and Pluto. Clearly, we all had a lot to learn and experience if we were to save the world! Barack Obama's parents symbolise the nature of the time – the linking of a Kenyan villager with a white American woman. That their son could rise to the most powerful position in the world expresses how much has been achieved in the years between then and now. That, on attaining this position, he faces massive difficulties created by the sad, self-indulgent and deluded actions of those intervening years is the darker side of his inheritance.

The Kennedy assassination led to the early Johnson years and, between October 1965 and June 1966, Uranus conjuncted Pluto. Understandings that desperately needed to be bridged exploded painfully within and between cultures. In the days leading to the first conjunction on 9 October 1965, the Indonesian army executed opponents accused of communism. Conservative estimates suggest half a million were to be killed by March 1966. On 15 October 1965, 'The National Coordinating Committee to End the War in Vietnam' staged the first public burning of a draft card in the United States. Generations of Americans faced each other head on. Equally revolutionary at the time, on 26 October 1965 The Beatles were awarded Members of the Order of the British Empire (MBEs).

On 6 June 1966, a few weeks before the completion of the Uranus/Pluto conjunction, black civil rights marcher James Meredith was shot and wounded after entering Mississippi. The dust was not to settle. Problems fermented and grew as Saturn sustained its opposition to Uranus until January 1967. Jupiter offered hope by trining Neptune and Saturn through 1966-67; building over-optimistically through the October 1968-69 conjunctions to Pluto, Uranus and Saturn. The young took the view that no one in power (or over 30!) could be trusted. Paris riots climaxed in 1968.

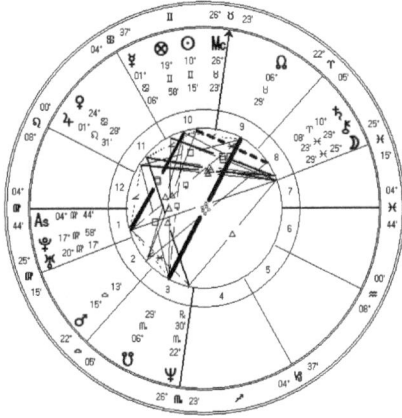

Sgt Pepper Launched
1 Jun 1967 12:00 BST -1:00
London, UK 51°N30' 000°W10'
Geocentric Tropical Placidus True Node

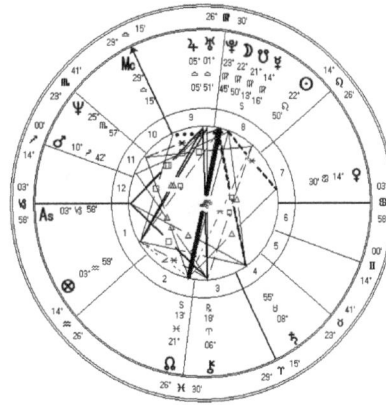

Woodstock
15 Aug 1969 17:07 EDT +4:00
Bethel, New York 41°N57'16" 073°W38'03"
Geocentric Tropical Placidus True Node

On 1 June 1967, with the launch of their *Sergeant Pepper's Lonely Heart Club Band* album, The Beatles are said to have started the 'Summer of Love' period, which climaxed with the 1969 Woodstock Festival.[100]

Appropriate to the music itself, emotional hedonism abounds in the *Sergeant Pepper* launch chart. This, combined with Mercury in Cancer applying to square Saturn in Aries, and Sun in Gemini to square the separating conjunction between Uranus and Pluto, implies immense social disruption. It symbolises dis-ease with the very root of social values. Ironically, the generation that had been so loved and provided for by their parents were in large numbers to 'leave home with a man from the motor trade'. This happened not only literally in those early hippie days, but symbolically in so many things that the Uranus in Cancer and Leo (1950s) generation have introduced and caused to dominate our twenty-first- century culture and economy.

Mid-August 1969 saw a late Virgo stellium building with Jupiter conjunct Uranus in early Libra. Terrorised by the dark, dank shadow of racial intolerance, their parents' obscene Vietnam war, brutal police reaction to protest, and armed only with the belief 'all you need is love' a movement grew and finally converged on a small town in upstate New York in mid-August 1969.[101]

It would be a fundamental mistake to dismiss the Woodstock Festival in the way we equally mistakenly dismiss many twenty-first century protests as degenerate, self-indulgent, naive and totally unrealistic. Quite the opposite, it is the contemporary world economy, its dream of competitive education and hard-working market competition leading to eternal growth and happiness for all that is naive and totally unrealistic. Woodstock Festival was a statement of intent and a demonstration that, even in the most modest and dire circumstances, people could made do, support each other and visualise decency and community for the whole world. It is the failure of societies and their leaders to sustain this vision and develop and institutionalise it in the forty years since that is the root cause of the economic and ecological disaster that we face.[102]

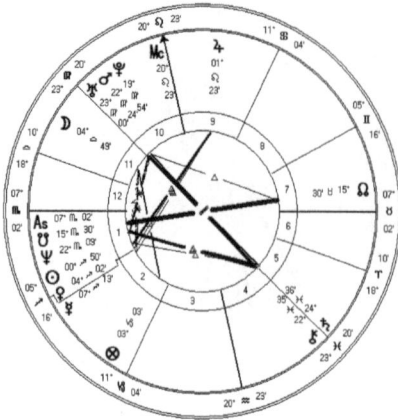

Nick Clegg and David Cameron
Composite Chart – derived ASC.
Nick Clegg 7 Jan 1967 05:30 UT +0:00
Chalfont St Giles, UK 51°N38' 000°W34'
David Cameron 9 Oct 1966 06:00 BST -1:00
London, UK 51°N30' 000°W10'

David Cameron, the UK Prime Minister elected in May 2010, and his deputy Nick Clegg were born in the midst of these traumatic events and astro-cycles. So, their destiny and very basic challenge is to master and transform circumstances developing in the decades after that time, of which they were not the mundane creators – in a nutshell, to sort out the problem of their generational inheritance.

The individual charts of both men have been studied in previous 'Working with the Planets' columns.[103] Here we study the composite chart. It shows that as a working unit both men have enhanced power and vision. With less than half a degree between each man's natal Jupiter, its composite position changes little. The composite Sun applying and the Venus and Mercury separating, all in Sagittarius, are trined by that Jupiter. The composite Uranus, Mars, Pluto opposition to Chiron and Saturn are within a degree or two conjunct/opposed the Woodstock Pluto. With so much focused on the Jupiter of the *Sergeant Pepper* launch chart, it is significant that this Jupiter is just eight minutes of arc away the Cameron/Clegg composite Jupiter, as well as within a degree conjunct to Jupiter in both of their charts. Study these charts and see the many other connections.

Significantly in 2010-11, Jupiter and Uranus transit early Aries opposed to their 1969 Woodstock position in Libra. At the same time, they T-square Pluto in Capricorn and Mars/Saturn in Libra – the key configuration this column has been exploring for two years.

To see solutions to our contemporary problems, we need to look objectively at the pros and cons of the decades since the 1960s. It is time to honour the progress, while addressing the counter-productive indulgence and waste. Honouring multi-cultural divergence in race, colour and gender, and support for the needy are developments to be celebrated. Greed-based wrangling, borrowing and short-term opportunism that keeps us 'rocking n' rolling' for just one more day curses us to constant disappointment. No *thing* can make us happy for long. Having the right state of mind always can. Achieving this involves difficult experiences of letting go on the way. It does not involve recrimination and accusation. Courage is essential, but in something much more than force of arms. Taking personal responsibility, seeking little in return; these are the attitudes that create the space for an ever-expanding summer of love and make it eternal.

Such idealism was common in those early days. Somehow since then, the world has kept their hedonism, but fallen short, even sold out on the harder principles needed to keep everyone right. On so many levels, we have created a world based on war and the training for war. Ever more frantically, we have expressed the rhythm and spaced out on the style, but lost sight of and allowed to wither the heart-caring purpose that made all this fun worthwhile.

The 'way back to the garden' will be in stages, guided instinctively along what seems the right way by partially sighted leaders, whose aims and methods may well be unclear even to them.[104] Constant adjustment may be needed on the way. The new politics must be founded on principles of decency and balance give and take between peoples and the people and the planet – the creation of a world, which is supported by everyone supporting each other.

The touchstone will be: does this correct us away from the self-indulgent nonsense that blew up in our firework-crazed faces at, and immediately after, the 2008 Olympics? Thinking this way... that's what I call the real way to 'rock n' roll'.

-o0o-

The May 2011 column opened with the first of many warnings of the upheaval that the upcoming Uranus-in-Aries squares to Pluto in Capricorn were to bring.

Battling with Authority

We knew it was coming! In the years leading up to the Pluto ingress into Capricorn, and even more so in 2006 when astronomers 'downgraded' Pluto to the status of a dwarf planet, astrologers were saying that Pluto's transit through Capricorn would see 'powers that be' (however they manifested in various cultures) seeking to assert their authority. Against them, populaces, better informed than at any previous time in history, would profoundly challenge their right to do so. Dimensional social upheavals, even more powerful than those seeded in those other Pluto-in-Capricorn days (early sixteenth and late eighteenth centuries) are occurring in the early twenty-first century. This time, will 'the people' not only take, but keep, power?

It will take some years to have a full, deep understanding of the change that is happening. Saturn may have completed its oppositions to Uranus and squares to Pluto – we have a real feeling of the profound problems we face. However, Uranus is only building towards the first of many squares to Pluto in June 2012 (they continue until 2015) – we are only beginning to discern on the distant horizon a faint sense of the vast consequential changes those Saturn 'delivered' problems are to force upon us.

More immediate transit combinations provide the impetus that carries forward each step in such long-term developments. The ongoing stellium patterns of the first half of 2011 are showing this very clearly. As I write, the revolutionary zeal and apparent humanitarian restraint of the Tunisian and Egyptian revolutions, symbolised by the Aquarian emphasis of the stellium, has given way to the suffering of the Libyan people as the inner planets enter Pisces. March's 'Working with the Planets' traced likely further developments as the stellium's focus including Uranus moved to Aries.

Before exploring the next stage in this process through May and June 2011, it is important to identify the breadth and depth of the change that is occurring. This is not just a story of revolutions in feudal monarchies, or people living under oppressive dictatorships risking everything to be free. In the USA, politics is brutally polarised. In Britain, arguments between the idealism of 'The Big Society' on one hand and 'dismantling of the welfare state' are only just starting. Economic breakdown in

Ireland and Greece struggles to keep rebellion at bay. The rapid growth in the Far Eastern economies threatens dire consequences for them and the world should the ecological threat get out hand or their boom bubble bursts. The massive social upheaval from all these could be far greater than that happening in the Middle East as I write. Ordinary people from anywhere in the world may, at some time in these Uranus-square-Pluto years up to 2015, feel the need to risk everything to be 'free of what binds them once and once for all'. They may see through the cheap temptations and empty promises of growth-obsessed political and economic systems and prefer to focus on family relationships and personal happiness. They may begin to resent 'qualified' (often self-serving) expert advice holding a determining control of their lives.

Times of upheaval also bring relationships that we struggle to control or may not be able to control at all. To what extent can we create an ecologically viable world and prevent the disruption and threat to our lives by extreme weather; hot, cold, fire, flood and landslide? How can we have any influence at all on what seem like regular earthquakes in Asia and on the Pacific 'Ring of Fire'?

-o0o-

The July 2011 column considered the upcoming Pluto-in-Capricorn/ Uranus-in-Aries square to the English 1066 chart and noted that in past centuries similar transits had come at severe turning points in British history. So many intense squares by transit to the 1801 UK chart, was particularly challenging. In the past, the subsequent recovery that followed saw a regenerative flowering. Could the upcoming London Olympics be the spur to a similar national regeneration and example to the world? If so how?

'Live as one'
Motto of the 2012 Olympic Games

Slogans often promise misleading contradictory 'good news' ideals, designed to mean different things to a disparate range of people. This one is less compromising and gives incisive advice to meet the challenges of our times. With just a year to go and Britain and much of the Western world going through hard times what, if anything, could we have to offer the world in our Olympic year? A deep look at the astrology suggests the upheaval Britain faces could point the way to positive world economic regeneration.

At first sight, the United Kingdom in 2011-12 seems destined to really become *The Country Formerly Known as Great Britain* described by Ian Jack in his book of that name.[105] Cutbacks, social resentment and upheaval seem to be our destiny, as we face the consequences of the sale of the nation's past, present and future assets by successive Conservative and New Labour governments over the past thirty to forty years.[106] The astrology is dramatically appropriate. The long-anticipated transiting Pluto/Uranus square is particularly focused upon England's precisely-timed 1066 chart. Pluto transits the progressed Uranus four times between February 2011 and September 2012 (the last and exact station) and the natal MC thrice between February and December 2012. Transiting Uranus squares its progressed position thrice between

May 2012 and March 2013. Then, up to February 2014, both transits move on to conjunct and/or square the natal Sun, and Uranus also to square the natal MC.

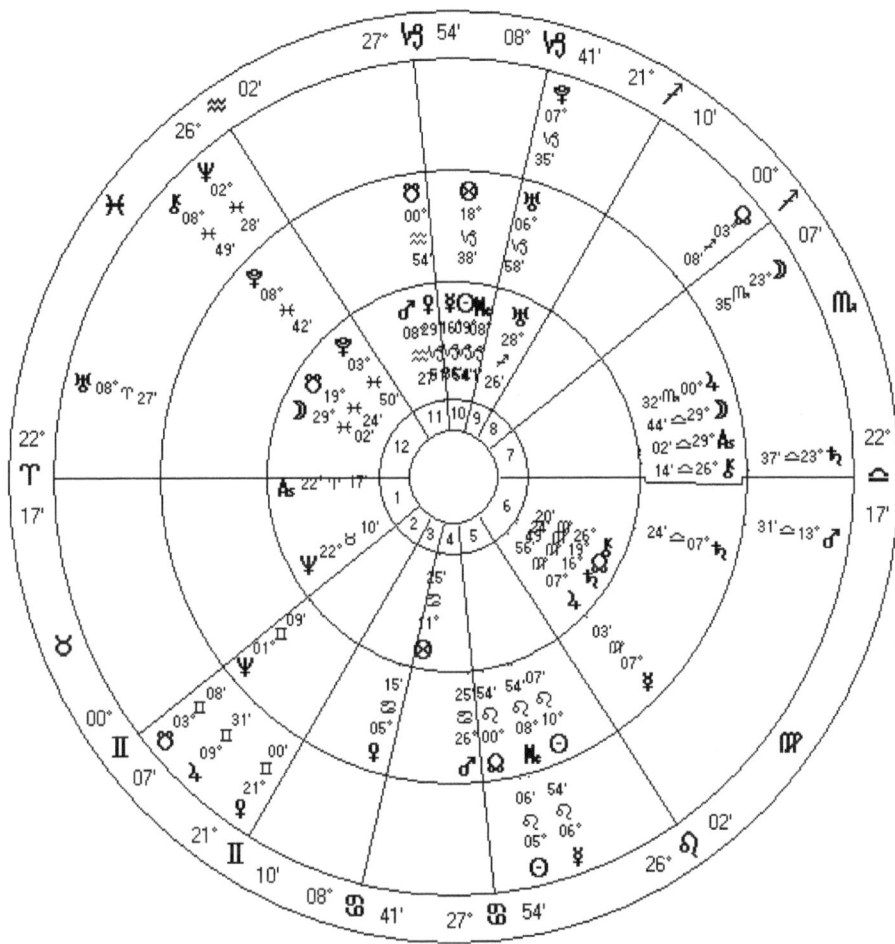

Coronation of William I
Inner wheel - Coronation: 25 December 1066, 12:.00 LMT +0:00:40
Middle wheel - Coronation progressed: 27 July 2012, 19:30 BST -1:00
Outer wheel - Transits: 27 July 2012, 19:30 BST -1:00
All charts: London, UK 51N30, 0W10 Geocentric Placidus True Node

The two   most recent previous transits of Pluto over the natal Sun and MC have been at times that seeded difficulties. In 1520, the infamously extravagant 'Field of the Cloth of Gold' meeting between the Kings Henry VIII of England and Francis I of France, triggered a series of events that were to isolate England from Europe and Catholicism and bring about the brutal martyrdom of Mary I's reign, when Pluto returned to its natal position in 1555-56. In 1765-66, the Stamp Act alienated the American colonies. This was to lead to American independence, which inspired the French Revolution and Britain's darkest times of the Napoleonic Wars (1803-15).

In 1800-01, Pluto returned again to mark the birth of the United Kingdom.

On both these occasions Uranus was sextile Pluto as it transited the 1066 Chart MC and Sun. As we have seen, this time it is in a powerful square. So, are the astro indications even worse? Not necessarily if we remind ourselves of the cleansing value of Pluto transits. Benefits can follow if minds are open to regeneration. After the horrors of her brother's and then her elder sister's reign, Elizabeth I's reign sired a golden age and sowed the seed of British colonial 'glory'. The British defeat of Napoleon left it ruling the seas and industrialising ahead of Europe, and so building an ever-expanding empire.

The difference this time is that Uranus is *squared* to Pluto as the latter transits the 1066 Chart MC. So, our regenerative influence toward the world may well be how we handle our problems and, in doing so, teach it how to handle its problems, which are all too similar to our own. This brings us back to the 2012 Olympics and the word which is the *theme* of the Games – '*sustainability*'!

We can never remind ourselves too often that the glorious prosperity Europe and its off-shoots in the Americas have enjoyed over the last 500 years came as a result of brutal and arrogant colonial conquest and the exploitation and often destruction of valuable ancient cultures. Attempts to set the record straight in the twentieth century often left the worst of both worlds, especially in parts of Africa where ruling elites aped the 'white man's' privileged dominance, but not always his 'burden' of responsibility. Countries bundled together without thought of tribal cultural cohesion have led to ongoing conflicts.

Worse still, we in the West, and especially Britain, never acknowledge that we have introduced to the world a system of doing business that may not be best for it, or even ourselves. Efficiency, virtue and hence happiness, cannot lie in ever-expanding economic growth. While such a notion may fit nicely when Europe was engaged in colonial dominance, it breaks down, or works against us, when every nation has the same rights and so seeks to do the same?

As the First World War marked the end of the European colonial project, the world economy, based on acquisitive capitalism, began to falter. Two simplistic alternatives were tried and found wanting. National Socialism was little more than incestuous colonialism – identify sub-cultures, and take their possessions. Soviet-style communism dishonoured the name, seeking, as it did, to macro-manage human endeavour and deny individual enterprise. These belief systems came into full force with Neptune in detriment in Virgo and led to horrific war. Their failure left the field clear for the only alternative, a half-baked inadequate version of 'free market capitalism'. Its shortcomings, having been propped up by Keynesian manipulation in both war and peace, in the early 1990s the hardly-questioned system was accepted as victorious. Planning for the future became increasingly out of fashion. The notion of competition, acquisition, ingenious invention of objects, new methods of delivery and processes made it seem there would be no end to the happiness-for-all potential of the competitive market economy. So, through heady Sagittarian and Aquarian times, the magic of scientific possibility seemed hardly to be faltered – only 'dinosaurs' would refuse to play the game.

The autumn of 2008 marked the failure of such *laissez-faire* optimism. However reluctant and in denial we are at present, however brilliantly the Far East and emerging economies seem to be performing right now, as Pluto transits Capricorn a new foundation for the world economy, beyond the colonial growth model, will have to be found. A system revolving around sustainability is the answer, having what you need, not being afraid to give, based upon not just rights, but also responsibilities. It was a system Britain struggled with and considerably mastered in the darkest days of the Second World War.

So perhaps it is no coincidence that Britain is the first among the triple-A-rated Western nations that has grasped the nettle of necessary cutbacks and talked about a regenerating 'Big Society', where increasingly numbers of us support each other and enhance our environment. Quite rightly, such developments face strong criticism, healthy cynicism and demands of fairness. For such a notion to succeed, a change is needed in what are socially acceptable values upon which to base business dealings. While there is nothing wrong with seeking riches, to do so at any cost of, by lying and cheating (even if it is legal) is to destroy the world and something to be deeply ashamed of. Until we believe that and act upon it, our hopes will constantly be dashed and the world will never be at peace.

So, can Britain run 2012 Olympic Games that inspire us all to 'live as one' in a 'sustainable' world? The symbolism of ceremony can be a powerful force. Using it to bring peoples together at times of great difficulty is an art that Britain's knack of royal choreography has achieved on more than one occasion. The recent royal wedding is fresh in our minds. An even greater example was the Queen's Golden Jubilee celebration. Britain led the way in 1948, after the foulest war in human history. When all is lost only the right answer will do. Often a key idea that strikes a chord is all that is needed to start moving minds.

Having demonstrated to the world how not to organise its affairs for the last 500 years, now is the time to sow symbolic seeds of a better way. Maybe we can do so by ourselves taking the medicine of restraint and realism first and then, as in those Second World War days, show that the working together for a sustainable future is the better way. Certainly, far better than acquiring wealth to finance endless shopping for what never satisfies or is even really wanted. If so, Britain will not be 'late great', but greater than it is has ever been. With the astro-event cycles that we have in the next few years, what else can the country and its people do?

Jupiter in Taurus makes the first of three trines to Pluto in Capricorn on 7 July 2011. The retrograde trine is at the same degree in late October. On 13 March 2012, the aspect competes a few degrees later. Now is a great time to start to instigate a break through!

-o0o--

The same July 2011 column concluded with a reminder of the role of Baghdad in the application of astrology to town planning and social organisation that was to become part of the rise of Islam in the first millennium CE. Traditional Western astrology, and much of our general academic knowledge, owe much to the Arabic preservation of ancient wisdom, at a time when much of Europe was in a state of barbaric disorder.

Astrology played a vital role in the foundation of the ancient City of Baghdad. Known from its earliest days as a representation of Paradise, as expressed in the Qur'an, the city was to become a grand world cultural centre, a resource of learning, beauty, imaginative design and splendour for nearly 500 years.[107] The simple symmetry of the chart drawn for noon on the foundation day shows how cardinal/fixed tension combined with determined harmony of vision and purpose are needed for any great endeavour to succeed. Firstly, we see the stress of cardinal endeavour indicated by a grand cross involving the Capricorn/Cancer Nodal axis with Mercury on the day of its station conjunct the South Node, against the opposition of the Moon in late Libra opposed to Uranus conjunct Saturn in early Taurus – a great time for revolutionary building. Secondly, we have the powerful harmony of Jupiter in Sagittarius trined by the Sun in Leo, challenged to advance learning by Mars in Gemini opposing it. 'Be proud, be wise, think deeply, take up your destiny, and build.'

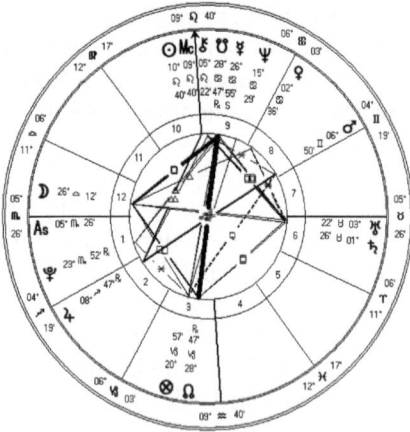

Foundation of Baghdad
31 Jul 762, 12:00 LMT -2:57:40
Baghdad, Iraq 33°N21' 044°E25'
Geocentric Tropical Placidus True Node

At a time in modern history when a dark decade in Islam's relations with the world is fading, it is important to remember the debt our Western culture owes to Islam for the very existence of much wisdom we take for granted today. High Islamic and classical learning emanating from Baghdad came to the great institutions in Córdoba, Granada and many other parts of Islamic Spain in the High Middle Ages. When we live as one, we have much to learn from each other. As today we face even direr cardinal tension involving Pluto, Uranus and Saturn may the Jupiter/Pluto trine in earth signs encourage the re-structuring of the global economy into a glorious future world.

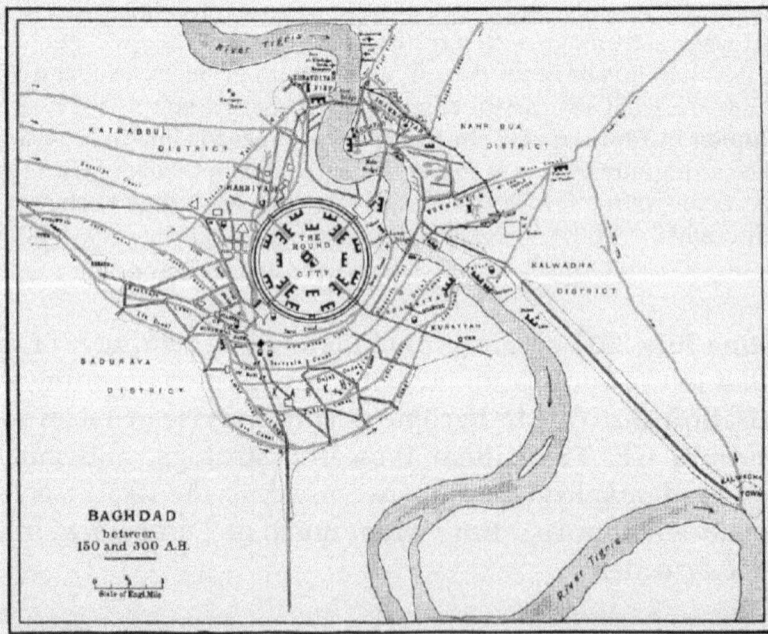

BAGHDAD
between
150 and 300 A.H.

Releasing funds to keep the financial markets buoyant allowed the few to benefit at the expense of the many. It clearly anticipated and warned about the inevitable social problems that we now know came after the 2012-15 years of seven Uranus-in-Aries squares to Pluto in Capricorn. Read this in Appendix A from page 255.

-o0o-

The November 2011 column urged readers for to prepare for the first of these seven Uranus-in-Aries squares to Pluto in Capricorn, due in June 2012, by studying the astrology of past major social changes. The traumatic change moments of the twentieth century could have worked out far differently, if contemporary astro-indicators had been understood and acted on in advance. The column mentions the early Arab Spring and other current events, which give a sense of what was coming. Were we to get it wrong again?

World Change – Before, During and After

Massive social changes do not happen overnight. The causes are sown in lots of little ways long in advance, and are then built up and nurtured by circumstances. As the tipping point approaches, resistance may strengthen for a while, but this only intensifies the pressure for change. When all is ready, a seemingly small event will trigger a massive process that turns assumptions and expectations upside down.

Mundane astrology's astro-cycles are ideal tools by which to chart and explain every stage of the process. Long outer-planetary cycles by sign and aspect describe the underlying, unavoidable changes in background fashion, social understanding and expectation. Retrograde patterns explain how the process of change seems to ebb and flow. For triggers, watch planetary angles to key degrees, eclipses and returns. Using these elements of mundane astrology is the key to genuine understanding of what has happened and is about to happen, not only in world societies, but also those times of turbulence in our own lives.

The past 100 years contain some notable examples from the wider world. Neptune in Cancer fuelled the confused patriotic attachment that encouraged the First World War. Saturn conjunct Pluto entering the sign in 1914 triggered and then described the intensifying brutality of the conflict. This in turn led to a post-war aftermath that questioned and undermined social authority. Alongside this in the 1920s, Neptune's move to hedonistic, risk-taking Leo, while Uranus transited excessively-tolerant Pisces, describes the circumstances that led to the 1929 Wall Street Crash. Neptune moving again, this time into Virgo, helps understand the nature of the desperate anxiety and guilt this seeded. It being in detriment there explains the dangerously simplistic knee-jerk reactions to the 1930s depression of extreme left- and right-wing politicians. Jupiter conjuncting Saturn and Uranus in Taurus, squared by sign to Leo, which Pluto was now entering, describes the intensification of hostilities in the Second World War.

In 1965-66 Uranus conjuncted Pluto in Virgo; their first major stressful aspect since the latter's discovery in 1930. All previous assumptions were put to a critical test. The build-up can be traced back to the outer planets all changing signs in the mid-1950s. The aftermath was so powerful that it has grown to this day into the Uranus/Pluto square that lies immediately ahead.

As Saturn, Uranus and Neptune built to a conjunction in the second half of the 1980s, the Soviet system faced strains it could not withstand. Triggered by Mars joining them and Jupiter opposed from late 1989 into 1990, governments fell, the USSR fragmented. Accompanying all this was recession in the West; a warning for the future of our capitalist system not clearly noticed at the time,

The seven planets in Taurus squaring Uranus in Aquarius in May 2000 marked the time that the dot.com bubble was brought down to earth. Pluto in Sagittarius and the Uranus/Neptune mutual reception in Aquarius/Pisces enabled the markets to devise methods to sustain a deluded optimism until 2008. Then Saturn opposed Uranus and Pluto entered Capricorn!

Use your knowledge of history and/or personal experience of these times to put your mind in the space before actual change occurred. The brave 1914 Cancer-driven patriots on all sides dreamed of very different battles than the slaughter they faced. The Leo-enthused thousands who borrowed expecting riches in the 1920s had no idea of the penury they were creating for millions in the 1930s and the horrific war that followed. The Virgo revolutionaries of the 1960s saw what was wrong, but lacked the experience and reasoned ideas to cleanse society. The people with Cancer ideals, who celebrated the end of the USSR, were not prepared for the opposing entrepreneurial Capricorns, who now control the spoils of previously state-owned assets. The Sagittarian optimism and Aquarian arrogance of early twenty-first-century bankers and economists, and the politicians that lauded and rewarded their 'achievements', really believed they had achieved the end of boom and bust. Now, we know all of them were wrong. Their worlds were to change beyond all their expectations.

The essential error during such world-changing historical events is to assume what we know will continue for ever, and so seek to solve the radically new problems we face with methods relied upon in the past. Looking from the twenty-first century, the patriotic assumptions of early twentieth-century European imperialistic patriotism may seem pathetically naive. Yet, are our assumptions about today and what we face in the coming decade any more enlightened?

Since 2008, this column has sought to explain the dimension of the predicament and suggest contemporary attempts to address it went nowhere near far enough. In 2011, we have seen hints of what might become sensational change, the 'Arab Spring' revolutions in the Middle East, phone hacking arrests, the UK riots, sovereign debt crisis in Europe, America and even Asian Japan. As we reach the last months of the year, expect to see these developments, tighten and take form: new Arab governments taking office; some very influential people arrested in the hacking crisis may face actual charges; authoritarian and liberal initiatives to answer problems revealed by the UK riots. Many nations' finances may again face pressure as the markets make realistic assessments of the profits to be made from the support funds being offered by central banks.

Yet all this in not even the beginning of the real change we can expect up to and after Uranus' first square to Pluto on 24 June 2012. To get a taste of how that might be, cast your mind back to July/early August 2011, when retrogression narrowly avoided a first square, but Mars sped through early Cancer to T-square them. The social unrest and financial sovereign debt crises were not solved then; rather, with the aid of retrogression, put off for the future.

-o0o-

The column then concluded with the special message below for those who had taken the end of the then current Mayan Calendar on 21 December 2012 to signify the actual end of life on the planet. Looking back, from 2021, on what actually came to pass, it may seem that humanity is now suffering the consequences of failing to be kind through the terrible upheaval of the 2010s. However, quite 'the end of days' yet. The jury is out on that!

2012 is better seen not as the end of days, as some have suggested, but as the beginning of something much better, a great new work in progress. Reconsider what we seem to be losing. Are we not glad to see the back of much of it? See the spaces of uncertainty left by failed past delusions, as great new opportunities to make our lives and institutions much more the way we want them. See 2012 as a new dawn. Like any dawn, it brings just the first trace of warmth. Who knows what new resources and opportunities a day ahead will bring, amidst the debris of yesterday's disappointments that still remain? Constant change in the years 2012-15 could well bring new opportunities and understanding. By relying on that hope, we avoid the impotent slavery that comes from serving and desperately sticking to past assumptions. Realise that genuine answers rely upon acceptance and understanding of decay as much as growth. Growth worshipped on its own can only lead to constant dissatisfaction and ultimate disaster. That kind of 'growth', which economists and self-interested traders insist on placing like a jewel at the crown of our endeavours, and politicians repeat as a meaningless mantra, is no more than a fatally tarnished piece of paste.

As we look inward to the returning light, amidst the darkness of this 2011 Winter Solstice time, visualise and welcome in great transformation for the good. Only by thinking that way can good be possible.

-o0o-

The May 2012 column prepares readers for the first of seven Uranus squares to Pluto. It comes in an intense threatening combination with other key planets, for which the world is ill-prepared. The functional foundation of our educational system assumes a faith-like amoral competitive life pattern, that creates conflict, rather than teaching the ethical compassion needed to resolve it. Consequences too horrible to describe are possible, if we do not change this.

Neptune's Pisces ingress on 3 February 2012 marked the first time since April 1995 that no outer planet had been in tropical Aquarius. Around UK breakfast time on 25 June, the day after Uranus (Aquarius' ruler) makes its first square to Pluto, Pisces' joint rulers, Jupiter and Neptune, are squared. This at the same time that Jupiter applies to conjunct the South Node in Gemini, while Neptune is opposed by the Moon, void of course in Leo.

We have become so enamoured with the brilliant benefits of the new Aquarian technology that we have failed to see the ignorant short-sightedness that came in its wake. These transits will intensify our recognition of the consequent price in suffering we have to pay. As we do, the questioning and challenging of the people whose 'expertise' has brought crisis to our world and our lives will go far deeper than attacks on the credibility of politicians and the greed of bankers. It will go to the very root of the assumptions and principles upon which modern society and its educational and cultural systems are based.

Secularism – a belief system we teach our children

The furore over Baroness Warsi's attack on 'aggressive secularism'[108] was compartmentalised at the time as just a debate about the social role of established religious institutions in the twenty-first century. Its implications go much deeper. They touch a nerve at the heart of what needs to be understood and corrected if we are to find real, lasting and happy answers to our problems. To solve contemporary problems, we have to address the counter-productive pervasive dominance of secular amorality that underpins our pursuit of knowledge and consequent decision making.

In traditional societies, upcoming generations were initiated into accepted social norms and values. In today's multicultural world, drifting away from established religious practice has created such diversity of values that most schools confine themselves to symbolic gestures of morning worship with opt-outs. They focus increasingly on teaching functional skills (mainly mathematics, language and science) to prepare for a competitive materialistic adult world. What is often missed is that such secular emphasis, albeit by omission, is itself a powerful religious teaching; one that assumes our lives should be focused upon, and measured by, this competitive materialism. Every school is a faith school. The majority, who teach this secular *religion,* inculcate the amoral values which our children take into adult life.

However vehemently proselytising secular lobby groups and militant atheists may argue to the contrary, reductionist science is no more than a contemporary dominant belief about universal reality, not the only reliable method to absolute truth for all time. It has ingenious and incredibly beneficial ideas and methods showing what we can or might do. Yet, it is no more capable of adjudicating what we *should* do and believe than was dominant Papal Infallibility in the sixteenth century. Just how dangerously harmful to humanity it can be to think otherwise was shown by the way Richard Dawkins' *The Selfish Gene* is said to have inspired the predatory corporate culture of CEO Jeffrey Skilling's Enron Corporation.[109]

A spur to search for twenty-first-century values

It is such thinking, such a lifeless world view behind which politicians and their advisors decide, that makes our problems seem insoluble. The educational and media systems, presided over by those politicians, cloud and trap our minds in material 'necessities' and a sad yearning for that 'all important growth'. This prevents our seeing the crux of the problem. Not that returning to social and educational principles based on narrow institutionalised religious prejudice would be better. Fundamentalism, be it spiritual or secular, prevents understanding and makes matters worse. Rather twenty-first-century societies need to transcend warring religious separatism and materialistic self-indulgence. Our decisions need to be based upon the best ethical principles found at the idealistic heart of all the great spiritual and humanitarian movements; open-hearted tolerance that recognises and learns from change, and so works for the benefit of all in a spirit of universal understanding.

The astro-cycles focused on 24/25 June 2012 symbolise our experience of living with a sense of traumatic loss in the midst massive technological advances, undermined by a crisis of belief. Could it be that such cycles indicate sufficient trauma to start off a process of radical questioning that recognises and reaches the root of our problems? If so, this will be a time to think less about what we want and more about what we have and how to use it to create happiness for each other. It will take time, but this in turn could lead to a root and branch reform to the aims and operation of our world economy, basing it on what we love to do rather than what we feel we *have* to do.

The astro cycles of June 2012 combine to represent intense difficulty. This time is best seen as a rare opportunity to question popular assumptions, cross boundaries of prejudice and consider radically different non-confrontational solutions with very different priorities than those we have come to take for granted. The more we 'stick to our guns', the more we will suffer consequences too horrible to describe.

-o0o-

As hysteria grew over the fast-approaching end to the Mayan Calendar at the Winter Solstice (21 December 2012), the July 2012 column opened with a detailed study of the Calendar's cyclic links with macro-historical change. Looking back, we can see that world society's reaction to the seven 2012-15 Uranus/Pluto squares (also squaring the Capricorn Uranus/Pluto conjunction at the beginning of the Calendar cycle) was naive, gratuitously brutal, and counter-productively intolerant. In the aftermath, the world culture was to lose its way, as it struggled and continues to struggle, to understand the enormity of change. We still seek a perspective high enough to navigate the way out of disaster.

Us as well as the Mayans!

Somehow, over the last 250 years or so, we have decided we can operate outside of the bounds that nature sets without having to pay a penalty…

All we wanted to do with this film is to show people that there is, perhaps, another way of looking at things now. We have carried on in a 19th-century approach to the way we operate for too long. We are now discovering that there are some limitations and we need to look again.

HRH Prince of Wales at *Sundance Festival* Premier of the film
Harmony – A new Way of Looking at Our World

The Great Year cycle of 25,820 solar (365$^+$-day) years can be converted into 36,500 'Tzolkin' (260-day) Mayan cycles. Each 260-day cycle equals the length of 9.55 lunar returns, the human gestation period, and marks other rhythms in nature.

The Mayans divided this great period into five lesser cycles of 5,125 years; the present one starting around 3114 BCE and finishing, it is claimed, on 21 December 2012.[110] The First Egyptian Dynasty started around 3100 BCE [111] and the Hindu Kali Yuga in 3102 BCE [112]. Work on today's site of Stonehenge commenced around 3100 BCE.[113] Is there something special about this time in history and how it relates to today?

Putting to one side the debate about the regularity and hence importance of the Winter Solstice Sun at Noon conjuncting the crossing point of Sun's ecliptic with the galactic plane, are there significant mundane astrology factors that suggest 2012 and the years around it are special? [114]

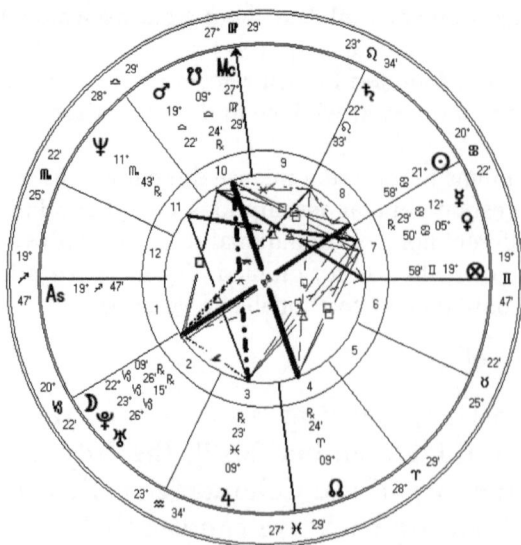

Long Count Start
10 Aug 3114 BCE 16:17 LMT +6:36:36
Mexico City, Mexico 19°N24' 099°W09'
Geocentric Tropical Placidus True Node

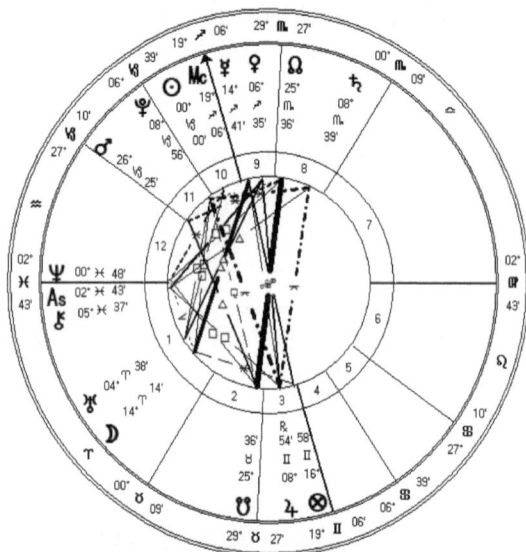

Winter Solstice
21 Dec 2012 11:11:37 UT +0:00
London, UK 51°N30' 000°W10'
Geocentric Tropical Placidus True Node

Dates in both 3113 and 3114 BCE have been suggested as the exact starting day of the Mayan Long Count. Especially interesting is that a few hours before the date given in Wikipedia the Moon was exactly full within a few degrees of Uranus and Pluto close to each other in Capricorn.[115]

On the Winter Solstice this year, Mars conjuncts that Uranus position exactly, while transiting Uranus applies to conjunct/oppose and transiting Pluto squares the Long Count's Aries Nodal axis. How often does this happen?

Solar Fire's electional search tool shows an irregular Uranus and Pluto phase in and out of Capricorn. Relevant to our times is their square by sign in Aries/Capricorn shown below.[116] Mars exactly conjuncts the Long Count Uranus on the Winter Solstice 2012. It is acts as a trigger. Firstly some explanation of…

How might astro-cycles work?
To some astrologers, and certainly to anyone who has not compared astro-cycles to behaviour and events before, the notion of drawing grand conclusions from comparing planet positions over hundreds or even thousands of years may seem at best bizarre. By what credible mechanism could bodies at such far distances from us have directly 'caused' such momentous changes on Earth? Of course, they could not have, but this is not what astrology is claiming.

The planets are merely reference points to help us map observed regular rhythms. Noticing and seeking to explain recurring events while trapped on planet Earth, ancient observers noticed that what happened seemed to be related to moving bodies in the heavens. As they learned more, the effect of cycles of the Sun and Moon were obvious and easy to explain. Cycles of individual planets and the interrelation between them indicated more subtle experiences. Perhaps their positions reflect the stresses, strains and flows experienced on Earth, which are caused by its dependence upon the combined dynamics of the solar system as it revolves and moves through space.

As well as thousands of years of earth-trapped observation, today we know of more planets and have the computing power to look backwards and forwards, and so relate cycles to our knowledge of history. This should encourage the wise and genuinely scientific to record, compare and discover the patterns that explain how consciousness changes and develops.

List 1: Uranus and Pluto both in Capricorn – 3200 BCE to 4000 CE

Phase 1 (last two examples)
3121-12 BCE
2869-64 BCE
Phase 2 (gap of nearly 2,000 years)
939-36 BCE
693-85 BCE
442-34 BCE*
190-84 BCE**
Phase 3 (gap of nearly 3,000 years)
2748 CE

> * High point in Ancient Greek philosophical, scientific and artistic culture
>
> ** By defeating Carthage, Rome is becoming world-dominant

List 2: Uranus in Aries, Pluto in Capricorn and Mars 26Cp15 – 3114 BCE to 4000 CE

Phase 1 (1,443 years from 3114 BCE)
1671-67 BCE (3 times)
1423-17 BCE (4 times)
1161-75 BCE (4 times)
921-19 BCE (2 times
Phase 2 (gap of nearly 2,500 years)
1516 CE (1 time)***
1762-66 CE (3 times)****

> *** Major church-authority shift and how humanity relates to the cosmos
>
> **** Seed time of modern industrial capitalism and democracy

21 December 2012-7 May 2018 (4 times)
2253-68 CE (4 times)
2515 CE (1 time) *(Next phase starts after search period)*

We seem to be at a key point of social change that corresponds to the very midpoint period of Uranus/Pluto in Aries/Capricorn 700-1000-year phase that occurs at intervals of 2,500 years. Today may be as significant as the early sixteenth and late eighteenth centuries. It is reasonable to expect a major correction and advance in the 500-year process that has led to today's world. It may be that humanity's understanding of the Universe is in the midst of an even more long-term realignment.

At the frontier of macro-historic change

This puts current trends and tendencies and our attempts to address them in a far grander perspective. To realise we may be at the frontier of such macro-historic change is a relief. Because there is no way back, we can let go of the pressure to take hasty actions to restore what has not worked in the recent past and now seems almost corrupt and wasteful. From the first Uranus/Pluto square on 24 June 2012, more and more people and world leaders will need to recognise and start to address rather than avoid the issues. By the second Uranus/Pluto square on 19 September, the credibility of the old authority systems will hang on a thread. This process will accelerate as Mars gathers speed towards its Winter Solstice conjunction with the Long Count Chart's Uranus. The truth will be obvious to an increasing number of people, as ethical integrity becomes more important than power plays and *using* the rules.

With Neptune applying to conjunct the Long Count Jupiter in Pisces, as we build to the middle of the 2010 decade, solutions based on interconnectedness and empathy will find favour and those that ignore these qualities will seem out of date, dysfunctional, even distasteful. How we do business with each other will need to reflect higher values. Policies and strategies based on short-term self-interest will seem tainted, and people that follow them regarded as lesser members of society.

-oOo-

The September 2012 column considered the upcoming Saturn Scorpio ingress trine to Piscean Neptune/Chiron, as a healing opportunity for social relations and refocus of the World Economy.

Real Change Happens in the Heart[117]

Realising this, we can see the importance of autumn 2012, which brings a serious change of emphasis with Saturn's ingress into Scorpio on 5 October. Methods of control will move beyond the Libran tendency to maintain the status quo and make things as easy for everyone as possible to the uncompromising taming of desire. We will feel less inclined to yield – the distinction between 'wants and needs' will become the dominant theme of the time.[118]

Events during the previous three transits of Saturn through Scorpio, especially each transit's final climatic year, clearly illustrate this denial of unrealistic desire.

- ❖ 1923-26: Saturn's Scorpio ingress coincided with the taming of several years of German hyperinflation. From 1924 the losses of millions of people were absorbed into a stable new currency. In Britain, poor wage and working conditions led to the unsuccessful 1926 General Strike. The defeat was to intensify the determination of the British Trades Union movement for decades to come. In Germany, Adolf Hitler established his leadership of the National Socialist party. In popular media, the death of romantic film hero Rudolf Valentino led to hysterical mourning all over the world.

- ❖ 1953-56: The Suez Crisis saw Franco-British duplicity exposed and Egypt defeated by Israel, but the Suez Canal successfully administered by non-Europeans for the first time. Although the Hungarian Revolution was to fail, the credibility of the Soviet system in the eyes of the world was profoundly undermined. The revolution against Batista (Cuba's American-supported corrupt leader) was to succeed and threaten the United States on its doorstep to this day. 1956 was the year of Elvis Presley's first single, Heartbreak Hotel, and also when his first album was released.

❖ 1983-85: during the last two years the brutal battles of the United Kingdom's miners' strike were fought. Interestingly, the two main protagonists were Capricorn (Arthur Scargill) and Libra (Margaret Thatcher). The latter stood her ground and prevailed. She had Capricorn's ruling Saturn in Scorpio exactly conjunct the Ascendant of her birth chart. This perfect symbol of the denial of other people's desires that characterised many aspects of the Thatcherite premiership was also expressed in her policies over the Falklands War, and nearer to home, Stonehenge's 'Battle of the Bean Field'. In New Zealand, the French secret service's sabotaging of Greenpeace's ship *Rainbow Warrior* was exposed, greatly enhancing the status of the organisation's various ecological campaigns.

Denial seeds future battles

As well as suggesting an irreversible denial in the face of intense desire, the above examples point to a powerful, deep underlying seeding of future battles. Each issue denied leads to a heartfelt, fixed determination that will create a cause that is destined to mould the future for good or ill. The Neptune sign position at the time gives an idea of the form the belief/commitment will take.

❖ 1926 (with Neptune in Leo): the humiliation of Germany prepared the way for Fascism. Trades Unions were destined to struggle to the point of actually achieving victory over the UK government in 1972. The Valentino hysteria was only the first of numerous subsequent public demonstrations of celebrity idealisation and grief.

❖ 1956 (with Neptune in Libra): although it was to maintain power for three more Jupiter cycles, the Soviet System as a people's popular movement was irreversibly undermined. The ability of Western powers to influence Israel or the Arab world was lost. An impoverished Cuba has been a thorn in the side of the US ever since. Rock 'n Roll continues to rule!

❖ 1985 (with Neptune in Capricorn): the defeat of trade unionism, while freeing enterprise, led to corporate control of the economy and an increasingly short-term, speculative and exploitative basis to decision-making. This is one of the key causes of our present economic problems and the inadequacy of our attempts to resolve them. In positive contrast, the growth of Greenpeace and ecological concern generally, Church reaction to materialism, even the meeting of minds over the 'Bean Field' discontent in the alternative community has shown how to broaden the base of decision-making. This now needs to become so main stream as to change the world economy and social relationships.

Real change happens in the heart

Which brings us back to the grand trine in the 21 April 2014 chart; with Pluto now in Capricorn, a profound regeneration of the way that power is motivated and works is the only way to answer our current problems. The realistic containing of desire represented by Saturn in harmony with Jupiter-in-Cancer's expansive care for everyone, driven on by the universal heartfelt concern shown both by the planet's 2012-14 trines to Neptune in Pisces, and the healing potential of Chiron and Venus in

Pisces come together to offer a profoundly powerful, yet sensitive force. This could underpin a new, much more sustainable, value-system/foundation to economic activity. By this time, we must have moved beyond the mindless parroting of 'solutions' based on ever-elusive 'growth'.

Lasting economic success does not come when citizens are whipped into production and consumption by manipulative marketing, hot-house education, family alienation and ever-longer hours of working to pay the bills.[119] Until we realise this, and change our motivational emphasis, political discussion will be fraught, resentful and blame-based, both within and between nations.

A truly efficient economy is stimulated and stirred to great sustainable success by the kind, devoted enthusiasm shared between all participants. Good economics is not 'unfortunately unavoidable' greedy, possessive, hard-hearted 'realism'. That only leads to unnecessary consumption, pollution and waste. Good economics makes our hearts feel good, in ever-wider contact with the good hearts of all around us. Good economics is motivated by the experience of joy, the reward of gratitude, the seeing of other people's pleasure. It is not about what we have, but how we experience life. The more we communicate this, until its realisation reaches those world councils whose decisions determine what happens, the more the relieving happiness of real change will emerge from the fearful circumstances we face.

Let go of anxiety over your possessions. Real change happens in the heart.

In the event, these Saturn-in-Scorpio years did see possible reform being rejected. As a result, much damage was done. The people's developing resentment with the over-confidence of the 'powers that be', was to lead to severely bitter outcomes through the second half of the decade.

-o0o-

Written with 'end of days' dominant in many minds, the November 2012 column explored the timing of the Mayan Calendar, using Western Astrology. Lessons were to be learned from the success of the recent London Olympics, especially if we were guided by what happened when past events had similar planetary combinations to those dominant in the mid-2010s.

Winter Solstice 2012 – Doom or Dedication

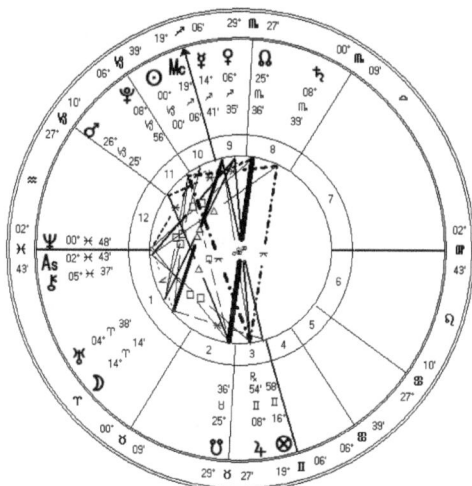

Winter Solstice
21 Dec 2012 11:11:37 UT +0:00
London, UK 51°N30' 000°W10'
Geocentric Tropical Placidus True Node

So at last it is upon us! That key day with its magical 11 hours 11 minutes 37 seconds time, when the Mayan Calendar is said to end and, with it some say, 'the world'.

Maybe there is something that suggests this in the number system by which the Mayans calculated. Certainly, it is generally agreed that this Winter Solstice is close to the end of the thirteenth b'ak'tun. Yet, is this more than the beginning of a new cycle, as would be the coming of a new aeon in Western astrology's Great Year? Is there anything in Western astrology that confirms such a momentous claim?

This chart for the exact moment of the solstice does not seem to suggest so. There are no major aspects. The most distinctive features are a sensitive Neptune and Chiron in Pisces around the London Ascendant, and a build-up of visionary action in the week or so before the moment, suggested by the Mercury and Venus transits through Sagittarius in trine to Uranus and Moon in Aries.

However, if we step back and see this Winter Solstice in the context of the larger picture it could indeed be special. We are, of course, at the central seeding point of that series of Uranus/Pluto squares. In 2012 this combines with the healing potential of Saturn in Scorpio trining Neptune/Chiron in Pisces and the lively wish to consider and communicate answers suggested by Jupiter in Gemini. All this suggests a fine time to bring people in the world together, to focus minds upon a new motivational attitude in the way we relate and do business together. Also, the northern Winter Solstice is always when the majority of the world's population, having felt the life force has been drawing away from them, find hope and renewal by promising a better way of doing things.

Greed and growth-driven competition and the idealisation of consumption have created a world of unsustainable credit, and a sense we are accelerating along the road to economic and ecological Armageddon. To address this, a whole series of ceremonies are being planned for the solstice at key 'energy points' around the globe. They will need to awaken far more people than the 'usual initiates'! Maybe the lesson of the Olympics could help show how.

'Winning' the Olympics

Now in November, after a challenging autumn, memories of the warm glow of our Olympian summer may seem to be fading far away. Yet, there is something about what we did then that is ever more and eternally glorious than the triumph of all those hard won Olympic and Paralympic medals. Britain showed the world in the opening and closing ceremonies not only how recent centuries had blown communities apart, but also how to build them together again. The actions of the game's volunteers were brilliant examples of the efficiency of willing commitment.

How it worked out demonstrates that positive understanding of astro-events can help turn potential horror into healing. The announcement of the award of the 2012 Olympic Games to London was at 11:50 BST on 6 July 2005, just before a New Moon at 14Cn31. This is in the English 1066 Chart's fourth house and UK 1801 Chart's Midheaven, five degrees before the latter's natal Moon; a command to create a home for the world to live, compete and play in. The circumstances in which this was to be done were far from ideal.

Overcoming difficulty

Some astrologers had made dire warnings for the intervening years. The week before the July 2012 opening, I was reassuring a colleague that the very difficult Mars/Uranus/Pluto transits did not have to mean terrorism, brutality and death, but a whole world of master competitors descending upon London. In November 2007, this column summarised and advised as follows:

> These Olympics will come after a four-year period of profound global adjustment. The bombing atrocities in London came just a few days after the announcement of the allocation of the 2012 games to that city. The reality and symbolism of both raise a range of questions. Will the world be in a condition to hold the games at all? What will be the inevitable issues of security for the games themselves and the lives of the people of Britain both before and afterward as a result?

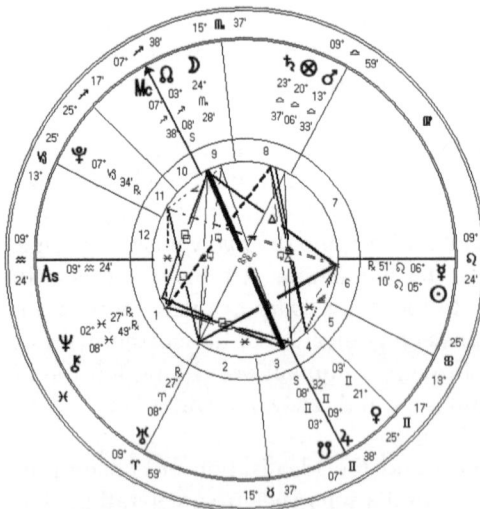

2012 Olympic Opening Ceremony
27 Jul 2012 21:00 BST -1:00
Stratford, UK 51°N33' 000°W00'
Geocentric Tropical Placidus True Node

As a country, Britain has the ability to face up to and transform the direst astrological configurations into ceremonies that turn disaster into celebration, even triumph, for a while. We saw how the Royal Wedding in 1981 eased world tension through a most difficult year. Great danger was transformed into community integration at HM the Queen's Golden Jubilee Celebrations in 2002. Both triumphs were caused by including not fearing, by opening out not defending, by making friends not enemies. If, in spite of all fears and temptations to the contrary, we can hold true within ourselves and engender in other nations the courage to trust in and respect each other, spend less time in seeking to profit and exploit, more on caring and creating happiness, this event may do a really great service of reconciliation. Harmonious aspects have their best potential when combined with tense and difficult ones. May the grand trine between Uranus in Aries, Sun/Mercury in Leo and North Node in Sagittarius help stage an event that helps bring the world together.

Such an aspiration will require a very different view of other peoples, and their beliefs and values, than the narrow-minded fear-driven policies and knee-jerk legal reactions of recent leaders and their policies.[120]

Why the Olympics were so successful

The chart drawn for Danny Boyle's selected exact opening moment of the games clearly reveals both the difficulties and the energy to overcome them.[121] Two T-squares focus the difficulties. The mutable one: Node/MC in Sagittarius (with void Scorpio Moon) opposed to Jupiter in Gemini, both squared to Neptune/Chiron in Pisces represents the pressure of so many activities and people coming together in a narrow space of time. The cardinal one: Saturn/Mars in Libra opposed Uranus in Aries, both squared to Pluto in Capricorn represents intense responsibility to guard against danger in turbulent times. From such configurations, it is easy for a simplistic sensation-seeker to prophecy doom.

Yet, that is to miss the positive potential to grow and advance if we work with courage and determination to overcome difficulty. Also, augmented by the Ascendant position, arising from the moment chosen to open the ceremony, the chart also has a six-pointed star. A proud and energetic fire grand trine formed by the Sagittarian MC/ Node, Leo Sun/Mercury and Aries Uranus suggests the great pride of going to any lengths of innovation to make everything possible. The restlessly intelligent air grand trine crossing it to make the star has Mars/Saturn in Libra trined by an expansive Jupiter in Gemini, both being presented by the Aquarian Ascendant!

The tension and the talent come together in a most remarkable way. The way that the organisers embraced both enabled thousands of athletes and millions, even billions, of people all over the world to come together in a remarkable show of cooperative achievement and entertainment. Most important of all it shows that, however dire the times, when we do the right thing the worst does not have to happen.

'Winning' the economic Olympics!

It is because there is a radical difference between sporting and economic competition that our everyday lives are so fraught and unhealthy. Sports lay down structures within which to compete. Although competitors stretch the rules as far as possible, anyone breaking them is labelled a cheat and rejected from the game and the respect of society. Furthermore, there are set restrictions on the timing and nature of the competition. Having won, a boxer is not allowed to continue to batter an opponent. Having won a match, the victor does not demand more time to humiliate and injure the defeated so he will never be able to compete again.

Unfortunately, in the running of our world economy there are no such restraints. Ever-expanding multi-national corporations get around rules to the disadvantage of everyone except themselves. Greedy electronic traders care for short-term profit, not economically viable investment. Bizarre buildings are sited uneconomically in deserts. Luxury cars and other goods are accepted, often celebrated, in the name of the free market and individual freedom. Caring for the needy is not so necessary, even though millions starve. Many will help if they can spare the funds, but not too often as it 'encourages laziness'. What has brought us to this way of running our world when we know so well how to play together? Can we learn from the Olympics?   That would involve a fundamental change in consciousness and motivation. Is this what recent exposés of public figures and their institutions are preparing us for? A wider look at the Pluto cycle might make this clearer.

Pluto in Aquarius – early considerations

With Pluto only just completing its fourth year in Capricorn and most people (especially economists and politicians) finding it difficult if not impossible to change their growth-obsessed Pluto-in-Sagittarius mindsets, it might seem a little early to look ahead to when the planet leaves Capricorn. On the contrary, knowing what might come *after* this Pluto-in-Capricorn driven restructuring of government assumptions and relationships with the people may help us let go of a yearning for past affluence and address present problems properly.

Guidelines from the past

The last two periods of Pluto's time in Aquarius saw questioning of authority, public upheaval and radical ideas destined to remould the centuries ahead.

❖   1532-53: From Luther's nailing of his articles to the door of Wittenberg church in 1517 near the beginning of the Pluto-in-Capricorn period, expectations of an optimistic future soon turned to a authoritarian struggle over control and individual choice. In England, Henry VIII finally rejected attempts to compromise with Rome and married Anne Boleyn in 1533, the year Pluto entered Aquarius. The subsequent years saw four more marriages for Henry, the creation of the Church of England, dissolution of the monasteries and redistribution of their wealth. They concluded with the insecure reign of Edward VI. He died as Pluto was entering Pisces in 1553. His sister Mary (born 1516) ascended to throne and restored Roman Catholicism for a while, until she died, leaving Queen Elizabeth I to stabilise the kingdom.

❖   1777-98: In the eighteenth century, the Capricorn period (1762-77) saw Captain Cook mapping the world for Britain, while its authority was being challenged by the American colonies and war with France. The US Declaration of Independence (1776) heralded the Pluto-in-Aquarius period and ongoing struggles for and against individual freedom. The French revolution was in 1789. The reign of terror 1793-94 and its aftermath created instability throughout Europe, with Napoleon coming to power as Pluto entered Pisces.

Today, we have had Pluto in our public consciousness since 1930, split the atom and seen amazing scientific advances. How will the next Pluto in Aquarius period show itself in such a world? The important lesson to learn from the past is that Pluto in Aquarius always challenges the status quo. In the sixteenth century, it was the absolute power of the Roman Church over the individual soul in life and death. In the eighteenth century, the absolute power of monarchy over the individual. Today, it is the absolute power of materialistic experts.

Materialism – the source of absolute power in the twenty-first century

The mass educational and communication advances for ordinary people in recent years place the issue of freedom far deeper than before. The present Pluto-in-Capricorn times are exposing hypocrisy and abuses of senior figures, who would have been 'too important' to be challenged fifty years ago. Since Pluto's Capricorn ingress in 2008 power-brokers have been 'under the hammer', the credibility of bankers, economists, politicians, senior journalists and media barons has been embarrassingly exposed. Is this the pot of revolutionary change that will be stirred through the rest of the Pluto-in-Capricorn period and form the stuff of the Aquarian period that follows? If so, is there an essential absolute power source that underlies and links these institutions?

There is and it goes to heart of the challenge of the human condition – materialism and the greed that goes with it. Unfairness in the allocation of resources has been behind the rise and fall of most conquests, political systems and revolutionary movements for thousands of years. In the centuries since the so-called 'Enlightenment' and Industrial Revolution, the notion of plenty and emerging democracy have given the impression that we can institutionalise greed and provide plenty for all. All we need is a series of rules and regulations, based on ever more advanced and sophisticated methods of collecting, compartmentalising and applying knowledge. The problem is that this bases the 'pursuit of happiness' on a purely materialistic foundation. Political argument is about 'haves' and 'have nots', ways of *measuring*, and then implementing fairness. Kindness, creativity, delight in life, care of nature, spiritual awareness are no more than desirable luxuries that the cut and thrust of the 'real material world' may oblige us to downgrade, even put aside.

Truth today is based on the notion that everything that is really 'real' can be measured and placed. By research we can learn how to do anything and, in time, solve all problems. The world and the Universe is a vast play room that we, like children, can manipulate and change as we wish. Without actually deciding we wanted it this way, as a 'matter of fact', from the advances and discoveries emanating from the 'Enlightenment', we have developed a scientistic world view that sees material reality as ultimate and absolute truth, and even seeks to marginalise and outcast the ways and resources of those who do not agree.

Questioning the custodians of power

From the institutions of such a world view come the academic experts, who advise politicians and show commerce how to profit. These people's ideas and products are sold and justified to the public by outlets, promoted by media consultants, skilled in the arts of psychological manipulation. The whole is overseen by a benign legal system that to maintain its objectivity can easily become lost in time-consuming complexity.

If Pluto in Capricorn represents challenges to the institutions that administer this world view, Pluto in Aquarius could see regeneration in the foundation and assumptions of this materialistic 'absolute truth', upon which we base knowledge. In the years 1995-2011, Neptune and Uranus in Aquarius marked the dominance of scientific and technological innovation for the 'common good', humanitarian revolution and people participation. So, with Pluto there instead, the world will experience the death and consequent regeneration of that scientific and technological innovation for the 'common good', humanitarian revolution and people participation. We will face and put in perspective the consequences of the rapid strides we made in those 1995-2011 years. Ideas and assumptions of experts and media manipulators, place holders, who insist they know what is best for us, or claim to speak on behalf if the public, have dominated to the point of oppression at times. They will be questioned. What technology is really needed? Does science, as practised today, hold all the answers? Do some aspects of it distort genuine understanding, even endanger our future? Is personal freedom possible without personal responsibility? Does pandering to encouraging the lowest common denominator tastes and opinions create happier peoples and societies?

Dedicate the 2012 Winter Solstice to a kinder world
When in 2005 (some well before) astrologers projected the nemesis of world economic system in 2008, it seemed ludicrously unrealistic, but it happened. To see the materialistic mechanical science philosophy that underpins the industrial revolution and human greed that has dominated our lives for far longer coming to a nemesis when Pluto enters Aquarius may not be that far-fetched. Let us be clear. This does not mean the end of 'sensible science', but a much better and wiser science. It does not mean the end of capitalism, but a much more responsible and decently motivated capitalism. It does mean an end to 'legalised' piracy in the contemporary financial market place. It does not mean the end of the world, but the birth of a better one, where rules and regulations are less important than doing the right thing. It means the birth of a kinder world, motivated toward individual happiness, as visualised in the preamble to the US Declaration of Independence, but so sadly misunderstood and distorted in some of the ways that great country has developed.

If our coming together on 21 December has this in mind, releasing counter-productiveness, working towards kindness, then Winter Solstice 2012 could see the end of the old and the birth of a new world. Nothing less will do it!

-oOo-

Addressing survivors at the start of the new Mayan Calendar period, the March 2013 column opened with cogent advice on how to master fear of, and in, the future.

What You Really, Really Want[122]

Although it was raining pretty hard in the run-up to the 2012 Winter Solstice, fortunately few people took Hollywood's popularisation of the end of the Mayan Long Count too literally. Yet, unwittingly or not, the promotional poster for the movie *2012* did symbolise, in somewhat startlingly graphic terms, the heart of the transformation the world is going through right now.[123]

A Tibetan lama apparently standing on the top of Mount Everest, as the world below appears to be covered by the ocean, could be a desperately hyperbolic representation of a world awash with attachment to greed – a very negative manifestation of the karmic consequences to be faced when Saturn is in Scorpio and Uranus in Mars' other sign – Aries. With Pluto in Capricorn (while Neptune is in Pisces), how else can efficient order be restored but by washing away all that negativity and starting again?

Taking away the meteorological exaggeration, humanity does need to find a way to escape from drowning in a world economy and educational system based upon self-indulgence and fear-driven possessiveness. In many ways, the build-up to the end of last year marked the nemesis of many of the delusions upon which our lives had become founded. The UK October Autumn Budget Statement announced the recovery of the UK economy was delayed from 2015 to 2018, which, in UK Treasury-speak, means indefinitely. The credibility of Britain's politicians, media and police forces was in crisis. Political divisions in the United States of America were forcing at best ineffective compromise in economic reform. The emotional response to the Sandy Hook school shooting, led by President Obama, promised a sea-change in attitudes to gun ownership. This will only be possible if the relationship assumptions that cause so many of its citizens to depend upon guns could also change.

The lesson to learn during Saturn in Scorpio sextile to Pluto in Capricorn times is that no weapon or insurance agreement, political promise, community we identify with, belief or interest we share, no thing, system, or person we feel inclined to trust can *guarantee* the protection of ourselves or those dear to us. Our insecurity is a fact of existence. It commences from conception, is reinforced at birth, and does not end until we die. Attempts to guarantee what can never be certain or permanent are at best futile. Frequently, they lead to a pointless waste of resources, or even greater danger. Attempts to defend ourselves against a supposed threat all too often make the threat worse, or can create a new one.

There are two central paradoxes of life that, once understood and accepted, hold the potential to seed and grow healthy relationships, and to create a better, happier world for everyone. The first is that we will always feel secure if we accept impermanence; recognise that everything we prize and value will not last for ever. Insecurity is the natural condition of our existence, not someone else's fault. The second is the best way to look after the interests of ourselves and those close to us is to be sensitive to our environment and to develop friendship by caring for it and everyone in it. Taking both paradoxes on board inculcates courage and clarity within ourselves, and friendship and support around us. Whether it is in our day-to-day dealings at home or international relationships abroad, the greatest efficiency comes from such an approach. For evil is the product of enmity, which we project upon those who do not seem to care for us.

The Saturn/Pluto sextile period made its first exact connection on 27 December 2012. The retrograde event is on 8 March 2013. Not completing until September, the harmonious relationship between this most formidable pair of planets will be a dominant healing feature of the year. This is a crisis we cannot talk or scheme our way out of. We have to *feel* our way out of it. The keywords say 'limitation of desire is harmonious with regeneration of control'. By understanding what we really want and accepting that we cannot always have it, we build a more sustainable, mutually supporting, happier world.

-o0o-

The May 2013 column drew on the history of the two previous Uranus-transiting-Aries periods, and then with Taurus, to guide the best way to respond to current transits. The dangers identified manifested with precise, increasing severity through the late 2010s. If only astrological advice had been heard in time to avert the catastrophe, the world mindlessly nightmared into 2014-20.

No longer a Rich Man's Game

> She was poor but she was honest,
> Victim of a rich man's game.
> First he loved her, then he left her,
> And she lost her honest name.
>
> It's the same the whole world over,
> It's the poor what gets the blame,
> It's the rich what gets the pleasure,
> Isn't it a blooming shame?
> *Traditional British music hall song*

Recent advances in social equality and changes of moral values make the risqué verses of this traditional song seem dated. One only has to follow contemporary media to see that in today's tolerant and liberated world, such abuse of the vulnerable would be exposed and punished by the full force of public condemnation. Change just one word, however, and the last verse has a remarkably modern ring:

> It's the same the whole world over,
> It's the poor what gets the blame,
> It's the rich what gets the *money*,
> Isn't it a blooming shame?

Astrology suggests that there is a common driving force behind the urge for both sex and money. Pure truth-like beauty is held safe and personally possessed in the Venus-ruled Taurean second house.[124] Here our acquired wealth is exclusively ours, as are our values and feelings. However, when we allow others in, we find ourselves in the Mars/Pluto-ruled eighth house of *shared* possessions and feelings. What was safely ours becomes exposed and vulnerable to the ravishing of others. When the barrier between yours and mine is less clear, letting go is both joyous and dangerous, as the heart opens to the seductive hiatus of intercourse. Do we dare to desire? Do we dare to risk losing everything, because we fear to desire? This experience of crossing the Rubicon that all new lovers know is little different from how it feels to make crucial business decisions. Fear and greed undermine the enjoyment of both love and money.

Successful financial market traders attribute their success to being able to control and manipulate fear and greed. By way of contrast, most of us only take risks when we have to. We prefer to protect ourselves by passing possibilities of trauma on to insurers, financial advisers, doctors, counsellors, reporters and other officially appointed experts. When these get it wrong, we all suffer. When they organise their area of society in their own self-interests, we become poor and they become rich; especially in bad times.

Half-baked solutions

Uranus in Aries times are especially unsuited to the finding of proper solutions to dysfunctional economies. Ill-considered, quick initiatives are implemented, not properly monitored, and then changed too quickly when they do not seem to work. So, over the last five years from Uranus in Pisces to early Uranus in Aries, we have moved on from bank bailouts, to artificially low interest rates, to 'quantitative easing' '(a way of creating money that does not exist by giving credits to banks against their government debt holdings). Recently central banks have offered billions in three-year loans to ordinary banks at artificially low interest rates. To avoid sovereign debt crisis and collapse of the Euro, the European Central Bank has guaranteed to buy back unlimited amounts of Italian and Spanish government debt.

Each of these initiatives, may 'kick the can down the road' for a while, but could leave the long-term debt exposure in even worse condition, when boom times fail to return. They also generate financial assets that those institutions and traders closest to the money can use for their immediate benefit. Equities and other assets increase in value, and quick profits with bonuses can be taken. Massive trading profit can be gained in seconds, while it takes years to agree (or fail to agree) on the rules and regulations to contain trading abuses, by when they are long out of use and new ways in place.

What remains, if any, trickles down at higher interest rates to ordinary enterprises. Depression remains. Businesses survive by employees accepting lower wages and part-time work. Government income is reduced, as its financial obligations increase. Cuts in services and increases in costs are passed on down the wage chain. Those at the bottom suffer the squeeze in their living standards most. Many millions of US citizens rely on food handouts and are even homeless in the world's richest nation.

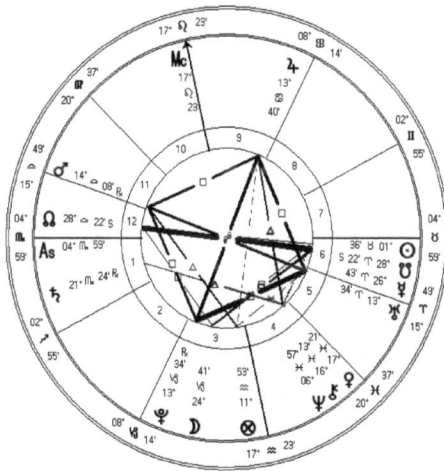

Uranus Squares Pluto
21 Apr 2014 19:20:52 GMT +0:00
London, UK 51°N30' 000°W10'
Geocentric Tropical Placidus True Node

In Britain, many, especially the young, are living in increasingly over-crowded conditions, and being forced to work for little or no money on government schemes. The poor and disabled are forensically assessed to cut welfare costs – even chased out of their homes. Are we on the way back to those dark Dickensian days of the nineteenth century? Public servants' work is contracted out to low-wage private alternatives. Sub-groups of the poor are turned against each other, while directors of large companies, financial speculators and owners of high-quality property see vast expansion in their incomes and assets.

Such unbalanced short-term profit making and exploitation is untenable. With Pluto in Capricorn, boom times for all are unlikely to return some time soon, if at all. So, Keynesian stimuli are unlikely to kick-start economies toward better times. At best they can do no more than delay the inevitable time of reckoning and make it worse when it comes. Times of nemesis lie ahead for rich and poor alike.

The spring of 2013 and 2014

There are two more Uranus/Pluto squares this year. Below is the chart for first, the third in the series. This ongoing aspect cannot be considered enough. Read again Dr Nicholas Campion's excellent application of Kepler's methods to these astro – events in the May 2011 *Astrological Journal*[125] alongside Darby Costello's 'Navigating by the outer planets in the astrological chart' in the November 2012 edition,[126] as well as 'Real Change Happens in the Heart' in my September 2012 'Working with the Planets' column,[127] which interprets in detail the key fifth-square climax in April 2014. As we move nearer that time, events on the ground are fine-tuning the shape and confirming the fundamental accuracy of these astro-projections.

Throughout the world, ordinary people sense injustice and are in revolt against, or largely have contempt for, those in charge of the processes that control their lives. The injustices outlined above make increasingly hollow the notion 'we are all in this together' that rang true at the time of the 2008 financial crisis, and again during the outbreak of the Arab Spring. The argument for the indispensability of our 'expert' leaders seems little different from the nineteenth-century justification of the aristocracy, with the new privileged class based not on *noblesse oblige* responsibility of birth, but wealth often gained by market manipulation, misinformation and the irresponsible exploitation of the vulnerable.

Learning from the past

Social unrest, leading to disturbance on the streets and electoral rejection of mainstream parties is already gathering a year ahead of April 2014. If injustices are not understood and addressed, it will continue to build. The experience of nineteenth and twentieth-century Uranus transits through Aries make worrying comparisons.

 ❖   1843-50 With Pluto also in Aries and Neptune in Aquarius until 1848, social disturbance was extreme. The neglect and lack of interest by absentee landlords left the Irish people to starve through the potato famine and to be driven off their land. Nearly half of the population emigrated, mainly to the USA. In Europe 1848 saw the publication of Karl Marx's *Das Kapital* and 'the most widespread revolutionary wave in European history', with many thrones toppled.[128] The same year, the British Chartist movement presented to parliament a six-million-signature human rights petition.

 ❖   1928-35 With Pluto in Cancer and Neptune in detriment in Virgo at the same time, these were years of savage hardship caused by world economic depression, following on from the inability of world leaders to solve the consequences of the 1929 Wall Street Crash. In Germany, Italy and Spain, revolutionary struggles led to fascism defeating communism and abolishing democracy. In the USSR Stalinist domination led to persecution, imprisonment and the death of millions.

These Uranus-in-Aries periods of global upheaval saw radically different outcomes. Opinions may differ as to whether this was due to the wisdom, or otherwise, of contemporary leaders, or the outer-planetary combinations driving their actions and decisions.

❖ As the Uranus-in-Taurus times approached (1850-57) combining with Uranus in Pisces, new democracies were formed in Europe. The United States expansion to the West, begun in the 1840s, was consolidated. Having avoided confrontation in 1848, the Chartists' aims were peacefully implemented. The 1851 Great Exhibition was a major contribution to world industrial development, focusing the British people on their nation's key achievements and of the time.

❖ Unfortunately, maybe because Pluto had been in paranoically defensive Cancer and Neptune in fanatically puritanical Virgo, the upheavals of the early 1930s were not so pleasantly resolved. The Keynesian solutions of the US New Deal created work and rebuilt the US industrial machine, but the defensive isolationism of the times kept the US apart from key international problems. In Europe and then the Far East, 1935-42 saw a crescendo of global destruction, flaring up (as Pluto entered Leo) into the Second World War, to contain German and Japanese expansion. Those Uranus-in-Taurus, Neptune-in-Virgo, late Pluto-in-Cancer times saw not the growth of a perfect new world home for humanity, but a mania of global destruction driven by factional obsessions of racial 'purity'. The years of post-war recovery were based on Keynesianism combined with state-funded intervention. From the 1980s, Keynesianism made an unholy fair-weather alliance with free-market monetarism. Its theories are a heavy deceptive chain around the neck of anyone seeking fundamental solutions to world economic problems. They are doomed to fail, because they assume we can avoid the consequences and trick the market by means of easy credit, tax incentives and creative accounting.

❖ Through the later Uranus-in-Aries years, approaching the Taurean ingress, radically different solutions are needed to enjoy its nineteenth-century-transit's outcome and avoid its twentieth-century disaster. Bes Being at the waxing of the cycle, as in 1840-50, gives reason for optimism.

Nineteenth century preparations for Uranus in Taurus
Knowing the history of last years of the mid-nineteenth century Uranus-in-Aries transit and a visit to the Royal Albert Hall and its accompanying Albert Memorial in Kensington, London, gives helpful lessons for our time. In 1848 with Europe in revolt, a mass procession of the British Chartist movement planning to present its human rights petition confronted the British army in London. Compromise narrowly avoided conflict. In the years immediately after, Albert, the Prince Regent, organised the 1851 Great Exhibition, which captured the minds of the nation. The two grand memorials to his efforts commemorate and celebrate the achievement and Britain's central role in the world at that time. To this day, the Royal Albert Hall is the focus of many cultural and ceremonial events. Buildings in the surrounding area are headquarters and museums holding the highest quality of art, science and learning. The Albert Memorial commemorates this in grand style. A life-sized golden prince on his throne, encircled by reliefs of great thinkers, artists and scientists, with the four grand corners representing the riches of world continents. As Uranus approached Taurus in 1850 (alongside Neptune in Pisces since 1848), this lesson of inclusiveness led to growing British world dominance into the early twentieth century.

Of course, because it started from a low base, this grand achievement obscured far more injustice and economic incompetence than it demonstrated. Slavery remained in much of the world; exploitation of the innocent was rife. In Britain, the rights and living conditions of the majority were harsh, inequality was extreme. Yet it showed what can be done when people work together.

Doing even better in the twenty-first century

In the twenty-first century, we start from a much higher base. Also, we approach the later years of Uranus in Aries, with Neptune in Pisces for six, not just two, years of its transit. Pluto is not in Aries, signifying sweeping away of the past and a completely new beginning, but the mature organising sign of Capricorn. In between the times, two Uranus cycles have ended empires and simplistic attempts to implement Marxism. The colonised are becoming the colonisers. Electronics is the master of heavy industry. Millions travel the world physically; most are gaining access to global communications. When else will be the time for the world's people to make a great positive leap forward to understand, tolerate and support for each other?

The last three paragraphs [below] have a pertinent message for the 2020s, overshadowed by the Covid-19 pandemic.

Today's seven Uranus/Pluto squares will 'rub our noses' in the self-created consequences of failing to grasp this great opportunity. The punishment for the selfishness of failure will intensify up to spring 2014, and then rumble on until the final completion moves out of orb in 2015-16. By personal responsibility we can gain the clarity and strength to move beyond a greed-based competitive world economy, and instead join together and create one based upon living together, without seeking to gain something for nothing. By doing the opposite we fall into the hands of far more unscrupulous players, who exploit us for their own benefit. Trying to beat others cannot bring happiness, be it by paper money, artificially creating growth, or the personal piling up of masses of gold.

The only lasting solutions are those that make increasing numbers of people happy. In the twenty-first century, with more mature outer-planetary transits, we can start to build not a British, American, Islamic or even Chinese empire, but a world where all live together in mutual admiration of the variety they express. This is the only true gold standard, upon which a sustainable world economy can be grounded.[129]

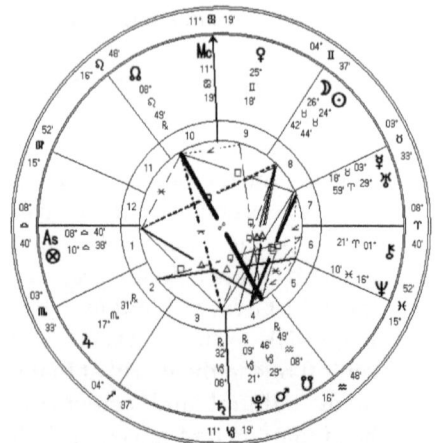

Uranus ingress Taurus
15 May 2018 15:16:41 UT +0:00
London, UK 51°N30' 000°W10'
Geocentric Tropical Placidus True Node

Uranus ingresses Taurus

Have a look at the Uranus ingress Taurus chart. Five earth positions and a trine to a Taurus new moon. The Mercury/Mars square separates. Does such idealism seem possible? Can it really be true that the truly practical solution is the enjoyment of a future society, organised for the benefit of all? Current suffering and uncertainty will not fade until, realising this, we refuse to be victims of a rich man's game.

-oOo-

The July 2013 column sought to apply the water grand trine that dominated the year to the history of welfare state and point to the dangers of its demise. These dangers were ignored, as the water energy turned instead to anxiety about 'balancing the UK nation's books'. The consequent hardships were to narrow popular opinion into blame-game nationalism and leave those in need uncared for and unsure about who to blame.

Do We Care?

A most moving and illuminating episode of the recent BBC television drama series *Call the Midwife* sensitively uncovered the story of a filthy female derelict, who wandered the streets, worrying mothers by staring closely into their baby's prams. Through kind care and diligent research, a nurse befriended and restored her to normal life, by discovering that she and her six children had been taken into a workhouse in the early twentieth century. Separated from her children (the youngest a new-born baby), she was put to work as a seamstress. When the workhouse system was disbanded in the 1930s, she had been left to her own devices. Thirty years too late, she embarked on a futile search for her lost baby. Only by visiting their childhood graves could she find closure.[130]

Today, we have moved on from such a savage application of the Dickensian Victorian notion that the poor bring their problems upon themselves, and should be put to work to compensate society for any help it gives them. Indeed, the UK government's welfare reform policy is said to be justified, because today this woman would be provided with a house and an income in excess of the average wage to care for her children. Yet, as the UK's pilot scheme to cap welfare benefits (started in Aries on 11 April 2013) is phased in throughout the country during July (Cancer time), the arguments surrounding this policy invite us to ask whether we are moving back to nineteenth-century notions?

The astrology of welfare reform

The idea that the state (rather than middle-class private and local philanthropy) should care for the welfare of people in need was born out of the Liberal Party's surprising landslide majority at the 1906 UK General Election.[131] In the years until 1914, improvements in universal free schooling and rudimentary provision of old age pensions, health insurance, employment support and benefits were introduced.

Uranus in Capricorn opposing Neptune in Cancer in the 'last day of polling' chart clearly indicates revolutionary change of government and belief in the needs of the people. The irresistible force of sensitive

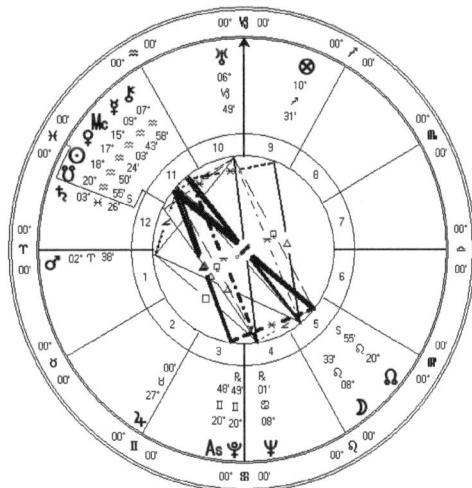

1906 UK General Election last voting day
8 Feb 1906 12:00 UT +0:00
London, UK 51°N30' 000°W10'
Geocentric Tropical 0° Aries True Node

change is marked by the harmonious connections that are to follow on from the Aquarian stellium led by Saturn in early Pisces. The Nodal axis has been retrograding back in harmonious aspect to the Uranus/Neptune opposition. Sun, Mercury and Venus apply to sextile/trine it in the coming weeks, while Saturn and then Chiron will apply to do so in the coming years. Now was a moment to address the needs that had been crying out for action for decades or even centuries.

After four turbulent decades, the years immediately after the Second World War saw massive expansion in welfare provision. The National Health Service became law in November 1946, doctors held back from joining until July 1948 – two months before Uranus entered Cancer. In the formative years of the service, it was to oppose its own and conjunct Neptune's 1906 positions.

In the ups and downs of the economic recovery and re-distribution of wealth through the decades that followed, the notion of the UK welfare state offering a cushion of support, below which no one should fall, was never questioned. The injustices of Victorian times were considered to be superseded history. Younger generations with no memory of the injustices of the 1920s and 1930s and the grand post-Second World War vision that led to the creation of today's welfare state, took it for granted; to some it seemed right to 'live off the system'.

Reversal

As planets cycle the zodiac and aspect an original key trigger point, what that point represents grows to a climax, and is then reassessed at the opposition to the original position. So it was that in the years immediately leading up to early 1984, when Neptune entered Capricorn that an eighty-year-old archetypal belief changed. It was time to think the unthinkable. Was welfare sacrosanct? The market was a far more important measure of efficiency. Full employment would no longer be subsidised. The individual must support himself, with less reliance on welfare. Work and enterprise should stand or fall on their intrinsic merits.

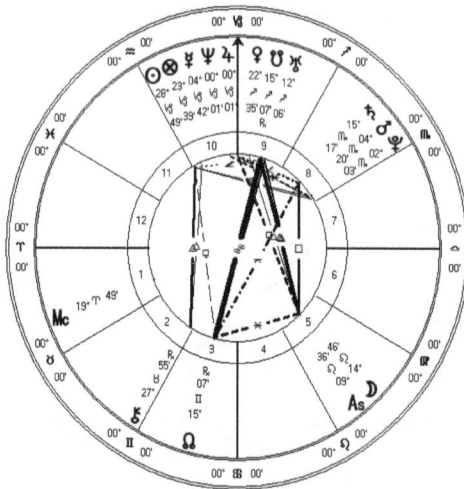

Transits 19 Jan 1984
19 Jan 1984 17:23 UT +0:00
Camberley, UK 51°N21' 000°W45'
Geocentric Tropical 0° Aries True Node

As Jupiter conjuncted Neptune in Capricorn in January 1984, the Nodal axis had been transiting the 1906 Neptune point less than two years earlier; Sun, Mercury and Venus were in the midst of opposing it, while Mars, Jupiter, Neptune, Uranus and Saturn were to make their opposing mark as the decade proceeded. Clearly a major struggle to realign the responsibility of governments for the welfare of their people lay ahead.

The mid-1980s boomed, adjusted and then recovered through the 1990s, hesitated at the turn of the century and recovered up to 2008. The prosperity of the 1995-2008 Pluto in Sagittarius, Uranus/Neptune Aquarian years, made life seem easier for a while, delaying the full impact of 1980s changing mindset. Then, as Pluto, the one planet yet to oppose the

1906 Neptune position in Cancer, entered Capricorn and proceeded to oppose that crucial 8 degrees of Cancer throughout 2012, the plans for a fundamental revamp of the UK welfare system were put in place.[132] Bear in mind the economic realities we face, and then add in the demands to correct past Western exploitation of other lands. How far back to the Victorian experience does this suggest the second half of the Neptune cycle, waning back to Cancer, might take ordinary citizens in the West?

The way to genuine caring
The lack of real recovery, the consequential deeper world economic crisis and the realignment of work and wealth between emerging and older imperial countries will not be solved by going back, blaming and depriving the poor, especially while increasing wealth is enjoyed by a minority who hold the reins of power. We have to find a better, kinder way.

All the key charts below and the whole of the year are dominated by a massive grand trine in water signs. Only Uranus and Pluto are not at one of its points at some time. Jupiter, Saturn and Neptune and Chiron are in a grand trine throughout the year. Expect powerful emotion-driven realignments of understanding. Against this will be those who encourage us to react with outrage, to harden and close pincer claws. So, destroying hope of real change.

These two months, indeed all through 2013, will see an ever-deepening debate about fairness. Used badly, it could generalise from the particular to boil up nasty archetypes into dangerous misunderstandings that drive us into warring camps. Used well, it could cross the boundaries of those misunderstandings, and so find solutions.

-o0o-

The July 2013 column then considered China's new leader, Xi Jinping. In the years since, the Moon (ruler of the Mars, Mercury and Uranus in Cancer conjunction to the South Node in Leo) has certainly explained his government's intransigent determination to sustain and expand China's dominant influence.

China is the world's most populated country with 1.35 billion people. Over the past ten/twenty years, the Chinese economy has expanded rapidly, people moved into towns and spent much more. The capacity of its totalitarian one-party system to contain the pressures of contemporary expectation and demand has become strained.

At the time of writing, Xi Jinping's time of birth is unknown, so noon has been used.[133] The Gemini Sun and Jupiter, with Mars, Mercury and Uranus in Cancer show the intensity of the struggle he will have to hold an ever-diversifying country together. The Moon conjunct South Node, with Pluto also in Leo, symbolise the certainty and purposeful self-belief that have become an

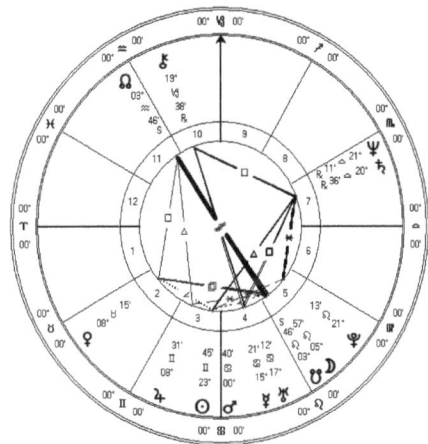

Xi Jinping
15 Jun 1953 no time AWST -8:00
Beijing, China 39°N55' 116°E25'
Geocentric Tropical 0° Aries True Node

in-built tradition for the Chinese ruling elite. As long as prosperity can be sustained, this self-confidence may be enough, but the combination of mutability .and the need to express cardinal Cancer care that otherwise dominate his chart suggest keeping the lid on a fast-changing society will not be easy. The communication of interactive empathy between himself and the people is the positive expression of the chart, but dare he let his guard down to that extent?

oOo

The September 2013 column clearly shows that understanding the outer-planetary transits, in hand and ahead, clearly anticipated the trauma to come.

Global Change (2008 to 2025) – 2013-14 progress report

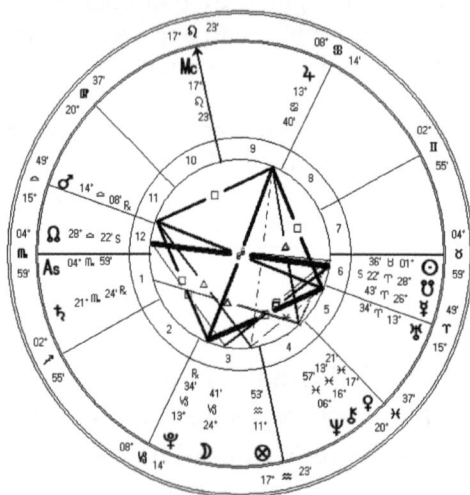

Uranus squares Pluto
21 Apr 2014 19:20:52 UT +0:00
London, UK 51°N30' 000°W10'
Geocentric Tropical Placidus True Node

It is nearly six years since Pluto entered Capricorn and only three since Neptune's 2011 ingress into Pisces. They will not change sign again for over ten years. Hence, the reorganisation of the structure of the world economy and deepening of global understanding is at an early adolescent stage.

The seven squares of Uranus in Aries and Pluto in Capricorn between June 2012 and March 2015 are stirring the pot of change in ways that conventional national and international structures seem unable to understand, let alone contain. Some nations are on the edge of anarchy. Institutions within countries are discredited. Solutions to problems are mouthed, but bear little relationship to what actually happens.

What has been bottled up erupts and takes us to unfamiliar places and extremes, for which we are ill-prepared.

Saturn advancing through Scorpio throughout 2013-14 could see us trying to contain and focus our passions, which many will find frustratingly difficult to accept. However, with Capricorn's ruler Saturn mutually receiving Pluto, Scorpio's modern ruler, great rewards will come from such restraint. At Saturn's previous time in Scorpio (1983-84) Pluto was there too. Then the mood was to take risks, to throw caution and controls to the wind. Simplistic monetarism and big bang electronic financial trading started us on the way to our present economic crisis. We may not be ready to admit it, but the world economy is at the end game of free market capitalist exploitation. The 2008-25 transits will force us to find a way that works for everyone and does better than privatise profit and socialise loss, or face destruction because we fail to make the attempt.

Jupiter starts 2013 in Gemini, moving to Cancer and a grand trine with Saturn and Neptune/Chiron from July to September. Its early-year sextile to Uranus will encourage lots of contradictory and immature demands, which will grow into passionate needs to be satisfied through the second half of the year. As explained in July's column, great hope and healing could come from this configuration.[134] However, suggestions that the world economy is over the worst and can recover without radical change of motivation and course will be cruelly disappointed. Also, with such strong flowing water planets and revolutionary fervour building from the Uranus/Pluto square, emotions could boil over into frighteningly pointless self-sacrifice.

We will experience a mixture of these possibilities, as a store of expectations and/or injustices to be redressed will pile up, while Uranus makes its direct station and moves unrelentingly towards its fifth and strongest square to Pluto in the series.

Uranus bustles forward to 21 April 2014 urging all kinds of change upon an unreceptive retrograding Pluto, already pressured by an opposition from Jupiter in Cancer and a destabilising square from Mars in Libra. The sense that we are not ready, but there is no more time and so we have to act, will be the dominating mood. Many astrologers have remarked upon the demanding, tense strength of this cardinal grand cross, with so many planets involved. The exceptions, Venus in Pisces and Saturn in Scorpio, together make a wide grand trine, seeking to temper Jupiterian excess with sympathetic realism. The emotions that emerge from the traumas of this time will be carried forward and transformed into forceful, perhaps foolhardy, action in July 2014, when Jupiter enters Leo and advances to trine Uranus in Aries. This is when actions, leading to major better-or-worse change start. We will move beyond excuses, spin and promises into an early beginning of new insights and approaches.

As events move beyond our ability to control them, the wise stop talking and acting and start thinking the unthinkable; are our fundamental assumptions untenable? Are these events moving the world towards a sea-change as game-changing as was the emergence of capitalist industrialisation in the eighteenth and nineteenth centuries? We are unlikely to know the answer to this in 2014, but, step back, retreat, look at the astro-cycles, we just might see what is coming.

Dominant World Image 2020

-oOo-

The December 2013 column warned of danger, if the healing potential of the current water-planet astro-cycles was missed

Differing World Reactions to the Same Transits

A water grand trine has dominated the summer of 2013 and will be within orb until after it completes in the late spring 2014.[135] It combines the expansive sympathy of Jupiter in Cancer with the fearless authority of Saturn in Scorpio and the spiritually sensitive sacrifice of Neptune and Chiron in Pisces.

Present crises in the Middle East show just how pernicious harmonious aspects can be, especially when triggered by a Jupiter/Pluto opposition. Events in Syria and then Egypt showed the Cancer/Scorpio/Pisces grand trine at the extremity of intolerance and destructive resentment. When feelings build to such a pitch, all involved become the terrorists that terrorise each other, especially when Mars is in fall in Cancer.   Compromise is unacceptable; death and self-sacrifice rule.

Turkey, Brazil, parts of Africa, Asia, and Southern Europe have seen similar demonstrations or intolerant reactions. Most not so extreme, maybe settling down, or are thy just not being reported?

In the UK, the EU, USA and much of

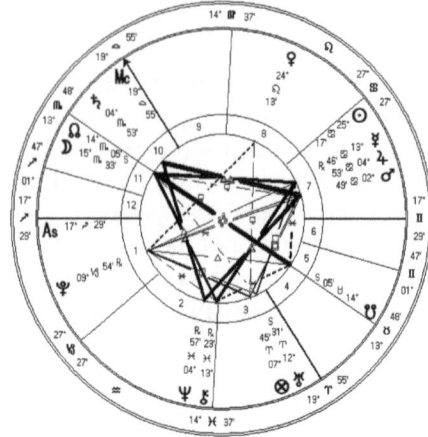

First Jupiter trine Saturn
17 Jul 2013 17:31:27 UT +0:00
London, UK 51°N30' 000°W10'
Geocentric Tropical Placidus True Node

the rest of the world, reactions to the transits seem to be more laid back. The International Monetary Fund and several governments are talking about economic recovery. When approached with constraint, the configuration offers well-being feeling our sacrifices had not been in vain, the cosmos is caring for us.

With Jupiter in Cancer, opposed to Pluto hints of danger are on the horizon. Is the system really fair to all? Should we accept and enjoy what we have? Will the current optimism last? Are we just avoiding, building up even-greater problems for the future? Are things really getting better – anywhere? The Middle East wastes the grand trine by using its passion as a weapon against opponents. The oil-rich Gulf States may be wasting their wealth by financing uprisings, alongside trophy projects, such as the football World Cup.

In one way or another are we squandering the real opportunity this water grand trine offers, by just reacting automatically, either with extremes of emotion or laid back over-optimism? The wise will see in this astro-event great potential power to change course and turn away from the globally destructive race to growth, and dominance of one group over another. Its deeper meaning urges us to turn back home to family contacts and community support, reduce our work and instead enhance our quality of life, to consume less and enjoy more.

In July 2014, Jupiter leaves Cancer and enters Leo, that December Saturn enters Sagittarius. How the world will be ruled then, is being decided now.

-o0o-

A note of desperation underlies the opening of the March 2014 column. With an intense cardinal grand cross building through April and the imminent centenary of the start of First World War, it invokes the warning of history. It contrasts the flippant descent into horror to Nelson Mandela's courageous wise way of cooperation. The lesson was to be largely forgotten by most of us for the rest of the decade and beyond.

Time to Forgive

> I don't think my father fought just for political freedom. My father also fought… to free yourself spiritually… he knew that if [he] didn't forgive he would be forever in prison spiritually… the lesson we can take away from his life is to have the courage to forgive other people… Because if we have the courage to forgive as human beings, there will be no wars… no crime… no violence… no conflict… Tata says none of us… are born hating another. We are taught to hate…if you can teach a human being to hate, you can also teach a human to love, to embrace, to forgive, and for me that's the greatest lesson. Makaziwe Mandela – Nelson Mandela's eldest surviving daughter, speaking to the BBC shortly after his passing.

> Father forgive them, they know not what they do.
> Jesus – last words on the cross

> Those who cannot remember the past are condemned to repeat it.   George Santayana

Early in the Christian Holy Week a lunar eclipse heralds the most intense days of the cardinal grand cross with that long anticipated fifth waxing square between Uranus and Pluto. Its intensity will build through Good Friday, the iconic day in the Christian Calendar symbolising the ultimate sacrifice, to climax on Easter Sunday and Monday. Much written and said by astrologers over recent years has explained the clear cause and solution to the many personal and social problems the grand cross and Uranus/Pluto symbolise. These will now be coming to a head. Problems that remain are caused by our failure to listen to each other, and realise they are solved when we do. When we stop pigeon-holing and condemning people as groups and instead listen to their story, we may understand and find it easier to forgive. If at that stage we still feel there is anything left to forgive! It is so easy to follow simplistic crowd views, stirred up by politicians and media, who seek to use prejudice to build a power base. It feels so good at first to be part of the outraged and righteous majority. Until, that is, the mass intolerance of our group is confronted by another mass holding with equal intolerance to a diametrically opposed prejudice! Celebratory joy sours as we sink into a consequential pit of self-created enmity all around.

The start of the First World War, whose centenary we will be marking this year, is a salutary illustration.[136]

War was declared on Germany on 4 August 1914. Three days later, the first troops from the British Expeditionary Force, under the command of Sir John French, landed on French soil. The government initially conveyed a 'business as usual' message to the British people. By sending a small expeditionary force to support France on the Continent and, by using naval muscle to exert an effective trade blockade against Germany, the war would be won by Christmas. [National Archives][137]

Four years later, after millions of lost lives and mourning families, the reality was horrifically different. Mercury opposed by the Moon and applying to conjunct Neptune explains the deluded optimism. Although this war is often characterised as a pointless struggle over a narrow band of muddy land in Northern France, the chart of the commencement indicates its traumatic consequences that still dominate world affairs a hundred years later. Through the coming months, Saturn was to conjunct Pluto three times in the early degrees of Cancer, while Jupiter and Uranus in Aquarius stirred revolt. The war changed the map of Europe and its countries' capacity to colonise the world. It led to other traumatic political and economic problems. Within societies, its aftermath was to transform family values, structures and relationships between the sexes.

-o0o-

We know now that the warning was to fall on deaf ears. In the extract (also from the March 2014 column) that follows, can be seen the first threads of specific feared negative attitudes. These were to degenerate and grow through the Scottish Independence referendum, the Brexit struggle and the US Presidential election of the following two years.

The astrology shows such changes were inevitable, whether or not there had been a war. Not for the first time, a low-level emotional reaction to an afflicted Neptune led leaders to the simplistic self-delusion that they could control and prevent change, rather than take the wise course of being willing midwives of global and personal transformation for the benefit of all. By taking the narrow, selfish, egocentric course, world leaders and the baying crowd that followed them condemned millions to death. Then, after that war, created even more problems that we continue to grapple with today.

What happens in its 2014 centenary year will show whether we have learned any lessons from this – not only in global affairs, but in the way we argue and judge domestic issues. Do we go with the crowd and assume everyone 'of that group' is responsible and guilty? When things go wrong, do officials own up and accept responsibility, or 'handle' and avoid by hiding behind their authority? Is our own personal motivation, in what we think, say and do, selfish or selfless? Do we accept responsibility or leave others to do our thinking for us?

Nelson Mandela gift of forgiveness
It has been noted that the passing of great souls enhances the global agenda by raising our consciousness above such narrow, self-destructive motives. Nelson Mandela's passing at the end of 2013 offered the gift of forgiveness, which has a key role to play

in resolving just about every problem we face, however great or small. To know the effectiveness of what we have said or done to others in our personal lives, or a negotiation, policy, judgment and punishment in public affairs, we have to listen and be sure we really know. For when we do listen often 'to know all is to forgive all'. When we step back and act without making the effort to understand, we condemn our future. We create the constant threat of First World War-like experiences in every aspect of our lives.

We entered 2014 with mixed messages. Christmas and the first days of the New Year were blessed with stories of economic recovery. Yet also, it seems more austerity lies ahead. The poor are living in increasingly crowded accommodation, or evicted into bed and breakfast accommodation. Bearing down on immigration is seen as a 'cure for all our ills'. The Middle East is descending into ever greater chaotic suffering. With the retrogression of many of the planets involved being so much a part of the final formation of the grand cross, issues avoided and not addressed could well return to haunt us. Avoid this, by seeing the future as a wonderful opportunity to ease through disaster to master challenges and grow. Start with your own life. Forgiveness is the way.

-o0o-

The May 2014 column continued to warn of the worst, and encourage the best, ways to resolve issues. How could we avoid unheeded 'love' intensifying into mere subgroup loyalty – its universal true nature lost in growing acrimony?

Learning to Love

Love, all alike, no season knows, nor clime, nor hours,
days, months, which are the rags of time.
The Sun Rising John Donne

The course of true love never did run smooth;
A Midsummer Night's Dream William Shakespeare

At the very heart of everything that exists is an irresistible urge to feel at one, to experience holding together in a harmony of understanding, even if we have to exclude other people to do so! However one-sided or fragmentary a conclusion our particular view of 'ultimate universal reality' brings us to, the need for the comfort of being sure motivates our quest. Fundamentalists forcefully fill the gap by proselytising. If they are believers, they insist we share their belief, if non-believers they insist we believe in non-belief!

Yet real harmony, the experience of everything being gloriously right in our world, is not to be explained, argued or fought for. It is far too deep for that. We know real harmony when we see and accept the true nature and place of everything around us. When we have let go of all struggle, have moved beyond need, and are truly open to anything that will happen, then we are ready to experience genuine love. Recognising and reflecting each other, lovers find heightened peace, togetherness and exhilaration, becoming as one in a sumptuous time of intimacy. Such ecstatic oneness also can be known by groups with common emotional, cultural, intellectual and spiritual understanding.

Beware of mistaking such amazing times in our lives as permanent, exclusive and dependent upon particular people or circumstances. Intrinsically, these experiences come, because we have let go enough to open a window to the truth underlying all things. We have become sufficiently aware to touch the essential ultimate harmony of the Universe that allows all to be as it has been, is and always will be.

Both before and after such intimate recognition comes great danger! At the calm point at the eye of storm there are clear quiet moments, but, at the eye's immediate periphery, the wind blows strongest and most dangerously. Similarly, in close personal relationships and strong group consensus, there will be moments of intense anticipation, even fear. Do we dare make that last vulnerable move across the hiatus of uncertainty that divides us from the other? Dare I look, say, touch, kiss, or hold? Will I be welcome, understood, liked, exploited, robbed, hated, or even killed? Then, if reassured and all being righter and more wonderful than we dared to hope, how long will it last? How to protect what we have? Shall we fight to recover the joy?

Around love and group devotion swell great storms of potential disaster. Confidence in the future fails, we can be tossed and torn apart, love turns to hate, loyalty to betrayal, wondrous contact with existential truth to disaster.

The suffering of separation

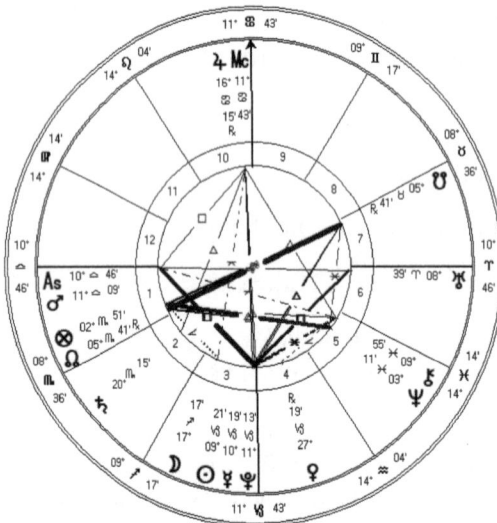

Syria Solar Return
30 Dec 2013 23:47:47 EET -2:00
Damascus, Syria 33°N30' 036°E18'
Geocentric Tropical Placidus True Node

From 1 March, Mars retrogrades through Libra, where it is in detriment. This symbolises ongoing disruption by completing a grand cross with Uranus in Aries, Pluto in Capricorn and Jupiter in Cancer. With Venus in vulnerable Pisces quincunx Mars through a turbulent April, stressful hurt feelings, resentment at being 'sacrificed' and fear of giving too much will have stirred up bad feelings. As well as resentment and frustration interrupting our own lives, this has been all too clear in dealings between groups and nations.

As I write, towards the end of February 2014, religious-driven atrocities in Africa increase and homosexuality is being criminalised. With the football World Cup approaching, the social fabric of Brazil is on the edge. The impetus of separatism grows in Ukraine, Spain and in the United Kingdom, the Scottish referendum comes close.

In the Middle East suffering has worsened to intolerable levels. The 2013-14 Syrian Solar Return chart, based on the date of its independence from the French, shows the entire breakdown of that country's physical and social foundation in graphic detail.[138] The grand cross on the angles, with Pluto in Capricorn almost exactly conjunct the IC and Mars/Uranus across the Ascendant/Descendant axis, has

Jupiter in Cancer near the MC, 'crying out in sorrow' at all the destruction around. This is an extreme example of what happens when groups force their view of 'harmony' upon others, and so attracts to itself other social groups with intensely different views of its 'true nature'. The Alawite fight to the last attracts suicidal attacks from extreme Islamists visioning their own idyllic heaven. Masses, caught between, are left to suffer and die.

In *The Value of Astrology* André Barbault shows the relationship between Sun/Jupiter conjunctions and peace negotiations.[139] The next conjunction on 24 July 2014 is in Leo. When they were together there in August 1955, outrage at the brutal lynching of Emmett Till in Mississippi led to the foundation of the American Civil Rights Movement. In August 1967, their conjunction in this sign saw the beginning of the nuclear arms non-proliferation negotiations. In August 1979 the Begin-Sadat accord between Israel and Egypt was agreed, leading to the first meeting between Israeli authorities and Palestinian representatives. August 1991 saw the coup against Gorbachev and the breakdown of communism. By August 2003 the US/UK administration of Iraq had been at least legitimised. The fire of Leo comes with brutality in the pursuit of peace. Something big has to happen to jolt minds from narrow sub-groups to open eyes to the larger underlying harmony, uniting us all in peace and happiness. So may it be in Syria!

Israel and Palestine

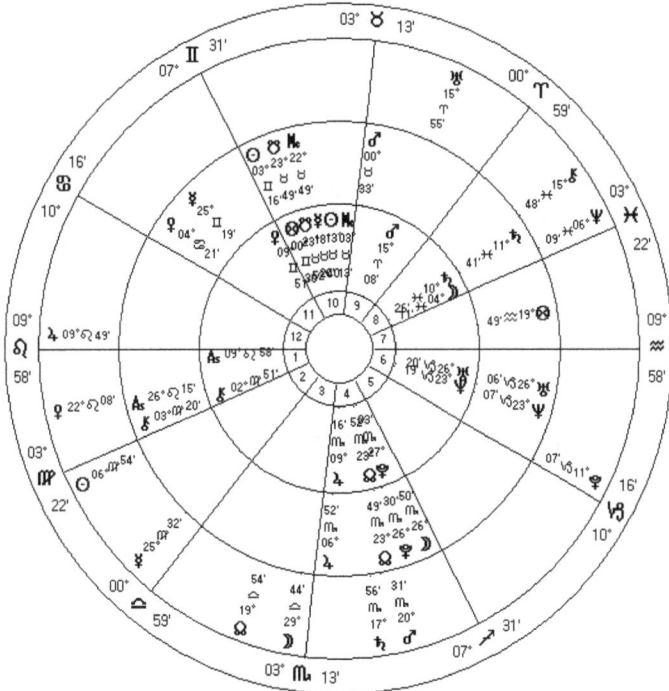

Inner wheel: Palestine Autonomy: 4 May 1994 08:55 UT +0:00
Middle wheel: Palestine Autonomy progressed: 30 Aug 2014 11:23:26 EEDT -3:00
Outer wheel: Transits: 30 Aug 2014 11:23:26 EEDT -3:00
All charts: Jerusalem, Israel 31°N46' 035°E14'
Geocentric Placidus True Node

January's 'Working with the Planets' used the Israel solar return chart to show the extremely difficult challenges that country would be facing in the spring of 2014, if it did not negotiate and accept change.[140] From the Palestinian perspective, after the late July 2014 transiting Sun/Jupiter conjunction, Jupiter goes on to square the Palestinian progressed Mars in early Taurus, and then squares natal Jupiter and conjuncts the natal Ascendant! on 30 August. Transiting Neptune in Pisces, building to conjunct the natal Moon/Saturn in the eighth house, will cast a cloud of spiritual and emotional confusion on any attempt to understand. Matters could deteriorate into mindless sacrifice, if progress is not made by then.

Finding harmony with others

Joining together in sub-groups with common interests or causes is not wrong. It only becomes so, when intolerant attachment to one side leads to the other being seen as the evil destroyer of our happiness. The test of this vital distinction comes when Venus enters Aries on 3 May and moves on to oppose Mars in Libra on 11 May. Now both planets will be in detriment.

There is magic in this combination. While both are inappropriately placed, because they rule each other's signs, they are in mutual reception. So, although Venus in Aries can be overwhelmed by impulsive ill-considered attachments, it can look across to Libra for ways of accommodating these for the greater good. While Mars in Libra may struggle to do the right thing in the midst of ill-tempered misunderstanding, it can avoid the consequences, by looking across to its sign of Aries. Then see how to move on and defend the space from where the love of Venus can save the day. Instead of the worst of both worlds, you can get the best.

Mercury's retrograde keeps it in Gemini (the sign it rules) for nearly all the period. So, opportunities for communication and reconsideration will be ongoing. Time to talk, to discover hidden truths and new understandings, to broaden the experience of harmony. Increasingly let go, see calm decency in everything. It will make us feel safe. With the Sun not conjunct Jupiter until 24 July, when both are in early Leo and approaching a square to Saturn, how we come together in May and June will mark the love we will share now and way into the future.

Great love is needed to resolve great conflicts. There is no other way. We need to cross the divide, even one marked by an iron barrier. See beyond ourselves, relax into empathy; let the sorrow out. Open windows to that harmonic oneness, which holds everything in the Universe together.

Do not squander this time for healing – learn to love.

-o0o-

A sense of hysteria underlies the opening of the September 2014 column. Struggling with the consequences of five Uranus in Aries / Pluto in Capricorn squares, and two still to come, the column draws on a wide sweep of history in a third attempt to encourage co-operation between people and peoples.

Bringing the World Back Together

> Things fall apart; the centre cannot hold;
> Mere anarchy is loosed upon the world,
> The blood-dimmed tide is loosed, and everywhere
> The ceremony of innocence is drowned;
> The best lack all conviction, while the worst
> Are full of passionate intensity.
> *The Second Coming* (1919) William Butler Yeats

In late April 2014, as the long-awaited cardinal grand-cross with Uranus squared Pluto was at its most exact, many horrible changes were about to happen, some unseen, just below the horizon. However, as events go, an outsider, with little understanding of how mundane astrology works, could have said things were no worse then than they had been in the preceding months and years. What had astrologers been fussing about?

How wrong the outsider would have been! Strong aspect patterns represent the background pressure for change, the desperate hopes, stocked up resentments, unreal beliefs, over-confidence – all pent up ready for expression. The moment of exactness is like a spring wound up tight. As it unwinds, events are triggered by lesser transits. Maybe a Full Moon, a retrograde, a square of Mars at a sensitive degree, or a combination of several events will activate the release of several traumatic happenings – maybe a death that leads to slaughter, an invasion, a word touches a chord that ignites a revolution. Anyone or combination of these will not be enough on their own. There always has to be major background intensity for something special to be triggered.

This explains the world since April this year. The promises of compromise in Ukraine went the other way. Atrocities in Pakistan worsened, Islamists overran Iraq; terrorised African communities always in fear for their lives. The politics of division have dominated the internal relationships of Britain, the USA and Europe. As I write this, the Sun is in Gemini, and every day brings more news of brutal words 'justifying' horrible deeds. The momentum of the unwinding of the spring of discontent continues to fire the blood.

What astrological explanation is there for our world and its people falling ever-further apart?

Crisis of belief and understanding – the Neptune/Pluto cycle
Seven remarkably disruptive Uranus/Pluto squares (with two still to go in the current series) is rare, but it is the Neptune/Pluto cycle that describes the atmosphere of impotent confusion, underlying the squares, that puts the dissolution of our times into a larger historical perspective.

This cycle, which takes between 493 and 496 years, represents seeding, grappling with, containing, confronting and finally settling into radically new orders of belief and understanding. The most recent conjunction in 1891-92 sowed the idea of modern science as a belief system for a better world, social movements to establish individual rights, responsibilities and ownership of resource.[141] At this early stage in the cycle, attempts to 'unify' world religions and establish universal co-operation have met with mixed success, against the resistance of established theocracies and materialistic self-interest. Fearful reaction to undisciplined rapid change leads many to prefer, even to fight for, a return to the past. Hence, the rise of fundamentalism.

From 1950 until 2032, the two planets remain in a long sextile to each other. Easy possibilities and impossibilities dream, excite, and then fade in and out of our consciousness – past beliefs, new beliefs, belief in no beliefs, confusion, and pointless sacrifice. In the absence of a commonly agreed purpose is there any purpose at all?

The conjunction in 905 CE came six years after the death of Alfred the Great and in the midst of pagan/Christian struggles in Britain and Northern Europe. The waxing square 1075-79 was soon after the establishment of Norman power and Viking acceptance of Christianity in 1066, and the completion of the Domesday Book, twenty years later. The conjunction of 1398 was just a year before the illegitimate deposing of Britain's Richard II by Henry IV. This led to war between France and England, the civil Wars of the Roses and religious conflict, until the waxing square (1568-75), when Elizabeth I was securely established after having ascended to the throne in 1558.

For us today, the waxing square of integrating order is fifty years away in 2061-65. Even then, the order it brings will not be welcome to all. In the meantime, behaviour is becoming ever more counter-productive all over the world – the opposite of coming together. Texan shoppers insist on their right to bear arms allowing them to shop and attend restaurants with automatic rifles on their shoulders. Suicide missions are the way to heaven for brave young men. Rape is the right and way to power for victors in wars. As more and more problems emerge, we seek regulations, other defensive structures and arms to protect ourselves against supposed 'enemies at our gates'.

So, bringing the world and our personal lives back together again may seem unrealistically idealistic, while the Uranus/Pluto square transit unwinds, amidst the ever-growing confusion of belief that is dominating the waxing phase of the Pluto/Neptune cycle. As you read this with the Sun in Virgo, anxiety could well have grown into ever-continuing battles fuelled by obsessive anxiety. Is there nothing we can do to reconcile those conflicting mindsets and the brutal realities they manifest? Is an uneasy truce on the way to a search for peace possible?

Working together in a dissolving world

There is a way of seeing beyond all this and making a breakthrough. Being in Capricorn, Pluto occupies the sign that rules control and structure. So this planet of death and transformation threatens the end of everything we value, unless we find a sufficiently all-encompassing structure to sustain a positive way forward. A house will soon collapse if only a part of the building has structural support. A business will be unproductive if only selected departments are properly organised. However diverse the materials and the people involved, all have to be appreciated and supported appropriately, their intrinsic nature recognised. By combining contra-pressures, diversity does not fight and destroy, but uses stress techniques to strengthen the whole – however bad the weather or the social/business climate we are operating in.

So, in our affairs, extreme views and horrible threats grow when we refuse to listen to and fail to understand what we consider to be alien in our personal, national and international lives. Rejections and refusal create space for alienated, extreme groups to seem credible and so to grow exponentially. With no middle way left to choose, reasonable people are left to decide between two diametrically opposed positions. Polarisation intensifies, conflicts lead to atrocities on all sides. Lacking an inclusive overall structure, the organisational force of Pluto in Capricorn is focused into separate warring sub-groups. So, we face traumatic upheaval, a world tearing itself apart; negative Pluto rampant.

The detailed analysis below reveals an important focus of astro-events around the Autumn Equinox this year. After an anxious first three weeks, a New Moon in Libra, a day after the Equinox, does offer a new beginning. For Britain, this will be just five to six days after the Scottish Independence vote, considered in detail in the last issue.[142] Whatever the result, the way things are afterwards could be an example to the world of how to bury differences and make a new beginning – maybe a chance to resolve similar difficulties in our personal lives too. The stakes could not be much higher.

-o0o-

Chapter 7
2015-20 - Confronting Reality
[Articles written November 2014 – September 2020]

Contemporary Background

Underlying the whole period was the destabilisation of the Middle East (due to the Iraq War and Arab Spring rebellions), consequent regional chaos, and worldwide terrorist attacks. A refugee crisis, European separatism, and continuing financial insecurity caused rejection of conventional politics. Popular nationalism grew, especially in Europe and the USA. Powerful campaigns in favour of climate control emerged. The US's world role weakened. Russian military presence and the Chinese economy continued to grow.

Through 2015	1.3 million refugees enter Europe by land and sea
7 May 2015	Conservatives win UK General Election
16 June 2015	Donald Trump announces his candidacy for US President
14 July 2015	Iran Nuclear Deal agreed
30 September 2015	Russia intervenes in Syrian Civil War
13 November 2015	ISIL terrorist attack in Paris
23 June 2016	UK votes to leave EU
4 November 2016	Paris Climate Accord comes into force.
20 January 2017	Donald Trump's 'America First' Inauguration Speech
29 March 2017	UK triggers Article 50 to leave the EU
8 June 2017	UK General Election – Conservatives lose majority
14 June 2017	Grenfell Tower Fire in London
10 July 2017	Mosul fully liberated from ISIL – begins end of ISIL power
15 October 2017	#MeToo Movement's impact grows
6 December 2017	US officially recognises Jerusalem as Israel's capital
8 May 2018	US withdraws from Iran Nuclear Deal
August 2018	Greta Thunberg rises to prominence
2 October 2018	Jamal Khashoggi murdered
7 October 2018	Extinction Rebellion's action in Westminster
23 May 2019	BJP election victory encourages Indian Nationalism
16 June 2019	Start of massive protests in Hong Kong
18 December 2019	Donald Trump impeached
From January 2020	Covid-19 increasingly spreads through the whole world.
20 February 2020	Stock market collapse, due to Covid-19 restrictions
18 March 2020	Crude oil price falls below $26 a barrel
31 May 2020	George Floyd killed by police – initiates BLM movement
3 November 2020	Joe Biden wins US Presidential Election.

Introduction

It is sadly fascinating to look back from the start of 2021 to 2014, when the brutality of the Uranus-in-Aries squares to Pluto in Capricorn was climaxing. All the terrible things said, done, and to be done created the cause for the subsequent destructive bitterness. Short-term ignorance was to turn the last years of the 2010s into an intensifying horror story.

Stuck with interpreting the transits and seeking to warn, the columns of these years take on an increasingly didactic tone, as one opportunity after another to open our hearts to understanding solutions, soured into blame games. The world was to listen to and follow the worst advice. The mainstream was to glory in the victimisation and rejection of the very people and actions that offered compassionate solutions. Tragically, this was just when such care was needed to re-structure the planet in the orderly, business-like fashion, demanded by the positive application of Pluto in Capricorn.

-o0o-

The next few pages from the November 2014 column seek to invoke a deep understanding of the lessons to be learned from ancient Athenian drama.

Catharsis
Going through it to put it right!

'Nothing forces us to know
What we do not want to know
Except pain.'
'ATHENA: You wish to be called righteous rather than act right. (...)
I say, wrong must not win by technicalities.'

Aeschylus, *The Oresteia*

In the fifth century BCE, Greek drama was performed before vast crowds looking down on the actors from the terraces of massive amphitheatres. The plays were strictly divided into two categories: tragedy and comedy, both playing a key function in an annual religious festival to cleanse participants by confronting players and spectators alike with the realities of existence.

In the tragedies, authors re-worked centuries-old epic stories. Actors were witnessed wrestling with their fate in the face of forces and consequences seemingly beyond their ability to control. However hard they struggled to be free, the Gods would appear to ensure they endured the consequences of their past actions. Throughout the spectacle a chorus danced and chanted, commentating and bemoaning the reasons for the horrific nature of it all to the audience. Agamemnon returns from the Trojan Wars to be assassinated by his adulterous wife, which her son Orestes avenges with disastrous consequences for the kingdom. Oedipus unwittingly kills his father and marries his mother. On learning the truth, he tears out his own eyes, to end his days a blind man wandering the desert.

From this, some say that the Ancient Greeks believed in fate and superstitiously accepted humanity was at the mercy of an imaginary pantheon of gods living on Mount Olympus. It goes much deeper than this. The Gods were humanised manifestations of the workings of the Universe to demonstrate that all actions have consequences. Free will to choose exists, but making the wrong choice leads to even more difficult future choices. We suffer the worst when we do not sustain our morality, fail to see clearly, and then act on our desires and gut feelings. We avoid the worst, and have far better experiences, when we honour the moral way. Catharsis is the fundamental benefit of Greek Tragedy. Spectators witnessing and so experiencing the tragic suffering of others recognise, regret and cleanse actions in their own lives. Seeing the consequences of others' delusions and attachments, we clear the decks to have the objectivity to really answer problems.

Today's theatre of public opinion
The 24/7 worldwide TV news media is our modern electronic amphitheatre. Today events in the real world are our dramas. Their reporters, commentators, and 'experts' act like a Greek chorus demonstrating, explaining, interpreting and bemoaning the narrative of world conflicts, social joys and tragedies, and violence interplaying with kindness between individuals.

Unfortunately, today's 'theatre' encompasses many culturally assumed contradictory 'truths', which are selectively applied and interpreted, depending upon the self-interest of the interpreter. One person's invasion is another's liberation; a terrorist can be seen as a freedom-fighter. Should media experts control or advise on our diets and drug/alcohol use? How far should they decide on the educational and lifestyle choices we make for our children? Are laws applied equally to all? Unlike in Athens, news dramas turn around not a commonly accepted *deus ex machina* truth, but individual and group choices as to where we *should* stand and who we decide to stand with.

This maelstrom of conflicting emotions and prejudices causes cathartic chaos. The deep empathy we feel for the predicament of a single child in one culture becomes more important than thousands in another. Death and destruction of whole communities can be less important than mild fear and inconvenience suffered by others. Profit and expansion can override people and places. The freedom to win caps the consequences of losing. Where values are erratically applied, outrage at injustice is not far behind. Horrified at what has happened, we take action to group together and protect ourselves rather than having the cathartic courage to see the cause within ourselves. Media channels shout distorted partial opinions across each other. Problems grow, as the theatre of world public opinion builds with ever-greater sense of unfairness and resentment. Nothing is cleansed; much is made worse.

Astro-cycles: clarifying arbiters of truth
Ancient Greeks and their contemporaries studied and used astrology to understand the ways of the gods, who represented the realities of the cycles of the heavens. Because astrology is culture-free, it is beneficial to use it today. By knowing the horoscopes of others, we cleanse away our negative gut reactions toward them. By understanding the transits of the past, present and future, we put the part we played then, in perspective. When we fail to do this, matters get worse and worse; more and more blind people thresh around in endless deserts.

Applying André Barbault's study of the relationship between Venus/Jupiter conjunctions and armistice/ceasefire negotiations to the Israel/Palestinian conflict illustrates this clearly. The two planets were exact at 7Le14 on 18 August 2014. An uneasy Gaza ceasefire held for a day or so, and then an open-ended one was agreed on 26 August. Regular readers will know the importance of the Jupiter/Neptune conjunction at 8Le45-8 in the 1920 Middle East Mandate chart, which set in motion the structure and contemporary problems in that part of the world.[143] As an uneasy peace was settling in Gaza, attention turned to advances and atrocities by ISIL in Iraq and Syria; the conjunction was squared to Mars applying to conjunct Saturn in Scorpio! What hope for peace in the face of such brutality? What have we done to deserve such actions, some of its performers brought up in the British educational system?

Keep in mind that Venus (the planet of love, but also attachment) is conjunct Jupiter (the planet of expansion and opportunity, but also out of control excessiveness) in Leo (the sign of generosity and fun, but also uncompromising dominance). August 2003 was their previous conjunction in that sign, a few months after George Bush deludedly claimed victory in Iraq. So, the possibility of loving expansive generosity tragically morphs to the opposite – excessive domineering self-obsession.

In the natural flow of our personal and social lives come great moments of karmic opportunity, when conditions are right for courageous insight to change the course of history, providing we are ready to let go of easy knee jerk reactions. The months immediately after the 9/11 attack was such an opportunity to put right mistakes made in the Middle East by European powers since the Crusades and (with the USA) throughout the twentieth century. Tragically it was missed. Trillions of dollars were spent unnecessarily and hundreds of thousands of lives lost. With Jupiter transiting its natal seventh house[144] after the 9/11 attack, the United States had the sympathy of all world cultures, except a small manic minority. Sadly, the US failed to marshal this sympathy for peace by correcting and cleansing past errors. Instead, within eighteen months, it alienated all neutrals and many friends, when, especially with the help of the UK, it embarked upon arrogant cowboy actions. This was to strengthen the terrorist threat within and between world cultures.

A new great opportunity
A proper understanding and use of the transits around the 18 August 2014 Jupiter/Leo conjunction suggests another such great opportunity, when common interests could bring opponents together and to build alliances across previously assumed divides. For this to become sustainable, many people and groups need to accept responsibility and show regret for planting the roots of the horrific problems they now face. If only Agamemnon had not preferred war to the life of his daughter. If only Cassandra had loved Apollo in return for his gift of prophecy! If only Oedipus' father had answered the prophet's warning by giving his infant son great love and care, rather than ordering his death and consequent abandonment! Narrow self-interest obscures clear decision making.

If only, the victorious powers had listened to T E Lawrence and Arab voices after First World War and not created those artificial kingdoms! If only the United States had monitored the 1948 establishment of the State of Israel and its development after in a more even-handed manner!

Astro-cycles offer us the objectivity to see and act fairly, beyond narrow self-interest. The struggles surrounding the Jewish state in the Middle East date from the beginnings of recorded history. Its astrology is illuminating. The chart for the destruction of Jewish Temple in 70 CE is especially relevant to our time.[145] It reveals a poignant tragedy, with negative consequences that would be kept alive for millennia by generations to this day. At Noon on the day of the destruction, Pluto was at 12Aq38. The day the State of Israel was established in 1948 Pluto was at 12Le38.[146] At the penultimate Uranus/Pluto square on 15 December 2014, Uranus is at 12Ar53. On 7 April 2015, Jupiter (whose transit through Leo since July 2014 has so stirred the pot of aggression in Europe and the Middle East) completes its retrograde phase, by making a direct station at 12Le35. Demanding order or control, Saturn enters Sagittarius on 23 December. Through the last two months of 2014, it is crucial to take advantage of windows of opportunity to put personal and international relationships in order. The alternative is to be confronted by the full face of aggressively fiery Aries/Leo /Sagittarius working together through 2015, to take the action to some pretty difficult places.

Learning from the show

At the end of the last play in the *Oresteia* trilogy, Athena persuades the Erinyes (the Furies pursuing Orestes for killing his mother) to relent. The play concludes with the end of his haunting being celebrated in a cleansed society. While we cannot change the past, by recognising and regretting the causal part we played in it, we can heal the future. Even when not directly involved, by witnessing the terrifying drama of the Middle East on the 24/7 World News amphitheatre, seeing the tragedy unfold, anticipating and then enduring the consequences, we can avoid making similar bad decisions in our own lives.

Learning by example, we accept that we create the cause of our own suffering, by what we do, or by allowing our confused, short-term prejudices to take us to places and people that corrupt and endanger us. Going through the catharsis of accepting this is the only way to be clear, and so have what we really want. By applying astrological objectivity to all we face, whether in the news or not, we can start the journey towards peace in our hearts and so in our world.

-o0o-

As the Uranus/Pluto squares built to a climax in early March that year, the January 2015 column reminded readers that the consequences of everything said and done to each other would not be over on the completion, but stay for long after. Feeling robbed, the unwise will remain trapped in past expectations and recriminations, straining at the leash to 'get' that person or culture who is 'to blame'.

The crucial need is to understand and master the proper use of Mars – the wise way to steer a path through the debris of consequences we will all be facing.

Mastering Mars

Victory attained by violence is tantamount to a defeat, for it is momentary.   Mahatma Gandhi *Satyagraha Leaflet No. 19*

The only thing that's been a worse flop than the organisation of non-violence has been the organisation of violence.
Joan Baez *Daybreak*

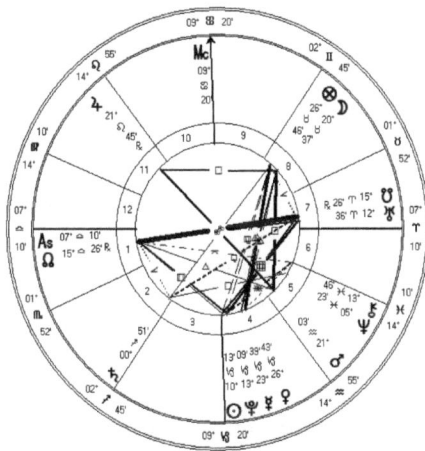

New Year 2015
1 Jan 2015 00:00 UT +0:00
London, UK 51°N30' 000°W10'
Geocentric Tropical Placidus True Node

This year's explosions may be much more real and their consequences longer lasting than the usual short-lived New Year firework extravaganzas. For, on the evening of the year's first day, Mars in Aquarius makes the initial non-lunar aspect of the year, when it opposes Jupiter in Leo (ego-driven rebellion). Over the coming five days, the Sun in Capricorn squares Uranus in Aries, and then conjuncts Pluto (uncompromising efforts to force through ill-thought out changes). Venus and then Mercury enter Aquarius in the build-up to a Full Moon the early hours of 5 January. Humanitarian idealism will fuel revolutionary new ideas, but insisting people act 'in their best interests' could lead to struggles, from which no one benefits.

Gasping with surprise, we will be left to pick up the pieces through the waning Moon days that follow. The wise will take this column's advice from the end of last year[147] and hold back; use the Capricorn New Moon of the 21 December 2014 Winter Solstice and ongoing stellium to organise and build resources. This will avoid dissipating energy and becoming victims of the ego-driven emotional excitement and will save us for grander issues that lie ahead.

Facing the consequences – the last weeks of the Uranus / Pluto square
The first two months of 2015 end just seventeen days before the completion of the period that had seen seven-Uranus/Pluto-squares, and started on 24 June 2012. Its

effect is far from over; the consequential fall out of the period's dramatic changes will be with us for a considerable time ahead.

On 1 May 2003, George W Bush stood in front of his troops on the deck of the *USS Abraham Lincoln*, in front of a large banner that naively declared his nation's 'Mission accomplished' in the Iraq War. He was speaking two days before the completion of the Jupiter in Leo / Neptune in Aquarius opposition that so clearly described the nature of his delusory 'mission'. Hundreds of thousands were yet (and continue) to die and millions to be displaced in the years that followed.

The aftermath of the Uranus/Pluto square series could be even more traumatic and far-reaching than that. The uncompromising determination of Capricorn with the impulsive immaturity of Aries is proving a lethal mix. It seems easier to undermine, even destroy, what is wrong than put anything better in its place. We can see this in conflicts and social unrest all over the world. Economically as well as politically, even medically, we point to scapegoats rather than take personal responsibility and accept hard choices. Whether in international affairs, domestic politics, or even our personal lives; we prefer to bomb enemies, either figuratively or literally, rather than seek to understand and address the root causes of our problems with them.

With its co-ruler Jupiter in Leo, Neptune in Pisces is expressing itself at the extremities: the most admirable are happy to risk all to care for the sick and hungry; the most degenerate offer and welcome mass death to achieve their ends. Could it be that the present outer-planetary mix of Pluto in determined Capricorn, Neptune in self-sacrificing Pisces, Uranus in immature Aries, Saturn obstructionist in Sagittarius and Jupiter self-importantly in Leo is putting our world and its people in the mindset of an alcoholic or drug addict? Constantly 'needing a fix', we see anything in our way as the pain-causing enemy that denies us the needed immediate satisfaction. Seeing this way, not recognising the limitations of such short-term addiction-driven life patterns, we are unable to learn from circumstances and come to proper long term solutions.

Spiralling further and further down, the stakes get higher, as the gap in understanding between us and the other widens. The worlds of having and not having the addictive agent (be it a substance, riches, or an emotional sense of righteousness) seem impossibly distant from each other. Grasping at easy solutions, desperately hoping we do not need to question or change ourselves, needing quick answers, we blame groups of people we do not know or understand, demanding they be punished, eradicated without delay. In the first months of 2015 the stellium helping to drive all this will move on; stirring rebellion through Aquarius, suffering through Pisces, and demanding the impossible as it reaches Aries.

Like that drug addict, it seems the world needs to hit rock bottom, before it is ready to decide between suicide and recovery. Only then will it be ready to change its ways. Maybe then from the most unlikely source it will accept and start on the right road. This happens, when we ask...

How much more of this can we take?

Take a desperately deep breath, ask this question and see change come like a flash of lightning on an oppressively humid summer's day. With clear recognition, the dark despair of past delusions will fall behind us and fade away. We do this when we are beyond relying on anything to dull the pain and are ready to take personal responsibility. Letting go of past baggage, we see with fresh eyes the clear way ahead is what we wanted all time; compromising with second best could never solve anything!

Letting go of fear and false assumptions of need will not be easy, but Neptune in Pisces can enable empathy and sacrifice; the acceptance of suffering for the common good. Also, Pisces' joint-ruler Jupiter can symbolise proud, generous creativity. Together at their best they offer unbelievably beneficial grand gestures capable of resolving major problems, providing our solutions leave no stone unturned to include everyone. For even our greatest enemies do not act without cause, however deluded we may think they are.

It will mean letting down barriers, accepting we may be the cause of our problems, accommodating differences, making friends of enemies. Turning away from resentment, Pisces can find this possible, even attractive.

Young people: society's 'litmus paper'

Let us start the search for solutions by asking why young people, born when Pluto was in Sagittarius, have adopted the negative and destructive manifestations of the planet and sign; being interested in vampire, zombie and generally violent films and video games, prone to piercing and self-harming; in some sub-cultures even turning the game into reality by finding idealistic reasons to fight and die for a cause?

It is the nature of every adolescent generation to be unrealistically idealistic, to seek simplistic answers that will eradicate and correct what they see to be wrong in their parents' world. The teenagers of the 1960s focused on universal love, in the 1970s punks rejected the status quo, in the 1980s yuppies restored materialism. The 1990s and 2000 generations worshipped the apparently limitless power of technology and scientific expertise. Could it be that the 2010s younger generation's focus of death and destruction in their culture is a symptom of the kind of world their older generations expect them to live in? To prepare for our frantic economically competitive world, their education is amorally short of values, and mainly narrow, mechanical and functional. On completion, they face a large personal debt burden, an increasingly large ageing population to support though their working life and financial barriers to acquiring their own material assets. The values of their own and foreign societies seem to be based on aimless consumption for the 'economic good', self-interest supported by brute power, and the all-importance of corporate profit ahead of a humane quality of life.

Faced with such a future in such a culture, the 'promise' of the uncompromising purity of fundamentalist Islam, aiming to sweep away all that 'is corrupt', may appear to be the best use some young Muslims can make of their lives. Such views need to be countered with higher aspirations. The naive following of death cults can only be mastered by channelling Mars into aspirations to act for the greater good – to serve all, not a selected group. To impress such values on an idealistic youth, there must be no backsliding from the purity of all our actions. Our hypocrisy and double standards have bought us to this. Only a grand strategy that offers youth ways of lifting the aspirations of our society to purity and tolerance is likely to lift all of us out of the suicidal morass our self-indulgence has brought us to.

Can we give up the expressions of self-destructive deceit that dominate our world? We owe it to our children to channel our actions wisely for the common good; teach them how to master Mars for the benefit of all.

For Mars is mindless. Its raw nature is to agitate, stir and force. The outcome of its action depends upon how it is channelled by the other planets, especially Saturn and Jupiter. With Mars joining Uranus in Aries, as the completion of the Uranus/Pluto square builds toward March 2015, making all four planets in a fire grand trine, the imposition of change in some way or other is unavoidable. Will it come through isolating and blaming, from ever-intensifying acts of destruction by warring parties? The alternative is to look inward, let Mars pull apart those self-defence mechanisms, which prevent us seeing and correcting opinions, policies and consequent actions that are our role in causing the crisis.

Mars in the months ahead means change. We fail to master it at our peril.

-o0o-

Recovering from a messy, mean-minded UK General Election, the July 2015 column drew on Richard Bach's book *Jonathan Livingston Seagull* to raise minds high above the fray to the clear objective perspective that astrology can give us.

Seeing Clearly

'Sing
As a song in search of a voice that is silent'
Neil Diamond album from the film of
Richard Bach's *Jonathan Livingstone Seagull*

Richard Bach depicts Jonathan Livingstone as an exceptional seagull, who rises above the flock's petty squawking and scrabbling over scraps of food, eyes ever focused downward, ready to swoop to grab, tear and selfishly take away as much as possible. Instead, by soaring upward ('seagulls spread your wings') and looking back from on high, Jonathan sees the whole world and the limited futility of his fellow seagulls' lives within it. I write as the UK is coming out of a time, packed with empty General Election utterances and conventional political debate, based on narrow-minded unkindness. So, the notion of 'a song in search of a voice that is silent' is a profound paradox to be prized. For the truth and the solution lies in rising above the fray, seeing the complete picture and acting without fear or favour.

The selfless use of astrology enables a similar heightened understanding of human behaviour that can be a saddening, as well as a blessed, experience. The charts, their progressions and transits reveal the pressures lying behind contemporary stresses and strains. Comparing people's reactions and knowing the cycles to come, astrologers anticipate outcomes. Far too often we see and act in our world as Jonathan Livingstone's fellow seagulls do in theirs. Most people are too close to their perceived immediate needs, and too often let down by idealistic alternatives, to focus on more than day-to-day survival. Most of us become prey to those who play on our fears and desires – to have that tasty scrap of 'bread', or fatty ham rind, before it is snatched away by someone swooping in.

Low-level motivation to grab what we can is the disappointing road to disaster. With still more than a year to go before the half way stage of the Pluto-in-Capricorn period, far more testing confrontations with reality are to come. Human beings can be more than seagulls. They can make friends, support each other and turn impossibility into possibility. When instead we seek to triumph and glory in that triumph, we put off supporters, who then fade away; except perhaps those committed to fighting and dying with us.

Creating happiness in confusing times
The fear of not having, the false pride of having too much, possession or power over others, both lead to constant disappointment and unending uncertainty. Hence

decisions and strategies based on such criteria create constantly unstable lives. Conversely, when we learn to cope and help others to cope, we create societies where more and more people are pleased. We can relax back into a comfortable quality of life, worrying less about what we do not have or need to do. When not competing over who has most, or should have more, we can focus on what gives greatest happiness. Worthy politicians of any colour, on the left or right, will understand this and make it the priority of their policies. Paradoxically, happy societies are far more efficient than those based on institutionalised money grabbing. The pursuit of happiness is the efficient answer to the challenges of our Pluto in Capricorn times.

The detailed summaries below show the next two months will not be easy and the next two years could be fraught with dangerous misunderstandings. Consider carefully the comments on the next long-standing outer-planetary configuration – the mutable T-square between Jupiter in Virgo, Saturn in Sagittarius and Neptune in Pisces. The more we "struggle at the sea shore for the best scraps" and so fail to broaden our vision to see and accommodate the needs others, the more resentment and consequent conflict we store up into the 2017-18 cardinal phase of outer-planetary transits that follows. Always and ever more so in the future, no political or cultural dogma on its own has complete answers; rather understanding, anticipating and positively applying insights offered by the astro-transits will be the true source of our salvation in the times to come.

This is the way to see clearly.

The July 2015 column then goes on to take a Jonathan-eye view of the outcome and consequences of the election.

UK General Election 2015 – Post Mortem
So, with all the party leaders but one failing to rise to the challenge of the times[148], the campaign sunk increasingly to the usual avoidance of key issues and low-level manipulation, appealing to a suggestible electorate's short-term self-interest. Congratulations to Nicholas Grier for his clear and most accurate prediction of the outcome[149], based on such leaders' and the electorate's low-level use of the transits.

The astrology of the result
Could the Conservatives greater-than-expected success be explained by the polling day Sagittarian Moon turning void of course (17:53 UT), and then ingressing Capricorn at 18:17 UT, making continuing uncertainty feel unbearable? Exactly what the electorate would see as the 'safest certainty' was established throughout the campaign by the candidates' ability, or inability to exploit Pluto. This was the key to the final outcome.

With Pluto transiting his fourth house in a square to his first house natal Sun, David Cameron had the relatively easy task of exploiting his incumbent status to reassure the electors that he knew their fears. His fears were similar to theirs. He would continue to protect the country from the dangers threatened by profligate socialists, scroungers, Scottish Nationalists and Europeans.

As outlined in the March study, Ed Miliband, with Pluto on his natal Mercury/MC, and Nick Clegg, with it on his Sun, had to confront death and danger full on. Both lost because they failed to do so. When afflicted by Pluto, compromise, weaselling out and evasion are seen as weak, even dishonest. Both men appeared to be running away from the key issues their opponents constantly repeated against them. Ed Miliband ducked the debate on Labour's economic record, when he should have welcomed it, quoting the words of his opponents in the mid-2000s, when they argued for even lighter bank regulation. Then asking if they would not have dealt with the 2008 world economic crisis any better. Everyone had been encouraged to overspend during those years; the better way now needed had to be fair to all. By posturing against the Scottish National Party during most of the campaign, he took ownership of an issue that was for all the parties to answer.

Nick Clegg should never have apologised for the student loan decision, but rather kept a precise record and constantly repeated every detail of the specific benefits that having his party in government had enabled. Both men could have raised the debate to a subject Nick Clegg touched on with some eloquence in his post-election resignation speech a battle against the politics of blame and division and for the inclusiveness of the liberal mindset. Focusing on fear is few people's first choice. Most feel much safer when different peoples are respected and we seem on the same side. To give the people confidence to see that way leaders need to be resolute, masters of their fears. Because both men did not demonstrate the stature to do this, the possibility of advancing the quality of British political debate has yet again been missed.

How different it was in Scotland, where Nicola Sturgeon was blessed with an ongoing transiting Pluto in Capricorn / Mars in Taurus grand trine to her natal / progressed Virgo stellium, as well as Jupiter transiting to conjunct from her Sun to Mars in Leo, triggered by the transiting Moon trining her MC and Mars in Leo on polling day.[150] Not surprisingly, she carried a whole nation before her, and will continue to do so into the future as Jupiter conjuncts her MC and moves on to cross the Virgo stellium.

The astrology of what comes next

For David Cameron the warning 'Beware of what you wish for! It may be realised' seems appropriate. Pluto retrogrades back behind the square to his first house Sun and only completes in January 2016. Saturn retrogrades to Scorpio near a square to his Mars in Leo, and then returns to conjunct his progressed Sun and Venus until August 2016. It will not be easy for him, or for us who have chosen him as our leader. Then, after a desperate internal struggle, Jupiter crosses his Ascendant, while Saturn applies to T-square his natal Saturn in Pisces, Pluto/Uranus and progressed Mars in Virgo. Then transiting Pluto squares his Sun through the 2017 deadline year. Will the budget be balanced, as promised? Will the UK's relationship with Europe be decided? Will Scotland still be with us? To carry a unified nation with him through such times ahead would be a true sign of greatness. We shall see if he has the compassionate flexibility to find and follow the way.

The Labour Party struggles to redefine itself. Could the reinstatement of policies that were successful in the past, and more recently rejected, answer the needs of the future? Having been punished, the Liberal Democrats are seeing a dramatic increase in their membership. Both need to rise above past petty assumptions. For, crucially, the Green Party will be busy in the wings. Its policy agenda may not seem unrealistic and radical should the conventional world economy run out of room for manoeuvre and fail to deliver. One of the less publicised outcomes of the 2015 election is the quadrupling of Green party membership and quintupling of Caroline Lucas' majority in her Brighton Pavilion constituency. The established parties depend upon older people. In five years' time, the emerging younger generations may well see the world they want for themselves and their children very differently. For then, Pluto in Aquarius will not be that far away.

In the meantime, with motivation for voting choices having been presented (and accepted by most of the electorate) in grossly narrow, self-centred ways, we can only say that the jury is out and pondering a most negative verdict on the state of the nation's soul.

-oOo-

Knowing now what was to happen in 2016 and its consequences in the years that followed, the opening paragraphs of the September 2015 column scream out with the pain of missed opportunity, reinforcing the value of knowing the astro-cycles. As matters and their consequences have come to a head, the astro-indicators that drive them are ignored at our peril. Understanding problems more deeply can move mountains, enable positive change, and prevent ever-increasing disaster that just will not go away.

Living Well with 'Alien' Worlds

> 'To strive so that all men may one day be able to understand each other, is that not the noblest of ideals?'
>
> Anim Maalouf *Leo the African*

If the events leading up to and during the 2012-15 cardinal square between Uranus in Aries and Pluto in Capricorn triggered traumatic disruptive change, the consequences of that change are shown by the mutable T-square between Jupiter, Saturn and Neptune that builds through this autumn to a climatic grand cross with the inner planets in June 2016.

The months from autumn 2015 to late spring 2016 will see a build-up of intense critical resentment (Jupiter applying to conjunct North Node in Virgo) about ongoing feelings of religious and personal vulnerability and victimisation (opposed Neptune in Pisces), exacerbated by frustrating obstacles (T-squared Saturn in Sagittarius). People and circumstances we cannot and 'do not want to' understand will be in our way, engaged in what seems like unreasonable, intransigent, sometimes brutal, behaviour. Feeling the need for ever-greater freedom, we will be frustrated and feel blocked by 'enemies' and 'strangers' who like us seek happiness, but from diametrically different perspectives; the clutter of too many contradictory needs.

An atmosphere of people being quick to judge and resent, while slow to understand and sympathise will lead to dysfunctional relationships within families and between groups within societies. In the United Kingdom, separation between

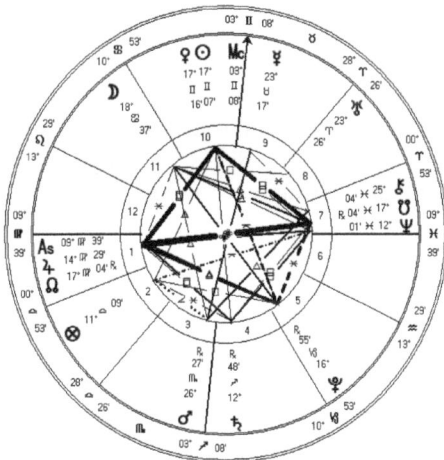

Transits 7 Jun 2016
Event Chart
7 Jun 2016 12:00 BST -1:00
London, UK 51°N30' 000°W10'
Geocentric Tropical Placidus True Node

rich and poor could move political debate away from the middle ground. The US Presidential election will be especially divisive. Violent fragmentation within and between countries and religious cultures will intensify.

The chart (alongside) drawn for a random moment in London on 7 June 2016 shows the mutable T-square approaching the Nodal axis and made into a grand cross by Sun and Venus in Gemini. Augmenting this tension to strain at the leash, break out and fragment is Mercury in Taurus, which, after opposing Mars (retrograding in Scorpio), accelerates to replace Sun/Venus and sustain the grand cross. Earlier that morning Moon in Cancer, still
anxiously full of the emotional intensity of its recent trine to Neptune/South Node in Pisces, opposes Pluto in Capricorn. Underlying it all, Jupiter in Virgo accelerates finally to complete its trine to Pluto in Capricorn. Whatever the circumstances, whoever does what, the mood will be to battle on to rise to the surface of our endeavours; not to sink, but to pay the price of swimming to what we see to be our salvation.

A better way
We are looking to these months so far in the future, because, in the period immediately before us, we can only avoid the worst in 2016 by opening our minds and hearts now, to learn from and go with the flow. Times of mutable astro-events can be refreshingly free, if we put our fixed attitudes and initiatives on the shelf for an exploratory while. This does not mean ignore or abandon them, rather be open to seeing additional possibilities that could enhance them.

Accept the truth of a relationship difficulty you have suspected for some time. Let yourself be relieved of a work responsibility that *seems* to give life meaning, but actually enslaves. Have the courage to see a doctor about a suspected worry. Open your mind to an opinion or situation previously always rejected out of hand. Move away from a protected environment to experience life through the eyes of enemies and strangers. Visit places that have always seemed alien. Spend much more or much less money than normal. Talk to strangers. Forgive or postpone debt repayments. Objectively seek to understand the minds of people who commit terrible acts. Negotiate with enemies, forgive and make peace.

Times of dominant mutable astro-events do not have to overwhelm. They can push us into wonderful new worlds and experiences, where we enjoy the differences, the debate, the excitement of so much that is unexpected. Do we want to live constantly pushing ever harder in a losing battle to hold back the door of insistent change? Would we prefer easing our assumptions, step-by-step to allow change in to play a part in our world? Mutable times can be truly liberating if we have the courage and kindness to allow the way.

-o0o-

The November 2015 column reminded readers of the Confucian insistence that an honourable, happy life is guided by principles, rather than rules. We now know that, in 2016, the building mutable grand cross, focused on Saturn's square to Neptune, brought out the worst in humanity. Delusion-fuelled prejudice drove the world to short-term decisions, informed only by a misconception of self-interest. In the early 2020s, those seduced by what they came to support in those times, are turning to ever-wilder negativities, to justify their wish to destroy opposition.

On 25 November, Mercury conjuncts Saturn in Sagittarius, just ten minutes of arc before their square to Neptune in Pisces and close to a T-Square with that day's Gemini/Sagittarius Full Moon. With the Moon having trined Mars earlier that day and Venus in Libra, having opposed Uranus in Aries only a few days before, what we believe and are going to do about our beliefs will be critical. Issues that have been building for some time will dominate the focus of the coming year, only fading after the last Saturn/ Neptune square on 10 September 2016.

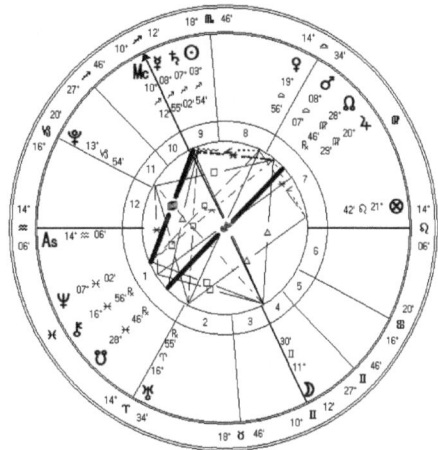

Saturn Square Neptune
26 Nov 2015 12:14:32 UT +0:00
London, UK 51°N30' 000°W10'
Geocentric Tropical Placidus True Node

So, what defines humankind's beliefs, especially at a time when the beliefs many people hold seem to lie at the core of the bloody conflict between them? Rather than arguing the case for various religions and their branches, it might be more fruitful to consider fundamental philosophies that influence the dramatically contrasting ways people behave, based on the creed they adhere to. The very different teachings of Confucius, Machiavelli and the Ferengi offer a crucial distinction.

The essence of Confucius' view was that men's relationship with men is the measure of all things; what you do not wish for yourself, do not do to others.

His approach placed emphasis not on rules, which were uncertain and prone to circumvention, but on the central principle that motivated an action. The intention an act is far more important than any rule broken in the committing of it? A perfectly ordered harmonious society could come from of the acts of human beings, providing they followed principles, rather than hid behind or sought advantage from rules. Every situation had to be considered in its context and judged by discerning the motivating principle behind each action, such as integrity, loyalty and respect, which came from moral values to be found in good family relationships. Good men should not devote their time to personal gain. If rulers become corrupt in this way natural disasters will follow and the people have the right to rebel. For Confucius, the ends did not justify the means and the further a society drifted away from realising this, the direr the relationships within that society and with other societies became.

Realising and accepting how far we are from this view lies at the heart of understanding the problems we face in personal, social and world relationships today. Indeed, the way we administer and adjudicate our contemporary life is much more akin to the ideas of Machiavelli, whom Wikipedia cites as the founder of modern political science and ethics.[151] Quotations from his ground breaking *The Prince* have a frighteningly pertinent ring in the modern world.

- ❖ It is better to be feared than loved, if you cannot be both... If an injury has to be done to a man it should be so severe that his vengeance need not be feared... A battle that you win cancels any other bad action of yours...

- ❖ It is undoubtedly necessary for the ambassador occasionally to mask his game; but it should be done so as not to awaken suspicion and he ought also to be prepared with an answer in case of discovery.

- ❖ A prince ought to have no other aim or thought, nor select anything else for his study, than war and its rules and discipline; for this is the sole art that belongs to him who rules, and it is of such force that it not only upholds those who are born princes, but it often enables men to rise from a private station to that rank.

More charmingly ironic, but just as pertinently ruthless are the Ferengi *286 Rules of Acquisition,*[152] well known to followers of Star Trek. Below are just a few.

> 13. Anything worth doing is worth doing for money
> 14. Anything stolen is pure profit
> 20. When the customer is sweating, turn up the heat
> 21. Never place friendship before profit
> 27. The most beautiful thing about a tree is what you do with it after you cut it down
> 28. Morality is always defined by those in power

Astro-cycles reveal both negative and positive possible outcomes. With traumatic clarity, they warn us of the consequences of addressing them selfishly, while with sublime clarity, they indicate the best way to master the potential of the time. As the tension of the unbearably expansive Saturn in Sagittarius square Neptune in Pisces bears down on us over the coming year, attempts to argue and fight for one belief against another will only make matters worse. The Machiavellian and Ferengi *me first* tactics may give us temporary mastery, for a while perhaps show us how to succeed in the global race *in spite of* others, but, by creating enemies rather than friends, this will only make matters worse in the long run.

In direct contrast, by showing us how to succeed *with* others, the Confucian principled approach will be lastingly successful, as well as making us much happier. So, whatever belief system you stand by, be it Christian, Islamic, Jewish, Hindu, Buddhist, Pagan, scientistic, humanistic, other secular, Keynesian, hedonistic, or the joy of family and friends, avoid disaster by keeping to the highest principles. Then everyone knows where they stand and we can progress along the only truly efficient way to solve all our problems.

-o0o-

Inspired by speculation in a recent issue of *Science* magazine the March 2016 column looked for astrological indicators for its suggestion that a new Anthropogenic Age started in the 1950s. The study below suggests a far earlier fundamental change, while explaining today's breakdown of traditional value systems, as humanity searches for something better.

Enlightening the Enlightenment

Recently, *Science* magazine reported on the progress of the Anthropocene Working Group, which is considering the possibility that the Earth is passing to a new geological Anthropogenic Epoch from the Holocene Epoch, which began around 12,000 years ago as the planet entered a warming period after the retreating of the glaciers of the late Palaeolithic period.[153]

The heart reason for such a change is the influence of human development on the Earth's geology. It is suggested that geologists millions of years in the future will be able to discern the crucial effect our activities today have had upon the planet. Such considerations play a key part in the scientific debate over the extraction of fossil fuels and global warming.

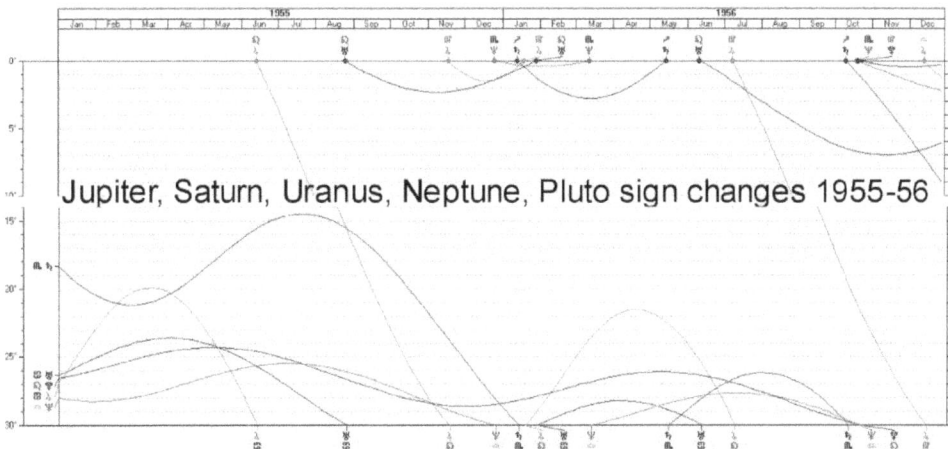

Jupiter, Saturn, Uranus, Neptune, Pluto sign changes 1955-56

The 1950s decade is seriously being considered to be the start of the Anthropogenic Epoch. Does astrology confirm this? The Graphic Ephemeris alongside, drawn with a 30-degree modulus, clearly shows a remarkable number of outer-planetary sign changes (moving from the bottom to top of the diagram) in 1955-56, at heart of the decade

Certainly, the pace of change quickened from those years, throwing out the past and diving recklessly into a Rock 'n Roll future of political rebellion, sexual liberation and other heady sensualities. An irresistible taste for radical change was picked up by the Uranus/Pluto conjunction in Virgo that then built through the first quarter of their cycle to a fundamentally destructive seven-hit square in 2012-15. Yet, for this to have a radical effect on the fabric of the planet much more needs to have gone before.

Astrology would support an Enlightenment-generated eighteenth century beginning for the Anthropogenic Epoch, symbolised by Uranus, and then Neptune and Pluto being discovered and so coming into human consciousness. The gross industrialisation of the nineteenth century followed, intensified by the discovery of subtle, even more effective electronic, fossil and psychological powers – symbolised by the Neptune/Pluto conjunction 1891-92, the Uranus/Pluto opposition 1901-02, and then the actual discovery of Pluto in 1930.

The 500-year pattern of outer planets returning in the twentieth century to their fifteenth/sixteenth century positions underpinned and dramatically accelerated today's human impact on the planet. In the 1940s Uranus was in Gemini, as it had been when the type-block printing press was invented in the 1440s. This exploded popular access to knowledge, enabling translated books to educate the masses. In the twentieth century it was electronic discoveries that expanded rapidly into information technology with the development of the World Wide Web at the turn of the twenty-first century – when Uranus and Neptune transited and then mutually received each other in Aquarius/Pisces.

The 1988-92 Saturn, Uranus and Neptune in Capricorn, triggered by Jupiter in Cancer's opposition, untied past world structures and left us on a dark and dangerous path that challenges us to regenerate into more enlightened ways of being with each other by the 2020 conjunction between the Jupiter, Saturn, Pluto conjunction in Capricorn, while Uranus transits Taurus; on its own a combination of astro-events that has not occurred for more than 4,000 years.

Using the big picture to understand and master immediate situations

Very interesting perhaps, but what has such macro mundane astrology got to do with March and April 2016? As we struggle out of the ruins that are the product of our greed, ignorance and hatred, moving toward the Spring Equinox of this most confusing mutable Saturn-square-Neptune year, it seems few people care to be mindful of what they say or do to each other. Wires of communication are crossed and consequential danger seems to threaten everywhere. It seems that all suggestions, solutions and paths of hope turn sour and are seen as no more than pretences, with unexpected and unwanted consequences, causing suffering for others and counter attacks from them on us. Generosity is met with insult, kindness taken advantage of, desperate cries of protest with unyielding barriers, invitations to explore understanding are seen as signs of weakness, offers of money are met with demands for more.

At such a time, the astrology of the larger picture can help us realise how new we are on a path of epochal change, with so few values to take refuge in and ground our lives upon. So, the first step must be to decide some common values, not engage in a punching match, hitting with puffed up gloves of self-righteous prejudice. The first step is to look at the world as it is; full of dissatisfied social fabrics, struggling to survive; over-confident about its future potential, over-dependent upon its worn-out past. Stop screaming unyieldingly with accusation against various gates of opportunity, which, if entered open-mindedly, would find us all in the same one place of mutual understanding.

We need the big picture, the realisation that we are in the midst of epochal change, where very few rules and customs of the past are likely to help us make the right decision. We are all in the same difficulty, needing as many friends as we can get to help us through. So, the answer must be not to accuse, but to make friends.

Understanding the big picture and realising how radically this is affecting the lives of so many others, makes it brutally clear that seeking to answer our problems at others' expense will only make matters worse. Little benefit comes from capitalism that is no more than picking pockets. There is no salvation in screaming at and attacking fellow crew members on the bridge of a ship that is heading for the rocks, or in a two-person kayak about to plunge over a waterfall. Working together is the only possible way to survive.

Time to stop clinging pointlessly on to the worst sub-cultural prejudices that have fuelled past wars! If we claim the right to discover and implement practical powers to change the planet in ways that could well last for millions of years, we must act with principles that match the very high standards of that power.

March to June and consequentially on to the end of 2016 the people of the world stand at a decisive point that will radically affect how we will experience our lives and determine ongoing actions that affect the planetary fabric. If we seek a good experience, let us start by cleansing our minds beyond base fears and narrow self-interest when making decisions. 'What's in it for me?' just will not do, when deciding whether to stay in the EU, the UK should keep Trident, who should be the next US President, fix policy on immigration, or just how we say 'Hallo' to the people we meet tomorrow.

Today, most of us have a common means to know each other and what lies behind events via the World Wide Web. A few clicks of a mouse or touch of a screen can take us into the unknown of the lives of other people and cultures. We can know the history of their experiences what they think and why they act as they do. There may be a few, but not many, who seek to spend eternity in Hell; burning, being frozen, or cut and torn asunder. Quite the opposite, most of us prize goodness. The problem comes when we see this as so precious, so pure and wonderful that we seek to bar those people who might 'pollute it'.

Distilling the essence of global transformation
Paradoxically, the high advanced principles we need to cut through all this are timeless. They have always been there enshrined in the essential ideals at the heart of all the world's spiritual teachings – once secular egocentricity, institutionalisation, power plays and commercialisation of the mainstream religious traditions are stripped away. They are compassion, everyone's wish for, and the right to, the pursuit of happiness, universal oneness and the rules of respect for all that the Universe contains. Whatever faith or belief in its wonders we follow, we speak and often take our joy in these principles every day. To transform the future, we must now enshrine them in every decision we make, every action we take. Islam, Christianity, Hinduism, Buddhism, Judaism, shamanism, naturalism and scientism – there is no other way out of our global impasse than to combine the essential idealism at the heart of the very best of every person's beliefs.

Move on from fearing the worst. This mutable year is ideally suited to explore and then distil the essence of our differences for the greater good of all. The eighteenth-century Enlightenment may have seen the beginning of epochal change, but it will be barren for us and its geological heritage, if we do not grasp this chance for spiritual unity, enabling global social understanding.

-o0o-

Written in March, the May 2016 column has a sense of almost-desperate foreboding in its warnings against allowing short-sighted selfishness to decide the key decisions. The three extracts below are agonising to read. How much better our lives might be today, if we could go back and use the transits in a kinder, wiser, positive way!

Cleansing the Confusion of a Lethally Vain World

History is littered with horrific decisions leading to terrifying consequences, but rarely has there been a time, such as now, when the wrong people have misrepresented so many wrong ideas, only to have them accepted by the very people whose interests those ideas undermine.

Fundamentalist Islam turning so many against all Muslims, enabling a US politician to claim all of them hate the USA, and so accelerate that trend. Simplistic nationalism points the responsibility for our hardships at the very opposite of the real cause. Job security and incomes of most people diminish, while owners' profits and off-shore assets continue to grow, yet the contribution to society of those businesses is reduced. Governments seek to force peace by acts of war. Violence increases and societies disintegrate, while each perpetrator fights ever harder, believing only their sub-group beliefs can solve the conflict. Like a boulder dropped into a pond, total war against ISIL seem to splash its influence ever-wider to all parts of the world.

Driving the above and many other misguided, counter-productive messages is the vanity of perpetrators. Both sides of the Atlantic, tub-thumping populists with blond hair combed nearly forward insist that they know the way to 'make USA great again', or Britain could be a much greater country if it left the European Union. Others boast their religion to be the only one and the best. Most see caring for suffering refugees as less important than their own comfort. Opponents are viewed as terrorists, but friends as freedom fighters. Leaders who risk everything to be kind to the needy have their hospitality abused. The very existence of desperate hardship is seen as threat by those who have more than they really need. Those in power sustain themselves by turning the poor against each other.

This is hardly surprising, as, consumed with self-interest, we build to the long-awaited mutual grand cross to the Summer Solstice, (Saturn squaring Neptune on 1 June, while Jupiter in Virgo applies to trine Pluto in Capricorn on 26 June). Everything that is happening seems terrible; we must do something, *anything* about it.

So much confused uncertainty around, the air of social decision-making is open and ripe for someone to stand up and take the people with them. Ideal for grounding new attitudes. A 'once in a lifetime decision'. Will it be a wise one?

How can we make the best out of a bad situation?
This question goes to the heart of just about everything that is being done and decided through these two months and the consequences for good or ill that will be felt for long after. As the grand cross intensifies with Jupiter, Saturn and Neptune in mid Virgo, Sagittarius and Pisces and inner planets emphasising the tension and triggering to square the four angles, one thing that can be certain is that any deception attempted or evil intended is likely to succeed for a short while. Then all selfish actions will be repaid with manifold brutality, as hurt and resentment about "what *they* have done" pours and spreads over all we thought we were achieving in these tawdry times.

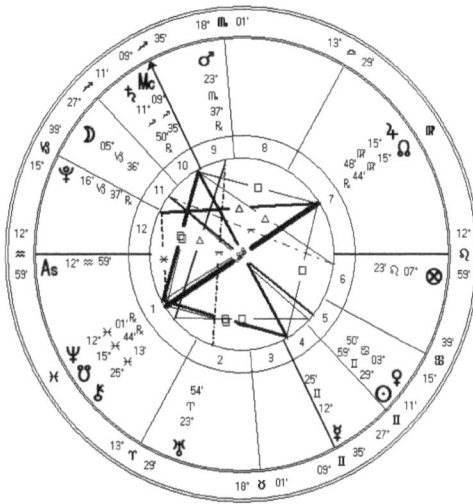

Summer Solstice
20 Jun 2016 22:34:08 UT +0:00
London, UK 51°N30' 000°W10'
Geocentric Tropical Placidus True Node

The solution is simple. If you do not want to be the victim, do not victimise others. If you wish to avoid problems, do not create them. However wrong what is happening seems, try to ride the storm and steer as many others as possible to a safe harbour. Shine the light that illuminates and melts the confusion away. Too much wrong has been done by too many on all sides for anyone to have the right of redress. We have to create generous spaces that leave everyone room to rebuild their lives. This way we transform all those mutable misunderstandings into expanding spaces of new opportunity. This way, people are too busy rebuilding their lives to wish to waste time seeking to carry on destroying the lives of others – however much they used to feel they deserved it. We see things improving and start to appreciate a much better world and more and more of those very different people who live in it.

The same edition announced publication of André Barbault's *Planetary Cycles*, with Cyclic Index graphs and his warning of challenges building from 2018 into 2020-21.[154]

> André Barbault comments:
> ...one can only wonder about the extreme depth of the trough as the wave plunges in 2020-21, the result of the next Jupiter-Saturn triptych which will be relatively close to Uranus and Neptune. It seems that will be at the epicentre of this dissonance...

In June 2012,[155] André Barbault had already considered the astrology of pandemics, looking at cycles as far back as the European Black Death (1347-48. From this study, he projected the possibility of one in the 2020-21, as well as describing the background conditions of the time.[156]

Cyclic Indices for the Twenty-first Century

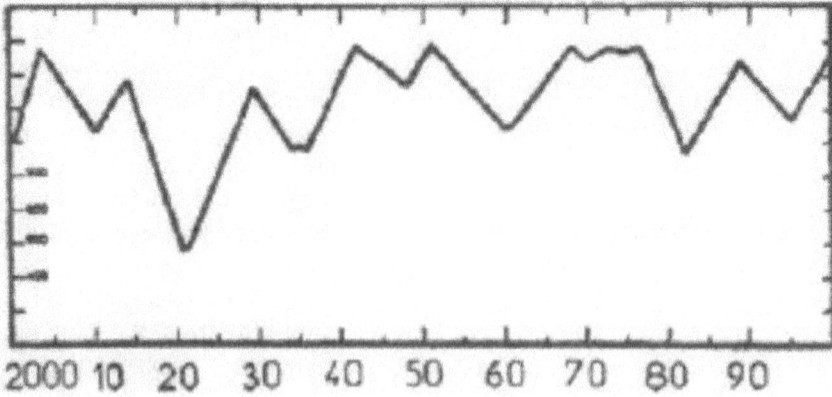

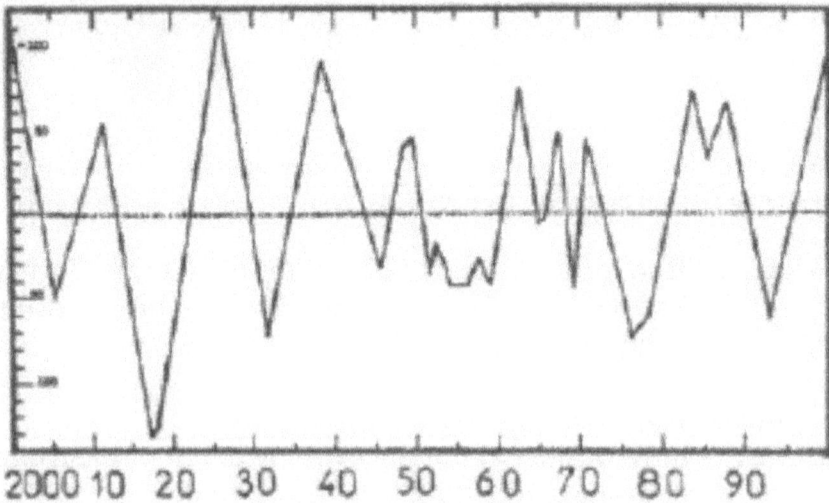

From André Barbault's *Planetary Cycles*.
The top graph shows the planetary distances, note the big bottom in
2020. The one below that is like a moving average which shows the
force for change building from 2018.

-o0o-

The astrological analysis of the EU Referendum (see next two pages) shows clearly the value of astro-cycles. Perhaps political strategists should pay more attention to them, rather than focus groups.

Britain's European Union Vote

Choosing 23 June as decision day for the EU referendum was a most risky gamble with the nation's soul. At the time of writing, Brexit versus Remain is little more than a cacophony of contradictory statistics that will for ever be incomplete and meaningless, while we aim no higher than personal gain.

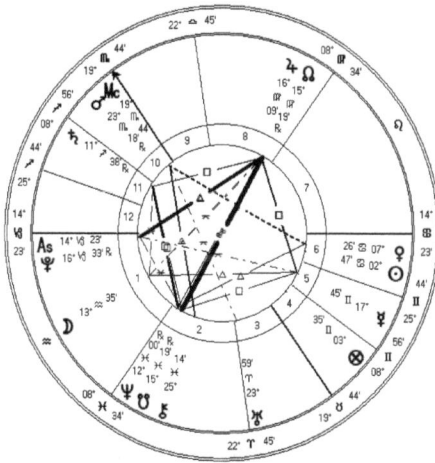

EU Vote Polls Close
23 Jun 2016 22:00 BST -1:00
London, UK 51°N30' 000°W10'
Geocentric Tropical Placidus True Node

The Closing of the Poll chart's tight grand cross between Mercury, Jupiter, Saturn, Neptune and the Nodal axis in mutable signs and succedent houses shows that this confusion will hold right through to the end. It will be difficult for either side to make a reasoned case. Also, whatever they say to the contrary, with Pluto rising as the polls close, both sides will be tempted to see the peddling of fear as the winning gambit.

However, those relying on this alone may well be wrong-footed. For, as the campaign approaches its climax, Jupiter will be moving in to trine that Pluto less than three days after the polls close. Also, crucially, the Moon in Aquarius, applying to trine Venus in Gemini will be just three degrees from the Venus of the 1801 UK Chart. Together these factors suggest: firstly, people will be fearless, ready to take a plunge into the unknown, and secondly, they will want to feel good about their decision. They are doing something beautiful for their country.

Predicting mundane events is sometimes possible, but more often outcomes are decided by the use the parties make of the astro-cycles, not the cycles alone. So, upon what strategies would victory for either side depend, bearing in mind that not just Jupiter trine Pluto, but Moon, Venus and Mercury in harmony are needed to illuminate the decision?

Brexit campaigners may gain considerable traction by citing out-of-control immigration and loss of sovereignty, but to secure a firm vote will need to move on to an intelligently explained positive glorious vision of the United Kingdom outside the EU. It has to has to be more than a resentment-based rush into 'freedom' from "other people telling us what to do", especially when the UK government will continue to do just that, whichever way we vote! People will want to know and feel good about the future and see beauty in what will happen the day after, and all the following days after, the country leaves the EU.

Remain campaigners gain some momentum by this 'what happens after leaving' uncertainty; those months and years of negotiation and how certain can we be of the country's financial stability through it all? However, that will not be enough to convince the doubters, with Jupiter trining Pluto and whetting appetites for the risk of the new. The Remain campaigners need to build on the natural pride of the British people of their role in the World; the nation's power to have global influence, using the EU as a platform. They need to show that within the EU the UK can lead reform, bringing a wise sense of perspective and so put right its excesses. Generally, it is best not to make the UK an orphan, trying to find new friends and new families to live with, but instead bring people and peoples together in an open-world commonwealth of nations. By this middle way of service, we could demonstrate how to help heal our fractured planet – a regeneration of replaying Britain's erstwhile imperial role.

Interestingly the 1801 UK Union Chart has the South Node rising in Libra trine Venus, both in a grand trine with the Moon/Mercury Closing of the Polls chart. An intelligent clean-clear invocation, bringing into the future the best that Britain's past stood for is the way for either side to win the referendum.

As I write this in March, it really could go either way.

-oOo-

This analysis of the post-Brexit-vote situation for the UK and the world was published in September 2016's *Astrological Journal*.

Astrology, Brexit and Global Healing

Predictive and descriptive approaches to astrology do not contradict, but complement each other. For astro-cycles describe the cosmic weather that influences our moods and actions, just as metrological forecasts indicate the high and low pressure behind mundane weather. How individuals or institutions will react to and experience either will depend upon the motivation and awareness driving their actions. Did we really have to leave the house in a storm; remember an umbrella if we did?

With astro-cycles the outcomes from our reactions to cosmic weather go deeper. Does immediate self-interest or a search to understand and help situations drive our quest? Depending upon this key distinction, the same astro-cycles (cosmic environment) will lead to vastly different outcomes. The cosmic environment of the Western Front in First World War led some men to feel the 'patriotic' need to devise and deploy armaments that killed millions, most to submit and go to the slaughter, while others worked tirelessly to rescue and heal the wounded. Change the motivational emphasis to the last of the three and the world still goes through the massive revolutionary social change the astro-cycles indicate, but this does not destroy, rather it heals society and individual lives.

It is when most people's motivation is focused on the first two, (ignorance, or self-interest, driven by greed and hatred), that the best long-standing methods of predictive astrology are likely to be accurate. For self-centred motivation puts the astro-cycles in control and makes what happens unavoidable. Mars in Leo urges immediate self-expression. Selfishly applied, it can easily cause conflict. Selflessly applied, it encourages happy, supportive teams under our leadership. Donald Trump's Leo Mars in the twelfth house, very close to his Ascendant, goes a long way to explaining his charismatic, no holds barred, 'cheeky-chappie' attraction, but also the likelihood of war should he become US President.

The astrology of the three most social-changing UK General Elections since Second World War and then the recent EU Referendum vote show clearly that victory came to those who understood and grasped the momentum of times, indicated by the contemporary astro-cycles. Would a wiser, selfless use of those cycles have led to a different result?

The 1945 General Election[157]

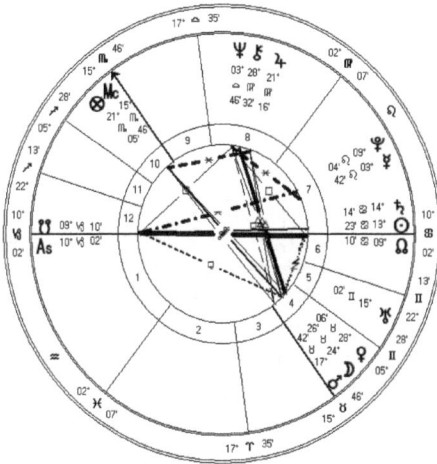

General Election 1945
5 Jul 1945 22:00 BDST -2:00
Westminster, UK 51°N30' 000°W09'
Geocentric Tropical Placidus True Node

Mercury applying to conjunct Pluto in Leo indicated Winston Churchill's charisma would not be enough to re-elect him to lead into the post-war world. His great words of heroism may have inspired and helped save the nation in times of peril, but there had been millions of other heroes who had given their lives in this cause. With the powerful Mars, Moon, Venus Taurus trine to Jupiter in Virgo and Neptune in Libra, now was a time of reconstruction, and, crucially, to set the record straight. To fight a common enemy, ordinary people may have put aside the massive social injustices of the 1920s and 1930s; now they needed to be addressed.

Clearly the Labour Party had the hunger and vision to grasp the momentum of those times. The Conservative Party was too trapped in the privileged interests it served to see, understand and act on the people's past resentments – far easier to hope that the nation's trust in their war time leader would re-elect him.

Because they knew the astro-cycles, both predictive and descriptive, astrologers, unlike most political commentators, would not have been surprised by Labour's landslide victory.

The 1979 General Election

With Venus, Mercury and Mars in Aries opposing it, Pluto, now in Libra, played a much more confrontational and destructive role in 1979. The mood for radical change was further driven by the Sun in Taurus opposing Uranus in Scorpio and trining Saturn/North Node in Virgo; all stirred on by the free spirit of Neptune in Sagittarius and explosive pride of Jupiter and Moon in Leo. Irresistible change was being forced upon Britain and the wider world.

So, perhaps this election result was unavoidable. People felt that any change was better than what they had then! In such circumstances, the role of descriptive astrology is to clarify and caution the decisions, following on from the Conservative victory. The astro-cycles may indicate radical change, but the dominant Aries should also warn of the disruptive consequences of cavalier insensitive, uncompromising

General Election 1979
3 May 1979 22:00 BST -1:00
Westminster, UK 51°N30' 000°W09'
Geocentric Tropical Placidus True Node

change. When the enemy is defeated, it is the time to make peace, bring all sides together; not lay out the groundwork for future social conflict. Margaret Thatcher's quotations of St Francis, as she entered Downing Street for the first time, was in keeping with this need. What was to follow drifted radically away from the quotation. Many feel we are still struggling to recover from the negative consequences.

The 1997 General Election

General Election 1997
1 May 1997 22:00 BST -1:00
Westminster, UK 51°N30' 000°W09'
Geocentric Tropical Placidus True Node

As the polls closed, Pluto rising in early Sagittarius was exactly squared by the Moon in Pisces. Jupiter in Aquarius was almost exactly squared by Venus in Taurus, which was only just past a trine to Mars in Virgo near the Midheaven. The mood of the times was an unshakeable and critical need to put right the hurts of the past.

Using astrology to look beneath the surface of the possibly dangerous over-optimism of the Pluto rising in Sagittarius, it can be seen that the strength that drove the change was the wish to be rid of unpopular people and the brutal memories they represented. The promise of a "new dawn", invoked by Tony Blair, the morning after Election Day, is not so evident in the chart. So it was that while certain shifts of priority led to important improvements in Northern Ireland, health and education, there was no real shift in the monetarist economic strategy, which has become the cause of the crisis we face in the twenty-first century. At the crest of the wave of victory, with Mars in Virgo, it is easy to rub in the failings of predecessors. More difficult to apply criticism to failings that remain in the new government's way of thinking. This could explain why many Labour voters turned away from the party at the 2016 Referendum. Notably, the Royal Assent of the Referendum Bill in December 2015 was given within a degree of the exact return of the Nodal axis of Labour's victory in this 1997 General Election.[158]

EU Referendum 2016

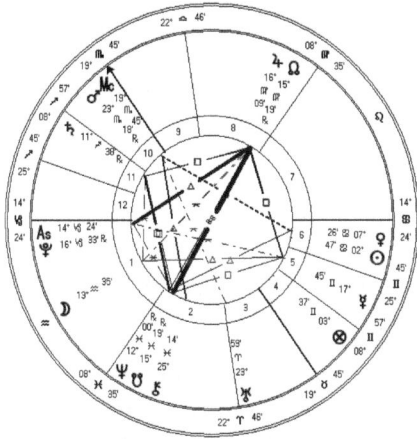

EU Referendum 2016
23 Jun 2016 22:00 BST -1:00
Westminster, UK 51°N30' 000°W09'
Geocentric Tropical Placidus True Node

If the three UK General Elections above occurred at times when the astro-cycles were ripe for unavoidable radical change, there could not have been worse astro-cycles than those of the months surrounding 23 June 2016 to hold a vote on an issue that was a far more important, constitutional change than any of them. The actual Bill that called the referendum was debated in the build-up, and received royal assent, three weeks after the first exact Saturn in Sagittarius / Neptune in Pisces square (26 November 2015). It called for a decision based on a simple majority of those voting. This may suit a by- or general election, whose result can be reversed in a few years. However, a constitutional change, designed to stand for at least a generation, usually requires a much more substantial decision – perhaps fifty percent of those voting, or sixty percent of all people registered to vote. The voting was to be on 23 June, five days after the second Saturn/Neptune exact retrograde square, when Jupiter in Virgo was three days from its reckless trine to Pluto that was rising in Capricorn.

With the associated grand cross, the astro-cycles clearly indicated the nature of the campaign. It was characterised by confusion, manipulation, fear (immigrants, especially Turks, if we remain, economic disaster if we leave), abandonment of reason, blame and intolerance. Far too many people would base their vote on

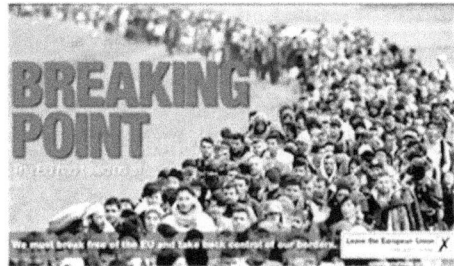

prejudice or treat the process as a by-election to teach the establishment a lesson.

The outcome and the way it was received could hardly have been more like the nature of the transits. 51.9% to leave was held to be a sacrosanct democratic lifetime decision, although it represented just 37% of the registered voters and 33% of the adult population. Soon after the vote was announced, key leaders on both sides either resigned or withdrew, leaving others to sort out the future. As Jupiter exactly trined

Pluto, Labour Leader, Jeremy Corbyn, was blamed and largely abandoned by his parliamentary party, even though his own constituents had voted overwhelmingly to remain, and most of his Labour MP critics' voters had decided the other way. Was a more long-term malaise in Labour support the real reason?[159]

When Mars made a direct station on 29 June, Michael Gove withdrew his support from Boris Johnson ('Et tu Gove?' was the front-page heading of one national newspaper). The Conservative Party originally decided to announce their new leader on 9 September, the day before the third and final Saturn/Neptune square. It seemed that the entire period of that square was to be taken up with the preparation, decision, and then indecision concerning the Brexit vote.

Then came Theresa May enjoying her Jupiter return on 6 July 2016 (could it be near the MC in Virgo with late Scorpio rising?)[160] This Libran with strong Virgo planets was dominant enough to spare the nation a bruising contest, but her task ahead will be far from easy. In the coming few months, transiting Pluto trines her Jupiter and Saturn retrogrades back towards her progressed Sun and Saturn, and then forward across her progressed Mercury,

Brexit, Europe and today's world events in their historical context
In the midst of this Saturn in Sagittarius squared to Neptune in Pisces time, as we struggle for survival out of the debris of the massive upheaval of the 2012-14 Uranus/Pluto squares, people all over the world are making massive, poorly conceived decisions and performing the most ruthless actions for short-sighted and selfish reasons. We are in one of the most unreliable periods in human history, when it is vital to learn from the past. The list at the end of this article shows how direly disturbing outcomes associated with Saturn/Neptune 90-degree separations can be.

The 2015-16 Saturn/Neptune square has been greatly empowered by its T-square to Jupiter in Virgo – all climaxing in a mutable grand cross through the late spring and summer, as inner planets transited Gemini.

Events for Britain and all over the world could well lead to terrible outcomes, for which our times will be remembered. Is it destined that we are doomed, or can astrological understanding guide us to doing something better with the future?

The Capricorn triple conjunction
With Saturn joining Pluto in Capricorn from December 2017 and connecting to the 1066 English and 1801 UK charts, which have their MC/IC axes reversed across Capricorn/Cancer, it would have been difficult for the UK to remain in Europe whatever the outcome.[161] The triple conjunction transiting across the EU's Uranus/Neptune conjunction (2017-20)[162] indicates that it too is due for radical change. So, should we have stayed and helped guide the transition? With less rush to decide, delaying the Referendum vote until the end of 2016 or spring 2017 would have enabled a less frenetic, more considered discussion of the idealism unpinning both sides of the argument.

Because it did not happen this way, the UK has to cope with the bad impression our unilateral decision may have created. Are the majority of British people motivated by self-interest, less concerned with the disadvantaged in the poor parts of Europe, only willing to help refugees if they stay a safe distance away, close to the borders of their country?

It is never too late to turn such impressions around. It could be argued that the EU is a club for the privileged that slowly allows in a few of the less well-off, but essentially operates at the expense of the under-privileged masses in the rest of the world. The astro-cycles since 2008 have been accompanied by so much destruction, suffering and confusion that an anarchy of blame and retribution screams out mindlessly on all sides all over the world. The Saturn/Neptune square eases into the autumn. Wherever we are in the world, negotiations that enable rather than defend selfish interests, include without exposing vulnerability, share rather than exploit, could go a long way towards easing tension. As boiling resentment and outrage cools, will we start preferring to solve our problems, turning away from the constant desire for revenge that only makes them worse?

UK – little Englander or champion of world compassion?
Underlying the justifiably admired idealistic kindness in Theresa May's speech on entering 10 Downing Street for the first time as Prime Minister is a crucial omission. The list of disadvantaged people she committed her government to care for referred exclusively to those in the 'Union' of the 'United Kingdom', as she put it. She is right to address the injustice and neglect experienced by so many working people who supported Brexit. The post-2008 recovery has benefitted the few at the expense of the many. Yet, the need to address injustice does not end at the borders of the UK. We cannot wash our hands of the responsibility to help to care for millions of people all over the world, whose experiences are far more dire than ours, as they seek to survive with little food, a proper home, or country.

Wealth, housing, laws and opportunities that favour, or even give exclusive access to, the rich and privileged are the root cause of conflict and rebellion within our nation. They are the cause of even greater global conflict between countries and cultures. Insensitivity to others' customs and ways initiates mutual enmity. Force of economic power and armed strength create desperate victims. Together they build to massive global misunderstandings and injustices that are the cause of today's ever-worsening world conflicts.

However successful the new UK government is in turning the fine intentions of its leader into tangible benefits for its people, its achievements will be empty and unsustainable, if good, kind relationships with others beyond the UK borders are ignored.

The window of flexibility to adjust to the new global structure will be hardly fifteen months before Saturn ingresses Capricorn in December 2017. Through 2018-19 a new way of doing business in the world will start to take shape, as we build towards the Jupiter/Saturn conjunction in the first degree of Aquarius on the day of the 2020 Winter Solstice. Through these years, the UK will be increasingly placing itself outside of presently existing certainties. It will depend upon new friendships it makes on the way, supported by just the dwindling resources of the Bank of England.

Turning our backs on helping the world and focusing on our little-Englander interests could leave us isolated and alone. Britain will need friends. These can only be made by the friendship shown to others in Europe and beyond. Capricorn demands efficiency. Friends working together create the greatest economic efficiency and social security. Seeing the way ahead as broadening our friendship with other nations, of making friends everywhere is the key to make the best use of our Brexit decision.

Two female Conservative Prime Ministers Compared

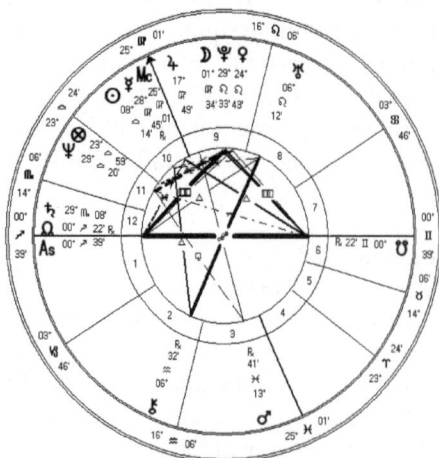

Theresa May
1 Oct 1956 12:00 BST -1:00
Eastbourne, UK 50°N46' 000°E17'
Geocentric Tropical Placidus True Node

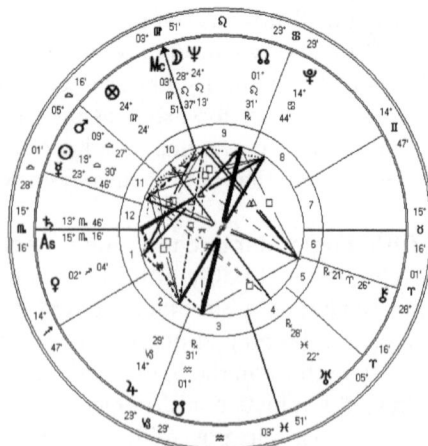

Margaret Thatcher
13 Oct 1925 09:00 +0:00
Grantham, UK 52°N55' 000°W39'
Geocentric Tropical Placidus True Node

Comparisons between Theresa May and Margaret Thatcher are difficult to avoid. Both have the Sun in Libra and Theresa May was born soon after the Thatcher first Scorpio Saturn return. Their style within this similarity is different. The Thatcher Jupiter in Capricorn squared Mars/Sun/Mercury in Libra explains her intransigence. The May focus on Moon, Jupiter, Mercury in Virgo opposed by Mars in Pisces points to her hard work and compassion.

The role of the fixed star Regulus in both charts is highly significant. The Thatcher Moon in Leo was just ten minutes of arc from an exact conjunction. The May Pluto is just twenty minutes of arc from an exact conjunction to Regulus, with her Moon in Virgo three degrees past and Venus in Leo five degrees before the star. 'Success if revenge is avoided' is how Bernadette Brady puts it. If Regulus is prominent, we can suddenly rise to great heights of recognition, but are in danger of falling just as quickly. Could Theresa May's exit mirror her predecessor's? The new cabinet is forming as I write. Reading this, as you will in the latter days of an inevitable honeymoon with the fresh new ministerial faces, seeds of dissent that could mature in the future may already be visible.

Much has been said of the finality of the Brexit decision, far less of the sixteen million who voted against. Looking at the traumatic astro-cycles for the rest of the decade, and the near-impossibility of any government delivering what so many Brexit supporters thought they were voting for, it will be interesting to see what kind of opposition develops. Even, in the end, whether, and in what way, the United Kingdom leaves the European Union.

-o0o-

Saturn/ Neptune 90 degree separations 1900 to 2030

European Colonialism-beginning of end
SatOppNep 16/08/1900 28°Sg39'R 28°Ge39'D
SatOppNep 04/10/1900 29°Sg15'D 29°Ge15'R

Suffragette hunger strikes begin
SatSqrNep 14/04/1909 14°Ar24'D 14°Cn24'D
SatSqrNep 19/10/1909 19°Ar20'R 19°Cn20'D
SatSqrNep 24/01/1910 17°Ar31'D 17°Cn31'R

First World War slaughter intensifies
SatCnjNep 01/08/1917 04°Le45'D 04°Le45'D

UK General Strike
SatSqrNep 16/01/1926 24°Sc08'D 24°Le08'R
SatSqrNep 23/05/1926 22°Sc06'R 22°Le06'D
SatSqrNep 06/11/1926 26°Sc49'D 26°Le49'D

Spanish Civil War July begins 1936
SatOpp Nep21/03/1936 14°Pi59'D 14°Vi59'R
SatOpp Nep04/10/1936 17°Pi26'R 17°Vi26'D
SatOpp Nep18/01/1937 18°Pi45'D 18°Vi45'R

Blanket bombing of Germany, V1 and V2 Rocket attacks on London, building the Atomic Bomb
SatSqrNep 02/07/1944 01°Cn34'D 01°Li34'D
SatSqrNep 08/01/1945 06°Cn25'R 06°Li25'R
SatSqrNep 06/04/1945 04°Cn45'D 04°Li45'R

Struggle for colonial freedom, Korean War, birth of modern consumer society
SatCnjNep 21/11/1952 22°Li46'D 22°Li46'D
SatCnjNep 17/05/1953 21°Li38'R 21°Li38'R
SatCnjNep 22/07/1953 21°Li12'D 21°Li12'D

Vietnam War, - escalation and opposition birth of generational counter culture
SatSqrNep 18/02/1963 15Aq39'D 15°Sc39'R

Physical and spiritual global travel grows
SatOppNep 26/06/1971 00°Ge51'D 00°Sg51'R
SatOppNep 27/11/1971 02°Ge52'R 02°Sg52'D
SatOppNep 19/04/1972 04°Ge46'D 04°Sg46'R

UK Winter of Discontent Thatcherism, Reaganomics, birth of Monetarism
SatSqrNep 14/09/1979 17°Vi47'D 17°Sg47'D
SatSqrNep 26/03/1980 22°Vi40'R 22°Sg40'R
SatSqrNep 22/06/1980 21°Vi00'D 21°Sg00'R

Collapse of Soviet Union, recession as monetarism shows it first flaws
SatCnjNep 03/03/1989 11°Cp54'D 11°Cp54'D
SatCnjNep 24/06/1989 11°Cp14'R 11°Cp14'R
SatCnjNep 13/11/1989 10°Cp21'D 10°Cp21'D

Internet stocks booming unrealistically, due to bust April/May 2000 Financial Services Modernization Act passed in USA – a major cause of 2008 economic crash.
SatSqrNep 25/06/1998 01°Ta29'D 01°Aq29'R
SatSqrNep 01/11/1998 29°Ar30'R 29°Cp30'D
SatSqrNep 06/04/1999 04°Ta07'D 04°Aq07'D

Unrealistic boom of loan/property markets
SatOppNep 31/08/2006 17°Le52'D 17°Aq52'R
SatOppNep 28/02/2007 20°Le14'R 20°Aq14'D
SatOppNep 25/06/2007 21°Le46'D 21°Aq46'R

Confusion, narrow-minded leaders encourage half-truths and hatred.
SatSqrNep 26/11/2015 07°Sg02'D 07°Pi02'D
SatSqrNep 18/06/2016 12°Sg02'R 12°Pi02'R
SatSqrNep 10/09/2016 10°Sg24'D 10°Pi24'R

A new beginning? Have we learned how to make things better?
SatCnjNep 20/02/2026 00°Ar45'D

The November 2016 column invited readers to study cycles (see above) that represented the development of modern investment-based capitalism since the late seventeenth century. We now know that in 2020 the worst economic figures for three hundred years were recorded.

World economic system past its sell-by date

Chapter Two of my *Reversing the Race to Global Destruction*[163] studies the foundation charts of the two institutions that depict the intrinsic nature of the World Economic System that for 250 years has underpinned the Industrial Revolution – the Bank of England[164] and the present US Federal Reserve.[165] Surprisingly, both show few astro-indicators of realistic practical control and good business sense. Instead, they describe speculation and manipulation, the exploitation of vulnerable untapped resources for personal gain.

In the eighteenth, nineteenth and even early twentieth centuries, when there were many untapped areas of the world to invade, settle and exploit, such a business model worked well for Europe and the US. Until recently, social movements even helped ordinary people in these privileged countries to struggle to comfortable lives. This was uneven and not to last, as the rest of the world adopted and mastered the economic model, offering low-priced goods from their low-waged economies. My book *Economy Ecology and Kindness* details the astro-cycles from 1980 to 2009.[166] It shows how these explain the futile monetarist strategies that led to the Western world selling its assets from the past, then its credit in the present, and, in final desperation, to massively mortgage its future. In the years since 2009, we have developed even more extremely unstable ways to sustain a financial system totally unsuited to our twenty-first century 'global village' world.

In 2008, the sub-prime property market collapse was caused by banks creating and trading unsustainable credit, based on inflated estimates of value and income. Eight years later, government policies encourage Central Banks to do something similar, using quantitative easing and artificially low interest rates.[167] Buoyed up by such credit, alongside international 'off-shore' finance, property prices and rents have boomed, especially in the luxury markets of the World's major-city prime locations, such as London and New York.[168] Traditional populations are being priced out of their family home areas. Those that scrape by enough to stay are exposed to ever-greater personal debt.

Will all these debts ever be repaid? What are financial assets worth if they are not? It seems the World Economy hovers ever closer to an Emperor's-New-Clothes type abyss. Is a day of reckoning close at hand?

Days of reckoning

In December 2017, Saturn will join Pluto in Capricorn. Both will be joined by Jupiter for the 2020 Presidential Campaign, with the US Pluto return looming on the horizon early in that next new administration. Wrong understanding, leading to wrong reactions to these astro-cycles, could spell doom for the US and the world. When the astro-cycles are easy and vast areas of the world remain untapped, the consequences of self-serving greed, ignorance and hatred can be absorbed. This building triple conjunction in Capricorn, with Uranus in Taurus from March 2019, will be uncompromising. Some of its interactions have not combined like this for five thousand years. Little of the modern world remains untapped. The reins of military power are in the hands of vastly different cultures, driven by conflicting beliefs. If each group, culture and country applies the intransigent Capricorn conjunction with uncompromising self-interest, not only economic collapse, but internal and international violence could build to horrific experiences. There will be nowhere to hide away and defend what we value.

How to seek a happier world
We save ourselves from all this by realising that narrow self-interest is never the answer. On the contrary, during this decade's remaining transits, it will be the very cause of the fearful things we are so desperate to avoid. Courage, not fear, is the answer. Celebrating hatred in group condemnation is how cowards create enemies. The courageous do not to rush to judgement, but seek to understand and accommodate the needs of strangers. The truly courageous make those strangers friends. It is far more beneficial to move over, make room, bring more and more people on to our side. Through kindness and understanding we can dissolve the bitter forces of intolerant fascism that have been tapping into the Saturn/Neptune square. These have spread vitriolic hatred, within and between sub-cultures; from the East, through the Middle East and now to the West and the very heart of our European and US elections.

To avoid global disaster, we must stand up and expose such scapegoating in all its nastiness – not only for its inaccuracy, but the complete lack of answers its message offers. Whoever comes to lead, whatever they said on the way to their victory, may they implement policies that bring us together to solve our problems by solving those of all people and the planet. As the nastiness of the Saturn/Neptune square separates, the positive way is not to allow Saturn in Sagittarius to drive us into creating more and more barriers to hide behind. When we feel the need for a barrier, or new rule, let us seek first the root cause and focus on resolving it. In the long term, endless conflict will ensure when we build walls and then close our eyes and ears to those screaming in pain outside. So, let us raise our consciousness to a wiser interpretation of the transits – to realise that just about every barrier, be it physical or procedural, is the cause of misunderstanding and conflict. In medicine, blocking the symptom makes matters worse, if we do not find and heal its cause. So it is in all things!

On the Winter Solstice 2020 Jupiter conjuncts Saturn in the first degree of Aquarius. Problems will be far from over, but may it be a time to see glimmers of a new approach to technology and relationships that simplifies and eases away the constant pressure to work. With more time for ourselves and the people we love, we could then understand and embrace more experiences and people. No longer feeling threatened, we could focus on bringing the world together.

-o0o-

The January 2017 column showed how the result of the 2016 US Presidential Election offered salutary lessons for mundane astrologers. Re-reading it now, the then contemporary analysis below gives a very accurate description of the consequences in 2020.

Lessons for Mundane Astrology

Despite the billions spent on meteorology, we only expect forecasters to tell us if it will rain tomorrow. Whether we will get wet is up to us. Even a psychologist could not say with certainty that we will go out and risk pneumonia. This is because life can be lived on three main levels of consciousness, which have vastly different consequences:

❖ Mindlessly – experiencing or falling into whatever comes along.

❖ Manipulatively – battling to survive and dominate in an unfriendly competitive world.

❖ Mindfully – seeking deep understandings for the benefit of everyone.

Using astrology to predict final outcomes is subject to the same above variables. Astrologers knew years ahead that Saturn in Sagittarius would square Neptune and Chiron in Pisces 2015-16, and then Jupiter in Libra would oppose Uranus in Aries. So, they forecast a period of religious and social confusion, frustration, resentment, brutality, a sense of victimisation, scapegoating, exasperation and thoughtless risk-taking. Nearer the time, the specific issues and personalities became clearer. Mechanical prediction of the level at which people would react was never reliable.

What exactly is a successful or beneficial outcome?
When it comes to general elections, a good outcome can often be for the worst and a bad one for the better. At the 1987 General Election,[169] Margaret Thatcher won an overwhelming victory. However, the closing of the polls' chart had transiting Saturn, Moon and Uranus trined her natal Neptune and Moon near Regulus. Due to her hubris, she was ousted by hidden enemies thirty months later.

Hillary Clinton may well be having the opposite experience. On the polling day of the 2016 US Presidential Election, transiting Saturn applied to conjunct her progressed Jupiter. Surely this represented the heavy responsibilities she was about to undertake! At 08:04 EST on 9 November that 270-delegate threshold was passed, just as Mercury was within 32 minutes of arc from an exact conjunction to her progressed MC near her natal Ascendant. How could the news be bad? The Sun had just transited her natal Venus and transiting Jupiter (about to conjunct progressed Moon) in Libra had just trined her progressed Venus in Aquarius. Maybe the outcome was not bad. Bear in mind this natal Venus was in her twelfth house. Consider the hatred Donald Trump had whipped up against her and possible continuing gridlock with Congress. Massive economic upheaval lies ahead for the world, with the ongoing Capricorn Stellium and triple conjunction in 2018-20 and the 2022 US Pluto return. Could to have lost been the kindest and happiest thing for her and the Democratic party?

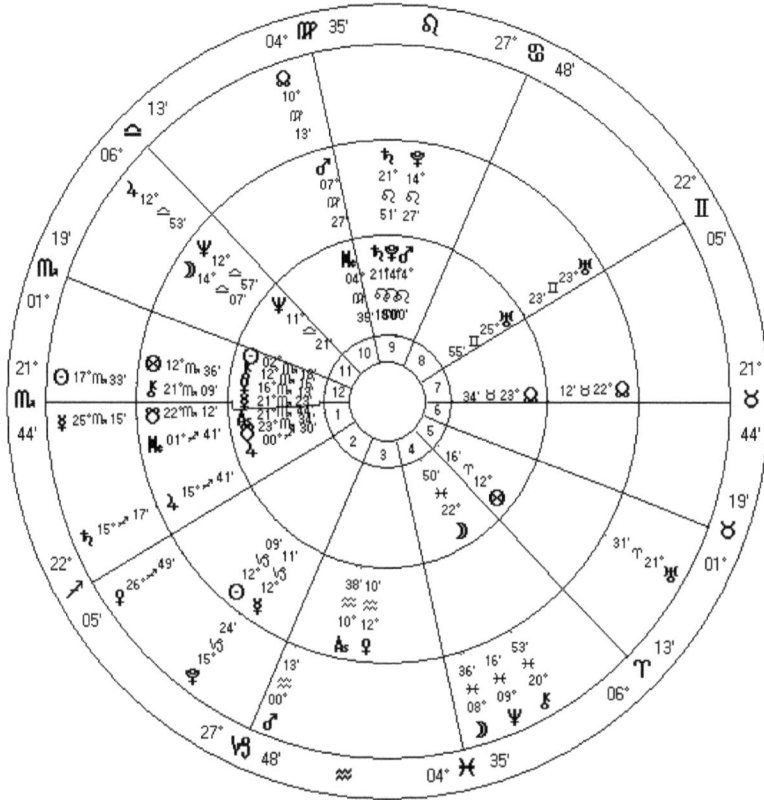

Hillary Clinton when Donald Trump passed 270 delegates
Hillary Clinton Natal Chart 26 Oct 1947 08:00 am CST +6:00 Chicago, IL
Middle Wheel Sec. Prog. SA in Long 9 Nov 2016 08:04 am EST +5:00 Washington, DC
Outer Wheel Transits Chart 9 Nov 2016 08:04 am EST +5:00 Washington, DC

Beware of what you wish for

In May 2015, David Cameron won a surprise General Election victory. In July 2015's 'Working with the Planets', [170] I wrote the following. We know what happened!

> Pluto retrogrades back behind the square to his first house Sun and only completes in January 2016. Saturn retrogrades to Scorpio near a square to his Mars in Leo, and then returns to conjunct his progressed Sun and Venus until August 2016. It will not be easy for him, or for us who have chosen him as our leader. Then, after a desperate internal struggle, Jupiter crosses his Ascendant, while Saturn applies to T-square his natal Saturn in Pisces and Pluto/Uranus and progressed Mars in Virgo, while transiting Pluto squares his Sun through the 2017 deadline year. Will the budget be balanced, as promised? Will the UK's relationship with Europe be decided? Will Scotland still be with us? To carry a unified nation with him through such times ahead would be a true sign of greatness. We shall see if he has the compassionate flexibility to find and follow the way.

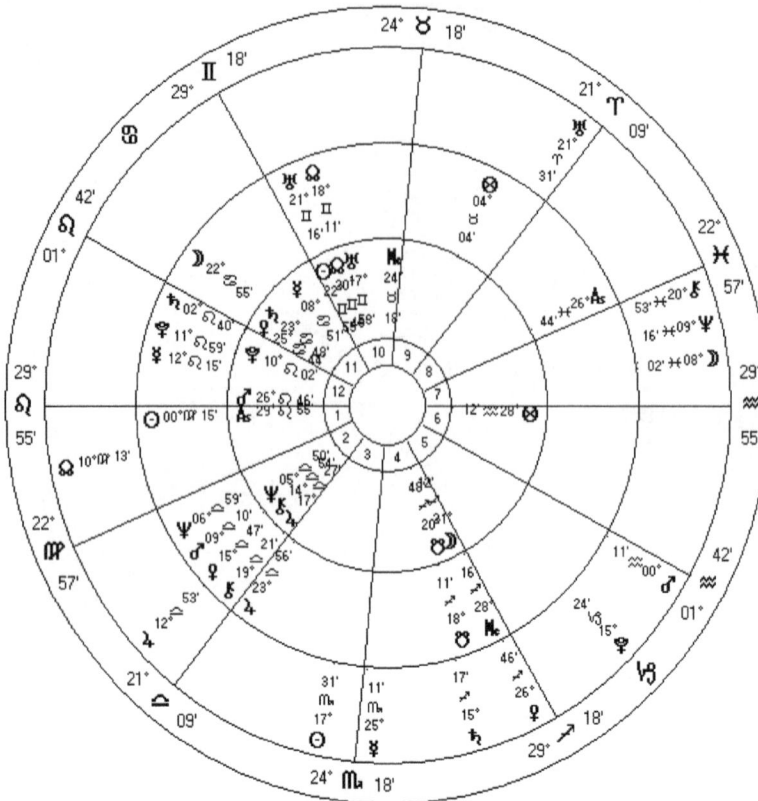

Donald Trump when he passed 270 delegates
Donald Trump 14 Jun 1946, 00:54 am EDT +4:00 Queens, New York
Middle Wheel: Sec. Prog. SA in Long. 9 Nov 2016 08:04 am EST +5:00 Washington, DC
Outer Wheels: Transits Chart 9 Nov 2016, 08:04 am EST +5:00 Washington, DC

Donald Trump when he passed 270 delegates

At that key triumphant moment for Donald Trump, transiting Moon was exactly trine to his natal Mercury, but it was applying to conjunct Neptune. Will the people get what they voted for? With Jupiter transiting his progressed chart's second house stellium in Libra, applying to trine his natal Sun, North Node and Uranus in the tenth house, it was easy for him to speak words of change and to be heard. Delivering all those contradictory promises may be a very different matter. Throughout his Presidency, Pluto in Capricorn continues to square the Libra stellium, being joined by Saturn and then Jupiter just as the 2020 election extravaganza gets underway. Unlike the business world, bankruptcy for a country is not such an easy start-again option. What other answers does he have?

Lessons for astrological prediction

All of which demonstrates to us in a very public way that mundane astrology can and should be used to describe and grasp underlying circumstances; to guide and enhance strategy.

   Whatever the motivation, attempts to make simplistic exact predictions are in the end destined to fail. Whether we take this on with the highest idealism or the sad need of self-promotion, the outcome will be counter-productive. Some, for the best of reasons, seek to prove astrology by precise prediction, but only narrow it into a straitjacket to predict again. Gauquelin found sceptics will go to any lengths to misrepresent astrology and 'prove' it wrong. Individual astrologers seeking fame and fortune risk being overwhelmed by selfish clients, after cheap advantage over others. Always just one bad prediction away from disaster, we trap ourselves in ever-greater intricate investigations to explain why it did not work this time.

   Far better to rest in the helpful certainty of the general picture. Guide, but always allow choice. See clients and events as working with the energy; not subject to what will happen, like butterflies pinned on a display tray. The great traditional and classical systems, often used as tools of prediction, are at their most valuable when we combine rulerships, dispositors, auspicious and inauspicious placings to create planetary pictures of multi-level meaning. In the foreword to *Christian Astrology* William Lilly insists:

   '...be thou humble, and let no natural knowledge, how profound and transcendent soever it be, elate thy mind to neglect that divine Providence...'

Astrology offers a wonderfully profound tapestry to enrich and strengthen our paths through life and enable the very best decisions, as when Joan Quigley advised Ronald Reagan on the timing of peace negotiations. It stands tall, when great mundane astrologers, such as André Barbault, Alexander Ruperti and Richard Tarnas, trace and describe the vast framework of world affairs. See the temptation to predict as a minor by-product, a distraction from the great work of understanding the cosmos and making the most of all experience within it.

-o0o-

As Brexit talks got underway, the March 2017 column used the astro-cycles to anticipate and explain the causes of what was to be ongoing, growing disagreement. By knowing and using them wisely, the negativity could be absorbed and a better way be found.

Changing Times Require Better Values

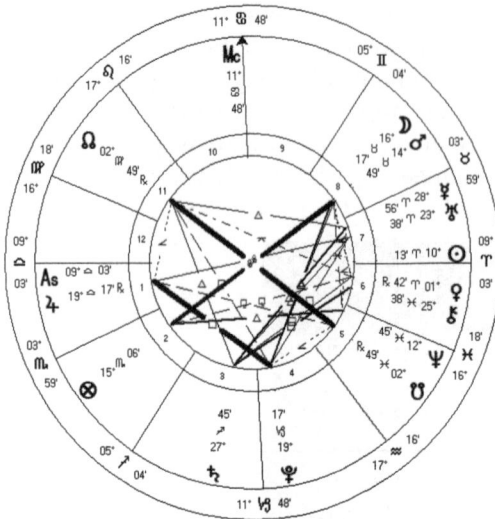

Jupiter squares Pluto
30 Mar 2017 18:18:44 UT +0:00
London, UK 51°N30' 000°W10'
Geocentric Tropical Placidus True Node

On 28 June 2016, the Sunday after the Thursday Brexit vote, Jupiter in Virgo completed its trine to Pluto in Capricorn ('time to take the plunge whatever the consequences'). On 30 March 2017, the penultimate deadline day for the triggering of Article 50[171], Jupiter, now in Libra, builds to complete its retrograde square to Pluto in Capricorn ('it's time to face the consequences of taking the plunge'). The aspect will make a tight T-square to Mercury and Uranus in Aries, sustained by a series of inner planetary connections until its final direct completion on 4 August. Expect tense talking and constant uncertain wrestling with reality.

Whether it is Brexit, 'America First', mainland European fascism, Chinese or Russian totalitarianism, the fundamental problem about negotiations based on self-interest is that greed quickly comes in to sour the agenda. As the Brexit talks start, Venus, just in Aries, is semi-squared to a close separating Moon/Mars conjunction in Taurus. The delicious salivating aspiration of wanting everything in *our* favour is quickly aggravated by the unpleasant 'bile' of others demanding the same for themselves. Even if we succeed by confrontation and superior power, a residue of resentment will lead to conflict, as the exploited count the cost of what they were forced to agree. Little peace or real profit in all this – just the need to arm to protect positions, agreed or not agreed, or to cheat, agitate and terrorise to correct and regain the advantage.

In such a world, anything agreed is not agreed for long. Instead, we face arguments over details, the imposition of sanctions. Intricate rules, seemingly 'made' to be broken; a treasure trove of earnings for clever lawyers and accountants and, when these fail armies and those that make their weapons. See all this in the 'Jupiter squares Pluto' chart above.

Better to see both sides
When you seek to take advantage of others, nearly always they will seek to do the same to you. Those of us left who were born and lived through the 1930s and early 1940s know the contrast between the dire consequences of the post-First World War

settlement (in the Middle East we suffer from them to this day) and the great global recovery created by the magnanimity of the post-Second World War Marshall Plan. Even the Cold War conflict that followed was between two social philosophies that were dedicated, nominally at least, to the benefit of all people in all countries.

The tragedy of the Uranus-square-Pluto and then Saturn-square-Neptune transits of the 2010s to date is that the Pluto-in-Capricorn need for efficient structural control is being expressed by turning away from such kind intentions. Instead, people are seeking ways to impose their will on others. 'America first', 'United Kingdom first', no need to care about the consequences for everyone else! How will it feel when such actions and attitudes toward others become the very ones those others lay upon us? The competitive business world is where a few people become rich at the expense of the many. Seeking to apply this to world affairs is a recipe for resentment and ultimate disaster. We need to deal with individuals and businesses, who have exploited globalisation for personal advantage, not delude ourselves into believing the everyone in the mass population of our individual nation can join these exploiters and take on the rest of the world.

Abandoning the wish for a kind and giving world that benefits everyone is directly opposed to our best interests. Because the present economic and social system is flawed and open to the few gaining unfair advantage, does not mean that the only way to succeed is to be better at exploiting others and forcing our will upon them. It means we have to question and radically change the fundamental ground rules of the system.

Our present system based on consumption and greed is exactly what we do not need. It leads to inefficient waste, unnecessary duplication, over-production, fraught, unfriendly relationships and conflict. The far better, truly efficient way to do business with each other is through cooperation, kindness and mutual support. For these are qualities of behaviour all but the most perverse in any negotiation would wish for. Paradoxically, dealing with others like this is the safest way to ensure our own interests are protected. Globalisation and immigration did not undermine our economies and take away our jobs. The way they were implemented to the advantage of greedy and selfish entrepreneurs did that.

The way to the best deal possible
Again, we should remind ourselves of November 2016's 'Working with the Planets'[172] description of the confrontation with reality that awaits us in the final years of this decade, as Saturn and then Jupiter join Pluto in Capricorn and intermittent earth inner planets build an ongoing earth stellium. These will be years when demands to be efficient, or die, will grow. If we cannot find kind values that enable us to cooperate, we may well return to a 1930-40s experience.

Have we advanced and become wise enough since then not to allow this to happen? Could it be that only the meanness of the mindset of each party in a negotiation is the root cause of the meanness in all the other parties? The capacity to realise this and so change and progress to decent final outcomes in three key world issues will be the litmus test of how our future is likely to go: Brexit negotiations in Europe, the actions of the Trump presidency, and our relationship with Islam and the Middle East. A time of truth is upon us. Only kindness, towards and from all sides, will see us through to happy outcomes.

-o0o-

The May 2017 column put the remaining years of the 2010s in a grand historical perspective. How were we to deal with the problems we had created for ourselves? Could we escape? The oft-repeated answer 'how?' was repeated, to be ignored yet again.

Settling Down to Change

We are at a paradoxical key turning point in the grand sweep of history.

- ❖ On the one hand, the last three hundred years have seen dramatic scientific and industrial transformation; the last hundred accelerating ever faster, with alarming irresponsibility, like a wild adolescent party. Now floundering with intensifying selfishness, we argue whether to face the global disaster of 'the parents coming home,' or pretend they 'won't mind'!

- ❖ On the other hand, Pluto, Saturn and Jupiter together (2019-20) in the righteous responsibility of Capricorn will symbolise a rare confrontation with reality (the only previous times since 1894 BCE were 549 CE and 1284 CE). On 12 November 2020, Jupiter conjuncts Pluto – the first time this has occurred with all three planets together in Capricorn since 2866 BCE.

Add to this the two previous Pluto in Capricorn transits (1517-32, the upheaval of the early Reformation, and 1762-77, the American Revolution and subsequent world struggle for democracy). Then begin to understand the frightening, contradictory struggles between disorder and demands for order that people seem to be facing all over the world, as they stand bewildered at this major turning point in the evolution of human history.

It's quite simple really
In spite of all this, when we look ahead at the outer-planetary transits of the next two months – even on into the last years of the 2010s – they do not show the massive aspects that symbolised the dramatic events of the 1990s, and years of the twenty-first century to date. Nothing like Saturn opposed to Pluto, just before Jupiter opposed Neptune, nor Saturn opposed Uranus across the Virgo/Pisces axis, or that horrific series of Uranus/Pluto squares and the mean-minded Saturn square to Neptune, whipped up by Jupiter in Virgo. Saturn in Sagittarius trines Uranus in Aries through 2017. After this, through 2018-20 the only outer-planetary events are Jupiter sextiles to Pluto and its trine, and then square to Neptune.

We are left with the routine annual inner-planetary connections to each other and the outers. All the angst will be focused on the building, ongoing stellium in Capricorn, augmented by the inners in earth signs at each third of the year. Between 2018 and 2020, Capricorn and earth sign planets will increasingly symbolise what dominates our minds, words and activities.

We have experienced amazing technological and economic advances. We have brutalised and been brutalised. We have built up intense resentment and responded to our changing circumstances with decisions and actions based on narrow selfishness. Now comes the task of clearing up the mess, dealing with the situations we find ourselves in. Whether it is Britain and the EU coping with Brexit, France with fascism, the US with President Trump, the massive issues faced by the varied cultures in the Middle East, the over-production of China and South East Asia, leaders out of their depth, megalomaniacs obsessed with their own power, indifferent populations only concerned with comfort and fun; everyone will be forced to roll up their sleeves and put right the circumstances they find themselves in.

We must face what has been said and done, repair the damage, put the planet and our relationships with each other back into good order. However difficult this will be, we can be reassured that there will be fewer new problems in the road ahead. Problems may be massive, but most of these were created by past errors and will be resolved by getting on with what needs to be done now. Just like clearing up after that wild night of festivities, or the dire destruction of a brutal conflict, it does not help to talk about who did what or caused it. Far better to develop mutual confidence, by working together on what needs to be done.

By focusing on what needs to be done in the present, our understanding may grow and expectations change. Ronald Reagan was elected in 1980 to defeat the 'evil Soviet Empire'. He started with the Star Wars defence system, but achieved much more by working together with that 'evil empire' for peace. Who knows what new friends we make, and outcomes we reach on the way, when exploring the implementation of the Donald Trump agenda, negotiate Brexit, or resolve global conflicts? With no new negativity to sour solutions, only past resentments will be in the way. The momentum for evil and dishonest intentions will fade. Unrepentant proponents will lose their energy, lose their legitimacy to continue.

Controlled by the ways of our Capricorn managing director, we can only address the circumstances as they are, get on with the job, think less about what we believe or want for the future. Focus instead on what is needed and feels right in the present; make friends, incorporate talents with eyes open to the way the cosmos shows us.

Get on with the job and see what happens. It *is* as simple as that!

-o0o-

Seeking to learn from the Grenfell Tower tragedy, the September 2017 column considered whether monetarist economics was merely a temporary business model, or just short-term simplistic economics, suited to the astro-atmosphere of the 1984 Jupiter/Neptune conjunction in Capricorn with Pluto in Scorpio. Would the system survive the 2020 Jupiter/Saturn/Pluto transit through Capricorn?

Authorities' failure to care

Affecting many thousands of people, directly or indirectly, the Grenfell Tower Fire exposed just how much in the United Kingdom has gone wrong, been misinformed, or neglected by those in power, over recent years. The event chart of the moment the fire was reported shows precisely the nature of the event, as well as the unyielding, persistent controversy it would lead to for many years to come.

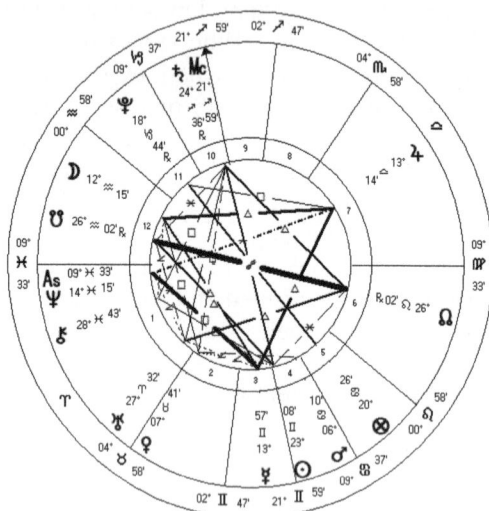

Grenfell Tower Fire
14 Jun 2017 00:54 BST -1:00
Kensington, UK
51°N30' 000°W12'
Geocentric Tropical Placidus True Node

A tightly applying fire grand trine is focused on Saturn near the Midheaven in Sagittarius, to which the Sun in Gemini on the IC applies to make a tight opposition. The Sun's ruler (Mercury) is in an air grand trine to Jupiter in Libra and Moon in Aquarius. The two grand trines, close to being an exact six-pointed star, demonstrate with tragic clarity that easy flowing-aspects do not always have pleasant outcomes. The only hope for good that could come out of this tragedy is if it leads to more care by the authorities to consider *all* the people they serve.

The Sun and IC ruler Mercury is in Gemini in the third house in a tight square to Neptune, which is rising in Pisces. Mars in Cancer in the fourth house will apply to square the seventh house Jupiter in the weeks that follow and, by progression, for years into the future. Just replace the technical information with astrology's plain language key words and the exact nature of what happened and its consequences are laid bare for all to see. When we do, questions and accusations follow fast and furious. Who planned the cladding upgrade? Were the fire regulations followed or adequate? Was the Fire Service's procedure appropriate? Was the after-event response adequate? Had tenants' warnings been ignored? Who was there to help afterwards? Underlying it all, was financial cheeseparing and a mentality based on privilege dominant at the heart of decision making? What are the implications for social housing policy and mobility?

As all this was happening, the need to counter-balance the relationship between ordinary people and the authorities erupted in an individual family's profound tragedy. The Charlie Gard case starkly revealed how medical and legal expert opinion can deny the right of loving parents to relate to, and make a decision about, their profoundly sick child.[173] Would Charlie have experienced much more harm, even pain if he had been allowed the experimental treatment his parents wished for, and so their relationship with him been allowed to follow the natural course they wanted?

The dire role of economics in our lives

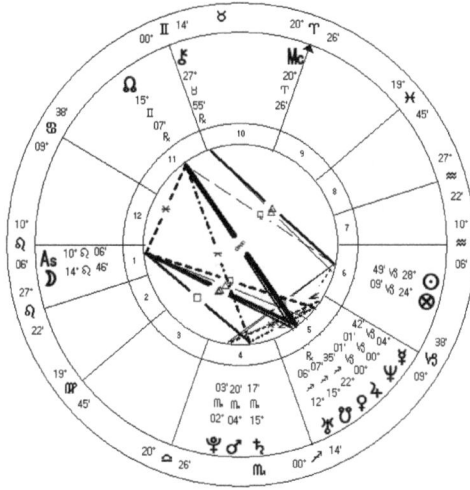

Jupiter Conjunct Neptune
19 Jan 1984 17:23 UT +0:00
London, UK 51°N30' 000°W10'
Geocentric Tropical Placidus True Node

It is the role of astrologers to describe and open doors of understanding, not seek to take sides and decide policy. Yet today's authorities seem to be floundering to understand, let alone act upon, the deep upheaval of the world and its systems, as well as the sub-cultures within their own nations. So, it might help to pick out an initiative that seems to be in tune with the Capricorn transits and offers insight into the issues they point to.

Could it be that the root problem is our obsession with money and things, making them the heart assumption behind all of today's decisions? Since January 1984, when Neptune and Jupiter conjuncted in the first degree of Capricorn with Pluto in early Scorpio, we have seen an ever-expanding dominance of greed-based economics in every aspect of our lives. Without any popular democratic decision to make it so, a particular way of economics has become the organisational 'scientific' root of how we relate, work and play with each other. Should this be the case and, whether it should or not, is our contemporary view of economics efficient?

The Econocracy is a key book published in 2017 by economists, who entered University as undergraduates around the time of the 2008 crisis.[174] They were surprised to find their teachers had little or no understanding of what was happening, or tools to deal with it going forward. Despite this, what they were then asked to study was little altered. Lecturers continued to indoctrinate students into a set pattern of mathematic neoclassical economic models. Their degree course uncritically kept to its fixed assumptions about the nature of society, and consequently the lives people had to lead. Intrinsically materialistic, the models make impersonal assumptions about human motivation and social realities. Being mechanical, they generalise or even ignore human nature. They encourage soulless competition, so losing the benefits of good will and cooperation. As a result, neoclassical models are inefficient and regularly fail to deliver expected results; even, at critical times, leading to boom and bust.

These complex technical models, upon which modern business practice is based, are not comprehendible to most lay people. The public are fed disconnected scraps of economic data – usually for self-interested commercial or political gain – by those seeking power. Hence, the very basis of day-to-day work, consumption and leisure is decided by unelected 'expert' technicians. No wonder the decision on Brexit was ill-informed on both sides, as has discussion about it throughout the year since. Slogans, rather than informed discussion have dominated the British media, blocking out time for other vital national and global issues. Now there is talk of another economic slowdown, a dangerous level of personal and national debt. Yet economic technicians tell us consumption and growth (even if is no more than the retail sales of imported goods) is the 'good news' way into the future.

The first of the Capricorn stelliums, no more than four months ahead, will profoundly question such facile analysis. Of course, not just in Britain, but most world economic activity, where such neoclassical economic analysis forms the very basis of nearly all decision making.

Time to change our minds

That young economists are beginning to ask radical questions about their discipline is significant. Such a debate needs to extend to other linked institutional areas that justify imposing the mechanical neoclassical economic straightjacket on ordinary people. My book *Reversing the Race to Global Destruction* showed how scientific, educational, legal, political and media experts disempower ordinary people's ability to make the lives they want for themselves.[175]

Recently, a contributor to the BBC's *Newsnight* floated the idea that news commentators should be elected for no more than two four-year terms! She pointed out that while politicians came and went, the people interpreting their actions continued to influence public opinion for decades. In addition to dominant individuals, editorial policy seems to be confined to a set category of opinions. The judgement of many editors and correspondents is limited to their education and upbringing. New ideas beyond this are denied balanced exposure. Radical new ideas in science, medicine, the law and politics are only reported to be dismissed, until irresistible grass roots public support thrusts them into the limelight, warts and all. Then, they may be reported as exciting surprises, or major issues of public ignorance to be challenged and dismissed.

Soon after his election as Prime Minister in 2010, David Cameron was mocked for suggesting measuring a happiness quotient should be part of policy making. Tragically, it was to be not much more than an idea, as he instead energised Britain to 'win' the global economic race. Maybe it should be resurrected, as we struggle to survive the consequences of politicians' facile promises to make, or think, America, China, UK and so many others 'first' in the race.

Back to basics in its most fundamental sense. What do we want of life? Surely not the everyone-for-themselves rat race of more and more possessions we never have time to use or consume fully, nor would enjoy doing so if we did.

Something to urgently consider in the months ahead, before it is too late.

-o0o-

As we came to the end of 2017, the November column made a strong statement about the value of astro-cycles in understanding the consequences and timing of our actions in public as well as our personal lives. Present problems were the product of past actions. What problems for the future were we creating by our present short-sighted decisions?

Actions have Consequences
(Astrology can help them to be understood and corrected)

Wise astrologers do not study the astrology of mundane events to pontificate about the foolishness of those in power, but to learn from these high-profile examples how to address similar problems in their own lives, and those of their clients.

Inspired by my comments on the Grenfell Tower Disaster in the September

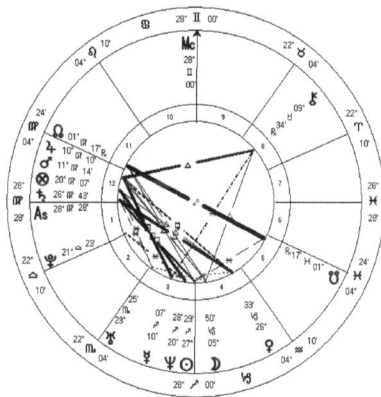

Right to Buy Bill Published
20 Dec 1979 00:00 UT +0:00
Westminster, UK 51°N30' 000°W09'
Geocentric Tropical Placidus True Node

column[176], I looked at the midnight chart for the day the Thatcher Government published the 'Right to Buy' bill. Although this enabled many council house tenants to buy at reduced prices and enrich themselves as homeowners, it was designed as a political statement to raise the status of home ownership. Many argue this marginalised those who could not buy then, or in the future. Councils received far below the market value for their housing stocks and had their ability to build replacement houses restricted. Council waiting lists have expanded dramatically. Dependence on a largely uncontrolled, often profiteering, private rented market has led to high rents and homelessness.

Belief-driven, some would say reckless, redistribution of resources is clearly shown by the stellium in Virgo squaring Neptune, along with the Sun and Mercury in Sagittarius, with Uranus applying to the square in the years that followed. Thirty-eight years on, the terrible symbolism of the Grenfell disaster has led to the UK's richest borough being accused of dangerous disregard for its poorest tenants.

The astro-cycles suggest this is the nemesis time for the 'Right to Buy' policy. Saturn (now transiting Sagittarius), Pluto and Neptune all square their 1979 signs, Uranus in Aries is under strain to Scorpio, the other sign ruled by Mars.

Squares, oppositions, conjunctions and sign changes to natal positions test the quality of the original action over time. They show what we did at the outcome will have consequences, and when and what these are likely to be. They also show all is not lost! The transit chart for the fire indicates hopeful ways to put right past errors. Alongside the grand trine of terrible conflagration, the Grenfell disaster chart also suggests what needs to happen next. Neptune in Pisces rising, squared to Mercury in Gemini, with the strong air grand trine, demands the reinstatement of compassion into the equation of social housing. Rigorous facing of the facts, beyond policy-posturing and watching-our-back legal strategies, is the only way to put right the past, and avert even worse social disasters in future.

22 November 2017 – Saturn return of 1929 Wall Street Crash

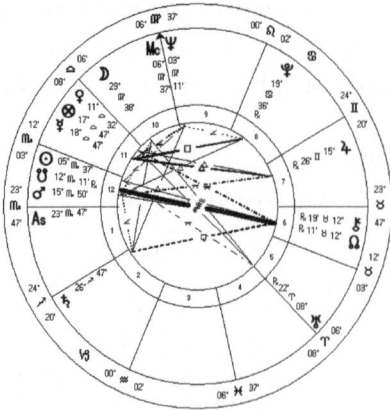

Wall Street Crash
29 Oct 1929 08:00 EST +5:00
New York, NY 40°N42'51" 074°W00'23"
Geocentric Tropical Placidus True Node

Wall Street Crash Saturn Return
22 Nov 2017 01:55:02 EST +5:00
New York, NY 40°N42'51" 074°W00'23"
Geocentric Tropical Placidus True Node

Housing was just one of many examples of 'loads of money'[177] Thatcherite 'family-jewel'[178] sale, monetarist policies, whose chickens 'came home to roost' in 1989-92, 2000, 2008[179] and will even more so in the earth-planet dominated years (2017-20).

The day Sun enters Sagittarius, a curtain-raiser to the coming years of radical reality, is Saturn's final 2017 return to its 1929 Wall Street Crash position. With Neptune in Leo, the 1920s saw unrealistic optimism that speculation could expand wealth without end. Until, that is, its Virgo ingress, with Saturn's Capricorn ingress in a stellium of inner planets imminent at the end of the year! The stock market continued to decline into the 1933 Uranus/Pluto square. A decade of global unease, and then, when Uranus entered Taurus, first in Spain then throughout the planet, great physical destruction and the loss of millions of lives followed.

Today, a massive global expansion of credit leaves nearly all nations with debt, upon which they struggle to pay the interest. Unbridled expansion of global enterprise has been allowed without regard for the lives of those left behind or the planet itself. Pluto is not in Cancer now, but Capricorn, and due to be joined by Saturn and then Jupiter, while again Uranus will soon be in Taurus. So, the reality will be about more than the destruction of homes and masses of individual lives, after which our economy returns to a more generous version of what we had before. This time we are due for a roots and branch radical restructuring of all we know and have come to expect. Many manual workers have already seen their livelihood and status taken away. Expect this to be faced by more and more people. To avoid the worst of outcomes, we must learn to live in a very different world.

The Winter Solstice 2017
Although the days approaching it seem to draw us down with an impotent darkening of creativity, the Winter Solstice is a time of hope, because it marks the shortest day of the year. At that solstice moment the Sun is furthest south away from the north.[180] So now, it can only return and with it the chance of rebirth and the possibility of glorious growth in the new year ahead.

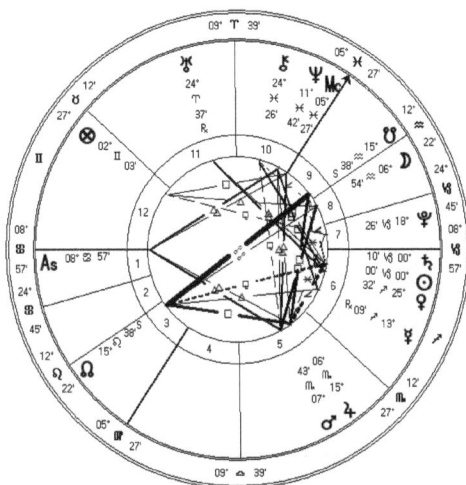

Winter Solstice
21 Dec 2017 16:28 UT +0:00
London, UK51°N30' 000°W10'
Geocentric Tropical Placidus True Node

The 2017 Winter Solstice is very special, because that day Saturn, and then the Sun, enter Capricorn and conjunct overnight before the next day's Solstice dawn. That annual faint but sure light of hope will be dependent upon a key condition, the need to be properly organised. Relax back from the constantly frustrated struggle with Sagittarian possibilities. From now on only what is real and realisable need be included. With Jupiter now established in incisive Scorpio, we have moved on from the distraction of mental anxiety. Now make a practical start by attending to your immediate concerns. Avoid confrontation. The time for talking is over, so confrontations could be bloody. The more that common sense takes over from posturing for the impossible, the better we will feel in ourselves and with others. Saturn in Capricorn is about sensible realism leading to effective and sustainable outcomes. Saturn in Capricorn has little time for dreamy aspirations. It soon despatches empty slogans, reduces pointless battles to rubble. It sees strength comes from integrity, leaves liars rejected without sustenance. It represents the energy of the Managing Director of the Universe, saying: 'Work hard, everything must be done to last'.

The cost of ignoring such authority is to lose and be left behind with little or nothing. These consequences will not only be for present failings, but for what we have failed to do in the past. Saturn transits insist we face and deal with them. Its transit, to be joined by Jupiter in 2019, approaching Pluto in Capricorn indicates rare Earth-shattering change. To get this wrong will not be a pleasant option.

The 2017 Winter Solstice's glimmer of light marks the start of a Capricorn focus due to build for three years, and to linger afterwards. Previous transits of Pluto in Capricorn saw the beginning of the sixteenth-century Reformation, and eighteenth-century revolution and democracy. The twenty-first century transit, powerfully accompanied by Jupiter and Saturn, will be more far-reaching than either; they merely opened doors to today's massive social changes.

A major shift in human consciousness

We can go further. The diagram alongside uses Solar Fire to study these three planets together over 10,000 years. See the 4,960-year gap between 2886 BCE and 2020 CE. Could we be at as great a shift in human consciousness as occurred with the development of the written word and

Electional Search Results
Criteria: FIND (Jup in Cp), (Sat in Cp) AND (Plu in Cp) AND (Jup Cnj Plu)
Search 4999 BCE to 54999 CE

22 Jan 4573 BCE	04:19:09
13 Jan 4336 BCE	06:47:42
9 Mar 3838 BCE	12:38:50
29 Feb 3601 BCE	11:34:18
24 Apr 2866 BCE	18:55:09
17 Aug 2866 BCE	13:35:24
1 Dec 2866 BCE	14:31:29
12 November 2020	**21:38:39**
3 Mar 2755	14:37:19
5 Aug 2755	18:01:51
8 Oct 2755	23:09:37
14 Dec 3253	17:48:03
9 Jan 3490	03:47:42

recorded history in the third millennium BCE? Could the glimmer of this 2017 Winter Solstice be that very first light of massive global change that only living scores of lifetimes would enable us to understand?

May we raise our vision beyond greed and fear to lightness of action, a worthy start to a radical new way!

Restructuring for a better way

We must stop using modern computerised technology to exploit, squander and scrabble over the planet's precious resources. This reduces power and wealth into fewer and fewer hands, leaving the rest working ever-harder for the pickings, with lives over which they have less and less control. This is the path to social discontent, even war, as it was in the 1930s.

We must start applying the brilliant capacity of modern computerised technology to use resources cooperatively, and hence more efficiently, reducing everyone's work pressure. It will require a radical change in what we expect and business methods. Through the coming Capricorn, earth-sign dominated years only radical restructuring to focus the world economy on willingness to care for everyone will create sufficient hope to avoid conflict.

The key that will unlock the gateway to this hope of happiness is the abandonment of greed-motivated growth as the sacred icon of our decisions and relationships. Replace this with mutual-support-motivated global sustainability. Then step by steady step new ways of economic, legal, educational, research and political priorities, laws and procedures will morph into our social experience.[181] Fewer hours to work each week, more to care for our family, be they young or old. Fewer things to buy, more time to enjoy what we have. Less to argue about, more to share. Less focus on protection, more on making room, cooperation. Fewer frowns, more smiles, less to fear, more to be happy about. Just as much to do and enjoy.

In short, the life most of us want *is* possible, if we welcome and use Jupiter with Saturn and Pluto in Capricorn against all we do not like or want. The positive lesson of Capricorn's ruler Saturn is that there must be limitation on limitation. By applying limitation to all that oppresses us, we set ourselves free.

Your personal way

For every 'oh so serious' idealist dipping into mundane astrology to advise on the way out of social conflict to make a better world, there are millions more people living their lives day-to-day, hardly noticing such trends and causes. For many, the joys in life are the ecstasy of music and parties, the intimacy of close loving relationships, the voice-driven communal roar of a sporting crowd, willing their team to victory. Then comes the need to pay for it all with work. So, organise childcare, and shop. Little time is left to study, to consider what to do about the pressures that shape our lives. Life experience is immediate. Ups are something to enjoy and downs to struggle through somehow. Politics are for tricksters or dreamers with empty promises.

It is OK, even good, for each of us to start from a state of mind that reflects exactly where we are. For realising this is the key foundation of our strength to make lives better. Focus on what is vital, a relationship, commitment, ambition perhaps. Do so without the fear of not being able, of dangers, even enemies. Be wary of those offering to protect you from such fears, or provide an unfair advantage. Anyone encouraging you to target others is nearly always seeking to use your energy to benefit themselves. Instead open your heart. It will open a way ahead of you. By dismissing the temptation to resent, hate and hurt, you will find supporting friends.

Illusory barriers fall away when we do not compromise on what we really need, or even want. By realising we are all in it together, confrontation falls away. We recognise what really makes good people and a good life for everyone.

When Britain leaves the EU

Vince Cable was laughed at, when he was the only leading UK politician to forecast upcoming economic danger in the early 2000s, well before 2008. So, his suggestion that, in the end, the UK may not leave the EU and he could become Prime Minister is fascinating! The astrology of the date we are due to leave certainly shows unfinished business, some might say a nation cut adrift from the world.

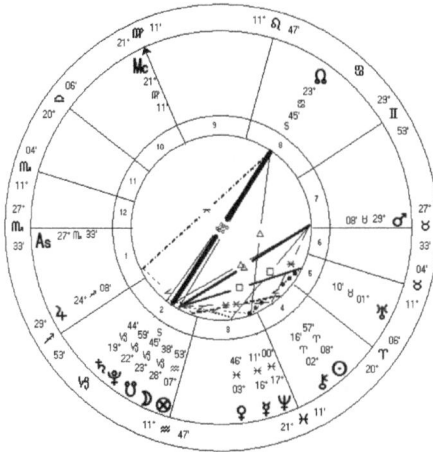

UK Due to Leave EU
29 Mar 2019 23:00 GMT +0:00
Westminster, UK 51°N30' 000°W09'
Geocentric Tropical Placidus True Node

Since such changes take effect from midnight (Brussels time, 23:00 UK time), a number of inner planets are bound to be below the horizon, but on 29 March 2019 all inner and outer planets are together down there. Just the North Node is above in the eighth, trying to draw in some sympathy from others for our second house material needs. Jupiter is rising in Sagittarius, just separating from a quincunx to that Node. It will return as it retrogrades through the summer. When it does go direct later in the year, it will quincunx the Mars' position. Chart-ruler Mars is void of course in late Taurus. It will progress into Gemini, urgently looking for friends, but, before this, will be moved into the sixth house of work by the advancing Descendant. Saturn/Pluto applying to conjunct in Capricorn, with the South Node retrograding back to meet them, all in the second house, does not bode well for the country's finances. Mercury and then Venus applying to conjunct Neptune in the third suggests communication driven by the need for sympathy. The Sun in Aries in the fourth house suggests a new courageous, if immature foundation. Uranus in the fifth house, squared by the Moon, about to enter Aquarius in the second house, suggests a very risky change.

As I write, it has become obvious there will be a transition period of at least two years (even less certainty on this timing from the Labour Party).[182] So it seems the UK will not leave the EU in more than name only until well beyond 31 March 2019. Between then and now, world economic events wait in the wings. Perhaps the flexibility in the Labour Party approach will be most in tune with the times.

-o0o-

This extract from the January 2018 column again puts our times in the perspective of a vast sweep of history thousands of years long.

The Seed Point of Incredible Change

```
Electional Search Results
       Tropical  Zodiac
FIND (Jup in Cp), (Sat in Cp),
(Plu in Cp)  AND (Ura in Ta)
Search:4999 BCE to  4999 CE

Enters    8 Jan 3838 BC
Leaves    15 Feb 3838 BC

Enters    2 Dec 2019
Leaves    22 Mar 2020
Enters    2 Jul 2020
Leaves    19 Dec 2020
```

Such new ways of doing business with and relating to each other will not be suddenly with us in early 2018! We have to put this seed point of change in context; consider it in a very long-term perspective.

The December 2017 'Working with the Planets'[183] included a search table, showing the rarity of similar concentrations of outer planets in Capricorn over the period from 4999 BCE to 4999 CE. When Uranus in Taurus is included, the result is even more remarkable. The only previous occasion when Jupiter, Saturn and Pluto were in tropical Capricorn and also Uranus in Taurus in the whole 10,000-year period was during the penultimate millennium of the Stone Age in 3838 BCE.

In the Fagan/Allen sidereal zodiac this has not happened at all during the period. However, these four planets, in the fire signs of Sagittarius and Aries from early November 2019 to the end of January 2020, have only been together there just one time during the period – 2430 to 2429 BCE. This was when the Bronze Age, having started in China, was about to come to Europe.[184]

```
Electional Search Results
     Fagen/Allen Zodiac
FIND  (Jup in Sg)  (Sat in Sg)
AND  (Plu in Sg  (Ura in Ar)
Search 4999 BCE to 4999 CE

Enters    6 Jan2430 BC
Leaves    5 May 2430 BC
Enters    1 Oct 2430 BC
Leaves    11 Jan 2429 BC

Enters    9 Nov 2019
Leaves    31 Jan 2020
```

To put in perspective and so understand the incredible changes that have been developing and are now being triggered in our own time, it might help to visualise all that has happened, been discovered and recorded in the thousands of years between the previous time these four planets were grouped together as they will be 2019-20.

Put your mind into someone living at the very end of the Neolithic Age, the very dawning of unbelievable change. How could that mind extrapolate from the new bronze jewellery and special tools and weapons made from it to the amazing new metal tools, and consequential power, new knowledge and changing social relationships all this would lead to? Visualise all that has happened since. How could someone alive at that time grasp any of it?

Now see all that has been building over the past five hundred years and accelerating through the twentieth century.[185] Just as Stone Age people, using tools, however well refined over the two and a half million years since its earliest Palaeolithic days, would not have the subtlety to assess the possibilities of the new metal tools. So, today, we cannot really grasp the changes that may emanate from computer technology and the breakdown of economic and sexual conquest that have been the exploitative driving forces of the past four thousand years.

The transition will be hard, as the certainties of past controls and assumptions we have relied upon are put to the test, found wanting and collapse. Seeking ways to hang on to and sustain past certainties will lead to increasing insecurity, resentment and conflict, even fruitless wars. Much better to visualise the liberating possibilities once all that old protectionist hierarchical repression is swept away. Seek to articulate fairer, more sustainable, less hyperactive ways of doing business. Rely on what you feel and need in relationships, while leaving the rightful space for others to do the same. 'You are you, and I am I and if by chance we find each other, it's beautiful'. This is the heart of all we need to know to lead happy lives.[186]

-o0o-

With Uranus about to enter Taurus, the May 2018 column compared notes to its 1930s time there. How similar and different would the events and challenges be this time?

Waiting for IT to Happen?

Remember and experience again those key moments of anxious anticipation waiting for an important someone to arrive, or something vital to happen. Then they do, or it does! Instantly the world is transformed; walking hand in hand down lovers' lane, perhaps engaging in stimulating conversation with an old friend, maybe a victory, or one's endeavour being rewarded. For those astrologers who risk precise forecasting, it may be prediction for good or ill actually occurring on, or near 'the button'.

Do not expect/anticipate the current ongoing Capricorn/Earth planet stellium to be like that. Over 2017-20 and then beyond, there will not be one major life/world changing event, but many that combine to pressure these years into a radical re-structuring of our personal power base, and/or the way the world's various constituents do business with each other. Capricorn is steady, determined, resolute, unshakeable and uncompromising. It and the other two earth signs hold out firmly for something real and lasting, not mere words, actions and emotions that rush us off in directions, and then lose their impetus and fade.

So, look for the deep re-structuring that is going on behind the various events that happen and our comments, reactions and feelings toward them. Avoid gut reactions to specific events. Instead, put them in perspective. Look for what is coming together. Encourage new, productive 'doors' to open. Turn away from futile, ever-weakening struggle to perpetuate our current economic system that has long passed its sell by date.

A vital stage in this ongoing three-year process is Uranus' ingress into Taurus on 15 May 2018. The monthly analysis (see detailed description below) shows many aspects, pointing to considerable wrestling action and forceful discussion around its key change of sign. This could be an important moment, but not the only one in these years of constant ongoing change. Between then and its retrograde return to Aries (6 November 2018 to 6 March 2019), enthusiasm for ill-considered inconsequential action will change into a search for effective, practical change. Whether this effectiveness will be for good or ill is an open question. Uranus' previous transit through the sign (1934-35 to 1941-42) certainly marked a most dire period in world history.

Then Neptune and Pluto were in the opposite signs to where they are today. Being in detriment in Virgo, Neptune-like Uranian change was obsessed with purity.

Dominant superior races had the right to do as they wished to those whom they considered inferior. Established in the 1920s, the fascist notion of racial purity rose to unassailable dominance in the early 1930s, particularly in Germany, Italy and Japan, while in the USSR, millions died in the Stalinist purges. Pluto reinforced this. The fight for 'my racial family' morphed with Neptune in Virgo into quests for the 'pure master race'. In Cancer since 1912, until the end of the 1930s, Pluto continued to explain the imperial upheaval, started in First World War. When, in 1934-35, Uranus entered Taurus, the three outer planets combined to consolidate and create the material resources to enable the ruthless imperial conquering zeal of the three axis powers. From 1936, they suited Franco's Spain. A few years later, Uranus in Taurus meant such rapid growth of German rearmament that is could invade Czechoslovakia and Poland. World War Two started, just a few months after Pluto's ingress into Leo, its new sign symbolising the heroic struggle and the sacrifice of millions to reverse the heartless force of fascism.

When Uranus transits Taurus this time, Neptune is in Virgo's opposite sign, Pisces. The news is dominated by myriad examples of suffering; some imagined, others terrifyingly real. The sick, wounded and dead from Syrian and Yemen wars, victorious Kurds with an opportunist new enemy at their back, refugees exploited by traffickers on their way to societies that have already rejected them, sweat shops in the third world, power-seeking politicians blaming hardship upon these innocents. Sympathy for all this is a dangerously selective battle between indifference and usually ill-informed bursts of outrage. Everywhere 'me first' movements emerge. To defend our families, we need more guns, more border checks and walls. In finance, more and more money is borrowed and artificially created to put off just that little bit longer the agony of paying our way.

Since 2008, Pluto has been in Capricorn, the opposite to Cancer the sign it was in from 1912-13 to 1938-39. So, we are in the midst of the death and regeneration of systems of control. We are seeing a constant push against restriction by individuals, and then governmental counter-efforts to contain the consequences with new restrictions; the erection of physical and judgemental borders between people. So, Pluto in Capricorn reinforces Neptune-in-Pisces sympathy *for the chosen,* with the legal and material means to put up defensive barriers against those undeserving 'Cinderellas', who threaten to take away what we (*the chosen*) have.

In 1934-35, as Uranus moved from Aries to Taurus to work with these two planets in Virgo and Cancer, fledgling resentment-driven fascism and Soviet purges matured into dispossession and even death for any who opposed. In 2018-19, as Uranus moves from Aries to Taurus, to work with these two planets in Pisces and Capricorn, the room for manoeuvre begins to close. The consequences of our Aries-time, ill-considered brutal thoughts and actions against others and our profligate financial arrangements will narrow. It will be time to 'pay up', literally and figuratively, or face the consequences.

The advantages of facing the consequences
Here comes the vital need to distinguish between short-term events and the larger context of change their combined effect is pushing us towards. The January 2018 column put these Capricorn years of change in a 'thousands of years' context.[187] Bear in mind that we may be living through the endgame of five hundred years of capitalist colonial exploitation, and even five thousand years of iron/male dominated chauvinism. So, it is vital to consider whether every barrier, problem, conflict we think we are facing is really an indication of the way that we really should not go. Is

what we see as a barrier to the continuation of past assumptions, really a challenge to incorporate the alternative into a way that answers all sides of the problem? Difficulties in building a wall indicates that the wall should not be built – find another way. The larger the existence of refugees, the more the need to find ways of sharing more fairly. When we see enemies massing on all sides, surely the wise course is not to act in ways that increase their number, but to try to answer, not reinforce, old problems, or create new ones.

See each of the many problems that will arise through these times as forcing us to confront reality. 'IT' is not just one event that will happen at one moment to change our world – rather there are and will be many 'ITs' that will pile up insistently, causing ever more pain and difficulty when we fail to answer them with true, objective understanding and compassion. The rapid advances that are forcing us closer to each other, with more power over nature, are indeed the core of a very different way of social organisation in the centuries and millennia ahead. To expand and enjoy the great power all this offers, we need to open our hearts to a more enlightened and supportive way of doing business with each other, and the natural world upon which we depend.

Or, as the last time Uranus transited Taurus, would we prefer another terrible war to complete the job of destroying life as we know it on the planet? As the earth-planet energy builds in intensity though 2018-20 surely, we can look beyond ourselves. Then the Pluto in Aquarius challenges in the years that follow will see us not marshalling science and humanity to destroy, but to find new ways of caring for the planet and each other.

-oOo-

The July 2018 column was inspired by Bishop Michael Curry's sermon at the wedding of Prince Harry and Meghan Markle, alongside a breath of economic fresh air from Mariana Mazzucato's *The Value of Everything*. Seeking to detract people from the difficult realities intensifying with the build-up of Capricorn planets, it urged humanitarian love – an even greater efficiency that also healed.

Love – the Second Great Human Revolution

British royal weddings have a way of distracting or re-focusing people along more unifying and compassionate paths. The union of the Duke and Duchess of Sussex was perhaps the most remarkable example of this to date – especially the sermon. Using the couple's obvious devotion towards each other to represent universal love, Bishop Curry invoked compassionate love as the force of a second great human revolution, as significant as the discovery of fire.[188] Indeed, a key message to raise up our age from its bitchy self-centredness.

It was especially heartening to see such a message gaining high-profile recognition, as it talked to a deep sensitivity in the heart of a new generation that my book *Reversing the Race to Global Destruction* had sought to invoke.[189] It was one of several indications that bright new minds are beginning to question and see through the destructive judgmentalism and futile cynicism at the heart of social satire today. Mockery and fault-finding need to be grounded on a vision of something better.

Bishop Curry's grand claim was that a revolution that put love for everyone at the very heart of world society would eradicate all human poverty and war. In short, the cause of all our problems is not the intrinsic nature of humanity, but a mere assumption of competitive greed insisted upon by mainstream opinion leaders, reinforced by the limitations of what is taught in our schools. As this column has regularly explained, with Pluto and now Saturn in Capricorn, monetarism based on competitive greed is the grossly inefficient business model that is being weighed in the balance and found wanting. Universal love is the answer. People and their supporters, who appeal to the basest human instincts, claiming this is impossible, and behave and legislate accordingly, are not only an inefficient enemy of common sense, but of the very people they claim to serve.

The flaws in simplistic monetarism

Even in its own terms our current world economic system is fundamentally flawed. A recent brilliantly argued analysis of how our world economy has gone wrong by adopting simplistic monetarism is Mariana Muzzacato's recent book *The Value of Everything*.[190] She shows that by classifying financial services as a part of GDP from the late 1970s, we have created an illusion of wealth that enriches and protects those that have, at the expense of everyone else. How far have we come from deciding what we as a people need, investing what is required to produce it and sharing the benefits of our endeavours? Nowadays, be you an individual financial trader, banker, hedge, pension fund, mergers or acquisitions manager, slipping in and out of ownership for a quick profit is all that is needed to get rich quick. Confronted by Capricorn reality, this casino world seeks to sustain itself by encouraging us to work harder to consume more. To succeed it relies on each of us matching its greed. We do this by borrowing more than we can afford, accepting rules that protect our sub-group at the expense of strangers. The system cares little for the suffering of others – just the occasional donation.

Unconditional love

True love is expressed with no conditions. When we truly love we are content to go behind, be considered last. We do not talk about a country, a culture or a family first. When the whole world and everyone in it comes first, and the lesson taught is to work for that ideal, the world and each one of us starts to get better. Do not be deceived into considering that the way of Capricorn is hard. Capricorn's aim is efficiency towards a harmonious universe. Harmony comes through tolerant recognition. Capricorn reflects its opposite sign, Cancer, the mother, the family. Capricorn uncompromisingly takes its responsibility to care for the family, leaving the inefficient to suffer the consequences. This will be so, however much those that run our world in their own self-interest twist, turn and legislate to 'kick the can' of the inevitable outcome of their erroneous actions down the road.

The remaining years of this decade will be difficult and confusing. Like a still-alive insect trapped on an entomologist's pin, the old ways will not give way easily. As we struggle to survive, blame and the projection of our own failings on others will grow in accusation, even hatred. Do not give in to believing such negativity. It is no more than the last throes of the old ways.

We must listen only to the heart we share, let the bluster of deluded simplistic greed-based economics wear itself out. Emerge and shake off the remnants of that old selfish world, long past its sell-by date. Let the sensitive subtle ability to touch, find information and make contact guide our first moves towards a gentle, loving, getting-better world. May everything needed be easily obtained!

Make better use of the new Uranus in Venus-ruled Taurus period than the 1935-42 one. Then, with Neptune in Virgo and Pluto in Cancer, revolutionary love became a brutally destructive obsessive illusion of 'racial purity'. With Neptune in Pisces until 2026, compassion and co-operation could become the answers to Pluto-in-Capricorn demands for true efficiency. If so, Pluto's movement into Aquarius will not see us under the thumb of a soulless mechanistic machine, as is often suggested. We can become masters of an immense subtle powerful resource, dedicated to the service of cooperating with evermore aware peoples throughout the world.

-o0o-

The September 2018 column saw little hope of clarity about how and when the UK would leave the European Union.

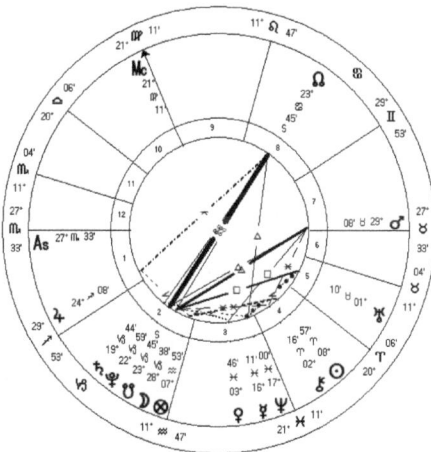

UK Due to Leave EU
29 Mar 2019 23:00 UT +0:00
Westminster, UK 51°N30' 000°W09'
Geocentric Tropical Placidus True Node

Over the years since the UK Brexit referendum, this column has mentioned more than once that Jupiter in Virgo was exactly trine Pluto in Capricorn on the Ascendant of the closing of the polls chart (a plunge into the unknown). Then it was in Libra squared to Pluto when we officially activated Article 50 of the treaty to leave the EU (faced with the problematic realities). In the first months of 2019, Pluto advances and the Nodal axis retrogrades, so that the day before the UK is due to leave the EU (if in the end it does!), Pluto conjuncts the South Node at 22 degrees of Capricorn.[191]

Many years ago, Stephanie Johnson wrote in Solar Fire the individual interpretation below:

Transiting Pluto Conjunction Transiting South Node
Fate plays a strong role in your life at the moment bringing to the surface people or events from your past. This can be as varied as someone important from your past reappearing to having to cope with a hereditary disease. You are being asked to pay your dues to society before moving forward with your own personal ambition.[192]

So, spring 2019 will be a time when decisions based on selfish disregard for, or intolerance of, others, greed, political expediency and other social diseases will confront their karmic consequences. We will be called upon to put things right, however difficult this might be to accept. Whichever way we campaigned and voted, time to face dire karmic consequences. Time to dig deep down to touch the unifying protective kindness shared all of good will, to see and correct errors.

Resting in an increasing sense of paranoia about the dangers of what is to come in the spring of 2019, now in autumn/winter 2018-19, we can see why myriad confusing, disjointed issues urge us pointlessly hither and thither. Are our opinions and strategies based on solid ground, or mere slogans and false optimism? Perhaps the most frightening possibility of this ongoing Uranus square to the Nodal axis is that all change, even that directly opposite to that we have been embarked upon until now, will seem just as hopeless. Even if we wanted to, is there a way back to where we were?

-o0o-

The one-hundred-year anniversary of the end of First World War, and the horrific global pandemic that followed, inspired the November 2018 column to focus on the lessons learned and how to avoid the danger of repeating past mistakes.

From Now On It Will Always Be
Kindness First... Kindness First!
(Transformed from the 2017 US Presidential Inaugural Address)

There are six archetypal states of consciousness in the Tibetan tradition.[193] Two have superhuman power, but limited awareness of the true nature of existence. In the godlike Deva realm, all experience is ecstatically delicious, but flawed because the beings there are unaware of the impermanence of their ecstasy. In the Asura demigod realm all attention is focused on jealously fighting for this Deva experience, but by the very act of fighting, denying themselves the capacity to have it.

This Asura mindset lies at the heart of the many 'me-first' manifestations that dominate today's world. Whether it is our religion, nation, sub-group, or my family first, it ends up with masses of lonely groups and individuals, deciding and sniping at each other from the fixed-position isolation of self-contained ignorance.

Without the reassuring ease of open interaction, definitions become increasingly frozen and sacrosanct. Everyone has to fit into a stereotype. It becomes impossible to express a public opinion without being labelled, threatened, trolled, or expelled. This is becoming so toxic in many parts of the world that to give specific examples, just to mention trigger words, could immediately alienate some readers of this column.

In such an atmosphere, digging in our heels, thinking only of ourselves, building more and more methods and instruments of power, unleashes fear. Accusation and acts of last-ditch aggression spread like a disease, corrupting in its wake all but the most kind and patient. War and economic hardship sire emigration and the social disruption of unfamiliar people in our midst. From this can come a process of polarisation that seems to justify rejection, then terrorism and, if we are not careful, all-out war.

Such attitudes and circumstances are typical when Pluto is in cardinal signs, especially when the sign is Capricorn, and even more so if joined by Saturn. The two are rarely together in that sign. Most recently was 1517-20, exactly five hundred years from today's transit (2017-20). Brutal persecution and conflict, sired by fixed-position self-righteous certainty, characterised the Reformation from its very early years. Superior religious certainty polarised conflict within countries. Enabled by the expansion of global travel, it was used to justify the oppression, even slaughter, of indigenous populations all over the world.

More recent horrors of polarisation – First World War

11 am 11 November 2018 marks the one-hundredth anniversary of the Armistice at the end of First World War. This war demonstrates the horrific consequences of 'me-first whatever the outcome'. Today, Pluto is in Capricorn's opposite sign, Cancer. When Britain joined the conflict, Pluto was in Cancer's second degree, with Saturn about to join it, squared by Venus and Mars in late Virgo.[194] The nation was told we would teach the Germans a lesson and be back in our Cancer 'home by Christmas'. As Saturn, and Jupiter towards the end of the period, joined Pluto's advance through Cancer, we saw a four-year conflict with 17 million military and associated civilian deaths; devastation that could only be endured by saying the First World War was 'the war to end all wars'.

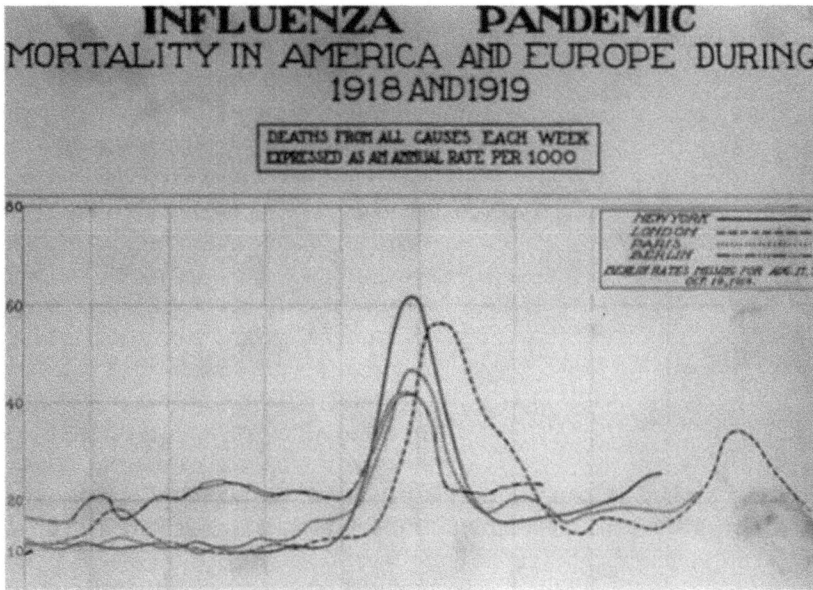

INFLUENZA   PANDEMIC
MORTALITY IN AMERICA AND EUROPE DURING 1918 AND 1919

♃	♂	♇	Tr-Tr	10 Aug 1918	21:02:05	06°♋02' D	06°♋02' D
♇	SR		Tr	7 Oct 1918	19:13:05	06°♋39' R	
♃	SR		Tr	3 Nov 1918	13:51:35	15°♋49' R	
♃	SD		Tr	2 Mar 1919	16:35:22	05°♋45' D	
♇	SD		Tr	19 Mar 1919	17:33:11	04°♋32' D	

Post-war celebrations were short-lived. Recorded through 1918 and becoming virulent from the 10 August Jupiter/Pluto conjunction came a horrific worldwide influenza epidemic. A macabre marker to the end of hostilities, October and November 1918 saw a massive peak in fatalities, as both planets in early Cancer started to retrograde back ever-closer to each other.[195]

It is said that twenty-five percent of the UK population were infected with 228,000 fatalities and estimated around a third of the then world population were infected, with between fifty and one hundred million deaths.[196]

The First World War and these horrific events at its conclusion symbolised the failure of European colonialism – ahead just a few decades of its twilight phase. Four hundred years of expanding exploitation had led to an orgy of fraternal blood-letting that climaxed with a global pandemic. For all its arrogant claims of superiority, and hence its right to conquer and control, Europe could not even save its own citizens – let alone the rest of the world. All families, be they imperial or everyday, were overwhelmed by a Saturn and then Jupiter with Pluto in Cancer force far beyond their capacity to contain. Radical change seemed unavoidable, yet still people preferred to sow seeds of conflict, by turning away from the pain of refusing to learn from each other.

The horrors of polarisation in the twenty-first century

The one hundredth anniversary chart sees Pluto now in the opposite sign of Capricorn. It is accompanied by Saturn, which is almost exactly opposite that agonising 1918 Jupiter/Pluto Cancer degree. Jupiter itself returns to that opposition point at the very end of 2019. 2018 sees the world infected by a very different, but even more dangerous disease, the consequences of everyone or every group at the other's throat.

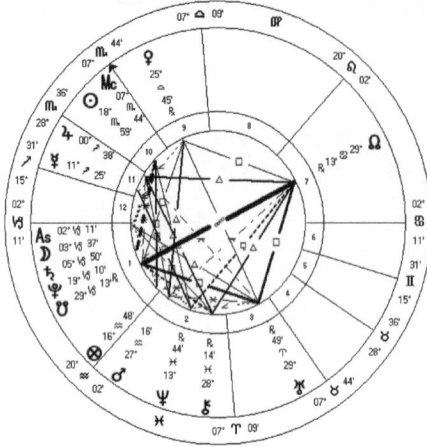

Numerous astro-cycle factors lie behind major trend changes, but perhaps a key trigger point to today's world mindset was Jupiter's conjunction to Neptune, one minute of arc past the cusp of Capricorn on 19 January 1984. This time in history, the world turned away from what was now considered 'dysfunctional Sagittarian idealism'. Instead, we would prioritise, put our faith in and organise everything around money. Money became the ultimate measure of success or failure.

WW1 Armistice Day 100th
11 Nov 2018 11:00 UT +0:00
London, UK 51°N30' 000°W10'
Geocentric Tropical Placidus True Node

Crucially, this left the question of how that money was obtained struggling to be heard. Was it economically viable long-term to: have one-off sales of publicly-owned utilities, buildings and land; private asset strip; sell interests and ease controls of financial institutions; ever-extend borrowing by individuals, institutions and governments; ignore environmental consequences? All made lots of money available. So, surely, they justified the Monetarist creed!

Such a monetarist philosophy is dangerously seductive. By appearing to give so much, it makes us want without thinking. We stop asking how much is beneficial or something we need. Even if we put to one side arguments of whether borrowing is sustainable, because it stimulates growth, or future scientific discoveries will resolve ecological concerns, monetarism remains most harmful to the human character and relationships. It acts like a cancer that disintegrates the fundamental criteria of truth and decency, by which we live with each other.

When an explosion of having things and evermore cunning ways of getting and showing them becomes the norm, it is everyone for themselves. Fairness and morality have little to do with it. The strong and wealthy make rules for themselves, gaining allies by offering a 'cut' to anyone supporting their agenda; join with them against the 'enemy'. Those left out are vulnerable to persecution, even used as scapegoats by those in power, to 'explain' any shortcomings. Rational fact-dependent debate is replaced by emotion-driven prejudice. The 'post-truth' of 2016 morphs into 'fake news'. The argument is 'won' by the 'how we want it to be' of those shouting loudest, as a maelstrom of anger and hatred stirs on all sides.

The world since the mid-1980s has been like an increasingly wild party for some, with far too many dangerously left out. Our children are being raised in a world where gut-felt emotion seems more reliable than objective truth. Exploited by costly higher education and low-paid insecure work, millions of them left stateless and hardly educated by war and economic collapse. All are vulnerable and 'ripe for the picking' by demagogues to stimulate and direct resentment against who knows what and where. Such is the *lethal* fertile ground, from which a global epidemic of terrorism and war is growing.

All this is stirring amidst desperate last-ditch attempts to keep the economic 'show on the road'. As the Saturn/Pluto in Capricorn transit unfolds and is joined by Jupiter, either the boom of recent years will bust, or the intrinsic nature of the world economy will lose all contact with reality. Facts will become arbitrary. Desire-driven wants will determine truth, and drive our actions against those we see to be in the way. It could feel like we are drowning in a hot accusational sea of adversarial emotion.

Capricorn is soft inside, but outside it is as hard as nails. When threatened, it seeks to control and order the world by persistent, indefatigable determination – however harsh the path, or dire the consequences. Imagine each individual or group with conflicting emotion-driven convictions reluctant to step back and look at the broader picture. Imagine the whole world suffering the social epidemic of everyone or group at the other's throat. Imagine a world where our minds have diseased into such Asura mentality, constantly struggling for what others have, motivated by fear they will take from us 'the little we have left'.

Or...

Do not despair! The history of Pluto and Saturn in Capricorn can be seen in a much more positive light. 1284, the most recent time that Jupiter also was with them there, is said to be the year the Pied Piper, for good or ill, enchanted the children of Hamelin with his music. 1271-95 were the years of Marco Polo's journeys to China, which led to the growth of Venetian trade and sea explorations for easier routes in the coming centuries. Venice established the ducat, which became the transactional currency of global trade for the following six hundred years. Then the sixteenth-century Reformation brought knowledge and power to ordinary citizens. This grew into the eighteenth-century Enlightenment and our capacity to transform the world today, providing we see our problems as opportunities to put things right.

There is always a better way, if we are ready to listen 'outside the box' of our own prejudice. There are powerful new practical possibilities if we are willing to learn when the problematic issues of Capricorn dominate the astro-cycles. Step back from simplistic accusations. Step out from the personal self and look objectively at what happens in the world. Particularly try to understand from the perspective of those we see as enemies. What is their story? What have they experienced? What is the history of their seeing things this way? Why do their numbers seem to be increasing? Really, can there be so many 'absolutely evil' people in the world, or are each of us merely *imagining* the other in this way? Are there skilful ways to open up tolerant channels of interaction? Surely, like us equally, everyone we meet seeks happiness. The best way to live in a happy world is not 'me-first and hard luck if that hurts you'. It is the very opposite. Happiness comes when we give to and expect kindness from everyone, when we do not create their problems, but seek ways to answer them. Think and say this more and more, louder and louder. It is the antidote to the social disease that threatens us all. Applied by more and more of us, it will make the world better.

Remember and keep on saying always: a kind, happy world is a truly efficient world. This is the message of the enlightened Capricorn... and there is nothing that turns on Capricorn more than everyone working together in a well-ordered operation!

-oOo-

The following special article was written for the January 2019 *Astrological Journal*. It clearly anticipates and explains the crisis and confusion that was to grow throughout the year.

A Key Turning Point in Human History

For six years in lectures and the 'Working with Planets' column, the rare combination of Jupiter, Saturn and Pluto being together in Capricorn has been anticipated with some trepidation.[197] Now we are in the middle of the Saturn/Pluto phase, with Uranus about to go direct and establish itself in fellow-earth-sign Taurus. Since 4999 BCE, only in 3838 BCE, 1660-01 BCE and 1517-20 CE have these three planets been in these signs at the same time. The current occasion (2018-20 CE) will not be repeated until after 5000 CE. This diagram shows when Uranus is in Taurus as well, only the 3838 BCE and 2020 CE dates remain.

Electional Search Results
Tropical Zodiac
FIND (Jup in Cp), (Sat in Cp), (Plu in Cp) AND (Ura in Ta)
Search:4999 BCE to 4999 CE
Enters   8 Jan 3838 BC
Leaves   15 Feb 3838 BC
Enters   2 Dec 2019
Leaves   22 Mar 2020

This comes after ongoing horrors, indicated by seven Uranus/Pluto squares (2012-15), were followed in 2016 by a Venus, Mars, Saturn and Jupiter grand cross in mutable signs, while Jupiter trined Pluto through much of that year. All this so unsettled humanity's common sense, it is little surprise that today we are still struggling to put right 2016's simplistic me-first decisions.

When trapped in a hole, the vital first step is to stop digging, and then look up, back and around to assess the situation. The years 2017-20 mark a momentous turning point in human history. 3838 BCE was in the late Neolithic millennium of the Stone Age, around the time of the first evidence of writing. Consider the massive advances achieved through the use of metal and the written word. In 7,000 CE, when our far-off descendants look back to the electronic developments of our times, will they see them as a turning point in human history just as significant?

Major events of the Pluto in Capricorn (tropical and sidereal) periods from 1195 BCE include the Trojan War, the building of the Temple of Solomon, the writing of the *Upanishads* in India and the Greek *Theogony* by Hesiod, and the construction of the Greek Parthenon.

In the early Common Era, just twelve years before Pluto's 277-331 CE transit in Capricorn, much of the Library at Alexandria was destroyed or moved to be further destroyed just over a century later. In the midst of the transit, Rome legalised Christianity and the Council of Nicaea dictated the form the religion was to take.

The 1515-44 CE period saw the Reformation, the first circumnavigation of the World, the expansion of Islam into Eastern Europe and also India. Copernicus' *On the Revolution of Heavenly Bodies* was published. Rapid expansion of colonialism and industrialisation during the next period (1762-92 CE) lead to radical upheaval in the way the whole world, and societies within nations, did business with each other. European nations, led by Britain, mapped and recorded the world, as if creating an eighteenth/nineteenth-century 'Domesday Book' of assets to exploit. Out of all this today's capitalism and the struggle for democracy were born.

The fundamental issue of our times

Now ponder how the events during the above Pluto-in-Capricorn years have grown into today's world. Clearly the coming of metals and written recording has increasingly heated up human activity. On the one hand, we are more inventive and capable of great things. On the other, darker, hand, humanity has become increasingly greedy. People demonstrate almost spoilt-childlike destructiveness if what they want is not provided. The ever-greater inventive force of the last five hundred years has made this tendency horrifically lethal. The problematical foundation that stirs this danger is the way we choose to measure success and failure in our day-to-day dealings; the financial system.[198]

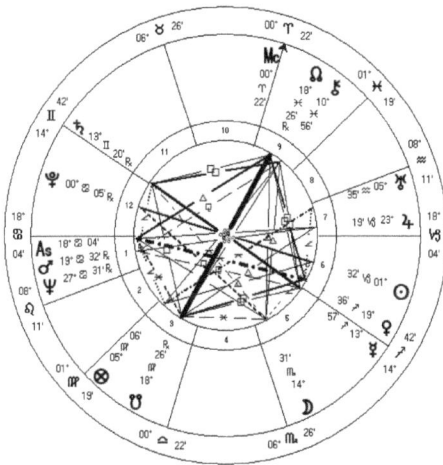

US Federal Reserve
23 Dec 1913 18:02 EST +5:00
Washington, DC 38°N53'42" 077°W02'12"
Geocentric Tropical Placidus True Node

In astrology, the three earth signs describe the crucial requirements of good business husbandry: the nurturing of proper sustainable, even beautiful products (Taurus); motivation to achieve the finest quality (Virgo); and firm controlling organisational structure (Capricorn). Without these qualities a business may grow, even blossom, but soon fade when challenged. A business may briefly exploit an easy resource, trick and use others' resources to sustain pretence of success. This is not proper earth-based business. We use air energy to manipulate value, fire energy to gamble, and experience fear and greed with water. Without responsible earth energy as well, booming value must bust, unsustainable riches be lost, and many people suffer so that a few can gain.

Ignoring this, after a struggle between various idealistic and individualistic methods of economic control, the latter part of the twentieth century seems to have bequeathed to the twenty-first century world a casino-like monetarist system with *laissez-faire* control. The horoscope of its heart beat, the US Federal Reserve Bank, shows this clearly.

The Capricorn Sun opposed by Pluto (fear it will not last); Mars applying to Neptune opposed Jupiter across the Cancer/Capricorn angles (confused risk-taking against all odds); Mercury in Sagittarian fifth house opposed Saturn in Gemini (reckless gambling against reality). Small wonder that just sixteen years later the system collapsed, leading to a horrific depression that blighted millions of lives and was a major contributory cause of the Second World War.

That was just a warning. The diagram overleaf (see links to full colour versions of the images in this article at [199]) shows that in 2017-20 the world faces an unavoidable and far more fundamental confrontation with reality. See that over the past hundred years major booms and reversals in equity markets, upon which today's economic decisions depend, have always occurred when there was a concentration of planets in earth signs. The 2020 concentration is far more powerful than any in these hundred years. On its own the Capricorn stellium is stronger than the one of 1517-20 and, with Uranus in Taurus, more power than any since 3838 BCE.

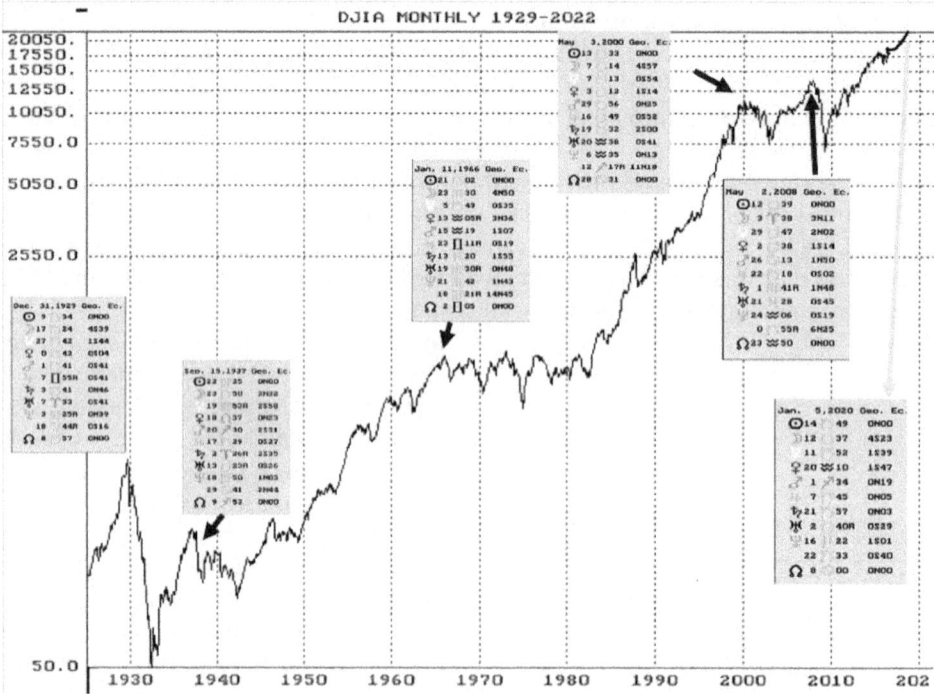

Below are three years highlighting just the earth planets. As well as Jupiter, Saturn and Pluto in Capricorn and Uranus in Taurus, note how the number of planets in earth signs intensifies in pulses throughout these years as the inner planets transit Capricorn, Taurus and Virgo.

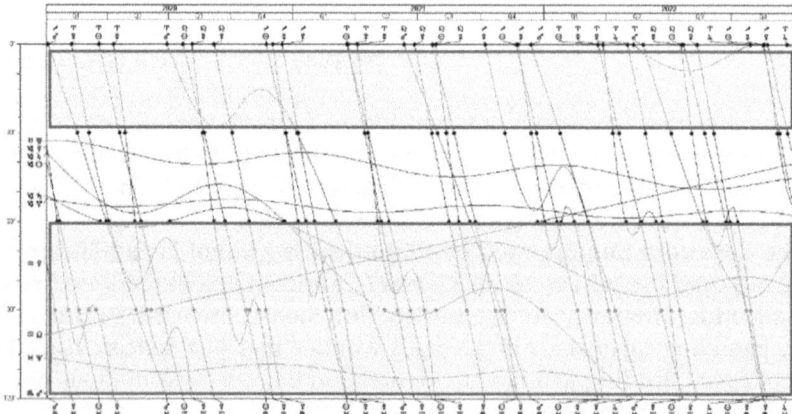

In addition, the diagrams below show the 26 December 2019 Solar Eclipse, focused on the East Indies and Asia, and then six months later another Solar Eclipse, on the Summer Solstice 21 June 2020, still in Asia, but now focused upon Hong Kong.

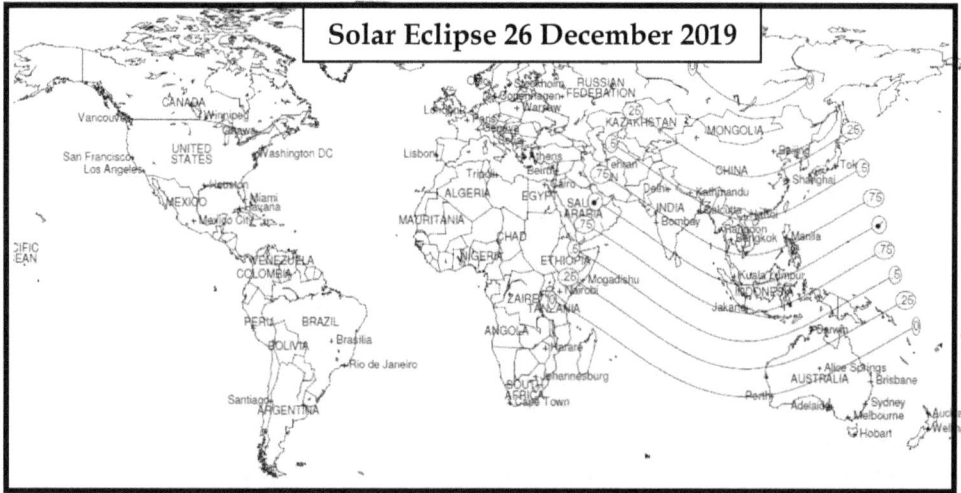

Solar Eclipse 26 December 2019

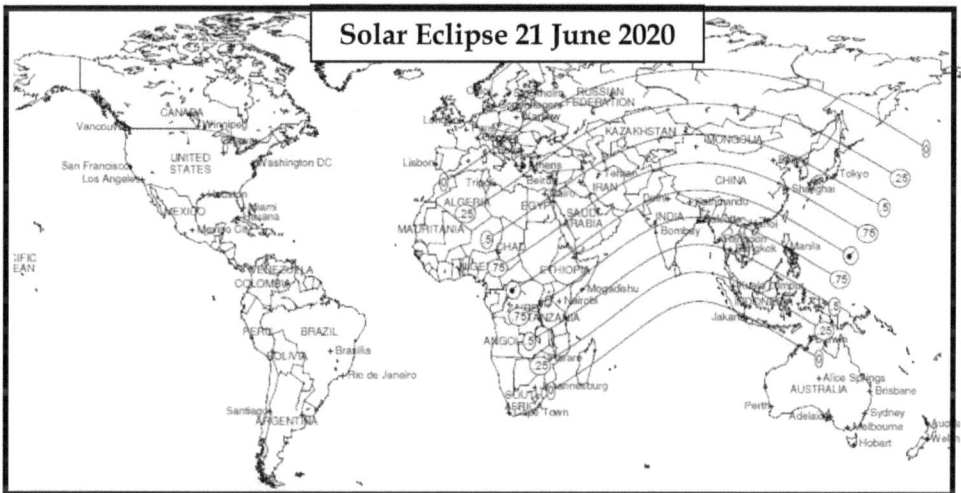

Solar Eclipse 21 June 2020

We are at a key turning point in human history.

What experiences and outcomes are ahead?
As the earth-planet concentration builds, the consequences of our previous actions confront us. Extreme weather, brutally destructive wars with no concern for human suffering, fractured schisms within societies, fear, the futile building of barriers to keep out the unknown.

Inadequate, worn-out economic and belief systems are unable to understand and contain an out-of-control economy. Debt is so over-extended that there is little hope of a bailout if markets crash. Will we be left scrambling for survival, with the force of arms determining the winner? Globalisation has indulged the masses, but left them helpless, as the few gain the world's wealth. Information technology tempts, and then traps us intrusively in systems we feel powerless to control. Five thousand years of male objectification of women and the feminine in all of us has made brute competition, social conflict, even war, seem inevitable.

Stopping the race to disaster

It does not need to go on like this. Our race to disaster stops when we question the assumptions of monetarist economics. The worship of growth leads to financial manipulation and the unbridled production of unnecessary goods, methods and services. The deification of the freedom to profit, whatever the cost, suffocates our oceans with plastic and chokes our air.

It is not too late to change course away from the insensitive destructive twentieth-century ways to a better twenty-first century political/economic paradigm. All that is wrong starts to turn around, when we abandon the politics of greed, when sustainability replaces growth as the measure. To have value, goods and services must last. Turn away from those who abuse their power. Work to reduce the need for barriers. Focus on kindness and respect. Appreciate life and each other. Celebrate the many male/female forms in our birth charts. Let personal, social and world affairs be based on respect and the celebration of differences.

Goodwill thus created would lead to radical changes in our economic, legal, educational, political and media institutions. No 'snowflakes' here! Enterprises based on co-operation are the truly efficient ones. Have the courage to trust and welcome in others. This is Capricorn beyond all the dangers we fear; Capricorn at its truly business-like best.

What of the Aquarian years that follow?

On the Winter Solstice 2020 Jupiter conjuncts Saturn in the first degree of Aquarius.

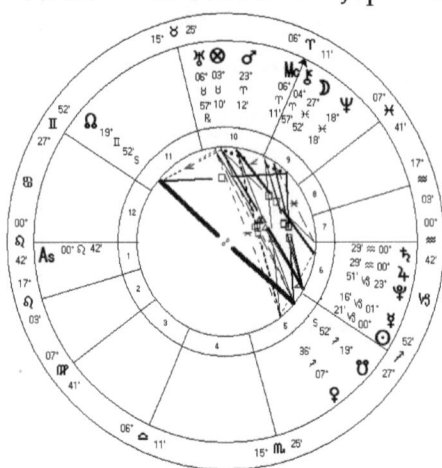

Jupiter Saturn Conjunction
21 Dec 2020 18:20:18 GMT +0:00
London, UK 51°N30' 000°W10'
Geocentric Tropical Placidus True Node

The Moon applies to ingress Aries and sextile the conjunction, but squares the Sun and Mercury in early Capricorn, while they apply to trine Uranus in Taurus. The pattern indicates pent-up wishes to be free, held down by the futile and horrific baggage of the 2010s. As Jupiter and Saturn apply to square Uranus in Taurus, dragging our way out of it will dominate 2021.

Many astrologers see hope, citing a new phase of Jupiter/Saturn conjunctions in air signs. There is the potential for both hope and despair in every aspect between any planets. We can be doomed or transformed by the tense aspects. We may indulge ourselves or make the most beneficial use of the easy-flowing ones.

Better to see this conjunction as the glimmer of a new agenda to come. The Pluto-in-Capricorn period has challenged and transformed humanity's structural relationship with the planet. The Pluto-in-Aquarius period will see a transformation of knowledge and technology and so change how we treat each other. The systems we create and our consequent experience will evolve from our behaviour through the 2019-20 last earth-planet years.

If the present selfishly destructive battle for growth continues unabated, expect unyielding, judgemental, paranoia-driven sub-group loyalties intensifying: social conflict, rebellion, drone and conventional warfare, terrorism versus authoritarian control of information. Trapped in a fight for survival against enemies we demonise and refuse to understand, we will passively submit to the 'higher wisdom' of artificial intelligence.

We can create and experience better lives through the Pluto-in-Aquarius period, if we now address today's problems. Realise sustainability is more important than growth. Cease labelling and condemning. Value each other. Bring down barriers. Produce no more than is needed. Use technology to reduce working hours. Devote more time to our families, and actual as well as virtual friends. By relieving the pressure of today's living patterns, we can feel less threatened, more accepting. Modern science needs to be less crudely mechanical, exclusive and over-confident. It should broaden its scope. It could incorporate astrology as an objective study of cycles that explain individual behaviour, and also discover it can help guide our adaptation to cultural change in the past present and future.

The chart of Pluto's first ingress with the Sun into Aquarius could suggest a strong commitment to such work in progress. The Gemini Moon square Saturn in Pisces indicates anxiety, but Mercury/Mars in Capricorn, having trined Jupiter and about to trine Uranus in Taurus, offers enduring resilience to transform.

An idealistic Aquarian icon for the 2020s

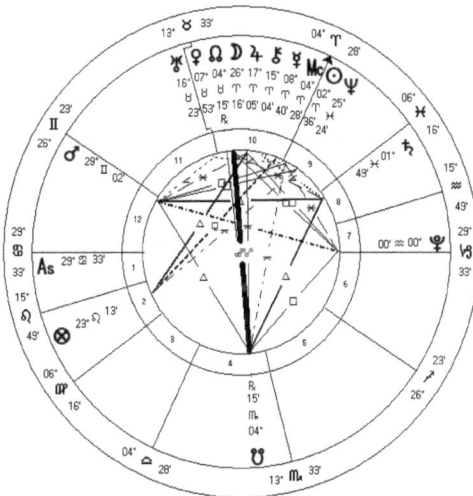

Aquarius Ingress of Pluto
23 Mar 2023 12:14:11 UT +0:00
London, UK 51°N30' 000°W10'
Geocentric Tropical Placidus True Node

To expect and work for a perfect earthly paradise is dangerously futile. Humanity is too fallible to know the way, too prone to brutalise others in service of 'the cause'. Yet idealism has a vital role, providing we accept the ends never justify the means. The world is happier when we take refuge in a kind ideal as our guiding vision, not an endgame at all costs. 2018 marks the Saturn return of my writing *The Anthem of Love*. Its message is so more vital today that it is reprinted in my book *Reversing the Race to Global Destruction*. Search online for 'Roy Gillett Anthem of Love' to hear me reading it.

The famous *Star Trek* series was set in the mid-twenty-fourth century, leading to the year 2384, when the Vernal Equinox enters Aquarius.[200]

This world had no need for money, because all is provided free at the point of use by technology. All knowledge was available in a vast computer database, but each person's space was respected. As a result, it was a highly efficient technically advanced, yet peaceful world.

As Jupiter strains forward into Aquarius through 2021, and Saturn there until early 2023, may we start laying the ground for a positive Aquarian transit of Pluto (2023-43). The last two Pluto-in-Aquarius periods saw profound instability. 1532-53 the social upheaval and brutal executions of the early Reformation. 1777-98 – the American and French Revolutions. *Star Trek* describes their society emerging from a devastating world war in the mid-twenty-first century.

Humanity stands at the gateway of a major leap forward in its consciousness. It has the capacity to mature its motivation. We claim to be wiser and higher than nature. Surely, we know enough now to be beyond intolerance, and so do much better than before.

-o0o-

Appendix A (pages 274-78) includes the March 2019 column's analysis of the thirty years from the destruction of the Berlin Wall until its Saturn return just after the midnight following the 2018 Winter Solstice. A truly sad tale of missed opportunities to transform our lives for the better, missed because no one in power took notice of the beneficial insight offered by the astro-cycles. So exposing the world to heavy circumstances that would increasingly show themselves in the coming years.

-o0o-

Re-read pages 39-42 to refresh your memory with an interesting analysis of the new UK Prime Minister – Boris Johnson.

-o0o-

With Jupiter's Capricorn ingress to join Saturn and Pluto imminent, the November 2019 column made a dramatic appeal for a change of approach in personal and social relationships. We now know that the planet had had enough of humanity's hubris. Firstly, with floods, tornados and fires, and then Covid-19, nature forced change upon humanity. A third world war, not so much with each other, but with nature was to be the story that started in December 2019 to build on through 2020 into the future.

…And This is Where the Story Really Starts[201]

This December we come to the trigger of the Capricorn/Taurus focus we have been anticipating for some years. The January 2019 *Astrological Journal* article 'A Key Turning Point in Human History' explained and illustrated in detail that 2019-20 would see a turning point of structural change. This would be as, if not more, significant as the development of writing and discovery of bronze, nearly 6,000 years ago. The article showed the significance of Pluto through Capricorn since then. Change has been accelerating from the Renaissance and Industrial Revolution, ever more so during the past hundred years. Read and study the article and diagrams in that January *Journal* and elsewhere online.[202]

The 'Major Astro Events' section later in this column gives a detailed commentary on the build-up to Jupiter's Capricorn ingress at the beginning of

December 2019 and after. The Winter Solstice is key moment each year, when the Earth's path around the Sun eases the Northern Hemisphere back into stronger solar beams. So, its chart is the key to understanding how its little light will increasingly grow within us and without through the twelve months ahead.

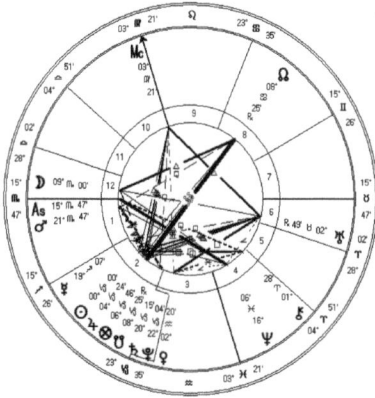

Winter Solstice
22 Dec 2019, 04:20 UT +0:00
London, UK 51°N30' 000°W10'
Geocentric Tropical Placidus True Node

The 2019 Winter Solstice (see chart above) has the Capricorn emphasis intensifying even more with the Moon there, plus Mercury and Mars coming ever closer to ingressing the sign. So, building through December into January and pulsing again and again through the year, the wild delusions of 2019's Jupiter-in-Sagittarius months will crystallise into hard-edged reality, causing real and possibly lasting harm. This is not inevitable. Capricorn can be brutally firm, but also it brings responsible structures for the wise to rely upon. This will be the choice of the year.

Four days after the solstice, the path of a major total Solar Eclipse is focused upon Kuala Lumpur, with its total line running from Saudi Arabia through Sumatra, the East Indies, and then out to the West Pacific Ocean.[203] There are many political, social and geophysical vulnerabilities in this region. The decency of the nations and people of the world will be of critical importance in deciding any outcome.

The irresponsible way to use Capricorn

The more irresponsibly people throw themselves into these months, the more unacceptable and irresolvable circumstances will be. As I write this, in the UK and many other parts of the world, masses of people have stopped talking intelligently to each other. Rather they are screaming constantly-repeated over-simplifications and refusing to consider any response. It is not so much the words used that cause anger, but rather the mindless brick wall of intransigence, the lack of respect and consideration for others' views. The shouting of slogans is the prelude to violence and even war. 'If they will not listen, I'll hit them where it hurts most'.

With the strong concentration of Capricorn and earth sign planets until the end of 2020, there will be numerous trigger points, from which economic and political change and even conflict could suddenly emerge. Many people have diametrically opposed opinions and positions about who and what should be first. If this continues, building through the decade, they will dig themselves deeper and deeper into their self-obsessed holes and destructively-dark mindsets, from which striking out violently will seem the only escape.

Opinions will be firm and strident, clashing with other opinions, as the world economy faces a radical confrontation with reality. Do we continue to 'print money', extend credit and consume ever more and more? Do we use our power to blame others and seek to cut them off from a share of the wealth? Me first! Me first!

This is a very negative expression of Capricorn, whose intrinsic and much more positive nature is to work hard and responsibly to construct what will last. To do this, it is vital not to shut ourselves away, but to marshal maximum support. The short-term 'party-time' approach consumes so irresponsibly that the temporary pleasure of the few leaves most people without what they need. The planet is sucked dry. Little is left for the generations that follow.

The responsible way to use Capricorn
The responsible Capricorn way is to rise above desire, and devise a system with more give and take, less work, less production, more cooperation. Not to continue to blame and fight against others, but to bring down barriers, to have the courage to walk across all that divides us, to care for each other and the planet.

At times like these, when opinions are polarised and the unscrupulous are seeking to divide in order to gain power, it is vital to commit to kindness and not do to others what you would not wish them to do to you.[204]

Thinking like this, dissolves the danger of labelling those we disagree with as demons, to feel justified in accelerating the 'anti' against them. When we encourage kindness on all sides, we may start listening to reason, rather than slogans, become clear just how empty of hope is relying on slogans to gain power.[205]

If you feel this is too optimistic a transposition of Capricorn to its opposite sign of Cancer, remember that Capricorn's essential aim is to succeed by orderly efficiency. Which of the below is more efficient?

- ❖ FORCING our view with enmity, and violence if necessary, on the reluctant, who we treat as mindless, unprincipled opponents,

- ❖ OR listening to and accommodating alternatives and working supportively with each other toward a common compromise goal.

The right Capricorn way to economic, social, personal and planetary happiness

Money is a great servant, but a bad master[206]

Monetarism as the foundation of the global economy is taken for granted by nearly all of today's mainstream economists, politicians and media reporters. Yet, in its present form, it dates back no further than the early 1980s, when deceptive Neptune was in Capricorn, Saturn poorly controlled in Sagittarius, and both were fuelling the passionate irresponsibility of Pluto in Scorpio. In the short time since, it has been accepted in Russia, following the end of the Soviet system, and, more recently, the emerging economies of India, South East Asia and South America and, from the 1990s, Chinese 'communism' morphing into state-controlled monetarism.

Growth measured by money-worth is extolled as the ultimate measure of success and happiness. So, the decades from the 1980s have seen the liquidation and spending of assets, deregulation to release more funds, by extending and artificially-creating credit, all the time keeping the cost of borrowing low. In this dash for wealth, lack of controls has allowed a free-for-all, which has enabled those with assets to acquire great wealth, to the disadvantage of the rest. In the East, availability of cheap labour has kept down production costs, at the expense of employees in the rich West. Energy-intensive over-production is threatening the fabric of the planet, and ordinary people's livelihood and services in the G7 block of countries.

Motivated by money-based notions of having or not having, nationalism and sub-group resentment has grown. Discourse has become harsh and authoritarian. Education has become increasingly functional, lacking in art and empathy. The legal system is becoming used more and more in the service of narrow self-interest in the civil courts, and retribution-based punishment when dealing with crime. The news and cultural media mainly pander to and exploit this status quo. The news rarely questions society's economic foundations. It even mocks radical alternatives. Entertainment and the social media are corrupted by constant promotional intrusions, put out there to exploit, not benefit, the masses.

Having suffered, but yet hardly learned from, the harsh realism of Pluto in Capricorn since 2008; with Saturn there for the last two years, and now Jupiter in Sagittarius, 2019 has seen last futile gasps of a global economy struggling to avoid the harsh consequences of its failure, and the inevitable social unpleasantness.

There is another way. Whatever you hear around you, turn away from condemning and shutting out what you do not know, try to learn from it instead. Look deeply into the implications of the #MeToo movement, not only to redress the exploitation of women, thousands of years old, but to awaken the true femininity and masculinity within everyone. By insisting on kindness and consideration, protect the wonderful world of knowledge and social sharing on the internet from those who seek cheap financial or political advantage. Throw in the dustbin any who try to use it this way. Welcome the unknown and the needy. Tread carefully, as you consider the motivation of the rich and famous.

May sustainability replace growth as the fundamental measure. May the natural process of give and take return money to its proper role, as servant to all we do. Abandon the politics of greed. Happiness and security do not come from things, but from a world where our actions and economic, legal, scientific, educational, political and media systems are all motivated by principled kindness towards each other and the planet.

-oOo-

The January 2020 column's overview of the year, included in full in the following pages, does not anticipate Covid-19. The different ways various parts of the world reacted to the described pattern of the astro-cycle focus could explain the different numbers of cases. Total immediate attention by New Zealand and parts of Asia, (appropriate to the March Aries/Capricorn focus) largely eradicated the virus for a while and contained subsequent outbreaks. Short-term economic considerations in the US, South America, India and the UK initially brushed warnings aside (lethal during a March Aries/Capricorn focus) and so these countries experienced the worst.

Dangerously on the Edge of the Old and a New world

Throughout 2019, the United Kingdom public have been increasingly impatient that the British Parliament 'get Brexit done'. In experiencing impatience, they have not been alone. In the USA, most Democrats just cannot wait to impeach Donald Trump, while their opponents wonder when constant attacks on him will go away. Ongoing rebellion in Hong Kong, horrific suffering in the Middle East and much of North Africa, rebellion in South America, burning forests there and in North America, South East Asia and Australia; all have the character of endless pushing against impasse.

Blame it on Jupiter in Sagittarius refusing to cease trying to change immovable Capricorn Saturn/Pluto/North Node resistance. In 2016, the year of the Jupiter/Saturn/Neptune mutable T-square, some very badly thought out reckless decisions were made worldwide. We have been failing to make sense of the consequences ever since. Should we, in many cases can we, go back? Perhaps that just might have been possible, while that ever-flexible Jupiter in Sagittarius was there.

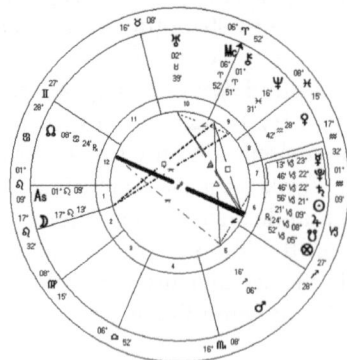

Saturn Pluto Conjunction
12 Jan 2020 16:59:16 GMT +0:00
London, UK 51°N30' 000°W
Geocentric Tropical Placidus True Node

New Moon
24 Jan 2020 21:41:52 GMT +0:00
London, UK 51°N30' 000°W10'
Geocentric Tropical Placidus True Node

However, by the time you read this, Jupiter will have left Sagittarius and entered Capricorn, a month or much longer ago. Now in 2020, we will be starting to experience, for good or ill, the reality of the outcomes we sought, or perhaps are being imposed upon us by those stronger than us.

In the November 2019 column,[207] we considered the impact of the 2 December Jupiter-into-Capricorn ingress and the Winter Solstice and Solar Eclipse that followed on 22 and 26 December respectively.

On the evening of 10 January,[208] the Moon will be eclipsed by the Earth shadow, as a prelude to Saturn's sole (in this cycle) exact conjunction to Pluto in Capricorn on 12 January. Mercury conjuncts both planets that day and the Sun the next, just as Venus enters Pisces. See this as the point that hard-headed realism will kick in alongside, or even in spite of, the needs of the vulnerable. This dichotomy will dominate most of the year. Consideration will take a back seat and be replaced by the need to put into place strong reliable organisation that is designed to stand the test of time. The problem is that different people and groups have different contradictory timescales and ways of organising. Goat-like pushing could harm those who resist and overwhelm the weak. As the momentum of determination increases, people could find themselves swept along into unexpected situations and experiences.

Before things go too far and become set in irreconcilable conflict, bear in mind that these intense days occurred in the midst of the third lunar quarter. This is a time to prepare, not to start forcing. Be systematic. Step by step note down what you feel is required. Take account of approaches and systems others may prefer. We can get more done, enjoy far better outcomes, if we seek mutual consent when approaching. Try it this way. Everything will make much more sense, not so irreconcilable after all. The Moon is waning (until it is new in Aquarius).

With Mercury in Aquarius too, see the Aquarian New Moon as the first of several of the year's previews to the much more substantial Jupiter/Saturn conjunction on the cusp of Aquarius at the 2020 Winter Solstice. With Jupiter approaching Pluto and Saturn, all still in Capricorn, the urgent need to address very serious problems will remain paramount. However, we will begin to see a glimmer of what might be different through the 2020s decade. So, people's ideas will not get in the way of each other so much. Paradoxically, relying on the creation of immovable, solid structures (especially walls!) to resist what seems to threaten only addresses the short term. It is likely to turn out unreliable, if not accompanied by a working understanding of what seems to oppose us. This is the message that Aquarius always gives to Capricorn.

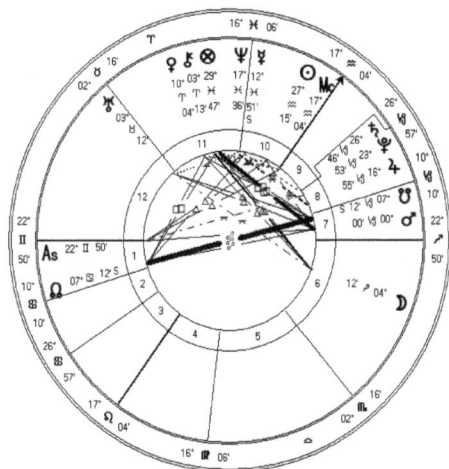

Mars enters Capricorn
16 Feb 2020 11:32:53 UT +0:00
London, UK 51°N30' 000°W10'
Geocentric Tropical Placidus True Node

Take advantage of opportunities to make friends through this cycle. For time is running short. On 16 February, the day after the start of the fourth lunar quarter, Mars enters Capricorn to stir the organisational 'pot'. Each person or group will 'urgently need' to get on with what 'we know has to happen'. Getting in the way will not be wise!

On 17 February, the day after Mars' Capricorn ingress, Mercury in Pisces makes a retrograde station. There it sextiles Jupiter in Capricorn and goes on to conjunct Neptune. Expect demands to answer suffering, especially in the last waning days of the lunar quarter, the 'suffering' of delay!

On 23 February, Venus in Aries squares Jupiter in Capricorn less than two hours after the Pisces New Moon. Mars in Capricorn hastens to conjunct/oppose the Nodal Axis and the Sun to trine/sextile it on 25 February. The best way to handle this new lunar cycle is to incorporate the best of the past to help understanding in the present, and so create a better future.

The Pisces period each year is the best time to understand, providing we do not allow past resentments lead to vindictiveness.

Key Moments and Trends for the Rest of 2020

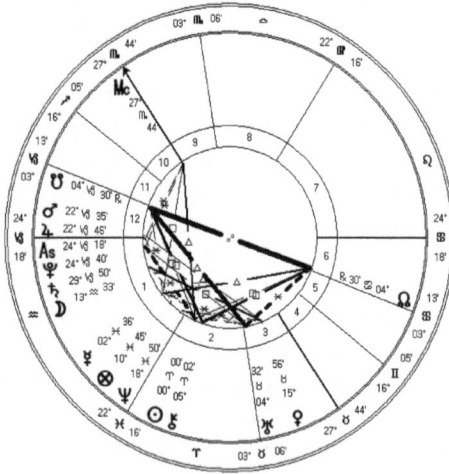

Spring Equinox
20 Mar 2020 03:49:30 UT +0:00
London, UK 51°N30' 000°W10'
Geocentric Tropical Placidus True Node

With Mars conjuncting Jupiter in Capricorn eight hours after the 2020 Vernal Equinox, the drive behind the early spring will be not only far more forceful, but more realistic, than usual. Expect anything instigated not to fade away, but to be sustained, as the Sun applies to square the Capricorn stellium through the month. Over-impulsive determination could find people forcing themselves upon one another without regard for the consequences.

Take advantage of any opportunity to broaden perspectives. With Mars and Jupiter in Capricorn driving the momentum of the time, and Aries-ruler Mars due to retrograde in its sign late in the year, the distracted and unwise could easily find themselves swept along in a process they did not expect, wish for and certainly do not agree with. The conscious and wise will understand and pace themselves, let the momentum work in their favour.

Being 'realistic' – the earth-focus of the year
Astro-cycles do not fix events. Rather they illuminate choices. A badly-advised choice at a particular cosmic moment will inevitably lead to a bad outcome in the future. The longer the bad choice persists, the worse the ultimate consequences. This is as much true of socio-economic decisions, as it is of individual actions.

Following the relaxation of regulation in the financial markets at the start of the twenty-first century, mortgage loans rose steadily for the first few years of the century. From 2003, with Saturn transiting Cancer, the sub-prime market ignored the need for structural consolidation. Deregulation allowed a massive boom in the housing loan market. This momentum continued through the speculative Saturn-in Leo period.

This led to a four-times increase in exposure, from the beginning of the century until 2008, when the sub-prime market, and with it the entire world banking system, all but collapsed. Only government and central bank rescues kept, and are still keeping, the world economic system afloat. The rescue mode used since (low interest rates with quantitative easing, tax cuts in the US whenever economic growth slows) has become so familiar that we have come to assume we can expand international deficits *ad infinitum*.

With six powerful planets in Earth signs (Mars, Jupiter, Saturn and Pluto in Capricorn, Venus and Uranus in Taurus) many financial astrologers have been expecting a major financial market correction just before or during 2020. If this does not happen our global predicament moves on to a far more fundamental crisis than the errors of 2003-07 brought to the world banking system in 2008. This time it will be a fundamental undermining of the fabric of the planet and our lives upon it. It may not be so sudden, but it will be far more radical, sustained and increasingly irreversible. Extreme-weather and health issues caused by hyper-activity. Social unrest caused by economic imbalance.

Reliance on increasingly short-term judgements. The world is becoming increasingly like a group of drunken teenagers driving a minibus at ever increasing speed and lack of attention to anything outside the vehicle. There is always another bottle under the seat, until there isn't... and/or we crash over the side of the road!

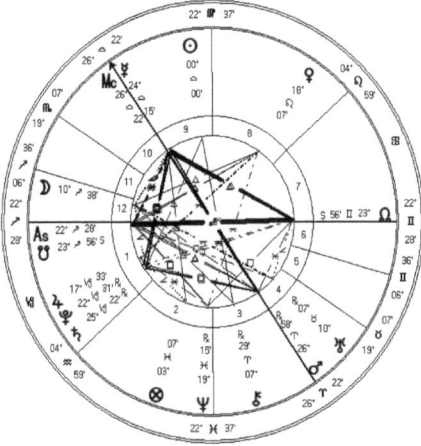

Autumn Equinox
22 Sep 2020 13:31 UT +0:00
London, UK 51°N30' 000°W10'
Geocentric Tropical Placidus True Node

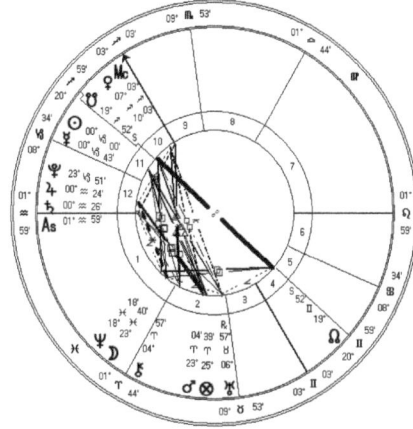

Winter Solstice 2020
21 Dec 2020 10:03 UT
London, UK 51°N30' 000°W10'
Geocentric Tropical Placidus True Node

Reconsideration - the first light of Aquarian change

From the Aries New Moon on 24 March there is the chance for surprisingly different approaches, as Venus in Taurus trines Jupiter and Pluto in Capricorn, and Mars joins Saturn in Aquarius. The discipline behind our actions could broaden, systems become more innovative, more intelligently considered.

Late April and May Pluto and then Saturn and Jupiter commence their annual retrograde phase until September/early October. Between June and late November Neptune retrogrades too. Each year this marks a period of reconsideration. From spring to autumn, with the weather warmer, outdoors more accessible, even in heatwaves the need to slow down and relax, the time is right to assimilate, ponder past decisions, and so to consolidate what we may have thought was desperately needed in those dark winter months.

Saturn hovering in the first two degrees of Aquarius from mid-March until the end of June, especially accompanied by Mars until 13 May, could direct the first glimmers of a radical rethink of the way the world does business. Could it be that, at last, the profit-obsessed world enterprises will listen the to the scientific community, whose discoveries have made possible the products from which they profit? The recognition that an ecologically caring, sustainable green economy may well not be a pleasant luxury we cannot afford, but in fact the efficient solution to the increasing debt crisis. Maybe as we reach the climax of these Capricorn intense years, we begin to recognise their lessons. Can we stop the nonsense of short-term fixes; see the first glimmer of what might be a better solution?

We well may not! The nature of retrogrades is constant reconsideration, going back to the past. In 2020, many will feel there is a lot of unfinished business to sort out once and for all. In the UK, a Boris Johnson government's promises would be tested, a Jeremy Corbyn one at odds with established interests, or a fraught hung parliament. The US Presidential Election, with or without Donald Trump, will also be fraught. As I write this in November 2019, all over the world governments are being challenged by the people. Aquarian energy struggling to find its feet out of authoritarian Capricorn could lead to some very revolutionary actions, just as short-term, restricted to immediate demands, not the long-term good of the world. Change at any cost! What we want right now! Little good to come out of that!

Summer Solstice Eclipse [209]

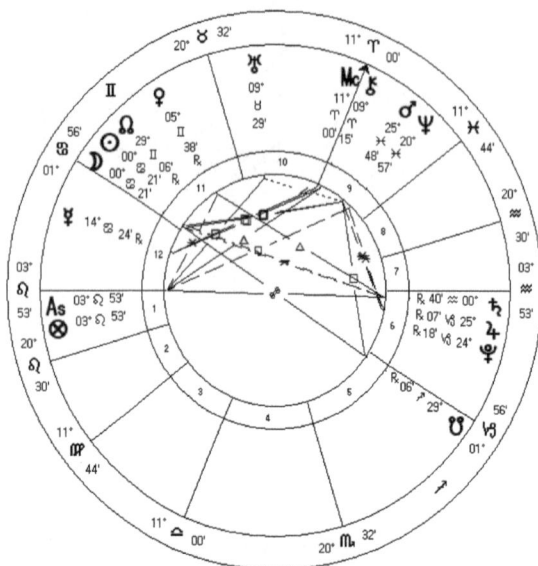

Solar Annular Eclipse
21 January 2020, 06:41 UT +0.00
London, UK 51N30 000W10
Geocentric Tropical Placidus True Node

Lack of understanding could make it very difficult to put right the anxiety and feelings of vulnerability that could well cloud the 2020 Summer Solstice. The Solar Eclipse's visibility (see map page 213) ends in Central Africa, having passed from the Pacific Ocean through Hong Kong, Asia and Yemen. It is at its longest at Mount Kailash in Tibet. Retrograding Mercury is unaspected. Venus, about to go direct in three days, is in a weak separating trine to Saturn.

The number of earth planets is reduced to Jupiter, Pluto and Uranus. It is the loosest part of the year, when breakthroughs should seem possible, but Saturn returns to Capricorn at the end of the month. Mars moves worryingly on in late Pisces; its hopeful conjunction with Neptune the previous week, now a distant memory. So much is needed! So little seems possible! The connections between the planets being insubstantial and hardly forward looking, this could be a dangerous time, when ill-considered actions could have dire consequences.

Avoid falling for the temptation. Sit back, watch, listen, observe. Let all feelings of negativity flow through and out of you inactivated. See and understand what is happening and its causes. In this way leave substantial focus and power within yourself to act effectively when the time is right.

Each year, whatever we have been preparing, wrestling with, adapting, allowing for through the spring and summer is brought back to balance at the Autumn Equinox. In 2020, the Sun is almost unaspected, making just three very weak aspects. By way of contrast, Mercury in Libra is applying to oppose retrograding Mars to make a T-square with Jupiter, Pluto and Saturn in Capricorn. Within ten days Venus will be in Virgo. Again, five planets will be in earth signs, Venus making a grand trine to Taurus and Capricorn. Time to draw together the threads and get down to business, something new and improved, or to do everything possible to recover from what has gone wrong.

However, sustained, all-out forcing will not answer practical necessities. Mars is to remain in Aries, not making its direct station until 14 November, entering Taurus in early 2021. Positive bursts of innovative actions and instigations will make it difficult to pin down and finalise anything. Bursts of aggression could arise, seemingly out of nowhere. With Venus in Virgo, duty will seem to call constantly, mixing dangerously with impulsive Mars. With the focus remaining on earth planets, any hope we had for change that we had not anchored down earlier in the year may now be clouded over by the apparent need to address old issues that have bedevilled the 2010s.

Whatever the difficulties, false moves, or disasters that have been experienced over recent years, the pressures building as we start a new astrological year will be very different. Any positive foresight that has averted, or cut through, error in recent times will start to feel vindicated and gather force. For this Winter Solstice has substantial indications of change, especially for the UK, where the chart Ascendant of the moment of the solstice is less than two minutes of time past the imminent Jupiter/Saturn conjunction in the first degree of Aquarius. Change is coming to the UK! Mars in late Aries is gathering speed to enter Taurus early January 2021 and conjunct Aquarius' ruler – Uranus. Sun and Mercury in Capricorn apply to trine Uranus in the coming week. Venus is in Sagittarius near the Midheaven.

Whether it is for the worst, but hopefully for the best, the general mood will be that we cannot be held back any more by narrow protectionist counter-productive impositions on our lives. People will be tiring of those that insist we have to put up with this or that 'way', of being told what is impossible, or against their interests. Any rebellion against the status quo could be a mixed blessing. Some may insist on outcomes that bring harm, even destruction. So, it is important to encourage the humanitarian side of Aquarius. Not seek revenge, but understanding. Try to avoid the arrogance of feeling and crowing about having been right all the time. Be ready to learn.

-o0o-

The March 2020 column dared to address immediate problems by looking ahead to how the world might find its way out of them in the future – and especially who or what might lead the way.

2020 – Preparing for Tomorrow

A film called *Tomorrowland,* shown in the recent TV Christmas-time extravaganza of movies, turns around a magic talisman badge in the form of a letter T, that projects its holder into visions for the future.[210] While gratuitous in its imagery, it concluded with a clear-cut message, accused of proselytising by some critics on its release in 2015. Hugh Laurie, playing the villain appropriately named David Nix, embarks on an elegant statement of despair that rings much truer today than it might have done five years ago. Originally intending to warn against the humanity's mindless dependence on constant growth of activity and consumption, he had devised a machine prophesying disaster, only to see it become a self-fulfilling prophecy and have the opposite effect. So now, in exasperation, he was intensifying its effectiveness, encouraging humanity to destroy itself as soon as possible!

As the problems and crass actions causing them intensify through 2020, more and more people may understand the sense of futility lying behind such an extreme attitude. When before has there been a time when the only people not being listened to are those with the answers? First World War perhaps, but that did not threaten the very existence of life on the planet. There were still vast areas the war did not touch.

In 2020, the Capricorn focus that has been nagging our errors back at us since 2008 comes into full force. Wrong actions will quickly have consequences, which reverse the intention and so lead to more wrong actions. What is right and wrong will be lost, as increasingly we jump and react to short-term explanations of cause. The problem is not Capricorn, but a global determination not to learn and act on its lessons.

> Just as the viewer reluctantly starts to accept the David Nix machine message, the bright young heroine, with a previously disillusioned older-generation idealist she has inspired to try again, destroys Nix's machine. The film ends with the magic talisman that has enabled the young heroine to travel between the present and the future, now held by each person in a crowd of clean, fresh, relaxed young people. Look inside yourself, feel it is possible to have the future you really want. Let the future emerge from the combined force of the best vision coming from within all of you. The film ends with shots of young people of all races in many different parts of the world finding the magic talisman.

Events and attitudes through the first two decades of the twenty-first century have confirmed the worst fears of astro-cycle observers. It was never going to be easy, as the century started with a mutual Saturn/Pluto opposition, alongside a fixed Jupiter/Neptune opposition, indicating the cause and futile response of the first ten years, followed in the next decade by seven cardinal Uranus/Pluto squares, all projecting into 2016's mutable grand cross year of delusion. The subsequent years to 2020 are climaxing the consequences of all this upon the world.

BUT, it could have been different, if, as was hoped at the end of the previous century, we had marshalled our inventiveness and resources less materialistically, been more accepting, less aggressive. Then the inventive humanitarianism of the Uranus/Neptune mutual reception in Aquarius could have combined with the dare-devil potential of Pluto in Sagittarius to have opened, not closed, our hearts to the unfamiliar. We could have tried to understand, and address the concerns of our attackers, not kicked back. We could have been better than the enemies who wronged us, not worse. Not losing the idealism in our souls, by dressing up our counter-actions with empty assertions of righteousness, degenerated into bloated consumers, demanding righteously never-to-have-had-enough.

There was another way to handle the turn of the century's Aquarian energy. The generation then in positions of power had been too spoilt and indulged through its post-Second World War lifetime to see and grasp it. In the slight figure of Greta Thunberg and the millions of her contemporaries who support her, we see a generation who have grown up in the midst of mindless waste, seeing brilliant science prostituted in the service of short-term polluting products and processes. The eldest, soon approaching their twenty-first year, are beginning to express the positive potential of that early-century Uranus/Neptune/Pluto potential. Perhaps their *Tomorrowland* talisman is the Jupiter/Saturn conjunction in the first degree of Aquarius at the 2020 Winter Solstice. If so, it will be just the beginning of so many needed repairs, alongside the vision to stop humanity submitting mindlessly to the machine, in an even more horrific repeat of the noughties. Years, decades, maybe centuries of this to take us all kindly into a truly sustainable world for our descendants to enjoy. Where all the wonderful technology and AI we visualise today is not there just to pile up cash for a few, but to enable a healing, sustainable family-focused world.

Facing the immediate future – preparing the ground

To start to make this so, return to March 2020 and start work on clearing the debris of events and our relationships so far; accept and address the consequences of having

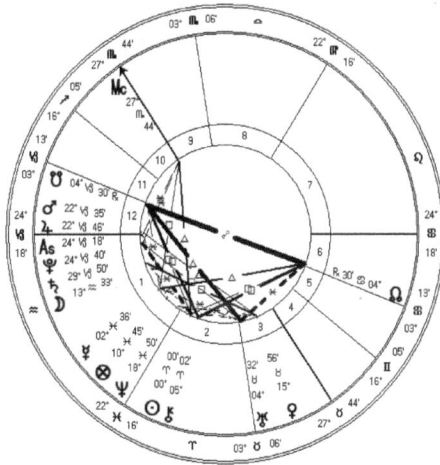

got so much so wrong for so long. In this strong, uncompromising year, little will be accepted, unless worked for really hard. The issues of the first two months of the year will seem minor, as the March Astrological New Year kicks in full on with the Vernal Equinox – the second, many say the first, key astrological moment indicating the nature of the year ahead.

Spring Equinox
20 Mar 2020 03:50 UT +0:00
London, UK 51°N30' 000°W10'
Geocentric Tropical Placidus True Node

The key 2020 equinox comments made in the January 'Working with the Planets' column are restated below.

> With Mars conjuncting Jupiter in Capricorn eight hours after the 2020 Vernal Equinox, the drive behind the early spring will be not only far more forceful, but more realistic than usual. Expect anything instigated not to fade away, but to be sustained, as the Sun applies to square the Capricorn stellium through the month. Over-impulsive determination could find people forcing themselves upon one another without regard for the consequences.
>
> Two days after the equinox, hope that the worst dangers may be avoided comes from Mercury in Pisces trine/sextile to the Nodal axis and the easing objectivity of Saturn entering Aquarius. Take advantage of any opportunity to broaden perspectives. With Mars and Jupiter in Capricorn driving the momentum of the time, and Aries-ruler Mars due to retrograde in its sign late in the year, the distracted and unwise could easily find themselves swept along in a process they did not expect, or wish for, and certainly do not agree with. The conscious and wise will understand and pace themselves, let the momentum work in their favour.[211]

Three months later, these words express the heart nature of 2020. With its irresistible authoritarian Capricorn dominance, 2020 will see all the problems we have created, or found ourselves in the midst of, come flooding in to demand attention.

What is not right in your personal life? In the larger world, nearly all the problems have not been addressed, just *talked* about. How will it be now the uncertainty of Jupiter-in-Sagittarius is over and we have to move beyond over-optimism or fear; now to do, decide and confront the consequences. Brexit, Donald Trump, impeachment/re-election, virtually every other part of the world has social rebellion and terrible suffering in the midst of insurmountable problems.

The power of Mars struggling to structure and build solutions, while new realities constantly show themselves and demand attention, can be seen so clearly in the Vernal Equinox chart. One old problem after another that there will not be time for, because yet another shows itself. So, we 'put them on the list'. Nor will they be resolved by old methods. A new way is not clear, let alone ready. Yet these problems cannot be denied. Expect a very difficult autumn, as the Mars retrograde then brings them back to haunt us.

Be uncompromisingly honest. As in *Tomorrowland* look deeply into yourself to find how you would really like things to be. Allow yourself to believe. Be patient. Prepare the ground. Be open to see new problems, as they really are. Prepare the ground, feel the growing force of clarity driving and incorporating all you have to do. So, whatever happens this year, you are ready break through to change.

Aries is often depicted as a pioneer bushman with a machete plunging into virgin undergrowth and cutting a way through for everyone to follow. It is the going that is all-important to Arians. Having blazed a trail, how to get others to follow is not their concern. This year, with the Mars conjunct the Capricorn stellium and the Aries Sun pushing against Capricorn through the following month, the force of Aries will be much more insistent.

At Aries 2020, we will be struggling with, most of the time falling foul of, the realities of seeing and trying to prepare a powerful path, along which to enforce new beginnings that will be strong enough to endure.

The May 2020 edition of the *Astrological Journal* headlined four articles revealing the incredible value of studying astro-cycles, when seeking to anticipate and understand how to handle something as world-shattering as Covid-19. How much better would our handling of the crisis been if humanity had heeded long-term crisis warnings from many astrologers, and exact predictions of the virus and its associated effects by André Barbault. Even today, the detailed understanding in the article below could help our ongoing interaction with what confronts the world.

Trapped in Today – Rebooting our World

Regular readers of this column will know its distaste for those who seek recognition by predicting future events, or, worse still, claiming to have done so, when what happened was one of a long list of general possibilities in their past 'prophecy'. Not only does this lead to unsustainable future expectations for the astrologer, but it implies all of us are at the mercy of 'good' and 'bad' circumstances. Unforgivably, it removes from the public mind that there are real and incredibly beneficial opportunities to shape our lives, when we understand astro-cycles.

The fact that for years many astrologers have been warning that the world is accelerating out of control, and that 2020 would be a major turning point (especially with regard to the world economy), is not the same thing. The distinction is crucial. For to predict specific events leaves the native at their mercy, feeling unable to prevent them. To identify trends and possible dangers in the road ahead, empowers every one of us to avoid, even change them, or at least protect ourselves. Putting the year in its historical and future perspective is to use astrology in the proper liberating, regenerative way.

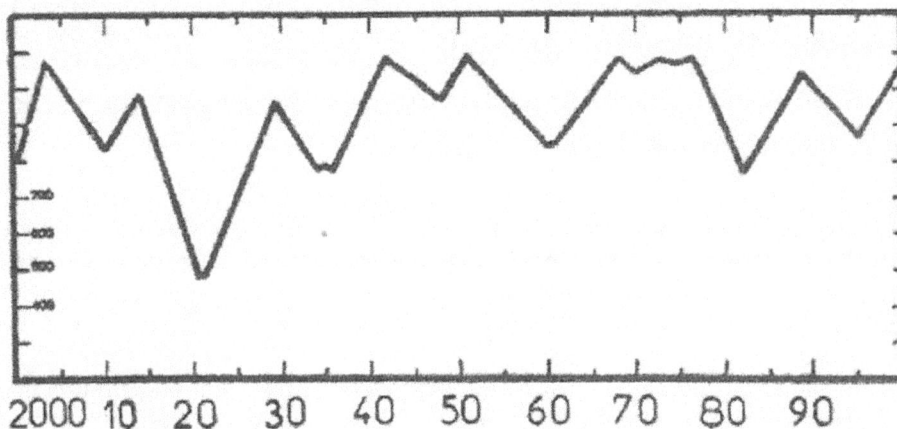

Exceptional among us, André Barbault not only performed this task, but managed to anticipate some pretty specific possible outcomes at the same time.

> Coming to the indicators for the twenty-first century in the… diagram of the interplanetary distances, we can see that the first low point (of the Cyclic Indicator[212]) is in the 2010s, which justifies the forecast of an economic crisis perceived two decades earlier, one can only wonder about the extreme depth of the trough as the wave plunges in 2020-21, the result of the next Jupiter-Saturn-Pluto triptych which will be relatively close to Uranus and Neptune. It seems that Europe will be at the epicentre of this dissonance, either compelled to reform itself or threatened with division because its space is limited. At least, that's if there are no natural disasters or a new pandemic, which would be suitable substitutes. In any case it will be a time of widespread discord.
> André Barbault *Planetary Cycles Mundane Astrology.*[213]

So, whether or not astrologers exactly predicted the 2008 economic crash or 2020 virus, knowing years ahead that such very special points in human history were coming could be extremely helpful. We may have cut back economic expansion years earlier, and so lessened the impact of the 2008 crash. We could have maintained our epidemic-preparedness resources, not devoted nearly all our focus on 'going for growth'; been wary, more prepared to come to terms to the terrible experiences many people are enduring as I write this column in late March 2020. Those that live and profit by expanding high values in financial markets, may well die at their fall.

Knowing the timing of the transits, the kinds of likely experience, can prepare our minds. It can guide our plans for the way we want our world to grow out it. Rather as the brutal horrors of Second World War, and the dysfunctional governance that led to it, made humanity ready to create a more caring and universally enabling world when it was all over.

André's projections can help us here as well. In the following paragraph he writes:

> with the great swing of the pendulum from the lowest to the highest point between 2018 and the peak of 2026 where here, conversely, there is a harmonic Saturn-Neptune conjunction at the central point of an encouraging double sextile to Uranus and Pluto which are trine to each other. It will probably be a change for the better when the headlines will be more agreeable and the civilization of our new mini Great Year at last becomes adult. André Barbault *Planetary Cycles Mundane Astrology*[214]

As we self-isolate and are turned away from the habitual pattern of our lives, our minds may tire of merely yearning to go back to how it was before. New doors of possibility may open our consciousness. New ways of seeing the family and friends we are 'trapped with', and the behaviour of those people and institutions we depend upon. How lastingly beneficial is it to grab and defend, selfishly looking out for our own interests? How much a relieving pleasure to step up to the plate with kind generosity?

Since 2014, numerous astrology talks to groups and conferences have anticipated a Capricorn stellium/earth planet focus building to the present intensity, not seen since 3838 BCE. These have been referred to frequently in this column, and in considerable depth in my 'Working with the Planets' articles: *From now on it will always be Kindness First… Kindness First*[215] and *A key turning point in human history* in the 2018-19 Astrological Journals.[216] A confrontation with reality for the world economy was clearly indicated. That it would be triggered and intensified by a worldwide pandemic was touched on, but not specifically predicted. Consultant astrologers will recognise that wonderful moment in many sessions, when the client feeds back their experiences that you have been describing blind, relying solely on the astro-symbols. So often comes the realisation, not that you actually 'got it wrong', but you were merely 'on the right lines'. Then, as the client feeds back their life experience, it reflects their chart meaning even more aptly. It is from moments, so many moments like this that we realise just how well astrology works.

For astrologers, seeing the world enduring Covid-19 right now is such a moment. In the vast sweep of history, it is a time that stops us in our tracks, creates room to think again, before it is too late. It stops us on that stupid race to disaster we have seemed to follow. It does this far more effectively than any demonstration, scientific argument, or worldwide conference could do. Rather it reaches into our homes, our very bodies, comes up real close in undeniable insistence that we take immediate responsibility if we want to survive.

Tom Wolfe's acclaimed book, *Bonfire of the Vanities*, satirised and laid bare the consequences of the deluded extravagances of 1980s New York. For every citizen in the entire world, Covid-19 blazes apart our assumptions about what we can do, or even wish to do, with our lives. What comes next? What hope is there for our future? It strips us of economic and political allegiances, profoundly disrupts the customary pattern of our lives. It seems to insist we push away many of those closest to us, as they are reduced to an image on a screen. Who knows when we will touch, let alone embrace them again? Does it really matter whether this or that sporting team triumphs? Will it ever matter in the same way again? When all but essential shops are closed, might we start again our view of the consumption/expansion obsessed world economy? How quickly will the taste for and confidence in world travel return? As selfless concern for others becomes the core enabler of our survival, will me-first selfishness ever return to drive the motivation of the World Economy?

Can we reboot our world?

Alternative possibilities – will it really be that bad?

Some may refer to stockpiling in the past for situations that did not turn out as bad after all. Certainly astro-cycles could indicate the hysteria surrounding possible bad outcomes rather than the outcomes themselves. To think and speak like this is not helpful for two reasons. If our worst fears are realised, then making maximum use of foreknowledge is of life-saving importance. If better than expected any transformation of human consciousness coming from thinking extreme measures were necessary, could well cleanse and regenerate our minds , so making our future lives and the world better. In this spirit, we consider below how 2020 might unfold.

Charting the way out

The pattern of the pressures of the year ahead was outlined in the January 2020 'Working with the Planets'.[217] As I write this, soon after the 2020 Vernal Equinox, the intensity of Mars in Capricorn's conjunction to Jupiter and Pluto is at its most intense, with the Sun transiting to square these two outers through most of the Aries period. The impact on Europe and the US is intensifying, as societies isolate and bunker down, dreading the threat they see ahead. It is a very new, so desperate, experience.

Two or more months ahead, by the time you read this, the Capricorn intensity will have relaxed just a little. Saturn will have entered more human Aquarius and Mars conjuncted it there, to enter Pisces at the end of the first week of May, a few days after Saturn makes its retrograde station, finally returning to Capricorn on 1 July.

This period includes the Summer Solstice, the climax of the Sun's growing power to expand creation, be it for good or ill. On that day this year (21 June 2020) across Hong Kong and central China all the way to Saudi Arabia, there is a strong annular eclipse; the line of totality having moved up from its Indonesian path on 26 December 2019. This is the third time since 1982 that the 18.6-year Nodal cycle has led to a solar eclipse that coincides with the Summer Solstice. On each occasion, it has been associated with a major world epidemic. In 1982, AIDS was being recognised and about to become rampant. 2001 saw foot-and-mouth disease sweep through Britain's cattle, leading to the slaughter and burning of millions of animals. The following year the SARS virus was to sweep through Asia.

So, by May and June 2020, however much we have tired of the restrictions, feel the worst is over, it is vital to be wary. As I write, East-Asian nations seem to be turning the impact of Covid-19 around, and are protecting themselves from the danger of it returning back to them from overseas countries. East-Asian countries seem to have achieved this by uncompromising authoritarian methods, when the building of the year's solar energy was not yet in full flow. So, even if the March measures in Western countries are equally sufficient and the virus does not mutate and return in another form, it would be a serious mistake to relax measures in May and June, to assume all is over. With Saturn back in Capricorn, Mercury and the Sun are in the earth-sign Virgo in the second half of August. On 9 September Mars will make its retrograde station in late Aries, to then move back to square the degrees of Capricorn it conjuncted so brutally in March. Not going direct until 14 November means pressure will build until it makes a precise conjunction to Pluto in Capricorn on 23 December.

The long-looked-forward-to Jupiter/Saturn conjunction in early Aquarius at the Winter Solstice may symbolise more than the usual Sun's glimmering light of hope returning to grow through that year ahead. Could a new Jupiter/Saturn cycle (now in an air sign) coming on that special annual day, leaving Pluto alone in its last Capricorn dog years, be a key starting point in a major social transformation? Could the world recover to a new age of understanding in human history, way beyond the imagination of anyone living today?

-oOo-

The July 2020 column considered how humanity's relationship with the planet might be educated by the dramatic change in its life patterns caused by Covid-19. Were we ready to learn and create a better future for ourselves, or just throw everything at desperate attempts to get 'back to normal' as quickly as possible?

A Personal Relationship with Our Planet

Readers living in the UK will have noticed that through the Covid-19 lockdown period the weather gentled down into sunny warmth. No longer bombarded by constant human hyperactivity, it was as though the planet had sighed in gentle relief and relaxed back its responses, leaving us space to rest and feed upon it naturally. We could notice more. With our bodily movement confined, our minds were freed to hear and feel all around us.

This seemed to have been so for much of the world, but not everywhere.[218] Just as I started to write this, came news of a tornado in the Bay of Bengal; strong, but fortunately not disastrous. Now, as most of the world blinks to ease itself out of the lockdown, little bubbles of thunder and wind reflect our complimentary hesitancy. It seems we and the planet are monitoring each other to see just how far back to a new normal we can go.

Personalising our planet like this may seem a little twee to the modern mechanical rationalist way of seeing things. Far from it! It is in perfect accord with the scientific notion that there is no action without a reaction. This applies to all we think, say and do, not just mechanical relationships. There are karmic consequences to everything. In some way or other, the tolerant equilibrium has to be restored. We may tolerate the odd ant in our house. When it is their season to swarm out and fly everywhere, the most kind of us find it difficult to avoid reaching for the killer spray!

So, in nature, when things reach an extreme imbalance, there has to be a similar measure of counterbalance. Crucially, humanity is not excluded from this process. In the grand scheme of things, we have created the cause for everything that happens to us – a key point missed by the disenchanted Christian, railing against what he conceives to be Divine cruelty, or the atheist mocking him. Advanced science may find ingenious ways to avoid consequences for a while, but, in the end, humanity has to face them – even more so, if it ignores the science as well.

The Covid-19 virus stops our misguided policies and actions in their tracks, forces us in on ourselves. It is the karmic consequences, coming at a time when the astro-cycles, its markers that describe the nature and timing of all our experiences, are at their most uncompromising.

With the extremely rare building Capricorn stellium through December into the January Saturn/Pluto conjunction, humanity was struck extrinsically by terrible storms, floods, and fire. Underlying all this was building the sinister, far more intrusive intrinsic threat of Covid-19. Is it too fanciful to put words in the 'planet's mouth', to reflect how it might react to humanity's brute arrogance?

'So, you will not hear and act upon climate warnings from the science that provides the wealth and health of the modern world, or even a movement of the next generation, inspired by a slight, determined Swedish teenager! If wind, flood, fire and social unrest will not urge a change in your ways, how about a virus that could reach deeply into each of you? How about a virus that puts a stop to virtually every activity you take for granted?'

At the same time, rewarding us with lovely weather. What a kind thoughtful planet we live in! How could we think to go back to things as they were?

What comes next?

Yet, somehow or other, that is what most politicians and business people see as the inevitable future. 'It may be gradual, take a little time, but there is no other way.'

With Pluto in Capricorn until 2023-24 and the apex of recovery on the Cyclic Index[219] between four and five years ahead from now, expect anything like this to be slow and disciplined. Also, expect dire planetary reaction to any excessive attempts by carpetbaggers to trigger short-term booms for personal advantage. At the most powerful Vernal Equinox in living memory,[220] the world virtually stopped at the very point of the year it usually sparks into action after a long winter. It stopped to turn in on itself, to think again. Do we really want to commute to work every day, normally leave our children in the care of others, rush around shops, buying everything that takes our fancy, whether we need it or not, spend fortunes on sporting events, be frequent-flyers to distant lands, short-change, even disregard, the very people who care for us?

As we ease out of lockdown, it might seem we are 'getting back to normal'. Every time it seems like that, the planetary reaction will encourage us to 'think again'. Countries and regions that neglect the planet most will suffer extreme reactions. The USA, socially and politically fragmented, its leaders old men with old ideas. Brazil, cavalier about its responsibility for its rain forest responsibilities, struggling to accept what is happening and organise for the consequences. Underdeveloped Africa. Central and South America, even some parts of Asia, unequipped to record and respond to what may still await them.

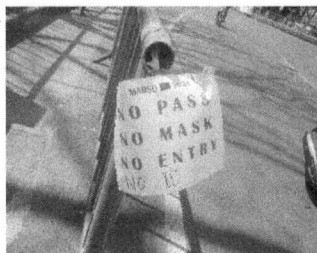

The days drifting from spring into early summer are a naturally relaxing time of the year in the Northern Hemisphere. No longer the need to defend ourselves against the elements, a time for fun and adventure. In 2020, this will still apply (just three planets in Earth now), but be conditioned with cautious hesitancy. Honouring those no longer with us, experiencing the gap between the recent absolute barriers and the freedom now opening up, will we be ready to want to shop until we drop, hug and cuddle, mass together, not 'give a damn'? Possibly not, but with the consequences not immediately discernible we may begin to take chances.

Saturn, retrograding in Aquarius through this time, provides a notion of caution to the wise. It returns to Capricorn on the first day of July.

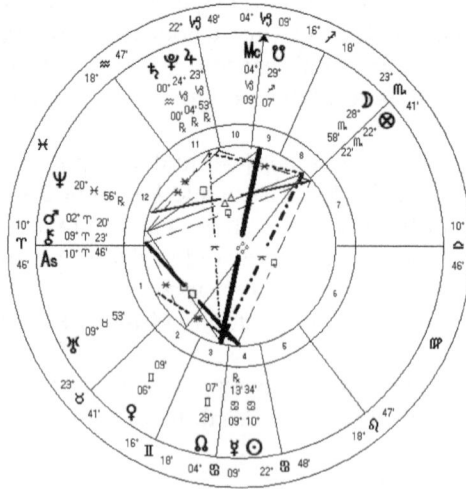

Saturn RX to Capricorn
1 Jul 2020 23:36:52 UT +0:00
London, UK 51°N30' 000°W10'
Geocentric Tropical Placidus True Node

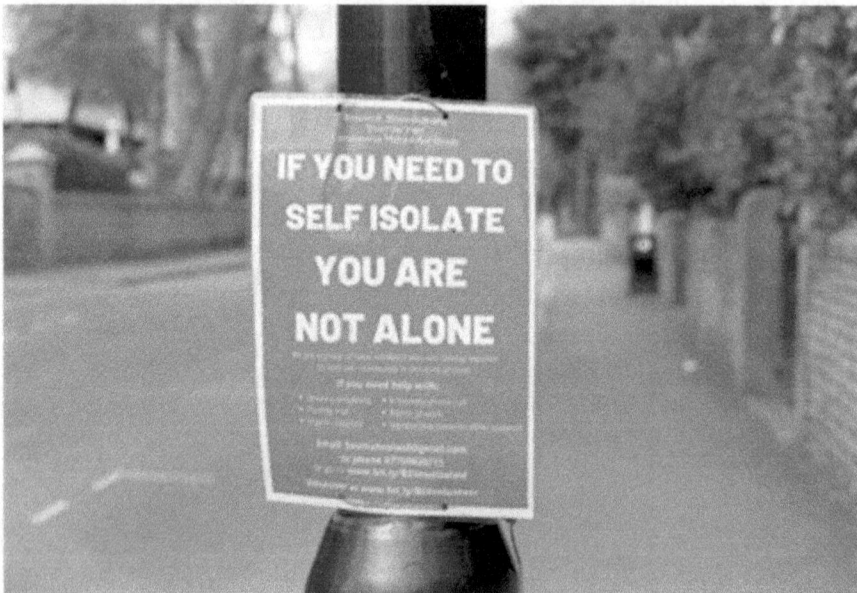

-o0o-

The July 2020 column also focused upon the astrology of the developing difficulties in world and especially US relations with China on the two pages that follow.

The Balance of Power

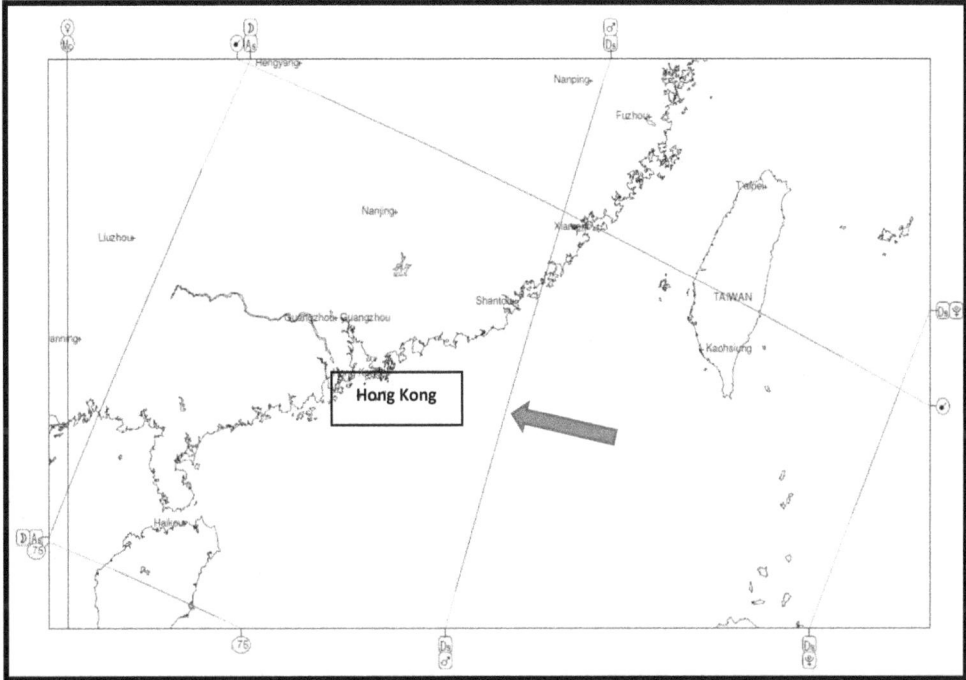

Hong Kong, China and 21 June 2020 Eclipse

By the time you read this, the Summer Solstice and its very special Solar Eclipse[221] will have passed. Its path of totality crosses very close to Hong Kong. Protests are erupting there, against new Chinese central government security laws, being drafted as I write.

Placing the Chinese 1 October 1949 chart on the eclipse path shows Mars, with Pluto not far away, on the Descendant always running through Hong Kong. On the Summer Solstice, 21 June 2020 (in China), the eclipse line of totality meets that Mars Descendant line. The always-difficult relations between Hong Kong and the Chinese central government may well come to a head at that time.

With the US government threatening, in response, to remove the territory's special status, its growing tendency to blame China for Covid-19, alongside the ongoing trade war, conflict with China could seem a helpful weapon in the US Presidential election campaign.

Of course, the relations between the two nations goes deeper than winning one election. Leaving the World Health Organisation separates the US from the mutual benefit of co-operation in its fight against Covid-19. Even more important than this, the consequent superpower balance in world relations is at stake. This is an emerging issue of fundamental importance that cannot be ignored, as the world focuses on defence against Covid-19 the changing roles of China and the USA in the world economy could affect all our ways of life.

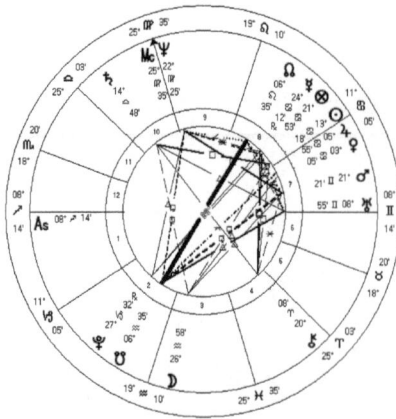

The USA, socially and politically fragmented, its leaders, old men with old ideas, almost blindly going into its first Pluto return, seems unready for this first karmic confrontation with all it has done, for good or ill, since its birth in 1776. As Pluto, Saturn and Jupiter have been opposing its Cancer stellium, the nation has seemed lost in fragmentary, contradictory policies and statements, centred around the interests and sudden ideas of a narrow, ill-informed leadership. Accusation splits the nation, when the amazing talent and generosity of spirit of its incredible range of people needs to be drawn out and integrated into brilliant solutions. It *was* after Pearl Harbour in Second World War. Why not now?

USA Independence (Sibley Chart)
4 Jul 1776 NS 16:50 LMT +5:00:40
Philadelphia, PA 39°N57' 075°W10'
Geocentric Tropical Placidus True Node

The Jupiter/Saturn conjunction in the first degree of Aquarius at the 2020 Winter Solstice, is in the same place as the Sun on the 2021 US Presidential Inauguration Day. By whom and how the country is taken forward through its Pluto return will be crucial to its future and status in the world.

The contrast with China could not be more extreme. Covid-19 emerged dramatically in Wuhan province, only a few days before millions were to travel to their family-home for the Chinese New Year. It seemed that massive spreading was inevitable and the Chinese economic miracle might be irreconcilably threatened. The present transiting Capricorn stellium is in the nation's twelfth house, so who can tell the truth about actual numbers and the measures taken to meet the threat? Yet, by taking unchallenged, clear decisive action, the nation seems to have navigated itself out of the crisis. Political and economic life there is returning nearer to normal.

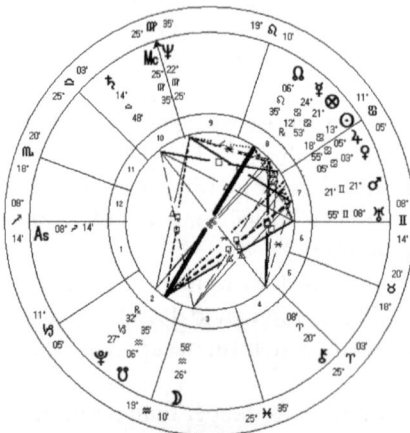

The world situation has reversed. At beginning, China was desperately building hospitals, while the Western daily news focused on a few hundred people trapped in a luxury cruise ship in a Japanese port. Four months on, it is major outbreaks in Europe, with the USA and Britain having massively more cases and deaths, that is destined to be the story of the pandemic.

Unlike the time of the Ebola crisis, now it is China offering help to the third world. In 2021, Jupiter, and then Saturn in Aquarius, cross the Chinese Ascendant and proceed to trine its Sun, Mercury, Neptune, North Node in its eighth-house Libra. For good or ill, its influence seems destined to spread ever-further beyond its borders into the economies and even the culture of the

China Communist
1 Oct 1949 15:15 CCT -8:00
Peking, China 39°N55' 116°E25'
Geocentric Tropical Placidus True Node

countries that will become increasingly dependent upon it for survival.

Resolution

Now, as much as any time in human history, it is important to cleanse our inner vision of all negative thoughts towards anyone, or anything. Then to shine a light outward to touch understanding in as many people and places as possible, especially those we feel like rejecting. If we do not like the world that seems to be re-emerging, we need ideas and ways of communicating that will bring together increasing numbers of supporters. We do this by answering other people's problems, not accusing and making them worse.

'Me-first' on its own leaves us alone, ignorant, unaided. You have to be pretty crazy to live like that. 'Me-first for everyone and the planet', is the happy healing lesson that our greatest friend, the planet we live and depend upon, will continually insist we have to learn.

-o0o-

Faced with a most powerful Mars retrograde period, indicating a savage second Covid-19 wave comparable to the Spring, the September 2020 column compared the world predicament to the experience of living through the Second World War. Then, it considered current world leaders. What qualities would be needed to lead the world out of this war against the virus?

Bluebirds
An Aquarian Vision for the Future

> Only when the tide goes out do you discover who's
> been swimming naked.   Warren Buffett

The passing of Vera Lynn in early July, at the grand age of 103, rekindled my young boyhood memories of what kept people going through the terrible Second World War years – the thought of what life would/could be like when it was all over. As well as the smile and embrace of loved ones and 'blue birds over the white cliffs of Dover', people had ideas for a better world. Not just words like First World War's 'a world fit for heroes', but real practical social changes that were to create a safety net for everyone and a 'free at the point of use' National Health Service.

Autumn 2020 has been anticipated with foreboding by health experts, as well as this column and many other astrologers. Will the easing of restrictions through the summer have encouraged contacts that create a second wave of Covid-19 infections and further economic collapse? Will the long Mars retrograde, squaring its potent March/April 2020 transit, express itself like this? Or, could a vaccine be ready and hastily, maybe unwisely, distributed?[222] Possible, but difficult to see the retrograde representing the infection just fading way,

The Capricorn outer planets ease back together to make direct stations (Jupiter, Saturn and then Pluto), as Mars retrogrades back to square them. Surely, the entire world will face an unavoidable confrontation with economic reality, the climax of what Pluto's Capricorn transit has been trying to teach us since 2008. The world faces debt created by the virus recession, Brexit in Europe, relations with China, the build-up to the US election, unemployment. A bankrupt world futilely trying to restore GDP growth with an economic system massively past its sell-by date. Greed-motivated capitalism floundering amidst spiralling debt that can never be repaid. Very few 'winners' in an ecologically worn out jungle of destruction. Very like that Second World War world of my childhood. So, is there another grand new vision to keep hope alive this time?

Today's commentators talk of an economic downturn, not seen for 300 years. The South Sea Bubble burst in 1720. It left a trail of debt and bankruptcy. It was the first of many failures of a system based on assumed, rather than real tangible value. Unperturbed, Jupiter/Saturn conjunctions in the fire element kept the speculative enthusiasm going through the rest of the century. Then these conjunctions in the earth element took over in the early nineteenth; heavy industry, colonialism, European and American expansion. The struggle for more and more possession rooted twentieth-century conflict. The worship of money drove ever-deeper into our social belief system; the heart motivation in our education, what we must devote our lives around. This now reaches the endgame of its illogicality. Like airline-crash passengers stranded in a jungle, confused and desperate we wonder what to do next.

Beware of seeing the 20 December 2020 Jupiter/Saturn conjunction as the simple beginning of a new wiser world, because it is in air. While the way of Aquarius is to know everything, some Aquarians can be impossibly misguided in what they are sure they know, as are the machines and systems that some Aquarian could create. The ingenuity of artificial intelligence (AI) could control a cashless system. Just link together shopping loyalty and credit/debit cards with a government revenue system. Then the income, expenditure and lifestyle choices of populations could be determined in the interest of its controllers. Drop-outs from the system would be abandoned in a rebellious dystopian counter-culture, which an oppressive central government could cite as the terrible alternative. The popularity of *The Hunger Games* quartet of films reveals the anxiety, as well as the hope, at the heart of the younger generation.

A positive Aquarian approach starts by dismissing the unprincipled, mistaken economic theory that lies at the core of today's global malaise. We need to a base our economy on practical reality, environmental reality and the social need of all beings, near and far. Only an eighteenth-century adventurer, about to exploit a near-untouched world, would believe growth was sustainable exponentially. Yet this has been the basis of economic theory for over three hundred years. Ordinary people at first exploited, now evolving into exploiters themselves. There is neither room nor resources for this. The planet and social cohesion is being brought to its knees. Covid-19 debt is destined to be the final straw. However difficult this autumn and winter may be, reject deluded short-term 'solutions'. Try to help as much as possible. Be reassured that we about to move on from what was wrong into what could be a much better future.

Towards a new world economy
Our lives could change, our eyes widen with hope, should we start to work from a new inclusive, sustainable economic model. As the warning signs have been screaming at us from the economic collapses of the year 2000, and especially 2008, young economists have been challenging the very foundation texts and course structures adopted in universities and business schools. This column has already mentioned *The Econocracy*,[223] which sought to free economics from a mathematical straitjacket, based on assumed reality, undemocratically imposed on society by self-

appointed 'experts'. Also, *The Value of Everything*[224] that revealed how most items included in conventional economic calculations were empty of real value. Alongside this, Kate Raworth's *Doughnut Economics*[225] has identified in great detail a sustainable alternative economic model. She replaces our current growth model, obsessed with making money and an ever-increasing GDP, with her 'Doughnut' image to illustrate what she calls a '…twenty-first-century compass.' She writes: 'Between its social foundation of human well-being and ecological ceiling of planetary pressures lies the safe space for humanity'.

Her diagram shows nine planetary pressure factors.[226] The social foundation consists of twelve. The sustainability of all these factors in interactive unison should be the basis for our economic plans for the future. This is the intelligent, positive-Aquarian way of decision making. What sense is there in growth, if it is based on assumed values that could collapse overnight and, at best, provide only a fraction of human needs, while destroying the planet's infrastructure? As we seek to recover from the debt burden of just one, or maybe several, waves of Covid-19 infection, it will be futile to indebt our economy to keep the GDP-based model afloat, hoping for a bounce 'back to normal' future. Did we ever really want that 'normal' in any case?

At first, in practice it will not seem easy. Basing investment on the Doughnut

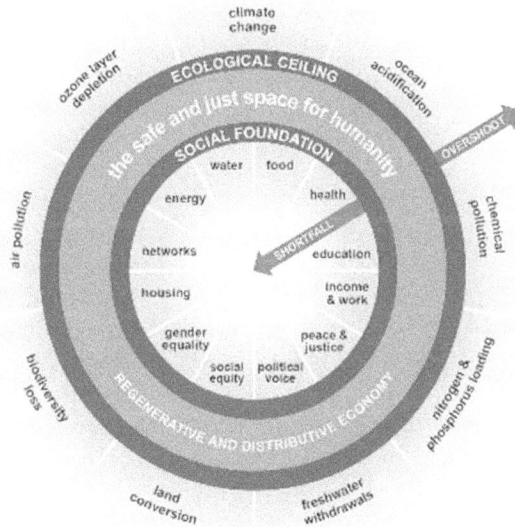

The Doughnut – a Twenty-first-century Compass

model will allow, even encourage, unemployment in counter-productive and wasteful areas. Less slave-labour-based over-production, expensive eating out, international travel, luxury house building for shell companies, quick profit financial trading and arms production. Instead, investment will be redirected to employment that provides for the planet's needs; what people really want, not what they are told they have to have to keep the economy growing. We will see the world we really want coming closer.

The consequences of the Covid-19 pandemic may be unavoidable, but the danger *will* end. So better to work towards that time with hope, not futile desperation, in our hearts. Being clear about the future, seeing it coming makes working through the difficulties of the present far easier.

With Pluto in Capricorn until 2023-24 and Jupiter moving into Pisces (May-July and from December 2021), the next few years will be transitional. Even with the wisest decisions, the demands of the old system will remain to resist change. The suffering of deprivation will bite deeply into many societies. The old ways will not relent without a struggle. Populist leaders may encourage scapegoating and narrow self-interest as the only solution for 'us'. After a Jupiter burst, how we handle the resilience of Saturn in Aquarius will be crucial if there is to be real change through Pluto's Aquarian post-2024 years. Be clear about what you want for the future. Look for, demand and also accept with glorious hope the inconveniences of real change.

Leadership – old style

A change of this dimension will require much more than conventional revolution. It will need a maturity of popular involvement never seen before, a new perspective of leadership and citizenship.

The astrology of today's key leaders shows them to be victims, trapped in the mentality of the times into which they were born. This, and their individual karmic shortcomings, makes them unable to see beyond themselves and the past they grew up in.

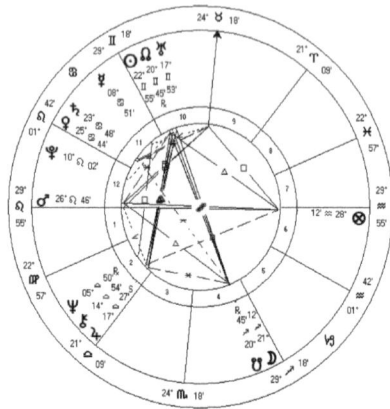

Donald Trump
14 Jun 1946 10:54 EDT +4:00
Queens, NY 40°N43' 073°W52'
Geocentric Tropical Placidus True Node

Donald Trump was born as the Saturn/Pluto conjunction in Leo was to signal the Cold War, and the start of the Second 'Red Scare' in the US, leading to the McCarthy anti-communist hearings (1947-57).[227] The mood then of mob hysteria, based on unsubstantiated accusation, has a familiar ring today. Individually, Donald Trump's Gemini/ Sagittarius Full Moon, explains not only his bombast, but its direction. His Moon, ruling Mercury, Saturn and Venus in Cancer in the eleventh house, conjuncts the South Node – emotional attachment to the familiar. All this is well suited to mass a crowd, by invoking simplistic traditional values, the Gemini words twisted to stir up, not shake into understanding.

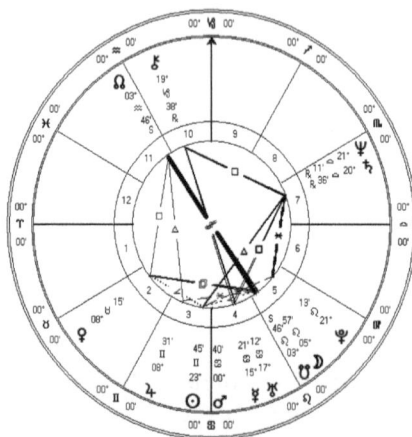

Xi Jinping
15 Jun 1953 No time AWST -8:00
Beijing, China 39°N55' 116°E25'
Geocentric Tropical 0° Aries True Node

Xi Jinping was born into a communist perspective of deluded hysteria, driven by the Saturn/Neptune conjunction in Libra. His formative adolescent and early adult years were through the 1966-76 Cultural Revolution, when Mao Tse-tung sought to hijack the contemporary revolutionary mood to serve the state. He is also a Gemini with strong Cancer planets (Mars, Mercury, Uranus). Xi Jinping's Moon too conjuncts the South Node, this time in Leo; the Chinese nation chart has Mars/Pluto conjunct in Leo in the seventh house. This explains his uncompromising focus on the cohesive integration and expansion of his nation.

Vladimir Putin's Venus rising in Scorpio with Pluto in Leo on the Midheaven represents a dark forbidding persona. His Libran Saturn/Neptune conjunction is in the twelfth house with Mercury. The Sun joined them by progression, when he was a young boy. He grew up through the rising energy of the Cold War. His nature is ideally suited to uncompromising manipulation and intimidation.

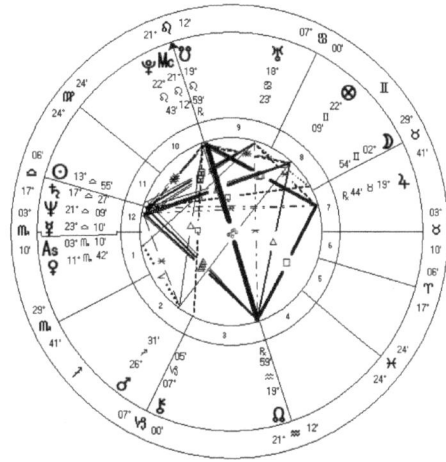

Vladimir Putin
7 Oct 1952 09:30 BAT -3:00
St Petersburg, Russia 59°N55' 030°E15'
Geocentric Tropical Placidus True Node

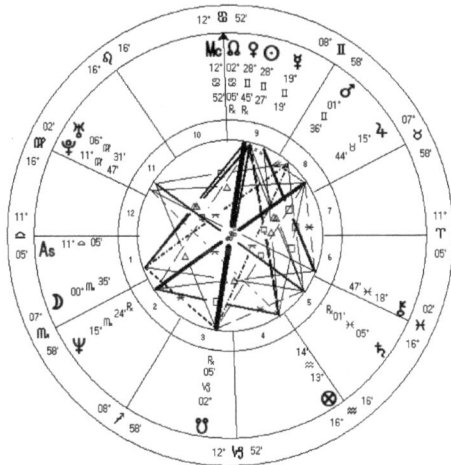

Boris Johnson
19 Jun 1964 14:00 EDT +4:00
New York, NY 40°N42'51" 074°W00'23"
Geocentric Tropical PlacidusTrue Node

Boris Johnson was born just before the Uranus/Pluto conjunction in Virgo. At the naive initial stage of this new cycle of social upheaval, it felt like a no-brainer to toss away the heavy-handed power politics behind the horrors of two world wars, colonialism, the Cold War and Vietnam War. His chart is dominated by Sun, Mercury, Venus and Mars easy going in Gemini. He will love the art of an idea rather than its responsibility and long-term consequences. The Moon in Scorpio applying to Neptune, opposed by Jupiter in Taurus, suggests the charming fixity of the time to enjoy without responsibility. This is tempered by his inner planets now progressed into Leo, Virgo, Cancer.

Leadership – new style

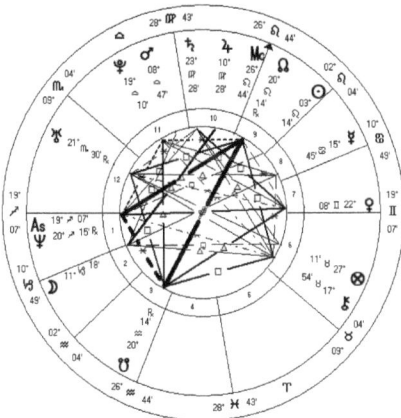

All these leaders are trapped in the brutality and/or ignorance of their past, unable to rise up objectively to see the needs of the future, or, in Boris Johnson's case, lacking the maturity of experience to do more than hang on to the coattails of his elders' assumptions.

Jacinda Arden was elected Prime Minister of New Zealand in October 2017. With Pluto in Libra and Neptune in Sagittarius, she

Jacinda Ardern
26 Jul 1980 13:59 NZT -12:00
Hamilton, NZ 37°S47' 175°E17'
Geocentric Tropical Placidus True Node

was born amidst an opening-out to the world, through young people's global travel and new liberal attitudes towards relationships. Understanding very different cultures could change minds. With the Sun in Leo and the Sagittarius ruler, Jupiter, in Virgo in the tenth, she clearly aspired to lead. At the same time, the Moon in Capricorn, ruled by Saturn also in the tenth, suggests responsible leadership is mixed strongly with a flair to express her splash chart by giving out protection in all directions.

The youngest world leader when elected, she comes from an entirely new generation and could herald very different focus that serves the need of the people, not the prejudices of special-interest systems.

Leadership of the people

We need to stop following the wrong leaders, stop listening to their simplistic 'solutions', which only make matters worse, while blocking our insight to learn from our mistakes. Yet, even a new kind of leader, however benign and far-seeing, will not be enough bring in the radical economic and social change the 2020 climax of the Pluto-in-Capricorn transit period demands.

For there to be real change, far deeper, more mature attitudes will need to grow within the heart of the majority. Not a leader's simple promise that touches a chord and stirs pamphleteering emotion. That soon fades, and instead forces acceptance of exactly want we do not want – a counter-productive false view that 'they' (the 'enemy') have forced all this upon us. No charismatic leaders, then!

It requires more and more of us to be wise; a growing majority to develop understanding, compassion and the courage and patience to endure radical, even uncomfortable change. An increasing majority need to accept the consequences of deciding decency, what is right is possible. Instead of seeking to reverse the limitations caused by Covid-19, keep those that save money and are more efficient. Do not travel to work unless you have to, or fly abroad just of the sake of it. Eat out only on special occasions. Spend less, buy less, repair more. Redirect investment such as airport expansion to green projects. Train brilliant technicians to create a new world. Transform employment away from low-paid work. Money saved can create new meaningful investment and jobs. Crucially, resist government attempts to squeeze out your savings on pointless purchasing.

This is a chance to rebalance the economy to a new-normal focus, where everything we work for has genuine value. Do not fear massive change. Take refuge in common sense and fairness. Demand all policies care for the planet, all its people and everything on it.

Realise real leaders grow from the wise will of the people at the root of society. Get ready for the possibility of real Aquarian change.

-o0o-

Chapter 8
The Way to a Better Future
[Articles written January to July 2021]

Contemporary Background
The crises of the US Presidential transition, last minute EU/UK Brexit negotiations, cases of Covid-19 intensifying, various vaccines being approved... the world seemed like a mother to be, suffering the last agonising pre-birth pains. Was the promise of 'a bright new baby in her arms' really possible? Having created the cause to suffer the worst that neglecting the world and its creatures had brought to us, could humanity be about to benefit from the brilliance of modern science?

With incredible astro-timing, would the Jupiter/Saturn conjunction at the first degree of Aquarius on the 21 December 2020 Winter Solstice mark not only mechanical science at its very best, but see humanity at last shaking off the selfish horror that rule by greed, ignorance and hatred can bring?

8 December 2020	First Covid-19 vaccination in UK
6 January 2021	Invasion of US Capitol
15 January 2021	Donald Trump Impeached
20 January 2021	Joe Biden Inaugurated as President of USA
13 February 2021	Donald Trump found not-guilty by 43 of 100 senators

-o0o-

Aware that there was so much more to learn, the January 2021 column was wary of over-optimism. Without compassion, humanity could degenerate and lose itself in different, but even more dangerous, ways. So, the column sought to put the immediate future in a broad historical perspective. To reach the highest Aquarian goal of genuine Universal Understanding, compassion is required, not only for all of humanity, but for the entirety of all creation.

The article below sought to show how the present time had developed from past centuries. It then lists important future astro-cycle steps leading to the Age of Aquarius. Clearly, we had a long way to go!

On the Path to the Age of Aquarius

Always keen to live in momentous times, some people have suggested the recent Jupiter/Saturn conjunction in the first degree of Aquarius marks the beginning of its Age.

Not that simple! Aquarius is the opposite of Leo. It does not seek to reign, rather to enable knowledge. For sure, its time is coming and has been coming since the Renaissance, but it is coming in stages, step-by-step. It is coming at a steady pace that ensures we, of lesser understanding, will not be overwhelmed by its characteristics and amazing devices. It is coming at a pace that ensures we do not become power-crazy with the incredible possibilities. Visualise anti-gravity machines and free energy in the hands of the today's world leaders. They can hardly handle computer technology and the many new scientific ways of exploiting the natural resources of the planet. Would we share more power kindly, or blow everything up in a morass of egocentricity? We just are not ready.

So, the Age of Aquarius is coming in preparatory stages, that can be tracked by studying the outer-planetary astro-cycles. Underpinning them is the five-hundred-year Neptune/Pluto cycle. The fifteenth-century radical change in the development of knowledge was heralded by the 1398 Neptune/Pluto conjunction. Significantly, this was the first of eight such conjunctions in Gemini that will continue to occur every just-under five hundred years right up to and including 4847 CE.[228]

The Underlying Neptune/Pluto Cycle
The 1398 conjunction was anticipated and reinforced by two rare Jupiter/Saturn cycles, commenced by conjunctions in Aquarius in 1345 and 1405 (the latter, the last in that sign before our 2020 one). It was further enhanced by the air of Uranus' 1439-47 Gemini transit. By providing the tools for ordinary people to exchange ideas, the fifteenth century accelerated communication and consequent cultural change. Around 20 October 1455, when the first moveable type book was published, Uranus was applying to conjunct Pluto in Leo.[229] From then printed publications, translated into the vernacular, increased dramatically. Individual free-thinking blossomed into the Renaissance. By the end of the century the ground was established, out of which was to grow scientific understanding of the mechanical workings of the planet, and its place in the Universe. As Pluto returned to Gemini in the eighteenth century, the Enlightenment and Industrial Revolution initiated three centuries of rapid advance to today's highly risky full-swing economy.

From the early nineteenth century, two hundred years of Jupiter/Saturn conjunctions in earth signs intensified the dominance of a material view of reality. As production methods expanded, decisions and disputes have centred around wealth creation and rights of possession.

Then came the 1891-92 first Gemini return of the Neptune/Pluto conjunction, just five degrees ahead of its 1398 position. This has fuelled ideas and asked questions that have moved aspirations well beyond simplistic gross materialism. Buoyed up by the powerful individualism of the capitalist revolution and major advances in scientific discovery, the ensuing twentieth century has seen upheaval, fired by revolutionary ideas. The consequences of the development of the internet and social media are comparable, on a higher dimension, to the development of writing at similar stages in the fifteenth century. These will grow ever more, as the Jupiter/Saturn cycle returns to its fourteenth and fifteenth-century sign of Aquarius and the Neptune/Pluto cycle, which we are in the midst of, advances to its waxing square. There will be ten square connections between 2061 and 2065. All of which will make available the tools to prepare humanity's consciousness for the Age of Aquarius, but when will it really be with us?

Stepping to the Age of Aquarius

On pages 544-52 of his *The Book of World Horoscopes,* Nicholas Campion lists eighty-six dates that have been suggested for the start of the 'Age of Aquarius', between 1457 and 3550 CE.[230]

From 1997 to early 2011 either or both Uranus and Neptune were in Aquarius, or in mutual reception, while Uranus was in Pisces. Campion lists five dates in or around this period – 1997, 1998, 2000, 2010 and 2012. Certainly, these years saw rapid electronic advances in the resources to communicate in our personal and business lives. Industrial production is becoming less dependent on intensive human labour, more on the supervision and servicing of automatic machines. These advances have transformed ordinary people's power. Using a small pocket device, we can have delivered to us, or order the creation and delivery to others of, a vast range of products. We can be in intimate visual contact with people all over the world.

Yet the way we have focused and used this capacity could hardly be more negatively Piscean. In a crazy expansive urge for more and more satisfaction, we techno-flood our minds with gratuitously meaningless hyper-sensational entertainment and self-indulgent communication on social media. We become obsessed and project our personal success or failure upon pseudo-celebrities or a special sporting team. Like Cinderella's ugly sisters, we see the slightest needs of the underdog, the poor and refugees as an irritating hindrance to our happiness. We invest in walls to keep them out. Yet ironically, society's capacity for selective kindness can well up into hysteria of generosity, when the news cycle or social media feed goes 'viral'. Aquarius' androgyny in relationships is over-focused on diversification and suffering, rather than happy release. We burn, pollute, and so destroy the very natural planetary resources that gift all that we so self-indulgently enjoy.

As the world experiences Covid-19, symbolising the terrifying consequences of such negative Piscean misuse of the turn-of-the-century's Aquarian tools, Jupiter conjuncts Saturn in the first degree of Aquarius. Exact on 20 December 2020, it offers the first indication of common sense. To keep our attention, Saturn stays in the sign until early 2023. This will be a bridge to the Pluto-in-Aquarius period 2023-44 that will regenerate our current way of seeing the world. Scientific understanding will advance in a radically different direction through the second half of the century, especially through Uranus's next transit through Aquarius – 2079-87. We could see ourselves at the mercy of the artificial intelligence machine, but it could also move the world on to a wiser, less adolescent Aquarian understanding.

Even bigger steps to the real Age of Aquarius

Returning to Nicholas Campion's list for a broader perspective, I prefer Ronald Davidson's date of 2376 CE as the start of the real Age of Aquarius. By then, the world should have advanced sufficiently to work safely with its possibilities. At the Vernal Equinox that year, the sidereal position of the Sun is just moving back to Aquarius, as the tropical Sun makes it annual entry to Aries (Fagan-Allan ayanamsa, or 2382 CE using the popular Indian Lahiri ayanamsa).[231]

Vernal Equinox of
Age of Aquarius - Tropical
20 Mar 2376 10:44 UT +0:00
London, UK 51°N30' 000°W10'
Geocentric Placidus True Node

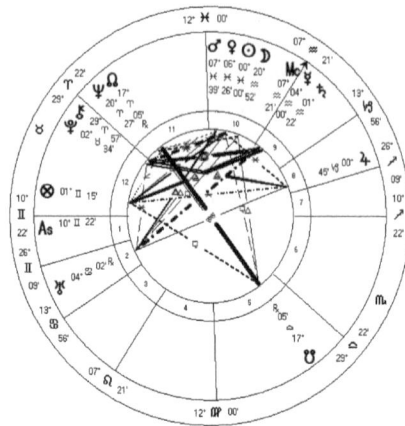

Vernal Equinox of
Age of Aquarius - Fagan-Allen
20 Mar 2376 10:44 UT +0:00
London, UK 51°N30' 000°W10'
Geocentric Placidus True Node

From the beginning of the twenty-second century until that time, Uranus, Neptune and Pluto initiate important new cycles with each other, and also transit Aquarius.

❖ **18 February 2104 – new Uranus/Pluto cycle begins in Taurus**
Hopefully the previous century has wisely prepared the way, by allowing the planet to recover from the abuse it endured in the nineteenth and twentieth centuries, without humanity becoming a mere minor machine-dependent functionary. Providing manic consumption is confined to past memory, practical technological wisdom could create a sustainable relationship between humanity, its economy and the planet.

❖ **21 March 2161 to 20 January 2176 – Neptune transits Aquarius**
9 February 2163 to 31 January 2171 – Uranus transits Aquarius
What was started, for good or ill, through those 1997-2011 years will advance (or degenerate) to a radical new level. Our twenty-first-century opportunities, hopes and fears, will by this future be in full

flow, inevitably taking our descendants to the sustainable best or dystopian worst we can imagine.

❖ **17 January 2165 – new Uranus/Neptune cycle in Aquarius.** Do we dare to hope this will be a century of belief in humane efficiency and selfless intelligence?

❖ **27 September 2221 – new Uranus/Pluto cycle begins in Libra**
20 January 2247 to 8 January 2255 – Uranus transits Aquarius
24 March 2269 to 14 December 2289 – Pluto transits Aquarius
The twenty-first century is seeing the unravelling of assumptions that have held sway for thousands of years. For all this time, human relationships have been based on a rigid patriarchal male/female divide. By twenty-third century, a new foundation for relationships that recognises each unique individual nature should be taken for granted. Within this new social structure, a proper political balance between a wide range of sexual identities will become natural.

❖ **3 March 2325 to 7 January 2340 – Neptune Transits Aquarius**
12 March 2330 to 6 December 2338 – Uranus transit Aquarius
As these planets come together in Aquarius for the second time, since 1997-2011, the world should be seeing and becoming really ready for the actual Age of Aquarius – now just on the horizon.

❖ **20 March 2357 – a new Uranus/Pluto cycle begins in Taurus**
❖ The balance between incisive method and beautiful, sensible care of the world around us, needs to be the essential focus for this cycle. Ask not what the Universe can do for me. Ask what can I do for the world.

❖ **2376 (or 2382) – the beginning of the Age of Aquarius**
❖ **20 May 2385 – a new Neptune/Pluto cycle begins in Gemini**
We will have come through much from the liberation of the soul from the fifteenth century, to the individual right to decide and change our world in the twenty-first and the many cycles of learning that followed. As humanity enters this cycle at the beginning of the Age of Aquarius may it have learned how to celebrate the riches and joy of a world that sustains life through consolidating interaction with its environment. May we live in a world that has put materialism and manic technology in perspective. A world where both no longer mould, but rather serve our lives for the greater good. May we will have matured enough for a world like that to be possible!

Then two thousand plus years to prepare for the next big step: the Age of Capricorn!

Back to 2021

While the Jupiter/Saturn conjunction at Winter Solstice 2020 may not be the start of the Age of Aquarius, historians in the future may well look back and say this was when humanity started to have the maturity to look forward to it. A growing acceptance of astrology as a diagnostic tool will be an essential part of the transition.[232]

By understanding astro-cycles, historians of the future will see the growing global change through the intervening centuries to the Age of Aquarius was seeded at this very present time – from the Winter Solstice 2020. The first twenty years of the twenty-first century have been two decades of mindless missed opportunity. Armed with remarkable new tools to understand the planet and communicate with each other, we have listened to and elected inadequate leaders and supported their short-term policies that indulgently waste planetary resources.

Our economic model worships growth. It is sustained by an educational system that initiates us into servicing a manic treadmill of work and quickly picked up and put down pleasures. So, our understanding and support for each other is similarly transitory and ill-considered. As a result, we are unable to understand the deeper needs and experience of people, whom we see as strangers, even intruders. Mindless prejudice can then degenerate our societies into rejection, often violent mindless conflict.

Missing the chance for a new idealistic start to the new millennium in 2000, its first decade focused on indulging in the amazing new technology and picking fights. As a result, ill-prepared for its challenging transits, humanity proceeded to tear itself apart through the 2010s, choosing ever more ecologically destructive false solutions.

Quite simply, Covid-19 is nature's corrective reaction. In some form or other, it will be with us until we accept that there is no bouncing back to the old short-term, 'kicking the can down the road' ways. We have to change the priorities of our economic and social relationships. It is no longer a question of not being able to afford a green, people-orientated way of working together. Rather, we will have no other choice and will be continually be pushed back on ourselves until we realise this.

See and celebrate the symbolism of the Jupiter/Saturn conjunction and their transit through Aquarius as broadening our understanding. Working together to share, not profit from, a Covid-19 vaccine. Not to blame other countries, but to welcome the chance to learn from them. In our personal lives, realise the precious gift of human embrace, as we slowly, slowly feel safe enough to hug each other again. Listen to nature, be pleased to be alive. Share, serve. When more and more of us put everyone else first, their experience of being cared for will flow back to us.

Then, bright-eyed tears of celebration can indeed ring out.

-o0o-

The last extract in this book is from the March 2021 column that identifies the kind-heart motivation needed, as the world struggles to free itself from social debris, caused by nastiness.

'A Journey of a Thousand Miles Begins with a Single Step', this famous Chinese traditional saying both focuses and relieves the mind, when faced with a great task. It brings the 'head in the clouds' idealist down to earth. Yet also offers hopeful, comforting advice that making a start is the way to go.

Compassion – Restoring the Soul of our Society

At this time, it is important to focus on the present stage of the Jupiter/Saturn cycle, which for thousands of years has been the vital foundation to understand the rise and fall of possibility. Jupiter, the planet of expansion, and Saturn, the planet of limitation and structure, work together to balance hope and realism in our lives. Without Saturn, Jupiter would explode in all directions. Without Jupiter all we know would petrify.

Working together, the twenty-year cycle of these planets waxes and wanes in two ten-year half cycles. On Winter Solstice 2020 began a new waxing phase in Aquarius. Expect optimism to jump ahead, as Jupiter separates from the slower Saturn into Pisces from 14 May to 29 July 2021, then is pulled back with Saturn in Aquarius again until 29 December. Over-optimism about the benefits of science and improvements in human relationships will wrestle with reality. Now is not just the beginning of a 200-year series of Jupiter/Saturn conjunctions in air signs. The Winter Solstice conjunction was the first of a series of four Jupiter/Saturn conjunctions in Aquarius sixty years apart. Furthermore, each of these series of four is around 600 years apart. 2021 for sure is a very small early start to major centuries-long developments in understanding.

That this year will not be that simple is emphasised by another outer-planetary cycle that will dominate 2021. Saturn/Uranus 90-degree multiple cycles over the past 130 years have been at key tension points of change. See below: the bold type indicates the conjunction, then come the years of the waxing square and the opposition. The last waning square (underlined) marks clearing out the debris of its cycle (the theme of the cycle is in square brackets).

❖ **1897,** 1909-10, 1918-20, _1930-31_ (conflict between colonialists and their failing economic system)

❖ **1942,** 1951-52, 1965-67, _1975-77_ (victory and post-war recovery that ends in futile conflict)

❖ **1988-89,** 1999-2000, 2008-10, _2021_ ('Triumph of capitalism' ends in intrinsic failure)

This Saturn-in-Aquarius waning square to Uranus in Taurus is exact on 17 February, 14 June and 24 December 2021, but will be in orb and not really fade until early 2022. Harsh events and practical realities constantly hold back progress. Consider! This may be for the good. Quickly applied half solutions often make matters worse. Rushing ahead when not ready can create more problems than it solves. So, while frustrating, even infuriating much of the time, see the positive benefit of how this can focus minds. Being held back to learn from our mistakes ensures a more substantial outcome. When and how to vaccinate against Covid-19 needs to be very carefully balanced, by minds cleansed of the urgent need to 'get back to normal' and the cost of not doing so. The eradication of resentment and hate between sub-groups will be an ongoing process. Give room to those that seem to oppose. Help everyone move to resolution. No room for victors in a world that is healing!

End of an era
In fact, attempts to 'get back to normal' will be futile and counter-productive. The 90-degree Saturn/Uranus cycle began in 1988-89, and so reaches the beginning of its final waning quarter. Disposing of the dysfunctional debris of that cycle will be its focus. Remember the notion of the 'triumph of capitalism' as the USSR fell? How does it look now? Russia and China have degenerated into capitalist oligarchies, while many Western societies have been losing their vision, turned inward and defensive. The world's nations have been either breaking down, or putting up barriers against immigration that they see as threatening to overwhelm them. The struggle between the impossibly simplistic desire for ever-continuing economic growth, amidst impending ecological disaster, is being upstaged by a global pandemic. The close interaction of Jupiter and Saturn in Aquarius against the Uranus square symbolises clearly the virus' threat to mutate and battle with scientific discoveries of vaccines to protect humanity. Ordinary people are confined to their homes. When out, they are required to hide their faces. What used to be the image of villainy has become kindness to our neighbour. What was the friendly, open-faced smile, is now seen as a lack of consideration for others – the face of a super-spreader!

Compassion – the heart of truth
What is 'truth' in the new world that is starting to emerge from this struggle with Covid-19, alongside its wastrel economic system that was on its knees before the pandemic started? The World Wide Web that overcomes privilege and so gloriously offers opportunity to more and more people, also provides them with a megaphone to pour out any unsubstantiated nonsense they happen to feel good about. 'I have heard… most people think…' Who says? We say and the louder and more often, the more credible it becomes. So easy to mock and condemn all this, but look deeper into the heart of normal everyday communities who appear to believe blindly. Most are kind, want happy lives for their families and neighbours. In an emergency, they would risk their lives to help out, even strangers. How different is this kindness from communities with directly opposite opinions, living in radically different worlds?

Wherever we are, come from and think, it is compassion that opens our hearts, and the mistaken belief that others lack compassion, which closes them. The crucial thing for us all to remember is that compassion that selects is not compassion at all. Approaching what you hear about others with compassion melts the ignorance that has hardened opinion and separated us from understanding. This is something we have to work on constantly, step-by-step clearing away misunderstanding, like opening up a path through a forest. Visualise clearing parts of a jungle of sharp, brutal misunderstanding to plant a harvest that will feed us, and more and more others.

As we find ourselves more at ease with each other, we can turn to how to ease our relationship with our environment. Just as we give and take and in human relationships, now is the time to learn how to give and take in our dealings with the Earth. Grabbing and expanding never was the way. It was just a greedy short-sighted delusion we thought was possible when there was so much virginal slack to take up.

So, in the last quarter of the Saturn 90-degree separation cycle that started with their conjunction in 1988-89, we need to use the new Jupiter/Saturn cycle to adjust to a sustainable balance between growth and consolidation in world economics. Produce products that are easy to repair, focus employment more on maintenance. Aim to work and produce less. Spend more time with friends and family at leisure. Balance the economy, so everyone has a home and food and medical care. See this not a benefit for certain countries, or groups within countries, but a human right without borders.

Such is a vision of the compassionate mind. Maybe it will never be entirely like this, but a world wishing for, moving there, this is the healing direction of the compassionate mind. Something to consider as Jupiter moves on to Pisces this year. It will leave behind Saturn in Aquarius to identify problems and re-structure. Then Pluto from 2023 to test and regenerate our scientific knowledge, education and social understanding. Crucially to accept the vital role that understanding astro-cycles could fulfil. In the longer term, Saturn transits Pisces, and then Pluto is there mid-century. Pluto was last there 1797-1823 – not the happiest years in human history. Hopefully, by relying on compassion we will be wiser this time.

Restoring the Soul of our Society

That the Covid-19 pandemic was said to generate the worst economic crisis for over 300 years fitted nicely the period since the foundation of the present world economy. To many ecologists it seemed like the planet was reacting with the full force of a Capricorn stellium insisting 'enough is enough'.

From its very beginning the current world economic system has been self-serving and based on a corrupt ethical foundation. Because it served the few in power, it was always incompetent and, in the end, doomed to fail for all but a dwindling minority. Ironic then, that it claimed practical common sense to be the basis of its legitimacy. Yet, how can ripping out and squandering limited world resources in the service of short-term profit be sustainable? It may have seemed so, when much of the planet was virginal, unexplored and scientific advances found ever-more ingenious ways to explore and harvest resources. For a few centuries, the system's need for an expanding market fitted nicely with ordinary people's hedonistic tastes. Life through those times became a celebration of sensuality, of consuming, fashion, travel, entertainment, game-playing. All going well then! 'It's so good. Who could want to take that away?'

Not for the first time should we compare such twenty-first-century economic judgement to teenagers, even young adults, hosting of a party of friends, while their house-proud parents are away. So, many things to enjoy, money in savings to use up by buying the drink, the drugs. No thought for tomorrow, even though the organisers sense increasing worry as the night progresses into day. The fun seems endless. Even awaking to the debris, the next morning, will be OK, if there are funds to go out for more. Then the visitors sulk off, leaving behind a reckoning for those who have to stay and pay.

Covid-19 brings that reckoning. There will be no way back. We need to care for each other, as well as ourselves. Start with compassion for all who suffer, wherever they live. Fair distribution of vaccine the first step. Food and shelter for all the next. Time to borrow, not to prop up the past, but to rebuild a more viable, fairer future.

Accept changing careers. Allow self-indulgent enterprises to fall away, however large and loud their protests. When hungry, we do not insist on caviar. Always consider the restoration of balance, sustainability. Rebuild an economy that will serve, not tempt human needs. Not self-serving financial systems, based on the artificial manipulation of market dynamics, but designed to give genuine value that serves our essential needs. This is not a Luddite, back to nature call, but rather to pick up what remains to enhance and make an increasingly efficient and intelligent world society for all its peoples.

As more of us work from home, office blocks can be refitted to be those much-needed homes. Dedicate education to understanding and care, not just functional mechanical operations in a wasteful competing marketplace. Introduce ethical ways of assessing people and social change – a role for astrology here. Encourage quality in the arts. Restore catharsis to drama.

Idea: Dissolve the power of unanswered misinformation that sets groups against each other, by developing internet filters that advance understanding. Extend the present systems that block hate speech and calls to violence, automatically to trigger counter-links of fact to any stated opinion. Let not false claims be left unanswered. Ensure opinions are balanced with counter-opinions. Then the brilliant potential of the internet can move on from underhand manipulation and irritating advertisements to educating open world understanding. This, whether we, they, and especially those in power, want it or not.

As we struggle out of the Saturn-square-Uranus so-called 'triumph of capitalism', may the opportunity of Jupiter and discipline of Saturn in Aquarius help us find such radical new ways to organise our lives. Ways that fearlessly cut back on what we do not need, and gently dissolve our hate against those who really have done us no wrong. May we value and repair all we find around us, not only things, but especially the people we meet. May strangers become our friends.

Step-by-step! It will take time and a radical new view of what is efficient. It will take kindness and compassion not to restore, but to advance, the very soul of our world society to a wiser, happier plane.

By starting on the path and starting in the right way, the right future will naturally unfold.

First beneficial Aquarian steps

Of course, the first light of the emergence of an Aquarian underlay to the astro-cycles does not mean an instant change to a more tolerant, idealistic, ecologically viable world. Rather, its possibility will be starting to edge its way into human consciousness. The old ways will still dominate, amidst the destruction caused by Covid-19. Many, most likely the majority, will still be blinkered in these old ways. Their actions may cloud the better options, push their society and the world at large into negative Aquarian-driven methods of social intrusion and control. The Aquarian year 2021 is no more than a first opportunity. We misuse it at our peril not only today, but increasingly into the future. Better to see it as fine way to start to sweep away all that has been misguided and wrong in recent years.

The first key trigger will be how we handle Mars's coming out of its 2020 rout of world society. Prepare your mind for this. We have now seen how the horrors of that year's spring, came back with a vengeance in the autumn. Not ready to learn, impatient to bounce back the economy, we enabled a super-spreader summer to bear a dire autumn harvest of sickness.

Mars is finally emerging from a brutal struggle to hold on to a degenerate past through its late retrograde and early direct return period in November/December 2020. It now moves forward into Taurus and, hopefully, a recovery phase. Below are the astro-events driving this:

Mar	Sqr	Plu	14:52	UT	23 Dec 2020	23°Ar55' D	23°Cp55' D
Mar	Cnj	Tau	22:27	UT	6 Jan 2021	00°Ta00' D	00°Ta00' D
Mar	Sqr	Sat	11:01	UT	13 Jan 2021	03°Ta04' D	03°Aq04' D
Mar	Cnj	Ura	20:37	UT	20 Jan 2021	06°Ta44' D	06°Ta44' D
Mar	Sqr	Jup	07:48	UT	23 Jan 2021	07°Ta59' D	07°Aq59' D
Jup	Sqr	Ura	22:49	UT	17 Jan 2021	06°Aq43' D	06°Ta43' D

May the final square with Pluto mark a farewell to things getting worse! Perhaps vaccine(s). A less slapdash, more sensibly determined breakthrough is possible with Mars in Taurus from 6 January. The pressure to act in thorough new intelligent ways is symbolised by its square to Saturn in Aquarius on 13 January. Be careful, it semi-squares Neptune in Pisces on 14 January.

Mars' conjunction to Uranus on 20 January, followed by its completing square to Jupiter three days later, suggest the early seeding of a radical new realism. Here is a chance to move on from the impossible, by railing against imagined obstacles. Instead, to see those imagined 'problems' that knock on our door, not the cause making matters worse, but as helpers with new knowledge to assist our finding and implementing solutions.

-oOo-

The July 2021 column defined astrology's essential role, enabling us to understand ourselves in the universe.

The Role of Astrology in Space, Time and Consciousness

❖ Time is the creation of humanity and all creatures caught up in its space/time continuum. Through time we develop notions of here and now, then and there, and so see relationships between things. By fixing relationships in this way, we make solid what is in essence a constant flux of energy. Just as we see endless space out there, with a powerful microscope we can see similar forces spiralling in inner space.

❖ Modern mechanical science is a belief system that is trapped in a relative grossly material world, finding ever more relationships, as it seeks ultimate answers that, by definition, it will never find. The more advanced the machine, the more, increasingly intricate relationships will be discovered. Cause will always have more causes. There is a predecessor to the Big Bang, which will have its own predecessor... ad infinitum.

❖ Fixed by the limited consciousness at our relative point in space, the cycles of our Solar System dispose our inclinations, mould our nature and motivate our actions. The Sun is a source of light and heat. The Moon's gravitational pull is close enough to draw and release liquids, tides and sap. Venus's interactive path with the Earth forms spirals that teach us how to love. The pull and relaxation of all the planets combine to bring subtle changes to the pliable bodies of ourselves, the people around us, and the world we share.

❖ How we react to our cyclic space/time relationships determines our experience of life. Are we tossed and turned by the winds of time, hardly in control, blaming, scheming to survive? Or do we train the mind to transcend discontent, stay on top of the flow, live a virtuous life to the full, and so become consciously ready for death. For the state of mind at death remains as a residue that forms a karmic pattern, which projects itself to the appropriate point of space and time of the next incarnation. This pattern sets a new lifetime of cycles to work through and master.

❖ Astrology is the bridge of understanding both within and between lifetimes. By applying its interpretive language of living names and definitions to planetary cycles, we understand our natures, experiences and opportunities. From the symbols of each birth horoscope we can understand, not only that individual's nature, but the cyclic pattern it will confront throughout its entire life. This helps us through a whole-life challenge to do even better this time round. Ideally, at the end, to be so conscious that we choose rebirth, solely to help everyone awaken to consciousness ever more widely.

These extracts end with invoking the motivation to apply ourselves to the challenges of the times, day-to-day with 'sleeves rolled up'. As long as samsara lasts, it will never be more than this. Yet, by applying a compassionate mind to all creation, as we work with the planets, we will experience and create increasing happiness.

Appendix A
The Astrology of Radical Economic Change

The July 2007 column included an incisive analysis of Britain's twenty-first-century rulers and the two men that were destined to lead the country through the imminent financial crisis.

Twelfth House Continues to Rule – Let Battle Commence!

'You have to trust twelfth-house people, or lock them up', was the focus around which my initial analysis of the 1997 Labour landslide victory turned. It could not have been more prophetic! Throughout the past ten years we have had accusations of 'spin', 'control freakery', 'in-group sofa government' and just plain 'lying'. We have been told by the media (via intermediaries) of secret battles between Tony Blair and his Chancellor. The latter has been accused by colleagues of 'personality flaws' and intolerance, the words of which read remarkably like a 'cook book' summary of twelfth-house characteristics.

Over the past ten years the twelfth-house tendency has spread with George Bush, Vladimir Putin and Ariel Sharon all having their Suns there. The consequent obsession with fear of others, the need to defend ourselves against what 'they might do to us' and insistence we must sacrifice our freedom in the service of security is now accepted as inevitable – 'the only game in town'. Looking back to the fresh sunshine of that early May 1997 days, life seems to have become ever more despondent and desperate. Does it always have to be like this?

As I write, it is expected that Tony Blair will announce his retirement very soon and, as you receive this, Gordon Brown will be, or about to become, Prime Minister of the United Kingdom. How will things change?

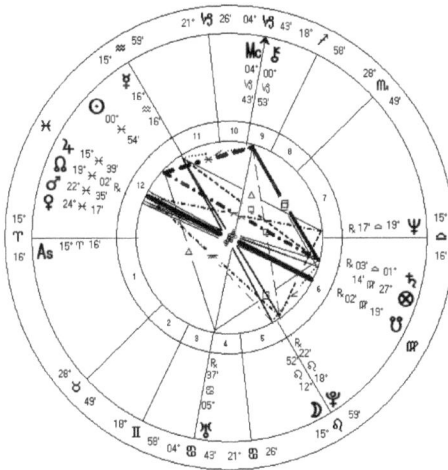

Gordon Brown
20 Feb 1951 08:40 UT +0:00
Giffnock, UK 55°N48' 004°W20'
Geocentric Tropical Placidus True Node

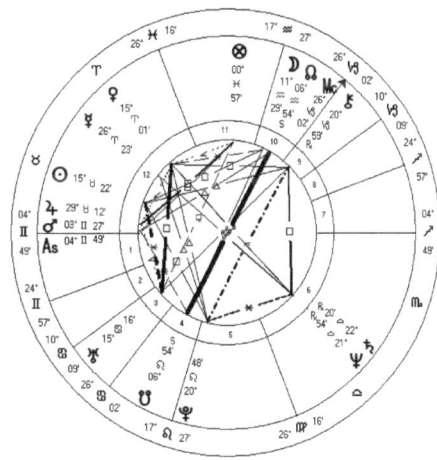

Tony Blair
6 May 1953 06:10 BST -1:00
Edinburgh, UK 55°N57' 003°W13'
Geocentric Tropical Placidus True Node

Intrinsically, the two men are not as dissimilar as it first seems, although it takes an astrologer to see it. The open and initially attractive, 'hail fellow well met', seemingly good-humoured and self-effacing public persona of the outgoing Prime Minister is deceptive. All you are seeing here is an Aquarian Moon conjuncting the North Node in his tenth house. This is his image, not the real driving force. That is explained by a tenacious Taurean Sun and Jupiter, an impulsively belligerent Mercury and Venus in Aries, ruled by Mars in Gemini just behind his Ascendant in the same sign. Lacking the maturity of vision to think through the implications of his decisions, but determined to prevail; he has manipulated and charmed his way through ten years in power. During this time much has been attempted, but little been done properly and completed. What financial and physical dangers for Britain and the world in the future have been created remains to be seen. Opponents point to Iraq as Tony Blair's legacy, whereas he himself would like to feel he has left the United Kingdom's education, health and public institutions ready to become leaner and much more efficient. Others may worry that, because of his twelfth-house-driven obsession with security and limiting legal rights, he has, albeit unintentionally, prepared Britain to be taken over by Orwellian fascism.

Gordon Brown[233] does not have the 'image-friendly' tenth-house Moon and North Node. So, with him, personality-wise what you see is what you get. He is dour because he is intensely anxious, conscientious and hard-working. The Piscean focus means he could not care more deeply. With so many planets in the twelfth house, he is intensely private. This explains the awkwardness of his progress toward the top job. That, with such energy he wishes to be Prime Minister at all indicates great kindness and idealism. He is a man with a mission.

Of course, that does not necessarily make his judgements and policies correct, nor indicate that his approach to government will be effective. The apparent financial successes of his Chancellorship may yet come to haunt users of hospitals, schools and transport systems. The drain of public finance initiatives (PFIs) will continue to bite, as infrastructures age and decay, but cannot be replaced, because we are still paying for them. The cost of housing, pensions, student and more general debt may become far less easy to sustain. For in time the property boom will burst and temporarily cheap Chinese and Indian products and services will no longer be with us. As a nation we are trying and working harder, yet being overtaken by Asia. For these reasons, the twelfth house Piscean devotion of Gordon Brown may turn out to deceive him, as well as us. However good his intentions, will the caveats of great chancellorship that are often placed upon him be his legacy? Or will he be seen as a leader who projected his own personality of obsessive hard-work upon a whole nation, but left it exhausted and failing?

However that goes, now the decks are cleared for a great political battle, which has very much to do with the twelfth house. As we observed during the Conservative Party leadership contest,[234] although David Cameron[235] has an attractively friendly Venus and Sun rising in Libra in the first house, his Moon and Mars are proudly and imperially placed in Leo. This Mars has now progressed into twelfth-house Virgo and moves between the natal and progressed Pluto and Saturn on both charts during the build-up to the next UK General Election. It will oppose Gordon Brown's natal Mars and Venus and be applying to oppose Gordon Brown's Saturn too – a critical 'up close and personal' battle in every sense!

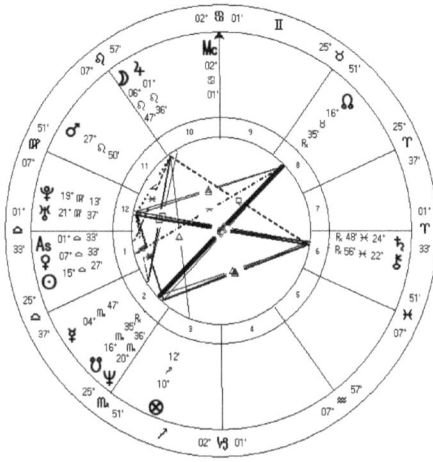

David Cameron
9 Oct 1966 06:00 BST -1:00
London, UK 51°N30' 000°W10'
Geocentric Tropical Placidus True Node

When Tony Blair was at this stage of preparation a few years before his 1997 victory, he was dismissed as 'Bambi'. Seeking to dismiss David Cameron as a lightweight publicist with little or no policies would be a similar error. The key question that needs to be asked is whether David Cameron is a manipulative, 'all things to all people' presenter whose actions in office would be as, or even more divisive and repressive than, Labour's? Alternatively, are his often-mocked statements, such as 'hug a hoodie' and 'rewarding the family' expressions of a healing vision that is vital for Britain? If so, has he the clarity and strength of will to apply these subtle insights to expansive benefit, like a homoeopathic political process?

Crucially, has David Cameron the capacity to help heal the psychotic trauma projected on the world by the twelfth-house paranoia of recent leaders and their policies? Or, with Gordon Brown's progressed Moon and transiting Jupiter about to activate his Midheaven in the coming year, will *he* mature into a much more open and publicly effective figure in the top job? Will his Piscean familiarity with the failure of fear focus a stronger and more effective healing? Or will the challenges of the turn of the decade be such that they can only be endured, whoever is in power?

It will be interesting to see how things develop.

-o0o-

Before continuing here, re-read Chapter 5. The November 2008 column was written just as the economic crisis was developing, following Lehman Brothers collapse on 15 September 2008 and during the last two months of the US Presidential Election. That article and some of the columns in the January and March 2009 *Journals* are an in-depth account of the circumstances that brought the world economy to its 2008-10 dilemma.

They were important considerations for the Pluto-in-Capricorn period ahead, showing why the hard won 'recovery', dominating the 2010s, was illusory, and so left the world in an ever-growing financial, social and ecological crisis as the threat of Covid-19 hit the planet.

-o0o-

The January 2010 column set the scene for the year ahead. Reading it from years in the future and knowing what actually happened, invokes a profound regret of missed opportunity. If only we had listened then, how different might the world have been, how much destruction, human suffering and waste could have been avoided. How well could we have healed the planet instead!

2010 – For Better or Worse?

We did not come here to fear the future. We came here to shape it. *President Barack Obama* – US Congress September 2009

In his keynote presentation to the 2009 Astrological Association Annual Conference,[236] Dr Nicholas Campion reminded us that, when writing *Mundane Astrology*, Charles Harvey, Michael Baigent and he had sought to encourage the use of astrology as Kepler had recommended in the early seventeenth century. Sound advice! Rather than making specific predictions, this column has always been a servant of this august tradition. So, what astrological advice does it have to help 2010 be a better year than expected?

Can we rely on economic recovery?
In 2006/7 observing the world economy booming and enjoying what was claimed at the time to be 'recession-proof growth', but aware of the upcoming 2008 Pluto Capricorn ingress and Saturn Uranus opposition (plus having some good old-fashioned common sense!), I was inspired to write:

> However, is the G8-, World Bank- and IMF-controlled world free trade economy as total, permanent, ideal and eternally happy as it seems? Have ordinary people really progressed from brutal exploitation, via the dictatorship of the proletariat, to a permanent aristocratisation of the proletariat? Or are we just in the middle of a lucky break? Are we in truth no more than a group of party-goers loaded with alcohol and other 'goodies' to indulge in and gorge on? Is all that lies ahead the jaded awakening of the morning after; to find our resources exhausted and the same old harsh realities of life confronting us?[237]

So, now writing in the late autumn of 2009, as the DJIA returns to 10,000, bankers' bonuses are back on track[238] and the increase in unemployment is slowing, do the astro-cycles confirm we have successfully navigated away from disaster, and that growth and happiness lie ahead?

Astrology aside, there are key economic and political reasons to question such early optimism. Since the mid-1990s economic growth has been more reliant upon the manipulation of confidence than fundamental industrial strength. As Robert Maxwell knew so well, encouraging high asset values (however you do it!) provides the collateral to buy more. Having spent reserves, borrowed vast sums and trawled for saleable assets to avoid catastrophe the world leaders, who presided over the 2008 economic collapse, have a desperately vested interest in sustaining the notion that their policies are leading to recovery.

Astro-events urge caution

The astrology of the immediate past, present and future urges a more sober assessment of current strategies. In the September 2009 'Working with the Planets', we noted that the recovery packages were conceived during a void of course Pluto in late Sagittarius with Mercury retrograde for the key conceptual time. Hence the strategy was strong on propping up the status quo and extremely weak at looking for and correcting the crucial cause of the problem. Some banks were allowed to fail. Others were temporarily nationalised, on the assumption that they could be re-sold at a profit later on. Those that remained in private hands (often propped up by government finance) were virtually re-floated in a less competitive trading environment. At the same time, the personnel and methods of financial manipulation were left largely unfettered. Hence, the first to appear to recover to profit are the investment banks, whose activities created the original crisis. With the Saturn/Uranus opposition still in mutable signs, have we learnt or radically changed anything? We continue to borrow and print the money that keeps the pain of hardship away from ordinary citizens. At the same time, it puts profits and bonuses into the pockets of those investment bankers.

How soon will there be a true time of reckoning? While this article is going through the publishing process, Saturn will enter Libra and square Pluto in Capricorn. On 13 January it moves into retrograde, to make a second square to Pluto on 31 January. In early April 2010 it is back in Virgo, to go direct on 2 May and build to the long-awaited T-square with Mars, Jupiter, Uranus and Pluto towards the end of July. In late summer and autumn, Jupiter and Uranus return to Pisces. So, 2010 will be a year of uncertainty that will see a constant struggle between the haunting ghost of fundamental cardinal reality and the self-delusion that it is not, and does not have to be, 'that bad'. Rather like at the end of a long party most people know they have to go home and get on with their lives, but a sad rump convince themselves the celebration can go on for ever and stay and spend the fare home on more indulgences.

This analogy does not fully reflect the seriousness of the situation. Pluto in Capricorn suggests the circumstances could become seriously uncompromising once the full cardinal changeover is complete. The price for continuing the party may be not only the financial reserve wealth and collateral assets of many nations, but a lack of energy capacity to continue familiar activities and the very ecological stability of the planet.

Astrology can help us make wiser choices

Astrology can help us avoid this happening, if we use it to understand Capricorn's harsh reality and embrace it as helpful. To make the right hard choice is the kindest way, because it ensures we do not make matters worse by putting off facing the problem. It answers it. 2010 will see a struggle between those politicians, economists, ecologists and citizens who see the sense in this, but find it difficult to be heard, against opponents who think it is much easier to gain democratic power by making pleasant noises and hiding the truth from the people – especially at election time! The voter who votes for the most pleasing political promise is just as dishonest as the politician who makes it. He or she deserves the consequences. Unfortunately, everyone shares the same fate, when such weak, indulgent governments fail.

Fortunately, there is hope for more intelligent and visionary attitudes gaining momentum this time. For Jupiter moves on from its Winter Solstice conjunction to Neptune and Chiron[239] to ingress Pisces, the sign it traditionally rules. In doing so, it heralds the second great trend of the coming decade – Neptune's transit through Pisces. Alongside the harsh, but necessary, kindness of Pluto in Capricorn, we are to experience (for good or ill) Neptune-like intimacy and sensitive wonder. It can encourage sympathetic contact, a healing impetus and willingness to sacrifice, outcomes that will help as many people as possible. Unfortunately, Neptune and Pisces, the sign it rules, can encourage personal sacrifice for misguided, fanatical reasons. Fear can be used by those in power to terrorise their populations, mobilise them against scapegoats, or to distract them from the real cause and solution of their problems. When governments and economic advisers deny the need for the radical change that is really needed, ordinary citizens become victims; exploited by the very bankers whose businesses they are underwriting.

With courage we can stand against such intimidation and insist on realistic and effective change. Happiness comes from accepting our needs are limited. If care, we will be cared for; be it by the people in our lives or the environmental resources we need to live. Over-dependence on governments and experts leads to life being invaded and ruled by 'alien' authoritarian brutality. Such authorities insist we sacrifice everything in the service of ideas and aspirations we do not understand, did not ask for, and certainly do not want. Astrology could be a key tool in helping us discern the difference and make wise choices.

-oOo-

With the 2010 UK General Election about to be called, the April 2010 column made an impassioned appeal that the upcoming Jupiter [with Neptune imminent] in Pisces period be used, not to continue to prop up short-term greed, but to transform the world economy with kind motivation. It was ignored and the time instead used to trigger a decade of finger pointing and exploitation of the disadvantaged.

The Crimes of the Centuries

> Poets starving children bleed
> Nothing he's got he really needs
> Twenty-first-century schizoid man.
> King Crimson *21st Century Schizoid Man*[240]

Those old enough to have heard these words for the first time in 1969 will remember feeling outraged at such negativity. Were we not at the 'dawning of the Age of Aquarius', when 'peace will rule the planet'?[241] Forty years on, and in that twenty-first century, it seems the Rado and Ragni dreamy hope for peace may have been seriously flawed and Robert Fripp's King Crimson nearer the mark.

For schizophrenia is indeed an apt way of describing the extreme irrationality of the two issues that dominate our contemporary world economy and the consequent assumptions that drive behaviour in our cultures.

- ❖ On the one hand we extol the 'success' of economic systems based on manipulation to cause expansion and celebrate consumption as a religious aspiration. We organise our education to serve it. Success is seen as basking in the glory of ever more possessions.

❖ On the other hand, we rely upon and literally swim in a petroleum sea, of which most of our clothes and other products are made,[242] while recognising the dangerous futility of exhausting in a few centuries finite reserves that took hundreds of thousands of years to create. Our scientists measure and we tremble at the global consequences.

Tragically, the having makes us no happier than does fear of the consequences. Instead, the potential glory of human endeavour splits psychotically into two desperately degenerate personalities. Both are self-destructive and a danger to everything they touch – all because we refuse to realise 'nothing he's got he really needs'.

The answer to a billion broken promises
Five years later, in 1974, the title song of the rock band Supertramp's album *Crime of the Century* laid out clearly our responsibility for the psychosis:

> 'Who are these men of lust, greed and glory?
> Rip off the masks and let's see.
> But that's not right, oh no, what's the story
> There's you, there's me'

Since then, we have experienced 35 years of ever-worsening booms and busts, experimented and failed with monetarism and returned to facile Keynesian intervention. We have been offered millions, if not billions, of hours of advertisements. Many have participated in focus groups designed to spin back to us what they think they heard we want. We have acquiesced in a society based on promises designed to massage greed and play to our fears. By accepting the highest 'responsibility' lies in more work to earn resources that enable more consumption, we have neglected our families and failed to create a caring society. In a Faustian pact, we have sold what would really make us happy in exchange for a billion broken promises.

With those to whom we gave the custody of our financial, economic and political institutions largely discredited, the late-spring 2010 British General Election offers a unique opportunity for the electorate. Now we know what they can be like, would not basing our vote on their promises make us even more complicit in their actions? Will we at last realise the crime we have allowed to be perpetrated in our name? Will we this time reject false promises and bribes, prefer realistic challenge that truly balances give and take? Will we demand the truth? Do the astro-cycles of the next few months support such a possibility?

A time of Piscean sympathy?
January's 'Working with the Planets' and those before have already outlined and interpreted the main cycles, including Pluto in Capricorn, a mutable Saturn/Uranus opposition that will complete in a cardinal T-square in July this year. For full information, read back issues of the *Astrological Journal*, or the broader analysis in my book *Economy, Ecology and Kindness*.[243] As expected, tales of optimism are in the air. We are told we have come through the worst. Recovery and growth are just around the corner. Asia, it seems, is a booming success story. Stock markets are making record gains. Yet the astro-cycles suggest all this lacks substance – it is

founded on sand, borrowed sand at that! Are we destined to repeat recent errors on an even grander scale, as whole countries, not just their banks, start to fail?

Encouraging selfish and dishonest individuals in a competition contained by regulation and enforced by surveillance and military control, is not a sustainable foundation for the world economy. To get it right, it is necessary to stop focusing on being better in the battle to get what we are told to think we want. We must start understanding what we need. To know this, we have to understand the needs of everyone and everything in the planet. It is much easier and more comfortable to assist creation, not disregard and destroy it to generate massive raw materials for manufacture. In short, our cultural and economic *raison d'être* needs to be sympathy and understanding, getting to know and helping – not learning tricks to steal a march on other people and the planet's resources. Fortunately, as the focus of outer-planetary energy moves toward Pisces, it is this need for sympathy that will be screaming out to be addressed.

How to work with Pisces
That does not mean it will be addressed. The consequences of Piscean misunderstanding can be dire indeed. While Mikhail Gorbachev's Piscean tolerance brought greater freedom and rapprochement with the West, it led to the dissolution of the USSR, the raping of the nation's wealth and a new kind of totalitarianism. Gordon Brown's Piscean good intentions to soften economic pain in the UK and the world may well prevent our addressing the key needs of the time, and so lead to far worse disaster in the end. Piscean sympathy can also turn to bitter resentment. Having 'put up with' unreasonable treatment, something snaps and excessive aggression ensues. As the outer-planetary focus turns increasingly to Pisces, with a Capricorn Pluto and Arian Uranus, the kickback from marginalised societies, age groups and religious cultures, who see themselves as left out or exploited, could lead to ever more brutal and unforgiving social disintegration and terror threats.

Because of all this and to avoid missing a unique opportunity of redemption that approaches, it is crucial we cultivate idealism and take refuge in Pisces at its empathetic best. Its great ocean of interconnected understanding can suck down and drown to nothingness any nagging demands of self-interest. We could create a very different economy based upon the principle of kindness. An economy that seeks to understand people's needs and the environment sympathetically is not only far more comfortable to live in, it can be more materially efficient and sustainable as well. By identifying with everything outside ourselves, we naturally want the footprint of our actions to disturb as little as possible. We seek to ease and support. We seek not to grow, but to balance our economies, to supply from excess in response to need. We do not do this because of some socialist dictate, but because it warms our heart to live in such a happy, understanding world. This ultimate blissful way of living has been taught by Jesus and every religious teacher over thousands of years. That the material existence of God is a matter of dispute in our modern scientistic world does not make the highest values such a God represents any less relevant. As Neptune transits Pisces, it will be easier and much better to focus upon this.

-o0o-

The May 2010 column continued to outline the lessons to be learned through the Pluto-in-Capricorn years. They were to be ignored, with dire consequences becoming increasingly true in the 2010s.

As the world economy boomed until 2008, we all became slipshod and dismissed the consequences of our actions. It was assumed that more growth would produce the wealth that would pay for whatever we needed. More working families would provide the wealth to pay for childcare, pensions and care in old age. The ever-increasing equity in our houses would cover borrowings, which in turn could be moved around from one provider to another. Only on the surface did all look fine. Young people were being made to incur debt to gain an education that in real terms was unlikely to improve opportunities. They were forced to live in crowded conditions, depending on parents to have sufficient equity to purchase a house – the very equity needed to cover elderly care costs. Such massive inefficiencies obscured only for a short time the consequences that were to burst upon us in 2008, when equity values collapsed with the dramatic depletion of pension funds, as well as the ability to float expansion by ever-increasing debt.

Because we treated what happened then as just another turn in the cycle to accommodate until boom-times returned, only in May 2010 will we be *starting* to address the fundamentals. Pluto in Capricorn's practical way, as the structural focus of Jupiter, Saturn and Uranus move from mutable to cardinal, is to face reality head on – to make needs answer each other. For example, three or four generations of each family can live and work together to answer each other's problems, by sharing homes and responsibilities. This way, a minimum amount of outside support is required to be purchased for both young and old. With less money required and work needing to be done, more time can be spent in caring for each other, enjoying and educating within the family. What better way to start the process of healing our society? Homes could become enriched foundations, not speculative assets. Extrapolate the philosophy and strategy that underpins such an approach into the larger economy and see that constant expansion does not have to be the root of all happiness. Truly sustainable societies come from strong structures not manipulated growth booms. Pluto in Capricorn says so!

-o0o-

As it became clear little had been learned in the years since the 2008 financial crisis, with an air of desperation, the March 2011 column continue to urge radical change. It stressed the only really efficient foundation for the world economy that would satisfy during the Pluto in Capricorn transit would be based on loving cooperation.

The Astrology of Monetarist Failure

Attempts to manipulate financial markets to avoid facing the consequences of their failure is no more than 'kicking the can down the road' is how a wise financier friend put it. The notion that growth-motivated free-market monetarism is the hard realistic answer all wise people must work towards, died in 2008. The worship of being rich, devotion to money, however it is obtained, is unrealistic and dangerous. The really empty, dreamy, false 'idealism' to think we all have a *chance* to 'get there', so being 'jealous' of those who succeed denies us that chance to do so.

The monetarist system is incompetent, because the people closest to the money control its supply to everyone else. They supply money we have entrusted them with, plus a massive margin of imagined money. This puts their hands tightly on the strings of all social activity. Their profit margins and capital gain needs determine what we should buy, how we should work, the culture we should enjoy, the way we care for our health, family life and the sport we play. So, denying banks and financial markets the oxygen of real or imagined money suffocates not just them, but the whole of society. Treat them too harshly and they will take the money elsewhere, even though it is not really theirs. However bad their decisions are, because the banks are holding paper credit representing our money, we cannot let them fail. We bail them out. Once bailed out, often with money we have borrowed against our future, the banks and financial markets are now closest to this new money. So again, they are the first to take personal profit, while making decisions that control our lives. Such a system is like a cancer that is eating up the very wealth of the planet and its people's endeavours. Nor is the Far Eastern miracle boom any more than the predators moving to the where the money is. In the end those ordinary Asian people will pay; as in Western countries we are now paying for 1980/2008.

A better way to organise the world economy
The difficulties we face with Pluto in Capricorn are forcing us to think again; surely there is a better way to organise the world economy! A good and effective employer, and Capricorn is the sign of such, knows that a good workforce is one that works happily within its capacity. It has a rich balanced personal life and a powerful belief in everyone working together to find the very best methods of production. The most efficient way to live and work on the planet is to respect and support, not manipulate, lie to and exploit each other. In really efficient societies, people share what they can and take what they need, always from the goodness of their hearts. They willingly behave with honour, not because rules say so and they may be caught. Effective rules measure and allow for kindness before profit. They make it clear what cheating is. This is really business-like, because right motivation efficiently broadens out benefit to more people over longer periods of time. Maybe Lennon and The Beatles were *fundamentally* right after all; *love IS the answer*!

The alternative of carrying on as we are is far from pleasant. Saying people are 'all in it together' is dangerous when so clearly some are not. The political safety valves where the dispossessed found refuge in the past are no longer available. The Soviet system collapsed long ago and China is now run by state-controlled capitalism. In the West, Liberals are in or were recently in power. With nowhere else to turn, raw protest by groups targeting injustice and the abuses of the privileged may well be gathering force. As we study the March/April 2011 planets anticipation, frustration, suffering, and possible outrage are clearly indicated.

Love IS the answer
The answer is wise policies that recognise economic rule by kindness is far more efficient than by conflict and competition; be this in households, family networks, social groups, nations, continents, even the whole world. Yes, indeed love IS the answer. It always has been! As we experience the consequences of the failure of capitalism, Marxism, Socialism, Keynesianism and Monetarism, maybe '*Loving Realism*' could become the catchphrase for a better way that is more likely to succeed.

-o0o-

The September 2011 column focused on the failure of 'Kicking the Can Down the Road' economics, specially referring to the Greek economic crisis. Funds released to keep the financial markets buoyant benefitted the few at the expense of the many. It clearly anticipated and warned about the inevitable social problems that we now know came after the 2012-15 years of seven Uranus in Aries squares to Pluto in Capricorn. Also, follow this thread in Chapter 4.

Are We Still Just 'Kicking the Can down the Road'?

Good financial market traders profit whatever the economic conditions. They succeed by freeing themselves from hopes and fears, personal expectations and the demands, even the needs, of others. Hard-headed amorality enables them to see circumstances with clear objective reality. So, their insights are likely to be far more valuable than those of politicians, who gain election by reassuring us, or the 'economic experts' who parade various contradictory theories in the media.

To see a trader's eyes light up with recognition at the words in the title (more lose money to trade and profit from!) reveals the real state not only of the world economy, but just about everything that is happening right now in social and individual lives. In one way or another, most people are taking stop-gap actions, delaying decisions, hoping time will 'take care of it'.

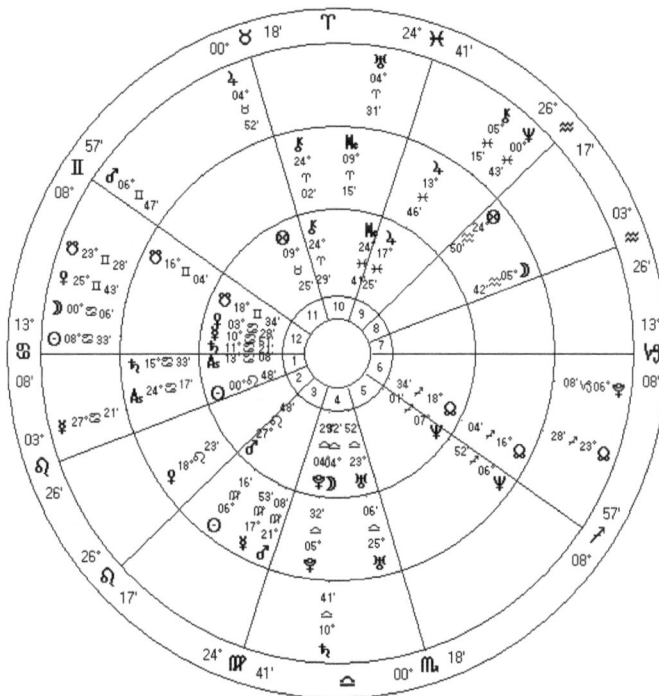

Greek economic crisis
Inner wheel: Greece declares democracy: 24 Jul 1974 04:00 EET -2:00
Middle wheel: crisis progression: 30 Jun 2011 19:20 EEDT -3:00
Outer wheel: Transits: 30 Jun 2011 19:20 EEDT -3:00
All charts: Athens, Greece 37°N58' 023°E43' Geocentric Placidus True Node

The trouble with decisions based on 'kicking the can down the road' is that, at the next catch up point, it is still the same can; just a little more battered. Since the dark days of autumn 2008, the talk has been of 'riding the cycle to the next upturn' by means of stimulus packages and/or austerity cuts to create lean and efficient economies, as 'the way' to restore growth and prosperity. The Greek sovereign debt crisis that raged June/July 2011 showed just how dangerously far financiers, who stand to lose or see a chance to profit, will encourage governments to use their asset collateral to keep the status quo liquid for just that little bit longer. As we come ever-closer to the Uranus/ Pluto square on the 2012 horizon, the futility of such avoidance in the financial markets is becoming screamingly clear to everyone. The consequent potential of social unrest is ever more alarming.

The tri-wheel shows that the astro-cycles developing at the time of, and in the years after, the Greek government acceptance of more austerity to obtain bailout confirmed what was obvious to most people at the time. The policy involved a dangerous risk of further financial exposure, a bailout would solve nothing. It would merely put off the inevitable, and so lead to an even worse outcome. The transiting Sun/Pluto opposition was in a grand cross to Saturn and Uranus as the decision was being made. This Pluto will be in an opposition to the natal Saturn and Mercury, approaching the Descendant and opposing the progressed Saturn until 2015. Greece cannot avoid change, all Greeks must accept that. However, to impose the 'solutions' of the 'economic experts', whose *laissez-faire* optimism created the crisis, upon the masses who see themselves as its victims is a recipe for social disaster. Non-cooperative dissent is certain; maybe something far worse will develop when it becomes clear just how much has been lost.

We do well to see the Greek experience as a clear marker for the UK, European and US predicaments. Even the apparent strength of other areas of the world that are currently booming is based the spending of assets. Investing reserves in infrastructure, and then spending the income generated on consumer luxuries is a very poor economic foundation. It is motivated more by optimism and short-term self-interest than any sure economic reality. The West is yet to recover from the deluded assumptions emanating from releasing capital assets and spending up large in the 1980s. Ever since, it has deluded us into seeking and manipulating ways to spend money we do not have. As we know to our cost, when booms turn to bust social consequences can be dire.

Earlier 'Working with the Planets' columns have questioned popular assumptions about the world economy. Encouraged by the first of three Jupiter-in-Taurus trines to Pluto in Capricorn on 7 July 2011, the previous issue's column urged a more enlightened use of the energy than the actions typified by the Euro zone's futile gesture toward the Greek economy.[244] For this ongoing trine is a special opportunity to make a major transformation of the practical structure of our lives.

This is not only in money matters, but in how we do every kind of business with each other – personal as well as economic – what we value and how we apply those values. What do we see as beauty and what is genuine order? How can we work together to organise our lives to make our ideals achievable and sustainable? To use such a trine to do no more than manipulate a bit more stopgap finance, or to make promises to ourselves or others that we cannot hope to keep, could be socially and personally dangerous. With Uranus due to square Pluto for three years, to use the trine as state power that forces those with little to have less, while the creators of the crisis continue to hold the purse strings and profit, is to invite unrest.

Jupiter trine Pluto is very much in orb for both the months covered by this article and on into spring 2012 when the aspect completes. The retrograde trine is on 28 October at the same degree as in July 2011. It completes a few degrees later on 13 March 2012. Throughout this time, judge developments in the world and your lives by whether they are opening exciting potentials that could lead to real change and growth in understanding and happiness. Would that be for an increasing number of people, not just a narrow sub-group? Anything else would be a tragic and extremely dangerous waste of time!

It is in human nature to put up with and master amazing difficulties, providing they cannot be avoided and everyone works together with a sense of unity and fairness. At the moment, people seem to feel the reverse is the case.

September each year is the time of the Autumn Equinox, when balance shows the way to reconcile opposites and marshal them into the achieving the most effective outcomes. A very special understanding of balance is needed this year! The Autumn Equinox of 2011 may well be the last chance for some time to understand, come to terms with each other and start to work positively together. Turn to those vital things in life and tools of understanding that it is difficult to accept, but without which we are incomplete. Make friends with enemies and see their value; be they people or alien ideas and options you have always dismissed as impossible. Explore the possibility of changing your mind. You will be amazed at what you can succeed at and with whom, if you will just let it be and grow. By making a start towards real breakthroughs, an atmosphere of hope will build. Whatever the immediate problems, people will start to believe and work together. Against all the odds, true understanding and hope may yet return to our lives.

-o0o-

After a detailed description of the Mayan calendar, due to be renewed at the end of the year, the column focused on the original intrinsic flaw at the core of the world economic system. The system would face crisis through the upcoming Uranus/Pluto squares 2012-15. Positive change based on higher principles was needed to avoid ultimate disaster.

The Astrology of the Current World Economy

Can astrology help us assess the nature of the capitalist economy that for over 300 years has underpinned dramatically growing modern industrial society?

The first investment offer that founded the present Bank of England was made to refinance the English navy after its seventeenth-century battles with the Dutch and French. The highly successful public response enabled a force to be created that would rule the sea and many lands throughout the world. During the eighteenth and nineteenth centuries British naval power stood behind the generation of great wealth for the nation. The same system of investment was adopted by European nations and their empires, as well as the emerging USA. It grew into today's world economic system.

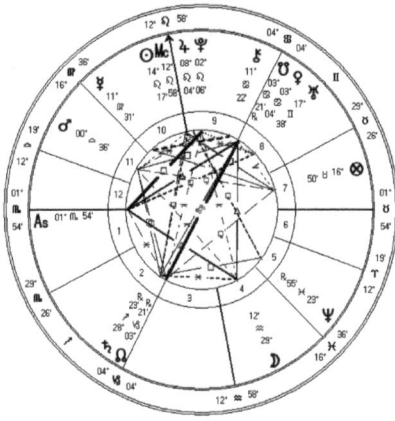

Bank of England
27 Jul 1694 OS 12:00 LMT +0:00:40
London, UK 51°N30' 000°W10'
Geocentric Tropical Placidus True Node

As the symbolic foundation of today's world economic system, the Bank of England chart has some surprising and very revealing features that have profound relevance to our twenty-first-century economic predicament. While speculation leading to great transformative success is indicated by the Jupiter, Sun, Pluto conjunction in Leo, either side of the LMT Noon Midheaven, the way that success is to be achieved is less gloriously indicated.

Ten days before the granting of the charter (Julian date 27 July 1694)[245] Mars in Virgo opposed Neptune, while Venus, in ambivalent Gemini, applied to oppose to Saturn in Sagittarius – investments were likely to be speculative and certainly not as they seem. By the day of the signing, Mars was in detriment in Libra, on from its square to Venus, but applying to square the Nodal axis, with Venus exactly conjuncting the South Node. With the Moon in Taurus in the seventh house through the morning of the opening day (Julian date, Wednesday 1 August 1694) trading was brisk. The Moon moving on to square Pluto, Jupiter and the Sun into the next day, speculation was intense. The offer sold out within ten days.

In less than thirty years the scandal of the South Sea Bubble's (1720) speculative deception was the first of a series of intermittent eighteenth and nineteenth-century booms and busts.

In 1913, today's US Federal Reserve Bank was created to underpin and stabilise business activity. Unfortunately, its foundation chart reveals a deception as great as, or even greater than, that of the Bank of England. Its mutable grand cross has Venus and Mercury in Sagittarius, opposed Saturn in Gemini, squared the Pisces/Virgo Nodal axis. Mars rises in anxious detriment applying to conjunct Neptune in Cancer and to oppose Jupiter in Capricorn. The sense of dominating others by projecting confused worry this suggests is made all the more traumatic by a Sun/Pluto opposition of the cusps of both Capricorn and the sixth/twelfth houses!

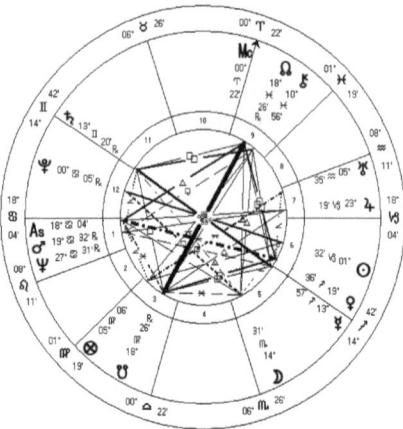

US Federal Reserve
23 Dec 1913 NS 18:02 EST +5:00
Washington, DC 38°N53'42" 077°W02'12"
Geocentric Tropical Placidus True Node

Even though the stability hoped for from the creation of the US Federal Reserve Bank was to fail with the 1929 Wall Street Crash and its terrible aftermath through the 1930s, attempts to stabilise and sustain the world economy, and much fundamental economic theory ever since, have been based on its model. National reserve banks and area institutions such as the European Central Bank control the issue of currency. International bodies such as the World Bank and International Monetary Fund have sustained national economies through the rocky road of the post-Second World War expansion and supported the modernisation of emerging countries.

Intrinsic flaw in the nature of our capitalist system

Unfortunately, as we see from the Bank of England and US Federal Reserve foundation charts there is an intrinsic flaw in the nature of our capitalist system as it has developed. Both show an amazing capacity to find ways around problems, but little or no capacity to find and implement fundamental solutions. As a result, the problems in the system exposed in the 1930s were avoided and then clouded by detrimental Neptune-in-Virgo/Libra beliefs through war and recovery. The crises of the 1970s, 1989-92 and 2000 were 'solved' by deferment. With Pluto in Capricorn, the one that built to 2008 is proving less easy to 'kick down the road'. In the years since then, a banking credit crisis has morphed into sovereign debt crisis. As we move into the Uranus/Pluto square years 2012 to 2015, this is likely to turn into central bank crisis. The world economy is profoundly unbalanced. It is building toward national, even international, bankruptcy in areas such as Europe and the USA. As their export markets dry up, the emerging world faces the consequences of excessive over-investment, unused industrial capacity and unemployment.

It does not have to be like this if we identify the root cause of the problem clearly shown by the two foundation charts. Short-term, personal-profit motivated financial manipulation has been the root problem from the beginning. There is little intrinsic difference in taking slaves and raw materials from African colonies in the eighteenth century, cheap labour and arms trading in the twentieth/twenty-first centuries, financial trading strategies that distort real value, acquisitions for asset stripping and job cuts, accountants employed to distort the real economic circumstances, and all those procedures that those in power hide behind.

Playing our part in necessary positive change

Ongoing Uranus/Pluto squares suggest we are at the beginning of three years of social unrest and surprises at all levels of our lives. Neptune/Chiron in Pisces will bring a hurt, accusatory sense to public life – especially June 2012-13 with Jupiter in Gemini squaring them. This cannot be avoided and will build until we accept and take the right action. Leaders spinning untruth or partial truth, false optimism, stonewalling and emotional manipulation create disappointment, anger and revolution. Yet, exposing who is to blame on its own will bring little more benefit than any other 'witch hunts' do. By doing the wrong thing ourselves, because it seems in our interest, we become cornered and just as responsible. While frightening at first, insisting on what feels fundamentally right generates the light that shows the way to hope and a better future.

Understanding and eradicating negative causes, and identifying and acting upon root needs create positive momentum. Amazingly, when things are moving in the right direction, everyone feels better and support grows, however difficult the present times may be. This is the way to talk, think and use Jupiter. Look ahead to its Cancer ingress and trine to Neptune and Chiron in June 2013. It is amazing what people will accept and can do, when they believe they are really working together. As all levels of society seek ways to make change beneficial, the more likely we are to demand that the institutions governing our lives stop preaching the pursuit of purposeless, often destructive growth. Think of how we can generate happiness for the world family as we would for our immediate one. Divert under-employment into feeding the hungry. Make do with less. Prefer unemployment to employment that destroys. Reform financial markets to make them genuinely businesslike, not exploitative. Do not compromise on making decisions toward that end, even if this means short-term personal loss. This is the way to balance the books both economically, socially, and in international affairs. We must find ways of morphing greed-based capitalism into kindness-based capitalism. There is no other lasting way to resolve the economic crisis.

-o0o-

Of course, we now know that actual financial breakdown was avoided, but the method of avoidance led to increasing social breakdown within and between nations and alliances. When world relations were at their most fraught and fragmented, the Covid-19 pandemic was to stop the world economy in its tracks.

The January 2014 column explored what attitudes needed to change. The extract below focuses on suggestions that could correct the structural failings of the world economic system.

Ignoring Astro-cycles Leads to Unwise Long-term Decisions

The first rule followed by a good consultant astrologer is to remind clients that their chart describes circumstances, not good or bad outcomes. Outcomes are gifts, which clients create for themselves from their understanding of life. Knowing how to use astro-cycles, for good or ill, enables supporting objective insight. This is an extremely useful way to relate astro-cycles to world developments and events.

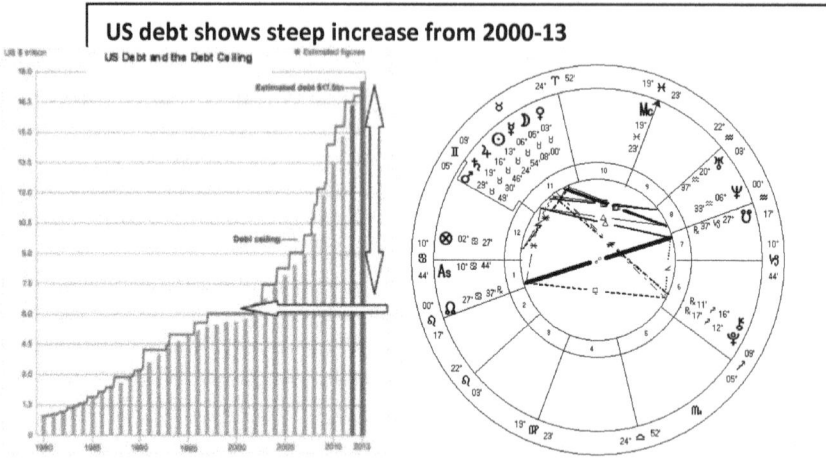

US debt shows steep increase from 2000-13

Taurus Stellium 3 May 2000 09:30 EDT +4:00 New York, NY 40°N42'51" 74°W00'23"

In finance, this is clearly shown by the handling of the national debt by the George W Bush and Obama US administrations and world economic leaders that followed their lead. Although rising steadily through the 1980s and 1990s, the debt could have been contained if astro-cycle warnings had been heeded.

Not for the first time, the week after the Capricorn New Moon saw the Dow rising to its previous highest so far (on 10 January 2000). With Saturn in Taurus due to be part of a seven planet stellium in that sign on 3 May 2000, a major correction to a booming stock market was clearly imminent. The unrealistic values of dot.com stocks meant it was the NASDAQ index that suffered worse. Seven planets in Taurus squared to Uranus in technological Aquarius could not have said it clearer! A time of consolidation was vitally necessary, but, with Pluto in Sagittarius and Aquarian Uranian ingenuity ever ready with clever avoidance of reality, few were willing to accept or even feel the need for belt tightening.[246] The near trebling of the US national debt from well under 6 trillion to an estimated 17.5 trillion in the succeeding twelve years is the price the US faces today for continuing to borrow and expand. Nearly all other world governments and central banks face similar debts burdens proportionate to their Gross National Product. Even if we ignore the ecological consequences of its overheated mechanised economy (which we cannot), the world can no longer pay its way. The three-hundred-year-old capitalist way of organising the world economy reaches its end game. Who really knows what comes next?

Avoidance no longer an option

The wakeup call of the 2007-08 financial collapse, upheaval in the Middle East and Afghanistan and elsewhere have only interrupted to lives of those directly affected. The agonies of Syrians, the hardships of Greeks and the hardships of the unemployed and foreclosed all over the world have been brutal, but, to date, the direst consequences have been kept away from the majority. This has been achieved by debt-created illusory assets; justified by the assumption that 'in the nature of economic cycles' growth will return to reverse and offset further debt burdens. So, the slightest increase in GDP, whatever the reason, is greeted with cautious hope that a recovery up-cycle has returned. Such grasping at straws ignores the astrological reality that Pluto remains in Capricorn until 2024 and in 2020 is joined there by Jupiter and Saturn to really test the efficiency of the world economy.

Through 2013, Jupiter's trine to Saturn helped make it seem that the strategy was working and a more radical means to address economical and human concerns was not needed. The trine created the notion that we had faced down the frightening worst (Saturn in Scorpio) and healing expansive ease was rewarding our acceptance of hardship (trine Jupiter in Cancer). Economically things were getting better. Iran was friendlier. We had done a deal with Russia on chemical weapons in Syria.

Causes to feel anxious were in the background; the problems of others. They may not affect us at all. We felt this way, because the Uranus/Pluto square was in a mid-way, retrograde phase throughout 2013. US debt crisis deadlines were averted by short-term agreements – 'kicking the can down the road'. The financial markets reacted happily at more money to spend and profits to make. Equity values rose. However, if the January/February ceiling deadlines are postponed for a further two to three months, the next crunch will come in the teeth of the most major of the Uranus/Pluto squares, the 20-21 April T-square between Jupiter, Uranus and Pluto, with Mars in Libra retrograding back to make a cardinal grand cross.

Crucially, issues put off at the retrograde Uranus/Pluto square on 1 November 2013 and struggled with again when Mars squared Pluto, on the New Year, come together with a vengeance and have to be fully faced in spring 2014. The more we fail to find early solutions, the more difficult it will be. Time is running out. We have to change minds and act while room for manoeuvre remains.

-o0o-

Refer back to the November 2016 column extract on pages 182-83.
The interpretation of the charts for the Bank of England and US
Federal Reserve describes the intrinsic limitations of the economic
system that has dominated the world for the past three hundred
years. The interpretation reveals why the system is well past its sell-
by date and so inadequate for the twenty-first century.

Several subsequent extracts in Chapter 7 develop the astro-
cycle background to the economic pressures as the focus on Jupiter,
and Saturn joining Pluto in Capricorn builds.

-oOo-

**The March 2018 column focused on the erratic response to Bitcoin's
public listing and construction giant Carillion's failure.**

Early Indicators of Return to Economic Realism

Right on cue, the Bitcoin plunged to a bottom of just above US$12,000 on 22
December 2017, less than a day after the Winter Solstice and Saturn ingress. This
was only eleven days after it was first listed and had risen near to US$20,000 on the
Chicago Board of Trade. Extreme volatility followed, plunging it below US$10,000
on 17 January 2018, the day of the first of three Capricorn New Moons with both
Saturn and Pluto in the sign since 21 December 1519.[247] Since then, it has fallen away
further to US$7,000 at the time of writing.

Two days before the Capricorn New Moon, Carillion, a UK major services
outsourcer announced its liquidation with debts of 1.6 billion pounds.

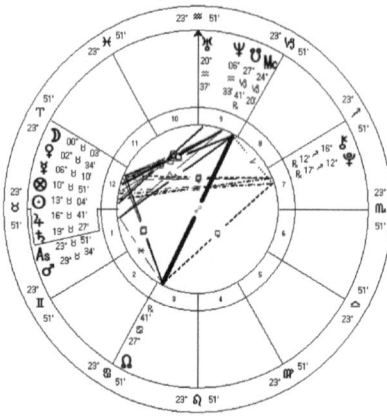

Midpoint of dot.com collapse
3 May 2000 06:00 BST -1:00
London, UK 51°N30' 000°W10'
Geocentric Tropical Equal True Node

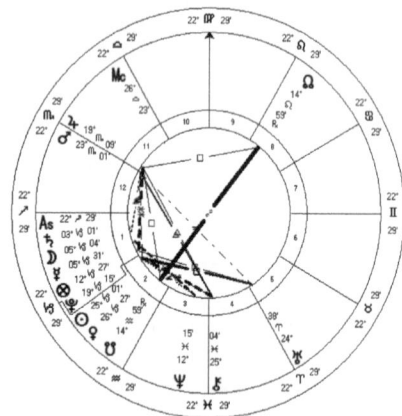

Carillion announces liquidation
15 Jan 2018 06:00 UT +0:00
London, UK 51°N30' 000°W10'
Geocentric Tropical Equal True Node

The early-day chart[248] of the announcement has Uranus in Aries squared by a major
Capricorn stellium. The Chart for the dot.com collapse in May 2000 has remarkable
similarities and a distinctive difference. In 2000, Uranus was squared by a massive
stellium in Taurus. A major confrontation with reality followed – rationalisation of

the emerging electronic revolution. The Carillion collapse chart is a clarion call. So much of today economy comprises over-stretched, half completed, possibly unsustainable projects. Now Uranus is not in Aquarius, but immature Aries and squared to the most mature of the earth signs – Capricorn.

By the time you read this, will the Carillion collapse be seen as a clarion call to cooling our over-heated world economy? How many other speculative construction companies will fail, because they have expanded by off-loading risk to sub-contractors and obtained credit, by using new contracts as temporary cover to growing existing debts? Is the boom in financial markets still being artificially sustained by the debt-financed give-aways of the US tax reforms?[249] Unheeding the 2008 warnings, when will we exhaust our capacity to obtain more credit?

Seed point of change

We are at a seed point of change, even more radical than five hundred years ago. The most recent previous Capricorn Moon with both Saturn and Pluto in Capricorn was in the early sixteenth century. Two others were close to it in time [13 Dec 1517 OS, 1 Jan 1519 OS and 21 Dec 1519 OS]. Luther nailed his 95 Theses to the door of the Wittenberg Castle church on 31 October 1517, six weeks before the first of these. In 1519, Cortes journeyed to the South American mainland to brutalise the Inca Empire. So, radical change in the nature of Christianity and European colonial conquest were born. The same year, the Texas coast was mapped for the first time.

Faced with a massive impasse of the crazy selfishness all this has led to, the world is readying for a major confrontation with reality that only a complete reboot of the world economy will answer. Resistance will be futile! It will only make matters worse. Remember when our computer freezes all those futile attempts to avoid re-starting, because we will lose all the careful work we have done, but not saved. Extrapolate that mindset to the whole world economy. President Trump feels he can put America First by bribing rich corporations with tax cuts to bring investment money back home. Financial markets boom up for a while, and then commence a steady decline. In the UK, little will be clear until Brexit is completed. In all established and emerging economies short-term extensions of credit may seem preferable to any radical change of course. This is wrong. The opposite is the case.

In Capricorn times, such approaches will be counter-productive. Capricorn takes time. Over the coming two years internal workings will churn away to clear the debris of confusion. Many enterprises will not work and remain unfinished eyesores – especially, those ill-considered, embarked upon for selfish short-term gain. To survive, projects must gain the devoted support of communities. They need to be sustainable for more and more people, not profit-cows for an elite. So, let go, allow the reboot, and turn our economy and way of life to a fresh workable world.

In May 2018, Uranus will be out of Aries. The destructive nature of its 1930s-40s last transit in Taurus is not inevitable, providing sustainable change is welcomed. Uranus comes close in September 2024, but does not exactly trine Pluto until mid-July 2026, when the planets are in Gemini and Aquarius. Hope and encourage everyone to wait, let go of 'pipe dreams' and allow relationships to return to how they should be. We really are all in it together. Try to work kindly to establish sustainability as massive change keeps on rolling in. In our short lives, we may never understand the full implications of what is happening in the world. Be happy and see it as a privilege to know we are an initiatory part of what is coming for the better.

It may seem a lot to ask, but nothing else is worth asking.

-o0o-

The July 2018, November 2018 and January 2019 columns of Chapter 7 (pages 203-16), track the build-up of financial crisis in the midst of the general social malaise of the times, revealing the role played by immature, short-sighted economic monetarist morals that had masqueraded as scientific for the past forty years.

-oOo-

What follows is from the March 2019 column that tracks key astro-cycles that reveal how ignoring, or not even knowing about them, led to missed opportunities to have the foresight to act in time, and so avert the economic disaster that the 2019 world seemed to be plunging into.

The Value of Being Guided by the Astro-cycles

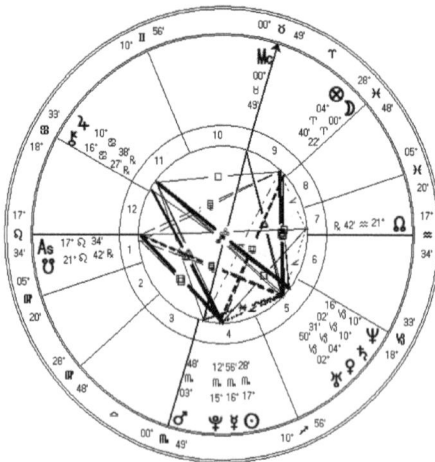

Berlin Wall Gates Opened
9 Nov 1989 22:45 CET -1:00
Berlin, Germany 52°N30' 013°E22'
Geocentric Tropical Placidus True Node

As the world builds to a climax of uncertainly, fuelled by blind selfishness, it would be helpful to consider how different it might have been. If only, in making key policy decisions, we had been guided by astro-cycles!

Just after midnight on the day of the Winter Solstice 2018, Saturn made the first return to its position when Lieutenant colonel Harald Jäger opened the checkpoint gates of the Berlin Wall. This key symbolic moment in the collapse of the Soviet system led to German reunification and what optimists at the time considered to be the 'triumph of capitalism'. Thirty years later, our world comes to its present predicament, because we have allowed the astro-cycles that followed to bring out the worst in us.

The Saturn cycle since the opening of the Berlin Wall
The powerful 1989 chart has Jupiter in Cancer in a tight opposition to Saturn applying to conjunct Neptune in Capricorn. Today, as Jupiter in Sagittarius hastens to join Saturn and Pluto in Capricorn, the 1989 optimism has reversed to arguments over trade agreements and the pessimistic creation of many kinds of new walls all over the world? Some triumph! Some capitalism! Wrong reactions to the astro-cycles through the subsequent Saturn cycle brought us to this. We can improve our lives by seeing past errors, and then make better choices today. How did get it so wrong? How might we have done better?

❖ **The 1990s:** Recovery from the shock and recession of the ongoing Cancer/Capricorn opposition at the beginning of the decade was slow. Then, from the end of 1994 the Jupiter/Pluto Sagittarian ingress seemed to support Alan Greenspan's low-interest Federal Reserve policies, which encouraged record-breaking price surges in the financial markets. The first quarter of the Saturn cycle completed on 2 August 1997, a time of triumphant optimism for the future. In Britain public-private investment financed extravagant infrastructure projects at high long-term costs. In Russia and breakaway ex-Soviet states, government wealth found its way into the hands of oligarchs. Rapid extension of credit facilities made life for everyone seem easier, freer, but for how long, to what purpose and, crucially, how would it be paid for in the end? Enabling all this was Uranus' transit through Aquarius, inspiring an unfettered electronic revolution.

Put into the context of the astro-events that were to follow, this over-optimistic free-for-all behaviour that marked the 1990s was clearly a missed opportunity. Using Sagittarian energy for short-term enjoyment is easy, but unwise. The world was crying out for change. Past assumptions had been found wanting, the world was ready for change, a new beginning. Credit was readily available. When better than now to redress the problems of the needy, to try ever harder to open out to the unknown, to make friends ? Instead, the second half of the 1990s saw spend and get-rich-quick indulgence in the now and 'belief' that new technology had ended the cycle of boom and bust. We could get away with anything, providing that Y2K problem did not spoil the show!

❖ **The 2000s:** In the event, it was not the Y2K millennium 'bug' that called a halt to the indulgence, but a rare combination of astro-cycles. Up to seven planets in Taurus squared to Uranus in Aquarius burst the bubble of mindless financial over-optimism.   Bust had not gone away. It returned with harsh reality. The market boom reversed. As the world struggled to recover from this, the September 2001 Saturn/Pluto Gemini/Sagittarius opposition across the angles of the US foundation chart symbolised the dire destruction of 9/11. Harsh reality came to mainland US for the first time. The following year the Jupiter-in-Leo/Neptune-in-Aquarius opposition, crucially connected to the chart of the post-First World War Middle East settlement, crazed our minds into the global delusion of the Iraq War. The dire reality of all that was to follow became increasingly clear at the opposition phase of the Saturn cycle (exact on 7 May 2004).

In the late 1990s, Neptune had joined Uranus in Aquarius and stayed there in the 2000s while Uranus moved to Pisces creating a mutual reception between the two planets. Pluto remained in Sagittarius until late 2008. Enabled by further easing of financial regulation at the turn of the century, an even greater 1990s-style boom returned with ever greater intensity. Aquarian ingenuity combined with Piscean false sympathy sought ways to give everyone what they wanted – subprime mortgages, the growth of Asian and especially Chinese consumer products.

So, the warnings of the early twenty-first century were obscured or just ignored. The Taurus stellium should have seen us crying out for sensible consolidation, not (with Saturn in Cancer) pouring credit into unaffordable housing. 9/11 should have shocked us into seeking to understand our enemies. The Aquarius/Pisces mutual reception could have eased us into putting right the West's relationship with Islam. We could have turned away from the reckless use of scientific discoveries, and instead focused on ingenious ways to stop our short-term throwaway mindset, which continues to pollute the planet today.

With Pluto on the cusp of Capricorn through 2008 that the deluded fragile foundation of the world's economy collapsed. The wonderful opportunity of Pluto in Sagittarius, with the Uranus/Neptune mutual reception in Aquarius/Pisces had not healed our relationships with each other. The ingenuity of the times had not moved away from exploiting the vulnerable. It did not seek ways to serve all needs, dissolve discontent, and so regenerate communities all over the world. We had the tools to do just this, but instead all this potential was recklessly squandered, channelling it into distraction and ways of avoiding problems, not solving them. As a result, 2000s ended with the world reeling, unsure how to recover, and, with Jupiter in Aquarius through 2009, ready for rebellion.

❖ *2010s:* The world entered this decade totally unprepared for the consequences of Pluto in Capricorn squared by Uranus in Aries seven times between 2011 and 2015. The beginning of the Saturn cycle's fourth quarter on 23 April 2011 marked the breakdown of hope for global regeneration, as brutality and hatred pulled apart many societies. Millions of people were forced to seek refuge far away from their homes, unsettling the stability of the countries they sought to enter. Austerity policies, consequent upon the *laissez-faire* economics of the previous two decades, alongside an increasing gap between rich and poor (within and between countries), fuelled growing popular discontent. In 2016, an ongoing mutual T-square between Jupiter, Saturn and Neptune, at its peak made into a grand cross by Venus and Mars, alongside Jupiter's trine to Pluto, saw populist movements gaining power throughout the Western World. All this paralysed attempts for mutual cooperation. Power politics degenerated into a glorified blame game. Bereft of astrological understanding, or memory of the causes in recent history; fear, mass hysteria, distortion, over-simplification led people to projecting their own short-comings on others. It became really easy to cast blame on just about anyone outside our immediate circle.

The karmic lessons of Saturn returns

Saturn's return to our personal charts brings all the realities we thought we had avoided back to haunt us. Edifices, strategies, relationships, even families built on unsure foundations, or forced on others against their wishes, come up against unyielding obstacles and tumble down.

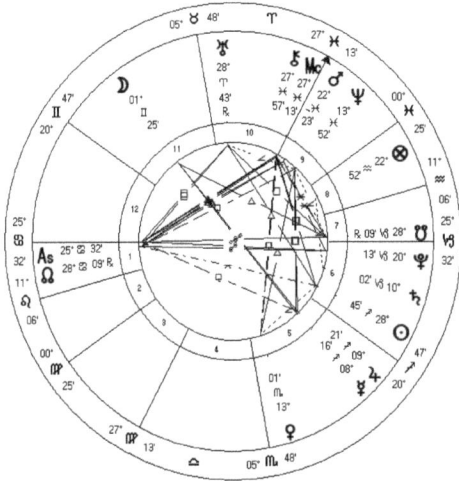

20 Dec 2018 17:59 CET -1:00
Berlin, Germany 52°N30' 013°E22'
Geocentric Tropical Placidus True Node

The first return, coming when the native has had the least experience in life, can be the most difficult. For many it is traumatically so. Saturn is uncompromising, yet in being so our wisest friend. If the time of the return passes with few problems, be pleased to feel you have faced and answered life's challenges clearly and kindly. Be just as accepting, if the time of the return brings difficulty, rejection, even breakups. Saturn, your friend, is pointing to the very things that have to be put right, so you can enjoy a deeply beneficial and happy future life.

It is the same with the Saturn return of event charts. The breakdown of the Soviet system from 1989 marked the birth of a great regenerative opportunity for the world. We have squandered this opportunity to heal and transform our world for the better. So, now at the end of the first Saturn cycle, we are at each other's throats in a me-first, squabbling world. This is destroying many societies and individual lives.

The building Jupiter, Saturn, Pluto in Capricorn and Uranus in Taurus focus of 2017-20 has been well covered already in this column and elsewhere. The confrontation with reality marked by the Saturn return in the face of these planets is being as historic as any before. With Jupiter still in Sagittarius through this year, the world is like a butterfly on a pin; futilely struggling to be free of self-created consequences. Jupiter entering Capricorn in December 2019 will end any such illusion of freedom. No more wriggle room. In Britain, for sure Brexit, or no Brexit. In US, the standing of the Trump presidency will be clear. In Europe, chaos or cooperation. Throughout the world, either truth and tolerance, or the horror of economic disruption and violence without end.

It is not too late to change. Realising how the errors of the past thirty years brought us to this point is the vital first step. We have these few months of 2019 to accept it is not 'them', but 'us' who created our problems. Step back from blindly forcing against the impossible, stop, listen, let go of everything we have assumed to be true. Let go of diatribe. Turn away from twisting everything to personal advantage. Anger itself is the enemy, not the person or idea that seems to anger us. Then everyone will see there is a better way. Make peace, change, allow in, be generous, care for each other and the planet, and be relieved at feeling so much better.

Astrologers often compare themselves to the Greek prophet Cassandra, who saw everything, but was never listened to. At this crucial time in human history is it too optimistic to hope the prophecy will be heard, acted on… and so avoided?

-o0o-

As the world (unwisely as it was to turn out) relaxed a little from Covid-19 restrictions, governments poured borrowed money into struggling businesses, seeking to restart economic activity. This reckless creation of liquidity sustained equity markets at unrealistic levels. While on the surface seeming to refute financial astrologers' predictions of a 2020 market reversal, it confirmed the forecast of economic collapse at a far more fundamentally dangerous level. Faced with the pandemic crisis, the world economy was reduced to surviving on a day-to-day basis, as one does during a war.

Clearly, as nations emerged from the crisis and faced the consequences, common cause would have to be found, if social unrest was to be avoided. The world economy would have to turn away from the simplistic, outdated, bodged-together exploitative colonial system to a model based on advanced intelligent accommodation of all planetary and human requirements.

Such an approach is outlined in Chapter 7 – pages 237-42.

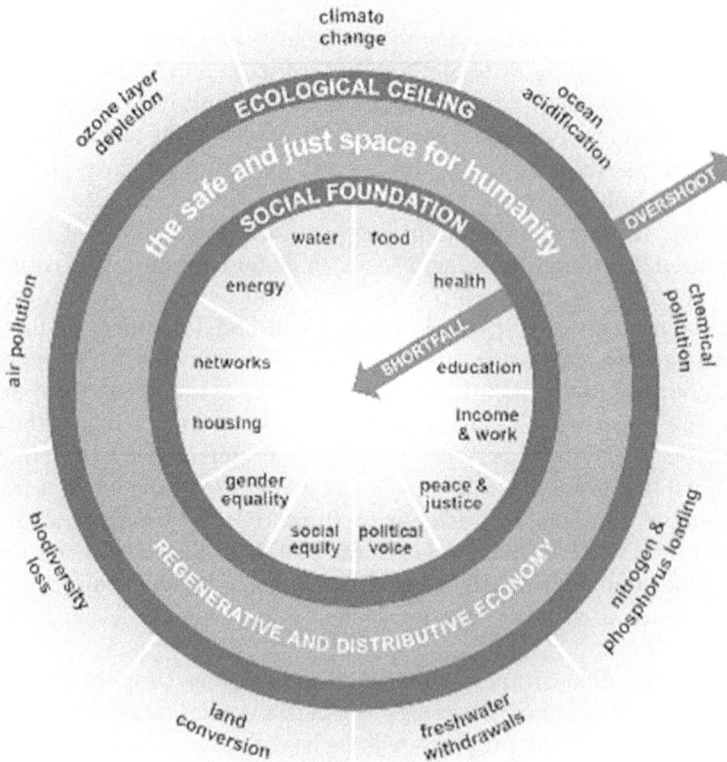

climate change
ozone layer depletion
ECOLOGICAL CEILING
ocean acidification
the safe and just space for humanity
SOCIAL FOUNDATION
OVERSHOOT
water   food
energy   health
air pollution
chemical pollution
networks   education
SHORTFALL
housing   income & work
gender equality   peace & justice
social equity   political voice
biodiversity loss
REGENERATIVE AND DISTRIBUTIVE ECONOMY
nitrogen & phosphorus loading
land conversion   freshwater withdrawals

-o0o-

Appendix B
Answering Astrology's Critics

This section includes pieces that give measured answers to reservations about the importance, or otherwise, of astrology's role in modern society. At what appears to be contrived intervals, familiar simplistic put-downs of astrology are repeated in the media. These are not covered here, but answered fully in 'Chapter 2 – A Conspiracy of Disinformation' of my *Astrology and Compassion the Convenient Truth*. Also in that book is a wealth of information about the valuable role astrology could occupy in the modern world.[250]

Since the end of the seventeenth century, the standing of astrology in society's intellectual mainstream was eclipsed and increasingly rejected by the upsurge of rational, reductionist theory, often referred to as the Enlightenment. So dominant has this view become that today it is supplanting religious traditions and becoming generally accepted as the only fundamental basis by which to understand our lives.

Astrology remained in the shadows for two centuries. When it was revived in the years leading to the 1891-92 Neptune/Pluto conjunction, it was immediately dismissed, even prosecuted as superstitious nonsense. In recent years, maybe still, the early pages of astronomy school text books for sixteen-year-olds make it clear that there is no role for astrology in modern-world astronomy. The reasons conventional academia gives for such an absolute, closed-minded position have become frozen in ill-informed simplistic ignorance. 'Chapter Two' of my book, mentioned above, lists and answers the misconceptions constantly appearing in the media. Legitimate, intelligent responses are not listened to. For reasons that are not true, and do not make sense, astrology is rejected as not worthy of discussion.

In doing so, today's anti-astrology sceptics do not see the crucial beam in the eye of their view of the world. Reductionist science is not only amoral, but by design the tools it has to measure human and social nature and behaviour are very recent and incomplete. Indeed, disciplines such as psychology and sociology are seen by many purist quantitative researchers to be (at best) on the very fringe of science.

Galileo is credited with the establishment of today's Scientific Method, which was based on 'Unprejudiced observation of natural phenomena as they happened, without reference to religious or philosophical views.'[251] So, by rigid application of reductionist mechanical research of the material world, science has come to dominate our experience with wondrous discoveries. We can fly around the world, even to the Moon and beyond. Ordinary people can participate, even control their world way beyond the wildest dreams of earlier times. We can cure, even avoid, sickness that ravaged populations in past centuries. Yet, we can also tear our world apart, extract and squander resources that had taken millions of years to create, poison and destroy species and vegetation in nature, pollute our atmosphere, overheat our oceans, destroy our climate.

Without a method to assess human nature or understand changing social trends objectively, humanity is left at the mercy of the worst aspects of its nature. For reductionist science lacks a framework to assess and then apply ethical principles. We choose/follow leaders for ill-considered, even the flimsiest of reasons, with little concern for their principles and reliability. Hence, we lurch in and out of both good times and bad, misunderstanding real causes, blind to any solutions, even though they are staring us in the face.

Astro-cycles – science's missing link

Hopefully, this book has shown that by understanding astro-cycles, we see other people and the times we are living through from those people's side. We realise the demands required to work together in the happiest and most productive way. Seeing the situation and/or person clearly, we are left with just two choices. Either make an enemy of the person or situation by being selfishly self-indulgent, or be supportively compassionate and make friends. The first stores up future problems. The second offers future happiness.

Astrology offers the framework; the rest is up to us. By using it we can fill a terrible void in the life of modern society. We become the best friend of mechanical science, by enabling its amazing advances to be used without those dangers of destruction we face, when using them today.

Knowing and feeling passionate about this, sensitive, intelligent minds were not to be deterred by astrology's critics. From the second half of the twentieth century, research proceeded, astrology schools were founded, examinations created, taken and passed. Beneath the surface, astrologers were consulted and some of the best decisions made.

Below are some extracts from 'Working with the Planets' that address these issues. This entire book demonstrates the benefits of doing so.

Soon after President Ronald Reagan's death, the September 2004 column reminded readers how the world benefitted from his clear courage in taking the wise advice of the astrologer, Joan Quigley.

Ronald Reagan passes on

Ronald Reagan's[4] use of astrology was greater than that of any modern world leader outside of the Indian sub-continent. Neil Spencer[252] reports Joan Quigley's and others' accounts of astro-timing peace treaties and summit meetings.[253] It could be claimed that astrology played a crucial role in ending the Cold War. Yet I did not hear a mention of this in all the tributes that greeted the announcement of his death on 6 June 2004. The honouring of the 'the great communicator' was glowing and loving. We would expect this. His memorial events were occurring during the 8 June 2004 Venus transit of the Sun. It could be said he died with the blessing of the 'stars' he lived by. In 1980, when he was first elected, who would have thought we would be talking like this today? That we can, gives hope for the future.

The column went on to argue for greater respect between the two world views. By combining the complementary strengths and weakness of both, we could create a much better world.

Academic Balance and Etiquette

> 'Hurrah for positive science! Long live exact demonstration!' Geologist, chemist, surgeon, mathematician, cartographer, lexicographer, the whole menagerie of exact demonstrators were welcome in his poetic parlor: 'Gentlemen, I receive you, and attach and clasp hands with you. Your facts are useful and real'.
>
> Gary Sloan in his *Walt Whitman: Sins Against Science.* [254]

Gary Sloan reports Walt Whitman, the great American poet's words in the 1850s, when material science was struggling for proper status in academia, rather similar to astrology's recent experiences. Indeed, it was not until after the Second World War that science was fully accepted at the 'Oxbridge' Universities.

150 years after Whitman's words, determined to maintain their now dominant position in our modern world, Indian material scientists have just failed in an attempt to have the Indian Court of Appeal block the allocation of government funds for the teaching of Vedic Astrology at twenty Indian Universities. From outsider to considering itself the only permitted insider in one and a half centuries says more about immaturity and poor academic manners that it does about defining and defending 'the truth'. For indeed in terms of all the knowledge that has been discovered, compared and shared over thousands of years of human history, modern material science looks more like a phase, even a fashion, not 'absolute truth'.

So, in honour of the Venus transit, now is the time to consider not only what and who we value, but *how* we measure our value system. We come to statistics.

It is an ironic paradox that 'there are lies, damned lies and statistics' is so oft-quoted, yet the popular media, government and industry have generally abrogated authority to a particularly narrow view of science that is based on statistics. Statistical studies lead to drastic changes in what and how much wine we drink 'for the good of our heart'. Possible treatments and 'cures' are announced as scientific 'discoveries', when only a statistical probability has been shown. In the case of BSE, taking the reverse position was the problem. Lack of statistical 'proof' kept lethal products on our butcher's shelves for years and even killed people.

Such criticism cuts deeper than the simple jibe, 'you can manipulate statistics to prove anything'. It suggests that over-dependence of government, medicine, industry and the public on statistical studies as the 'be all and end all of truth' fundamentally threatens the freedom and health of twenty-first-century humanity.

Research funding goes to studies that have an emotional appeal, or profit potential. Academic bureaucracy perpetuates research teams once they are set up. Amazing cures have been discovered and refined and it is vital to re-examine findings 'to be sure'. Yet far too often the never-ending 'scientific method' quest to discover and refine the 'nuts and bolts' of the Universe becomes the 'sacred cow' that dominates not only what we can do, but what we believe. It tells how we are 'allowed' to live our lives.

Material mindsets dominate research and academic activities, leaving no room for approaches not following a strict reductionist 'scientific method'. These are at best seen as rather 'quaint' childlike activities – at worst downright dangerous and 'ought to be banned'.

Yet, is it not how and what we love that 'stirs the juices' and brings magic and excitement to our lives? Our values make us break our necks to be there, to do that, to celebrate. Our experiences motivate our actions. They cause very practical things to happen. Should we not seek the structure of feeling, before we consider paying for complex machines to measure the consequential electrical currents in the brain? The best that the motor-mechanic mind of the material scientist will make of the Universe is a finely tuned Porsche with no people inside.

To become acceptable, astrology does not need to prove itself before the hard-edged, unyielding edifice of the modern material scientific view. To suggest it does shows the extent to which modern science has forgotten, and wishes us to forget, that we are constrained by the facts of living on planet Earth. Far better for all concerned to realise where we are and learn how to work with the planets, whose motions keep the Earth and ourselves on path.

-o0o-

Refer to Chapter 4 to read the commentaries on pages 62-64, including the chart diagrams relating to Israel and the 2003 Iraq War. These are from the May 2011 column, put together when the dire consequences of that war were becoming frighteningly clear. They also show how astro-cycle indicators link events across millennia, and into the birth charts of those who instigate new events. This column goes on to show the links are rare, not cherry picked, but specific and focused.

Astrology detractors may respond to this demonstration with the three criticisms that are shown and answered below:

❖ *How many other times have similar astro events occurred without similar results?*
    Since 70 CE: Sun and Jupiter in Leo with Uranus and Pluto in Aquarius has never occurred; Jupiter has conjuncted Neptune in Leo eleven times, but only twice as close as two degrees and never so near to exact as March/April 1920. The 1948 chart's four Leo planets have been together only five times, but the period leading up to the foundation of Israel in 1948 was by far the strongest and Pluto has never been anywhere near exactly opposed its 70 CE position at the same time.

❖ *Astrological interpretation may seem to work in retrospect, but not so well when looking ahead.*
    Using this information, the outcome of the war in Iraq was clearly foreseen at the time, as well as the inevitable failure of policy initiatives, because none of the parties was able to see and accept the real issues, which the charts clearly revealed.

❖ *Astrology uses generalised statements that could apply to almost anything.*
    Basic keywords clearly describe the above events and connections.

-oOo-

In the 2010s Professor Brian Cox was a popular figure offering dramatically illustrated understanding of the Universe to television audiences, while being increasingly against any possibility there could be any interactive connection between astro-cycles, human behaviour and social trends. He went to extreme lengths to demonstrate his ignorance of astrology and prejudice against it to millions of viewers. Belying all these protestations, the May 2011 column showed that he too was both the victim and clear beneficiary of his birth chart.

Professor Brian Cox
Brian Cox was revealingly cagey, when asked his birth details during a BBC 5 Live interview on 2 February 2011. Of course, the date and place is a matter of public knowledge. Then a birth time of 07:31 am was offered by a confidential source with the claim it is very reliable. While not independently verifiable, let us see if the chart fits.

Certainly, the first house Pisces/Aries stellium suggests a powerful presenter of pioneering breakthroughs. That these presentations should creatively stir people is shown by the Aries Moon being in a tight trine to Jupiter at 29Le20. This fits with Jupiter being close to the Descendant; even more remarkable is that, at the time of his birth, Jupiter was within three minutes of arc of the position of the royal star Regulus. The tendency of BBC producers to place Professor Cox at sensational viewpoints to illustrate his exhilarating subject matter could not be a more appropriate way of expressing the astrology – 'Wonders of the Solar System and Universe' indeed!

Professor Cox's clear emotional devotion to his subject fits the Pisces Sun being the first planet to rise in his first house. Saturn, the traditional ruler of his late Aquarian Ascendant, being placed in Aries conjunct Mars, makes him a powerful initiator. Both being sesquisquare to Neptune, which is squared to Jupiter, suggest he will be a resolute fighter for such causes. The Moon is quincunx to the separating generational Uranus/Pluto conjunction in Virgo in the seventh and separating from a weak semi-square to the Sun to leave it unaspected. This suggests he has emotional issues with the unconventional. With Venus and Mercury tucked away in the twelfth in an applying trine/sextile to the Nodal axis in the first/seventh houses, we see him as having endless hidden reserves of scientific wisdom.

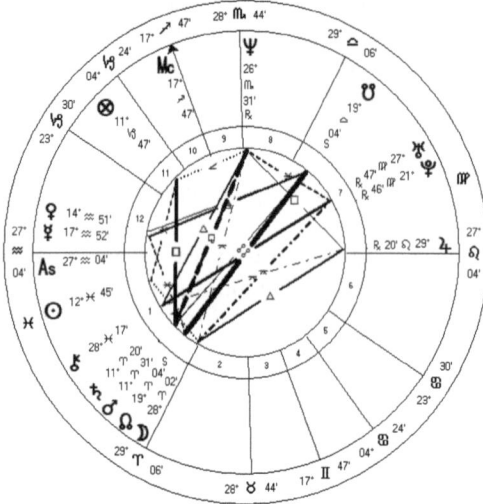

Professor Brian Cox
3 Mar 1968 07:31 BST -1:00
Oldham, UK 53°N33' 002°W07'
Geocentric Tropical Placidus True Node

If the time were different the main force of the chart would remain, but the focus would change. While lacking information to check the chart against events in his life, we can track the progress of transiting Jupiter, Mars and the Nodal axis in terms of the broadcasting of his highly successful television series. Jupiter transited the Ascendant of the 07:31 chart on 4 January 2010 (when did final filming start?). When the first programme in the *Wonders of the Solar System* was broadcast (7 March 2010), Jupiter was moving quickly forward at 11Pi30 and had crossed his Sun before the second programme the following week. The day of the second programme in the series (12 March) the transiting true Nodal axis made an exact grand cross to its natal axis. He said astrology was 'rubbish' on 28 March 2010, the day after Mercury crossed his natal North Node. When he supported Dara Ó Briain repetition of this opinion about astrology on 3 January 2011, Mars was at late 19 degrees of Capricorn separating from an opposition to Saturn that was advancing in late 16 degrees of Libra. Together these were making a grand cross to his natal Nodal axis (Mars almost exact). At the time of writing, I note that his new series *Wonders of the Universe* is scheduled to occur with Jupiter moving between 9 and 12 degrees of Aries across his Saturn/Mars conjunction. The Moon is at 7Ar47 when the first programme opens. Were any of these times elected or are they just the natural wonders of solar system?

Either way, once you know the language, it is clear astrology works.

-oOo-

The March 2012 column considered whether the British *Royal Society* was true to its original aims in being so dismissive of astrological methodology.

'Take nobody's word for it'

The Royal Society's motto 'Nullius in verba' roughly translates as 'take nobody's word for it'. It is an expression of the determination of Fellows to withstand the domination of authority and to verify all statements by an appeal to facts determined by experiment.

History Section – The Royal Society's web page.[255]

Abstract: *Few reasonable, rational and open-minded people would have anything but admiration for the above aspiration, providing that, in the spirit of the essential meaning of 'Nullius in verba', what is meant by the word 'experiment' is rigorously questioned.*

In the years since the foundation of The Royal Society in the late seventeenth century, the word has taken on an increasingly fragmentary and reductionist meaning; rather like creatures in nature, collected, categorised and pinned in cases and compartments, as if systematic understanding in death brings greater clarity than observation in life. Yet, while knowing the elemental fragments and mechanics of an object or process is vital, rearranging or even putting the pieces back together again does not necessarily create or re-create the living being or experience.

This distinction is so critical that we have to ask whether today's notion of 'scientific method' is so narrow that it itself is becoming no more than a dominant authority that needs to be questioned? Its treatment of astrology suggests this.

Modern scientific ingenuity

To find an answer, we must consider the very essential nature of the Universe, which exists both inside and outside us. Our observations suggest it has infinite possibility. While there are rules to follow and reactions to actions, modern science has shown that the ingenious mind, willing to go to sufficient trouble and expense, can find a way around almost any barrier to our understanding and actions. This is because the method we use determines the facts we will find, and hence the experience we will have. Any truth established by experiment is limited to the experimental design. A telescope sees over long distances, a microscope within small spaces. Looking both ways sees more space than substance. Even keeping our focus on our earthly lives, we see differently at night and day and at night by infrared. X-ray and heat-seeking machines see nature very differently. By containing the experimental circumstances, we can build machines to travel through a vacuum to the Moon and beyond or a vast underground machine to map the movement of the minutest particles. New medicines and interventions can cure diseases, heal bodies and extend life.

Ways of understanding of the Universe

Modern science is not the first to tap into, discover and remake the natural rhythms of the Universe. Archaeology reveals many different civilisations that created very different worlds. Some of them flourished for far longer than our own to date.

Frequently, what these civilisations knew is rediscovered and confirmed by our modern methods. Ancient Kundalini visualisation, as an essence of healing attunement, is remarkably similar to the DNA spiral. For many centuries, Hindu cosmologists have known and explained the cycles of a regenerating Universe lasting billions of years in terms that the modern cosmologists only started to talk and dispute about in the twentieth century. Even today, the methods psychiatrists use to help mental illness range widely. Electrical and chemical behavioural and structure-based techniques have measurable effects, but often come with dangerous and difficult-to-control side effects. Regression and a wide range of gestalt and counselling therapies are less mechanical and not easy to pin down in research, but often more satisfying and effective. When our descendants look back from 500 or 1,000 years in the future, it is unlikely they will interpret the Universe as we do today? They may well see our scientific focus as narrow and doctrinaire, just as we now view the eleventh and sixteenth-century world pictures.

Appropriate experimental models

So what would be, and who should determine what would be, an appropriate experimental model by which to test the facts in a particular field of knowledge? The key is that the experimental design should be appropriate to the subject under study. We do not expect a meteorologist to predict whether a person will become wet or sunburnt, rather to describe the environment, to help individuals decide what to do. However hard seismologists try, their expert machines are much better at explaining earth movements than predicting them – rather like astrologers!

Where activities can only be safely undertaken if reliable predictions of mechanical cause and effect are possible, precision is vital. However, in most areas of life, giving people an intelligent knowledge of the environment and possible consequences is all they need or want. What kind of person is it who seeks rigid control of a loved one or prior knowledge of every moment of their lives? We seek knowledge of ourselves and our circumstances, help in recognising and coping with opportunities and change. In these things, mature understanding of astro-cycles has been invaluable for thousands of years and has the same potential to this day.

How to experiment with astrology

So, what would be an appropriate method to experiment into the workings and reliability of astrology? The answer becomes clear when we realise that every astrologer who engages in an objective, non-deterministic interaction with a client or phenomena is engaged in empirical research. The key concepts we work with are no more or less unyielding authorities than mathematical number systems and rules. Like them, astro-concepts are a framework used as reference points, upon which to place and systematise our observations. Two will always be two and become three when one is added, but the ways that oneness, twoness, and threeness can be understood and applied are numberless!

Every time we use and share our understanding of astro meanings, we extend our knowledge of human nature and the way the Universe works. Yet, like numbers, each astro concept has a clear focus range that not only disciplines, but enhances judgment. We start to systematise an experimental design when astrologers share and compare their findings. We should not seek to prove specifics, but use specifics to extend understanding. Some factors, such as those studied in Gauquelin's work, are so strong they look like mechanical proofs, but to rely on them alone will not 'prove' astrology. A more fruitful approach would be to develop broader and more disciplined systems of recording.

Royal Society's foundation role – to ensure practice is beyond authoritarianism
Knowing this, it is a great loss to larger society, as well as astrologers, that astrology has been so sidelined away from modern education, and misrepresented in the media, that it is little understood today. The encouragement of its absence from genuine academic study and debate points to an essential flaw in the practice of modern science and the Royal Society's foundation role – to ensure scientific practice is beyond authoritarianism. Broader experimental designs do not threaten, they enrich scientific advance. They enable science to help us celebrate and enjoy life rather than manipulate it. Instead, science today is focused on a rather 'boyish' enthusiasm for extravagant reductionist mechanical studies that presume to explain all space and time, but give results mainly valued for their commercial applicability. These dominate a competitive society that is dependent upon expert judgements and devices. While these often heal, help and titillate its citizens, they also disempower. People are offered many choices, but few skills to drive their own destiny.

The science of life is the highest science of all. Science that excludes it is an empty shell of itself; just fundamentalist old-school scholasticism reborn, with a mechanical God at the helm this time!

-o0o-

The July 2013 column wondered whether a key law of quantum physics showed astrology's critics were demanding of astrologers what they did not require of themselves.

The Uncertainty Principle

The Heisenberg Principle is a key law of quantum physics, which suggests that the way we look at things may affect what we see or know. For example: the more precisely we measure the position of a particle, the less precisely we can understand its movement. Astrology is concerned with cycles: i.e. the changing relationship between particles' positions. Hence a physicist who insists that astrology be proved by predicting a precise outcome to a set combination of particles, which are in cyclic flux, is demanding what physics does not demand of itself. We should not expect astrology to predict events, but to describe and anticipate tendencies, pressures, and qualities of environments. If people listened to such information from experienced astrologers, the world and our lives would be much happier.

Endnotes

[1] Roy Gillett, *Astrology and Compassion the Convenient Truth* (Oxford: Kings Hart Books, 2007), Chapter 3.

[2] André Barbault, *Planetary Cycles Mundane Astrology* (London: Astrological Association, 2016) tr. Kate Johnson from *Les cycles planétaires*, 2014.

[3] A popular introduction to astrology: Roy Gillett, *The Secret Language of Astrology* (London: Watkins, 2012).

[4] https://www.astrologicalassociation.com/astrological-journal-shop/

[5] Roy Gillett, *The Secret Language of Astrology.*

[6] At the time of writing [2021], highly-regarded sources are: https://alabe.com/freechart/and https://www.astro.com/cgi/chart.cgi

[7] Mandalas are generated by Rique Pottenger's 'Astrological Mandalas' software. Obtainable from: https://crucialastrotools.co.uk/astromandalas.html

[8] Roy Gillett, *The Essence of Buddhism* (London: Caxton, 2001).

[9] *The Ascent of Man.* BBC television series first broadcast in 1973; written and presented by Jacob Bronowski.

[10] Tony Blair birth data: 6 May 1953 06:10 BST, Edinburgh, Scotland (55N57, 3W13). Rodden rating AA, from birth certificate.

[11] Gordon Brown birth data: 20 February 1951 08:40 GMT, Giffnock, Scotland (55N48, 4W17). Rodden rating AA, from birth certificate.

[12] George W. Bush birth data: 6 July 1946 07:26 EDT, New Haven, CT (41N18, 72W56). Rodden rating AA, from birth certificate.

[13] Vladimir Putin birth data: 7 October 1952 09:30 BAT, St. Petersburg, Russia (59N55, 30E18). Rodden rating DD, source provided by the webmaster of the President Vladimir V. Putin website in 2000.

[14] David Blunkett birth data: 6 June 1947 07:00 BDST, Sheffield, England (53N23, 1W30). Rodden rating A, from his memory in a letter to Caroline Gerard.

[15] On 28 December 2004, the *India Daily* printed the full text of the paper by N. Venkatanathan, N. Rajeswara Rao, K. K. Sharma and P. Periakali.

[16] This is the number of deaths estimated on 20 January 2005.

[17] Roy Gillett, 'Working with the Planets', *Astrological Journal* 48.3, pp.42-49.

[18] Nicholas Campion, *Book of World Horoscopes* (Wessex Astrologer, 2004).

[19] 'God called the light Day, and the darkness he called Night. And there was evening and there was morning, the first day.' Genesis 1:5 NRSV.

[20] 'Th' Eternal to prevent such horrid fray, Hung forth in Heav'n his golden Scales, yet seen Betwixt Astrea and the Scorpion signe, Wherein all things created first he weighd', John Milton, *Paradise Lost* (1667) Book IV, lines 990-999.

[21] John 1:1 and John 1:14, NRSV.

[22] The six innermost planets in ruling signs.

[23] Pam Crane's asteroid study considers February/March, but seems to be suggesting that the interesting date is 20:05 on 2 March 5 BCEE, on her website: http://revpamcrane.weebly.com/01-the-prince-of-peace.html

[24] My thanks to Wayne Turner for drawing my attention to this possible date in a personal email. He writes, the data 'is based on the research of Dr Ernest L Martin which came out in the 1980's and which I was alerted to by an article in Sky Telescope, December 1986, pages 632-635, titled Computing the Star of Bethlehem by Roger W Sinnott. It was Sinnott who first noticed this Jupiter/Venus conjunction back in 1968 according to the article. A follow up letter and illustration of the conjunction of Jupiter and Venus was printed in the April 1987 issue, pages 357-358, from James DeYoung and James Hilton of the US Naval Observatory'. http//askelm.com/star/star000.html

[25] Jim Shawvan states 'On. Oct. 29, 2000, I made public my speculation on the probable delay in the results of the US presidential election of Nov. 7, 2000. That speculation appeared on StarIQ.com starting on Nov. 1st.' at http://www.stariq.com/Main/Astrologers/A0000807.HTM

[26] Although it is reported at http://www.stariq.com/Main/Articles/P0005478.htm that the Great American astrologer Evangeline Adams did predict the US entry into that war.

[27] Charles Carter, *An Introduction to Political Astrology* (Essex: Fowler, 1980).

[28] Alexander Ruperti, *Cycles of Becoming: The Planetary Pattern of Growth* (Santa Monica, CA: Earthwalk School of Astrology, 2005).

[29] Richard Tarnas, *Cosmos and Psyche: Intimations of a New World View* (New York: Plume, 2014).

[30] Michael Baigent, Nicholas Campion and Charles Harvey, *Mundane Astrology* (London: Thorsons, 1992).

[31] Nicholas Campion, *Book of World Horoscopes* (Wellingborough: Aquarian Press, 1988; republished Wessex Astrologer, 2004).

[32] Rupert Sheldrake, *The Science Delusion* (London: Hodder & Stoughton 2020)

[33] Peter Berger and Thomas Luckmann, *The Social Construction of Reality: A Treatise in the Sociology of Knowledge* (New York: Anchor, 1966). Although it may not have been the authors' intention, this book prepares the way for the study of astro-cycles, as a method to explain and anticipate how societies change their 'realities'. While astrology itself may be a social construct, its dependence upon measurable cycles makes it constantly self-correcting. This is why there are so many astrology systems. Tibetan Buddhism teaches that 'anything labelled dependently arises'. So, it is good to have a system that helps us step back, accept and work systematically with relativity. Astrology is content that its methods be accepted as a work in progress. Thankfully, it avoids insisting they are absolute truth.

[34] Roy Gillett, *Astrology and Compassion*, Chapter 12.

[35] At the time of writing the time of birth is not known, so house positions and the exact degree of the Moon are unreliable.

[36] The 17 December 2012 edition of the *New Haven Register* newspaper reported the possibility that Adam Lanza suffered from the autistic Asperger's syndrome.

[37] See Roy Gillett, *Astrology and Compassion*, Chapter 12, which demonstrates how the birth charts, progressions and transits of Mark Chapman (John Lennon's assassin) and Cho Seung-Hui (the Blacksburg, Virginia campus mass murderer), not only showed their potential for such behaviour, but crucially that they acted at a time that could have been predicted.

[38] Roy Gillett, *Astrology and Compassion*, Chapter 12.

[39] 'Astrological Forecasting – the Facts' in André Barbault, *The Value of Astrology* Kate Johnston (trans.) (London: The Astrological Association, 2014), Chapter 7. This book, translated from *L'astrologie certifiée : connaissances, statistiques & prévisions*, is the first book by this great French astrologer to be published in English.

[40] Nicholas Campion, *History of Western Astrology* [2 vols] (London: Bloomsbury, 2009).

[41] Roy Gillett, *Astrology and Compassion*.

[42] 26 June 2015 12:00 CET, Sousse, Tunisia (35N55, 10E35). For details and discussion of time of the incident see https://en.wikipedia.org/wiki/2015_Sousse_attacks

[43] This bizarre incident (which happened the day after the others mentioned) wasn't a terrorist attack but a 'colour powder party' when clouds of corn starch were sprayed towards participants, and the starch ignited, burning 508 people and killing fifteen people.

[44] 24 March 2015 10:40 CET, 24 March 2015, Prads-Haute-Bléone, Alpes-de-Haute-Provence, France (44N17, 6E26). For full details see https://en.wikipedia.org/wiki/Germanwings_Flight_9525

[45] A radical Islamist preacher, who was expelled from the United Kingdom in 2014 after a long court battle.

[46] Andreas Lubitz birth data: 18 December 1987, Neuburg/Donau, Germany. Time unknown. Source Astrodatabank: https://www.astro.com/astro-databank/Lubitz,_Andreas

[47] See references 37 to 38, which refer to Mark Chapman (John Lennon's assassin) and Cho Seung-Hui (the Blacksburg, Virginia campus mass murderer) and Adam Lanza. All not only showed their potential for such behaviour, but crucially acted at a time that could have been predicted.

[48] It has been noted to be significant indication of his shortcomings is that his 'do or die' approach to leaving the EU seems to be based on a rather unfortunate misquote from Tennyson's *Charge of the Light Brigade*. See below:
'Theirs not to reason why,
Theirs but to do and die.
Into the valley of Death
Rode the six hundred.
Cannon to right of them,
Cannon to left of them
Cannon in front of them
Volleyed and thundered;
Stormed at with shot and shell,
Boldly they rode and well,
Into the jaws of Death,
Into the mouth of hell
Rode the six hundred.'

[49] Daniel Yergin, *The Prize* (New York: Free Press, 2014).

[50] Roy Gillett, 'Pluto Death and Hope', *Astrology Quarterly* 71.3 (Astrological Lodge of London, 2001).

[51] This made sense when it was first published in the *Journal*. Rather late now, of course, but interesting to look back and reflect.

[52] So fully outlined in the excellent articles in the *Astrological Journal* 45.2 (March/April 2003).

[53] Roy Gillett, 'Working with the Planets', *Astrological Journal* 45.1 (January/February 2003).

[54] 4 July 1776 NS 16:50 LMT (+5:00:40) Philadelphia, PA (39N57, 75W10).

[55] 'You may say that I'm a dreamer, but I'm not the only one' John Lennon, *Imagine*.

[56] John Milton, *Paradise Lost*, Book IV.

[57] Ibid. This great poem's epic dimensions benefit from rich astrological imagery. In books IV and X, Milton details planets, aspects and other technicalities, such as the tilt of the earth on its axis.

[58] Stephanie Johnson, 'Standard Natal Interpretations', Solar Fire v5.1 software, Astrolabe Inc.

[59] http://www.rosemaryclooney.com/LyricPages/whossorrynow.html

[60] Roy Gillett, 'How the planets work' in 'Working with the Planets', *Astrological Journal* 45.1 (January/February 2003), pp.35-37.

[61] Jigsaw version 2, created by Graham Dawson and Bernadette Brady. Published by Astrolabe Inc.

[62] 'Sunnis and Shia: Islam's ancient schism', *BBC News Website*, 4 January 2016. https://www.bbc.co.uk/news/world-middle-east-16047709. As of January 2016, the global population of Shia Muslims was estimated at between 154 and 200 million.

[63] On 7 July 2005 several lethal terrorist explosions occurred in London.

[64] From *Lam Rim*, the traditional Tibetan Buddhist teaching foundation teachings.

[65] Roy Gillett, 'Working with the Planets', *Astrological Journal* 47.6 (November/December 2005).

[66] *New York Times*, 8 October 2005.

[67] Using time zone based local clock time can distort the actual local LMT MC by up to 15 degrees. Also, latitude affects the Ascendant.

[68] I have not been able to find the exact location of the test. So I have estimated the coordinates from maps that were shown on the media at the time. The more westerly the site, the nearer the MC will be to the South Node.

[69] Still 'working' in spite of attempts by that IAU conference 'rump' to remove it from text books, along with so much more astrological wisdom they never allowed in at all.

[70] Foundation of North Korea: 10 September 1948 12:00 JST, Pyongyang, North Korea (39N01, 125E45), cited in Campion, *Book of World Horoscopes*.

[71] See endnote 25.

[72] Inauguration: 20 January 2001 12:00 EST, Washington, DC (38N54, 77W02).

[73] John McCain birth data: 29 August 1936 18:25 EST, Colón, Panama (9N22, 79W54). Rodden rating AA.

[74] Barack Obama birth data: 4 August 1961 19:24 AHST, Honolulu, Hawaii (21N18, 157W52). Rodden rating AA, but at the time the article was written the birth time was unknown.

[75] Hillary Clinton birth data: 26 October 1947 20:00, Chicago, IL (41N51, 87W39). Rodden rating DD.

[76] Roy Gillett, 'Working with the Planets', *Astrological Journal* 49.6 (November/December 2007).

[77] Roy Gillett, 'Working with the Planets', *Astrological Journal* 50.1 (January/February 2008), p.24. I have paraphrased the text from my original article to make the meaning clearer.

[78] For an in-depth analysis of this projected economic rationalisation, see Gillett, 'A Key to Better Economic Planning', *Astrology and Compassion*, Chapter 14.

[79] See 'Working with the Planets', *Astrological Journal* 49.5 (September/October 2007) and the 2008 issues 50.2 to 50.5.

[80] Ibid.

[81] Roy Gillett, 'Working with the Planets', *Astrological Journal* 50.2 (March/April 2008), p.41. The copy deadline was early February 2008.

[82] The crisis in the US mortgage markets, which involved most world financial institutions, was based in the selling of a risk that others would default on their debts. Unlike conventional house, motor and life insurance, a lack of regulation allowed speculators to insure other people's debt risks that they themselves did not face. In the summer of 2008, the exposure of just two major British-based banks was equal to four times the UK government's annual expenditure. World-wide, it was estimated to equal 62 trillion dollars, or $10,000 for every man, woman and child on the planet.

[83] This and data for 1, 2 and 3 quoted from Bill Meridian, *Planetary Stock Trading* (New York: Cycles Research, 2002).

[84] Both dates taken from Trading History generally available. Timings may be out by up to a hour. London Stock Exchange now opens at 08:00 London time am, but previously opened at 08:30 and 09:00.

[85] http://en.wikipedia.org/wiki/Shanghai_Stock_Exchange#Chronology

[86] 20 January 2009 12:00 EST, Washington, DC (38N54, 77W02).

[87] See endnote 74

[88] *Pleasantville* (1998). Film written, produced and directed by Gary Rossis, and nominated for an Academy Award.

[89] It went on to refer to the *West Wing* (series 7) television series and ask 'Could McCain and Obama bring the Alan Alda/Jimmy Smits battle to real life?'

[90] See endnote 74.

[91] With Aquarius rising, but a Leo Sun and Gemini Moon, Barack Obama will control the agenda with calm intelligence.

[92] Chancellor of the Exchequer, the chief financial minister in the UK cabinet, similar to the US Secretary to the Treasury.

[93] Alison Murdoch and Dekyi-Lee Oldershaw, *16 Guidelines for a Happy Life: The Basics* (London: Essential Education, 2008).

[94] That is from the trade unions to the performance of the financial markets. Seeing performance on Wall Street and other markets as the touchstone of successful economic recovery is a major error. Financial markets respond positively to easy money, which itself is the very cause of our current crisis.

[95] Hans Christian Anderson tells a story most apt to recent developments in the credit market. In the story, no one but a 'stupid ruffian' dared tell the King that a trickster had deceived him into paying for a suit of clothes that did not exist. So, he was walking naked before the entire populace.

[96] The original research did not allow for the Chiron ephemeris starting at 675 CE. However, the two CE dates given remain the only ones in the period from 675 to 2500 CE.

[97] Nowadays, parental age can vary more widely than in the past – especially due to modern IVF methods. It would be interesting to research connections between this, the Uranus cycle and generational relationships in the twenty-first century.

[98] Of course, the role of karma in the reincarnation process makes the child the responsible co-creator of this birth process. However, most children and growing adults are unaware of this. Indeed, coming to realise it as the child/parent relationship matures is an important step on the liberating path to enlightenment.

[99] See endnote 74

[100] The Woodstock music festival was held 15-18 August 1969, Bethel, NY, on a farm 40 miles southwest of Woodstock.

[101] The single 'All You Need is Love' was launched by The Beatles just over 3 weeks after the *Sergeant Pepper* album on 25 June 1967 in the first live global television link, watched by 400 million in twenty-six countries.

[102] Gillett, *Economy, Ecology and Kindness*

[103] Roy Gillett, 'Working with the Planets', *Astrological Journal* 52.2 (March/April 2010), pp.38-39.

[104] '...we've got to get ourselves back to the garden', Joni Mitchell *Woodstock* (song, 1970)

[105] Ian Jack, *The Country Formerly Known as Great Britain* (London: Vintage, 2011).

[106] Fully explained in Roy Gillett *Economy, Ecology and Kindness*.

[107] For full details of the advanced planning, design and beauty of the ancient city visit http://en.wikipedia.org/wiki/Baghdad

[108] Co-Chair of the governing British Conservative Party, in her speech in the Vatican February 2012.

[109] Sheldrake, *The Science Delusion*, p.184.

[110] http://en.wikipedia.org/wiki/Maya_calendar#Long_Count

[111] http://en.wikipedia.org/wiki/List_of_ancient_Egyptian_dynasties

[112] http://en.wikipedia.org/wiki/Kali_Yuga

[113] http://en.wikipedia.org/wiki/Stonehenge

[114] http://earthsky.org/astronomy-essentials/will-earth-pass-through-galactic-plane-in-2012

[115] http://en.wikipedia.org/wiki/Maya_calendar#Long_Count

[116] Owners of Solar Fire are encouraged to use this tool. It is fine way of discovering how often a combination of events happens and hence putting its significance in perspective.

[117] Title of HH Dalai Lama's Public Talk given at Manchester Arena 17 June 2012.

[118] 'You can't always get what you want. But if you try sometimes, you just might find, you get what you need.' From 'You Can't Always Get What You Want', track on Rolling Stones, *Let it Bleed*, 1969.

[119] As I write, a report in the UK newspaper *Daily Mail* points out that the average working week for many in the UK has increased from 9 am to 5 pm to just after 7 am to 7 pm. With so many other people unemployed, who gains when one person does one and a half person's work, while wage levels are frozen or reduced?

[120] Roy Gillett, 'Working with the Planets', *Astrological Journal* 49.6 (November/December 2007), p.22.

[121] The choice of 9 pm was chosen to ensure the best lighting effect. Could that this was when the Ascendant completed an air/fire six-pointed star also be relevant – synchronicity?

[122] Spice Girls, *Wannabe* (debut single 1996).

[123] To view this picture, visit http://www.impawards.com/2009/two_thousand_twelve_ver6.html Film made by Centropolis Entertainment, distributed by Columbia Pictures (2009).

[124] 'Beauty is truth, truth beauty – that is all ye know on earth, and all ye need to know.' Keats, *Ode on a Grecian Urn*.

[125] Nicholas Campion, 'Exploring Johannes Kepler's planetary politics: the Uranus-Pluto square', *Astrological Journal* 53.3 (May/June 2011), pp.19-26.

[126] Darby Costello, 'Navigating by the outer planets in the astrological chart, in particular the Uranus-Pluto square', *Astrological Journal* 54.6 (November/December 2012), pp.30-36.

[127] Roy Gillett, 'Working with the Planets', *Astrological Journal* 54.5 (September/October 2012), pp.39-43.

[128] http://en.wikipedia.org/wiki/Revolutions_of_1848

[129] The idea of a true economic gold standard being kindness is fully discussed in Gillett, *Economy Ecology and Kindness*, and further developed in Roy Gillett, *Reversing the Race to Global Destruction* (Camberley: Crucial Books, 2017).

[130] All had died not long after being separated from their mother. https://callthemidwife.fandom.com/wiki/Mary-Anne_Jenkins

[131] Voting was spread over several weeks in those days, so the chart is drawn with a 0 Aries house system for noon on the last day.

[132] Readers living in the USA and other parts of the world may recognise similar restrictions in welfare in their neighbourhoods.

[133] https://www.astro.com/astro-databank/Xi,_Jinping gives this date of birth.

[134] Roy Gillett, 'Working with the Planets', *Astrological Journal* 55.4 (July/August 2013), pp.46-51.

[135] The chart is drawn for the first exact trine of Jupiter to Saturn; the retrograde trine is on 14 December 2013. Completion is on 24 May 2014.

[136] Britain declared war on Germany at 11:00 GMT 5 August 1914. London, UK.

[137] National Archives, 'Over by Christmas' in 'The First World War, 1914-1918', http:/www.nationalarchives.gov.uk/pathways/firstworldwar/first_world_war/over_christmas.html

[138] Foundation of Syria: 1 January 1944 00:00 EET, Damascus, Syria, cited in Campion, *World Horoscopes*.

[139] Barbault, *Value of Astrology*.

[140] Roy Gillett, 'Working with the Planets', *Astrological Journal* 56.1 (January/February 2014), pp.58-63.

[141] It is interesting to note that the next conjunction occurs in 2384, just seven years after the Synetic Vernal Point, as defined by Cyril Fagan, retrogrades into Aquarius.

[142] Roy Gillett, 'The Scottish Independence Vote', *Astrological Journal* 56.4 (July/August 2014), pp.62-63.

[143] 25 April 1920 11:22 am CEDT San Remo, Italy.

[144] The Sibley Chart 17:10 LMT, 4 July 1776 Philadelphia, USA

[145] Noon chart for 4 August 70 CE, Jerusalem.

[146] 14 May 1948 16:00, Tel Aviv, Israel.

[147] See Roy Gillett, 'General Election 2015: the struggle for the nation's soul', *Astrological Journal* 57.2 (March/April 2015), pp.20-22.

[148] See Nicholas Grier, 'UK General Election 2015: the likely outcome', *Astrological Journal* 57.2 (March/April 2015), pp.15-17.

[149] Ibid.

[150] 19 July 1970 15:16 BST, Irvine, Scotland. Roden rating AA, from birth certificate.

[151] https://en.wikipedia.org/wiki/Niccol%C3%B2_Machiavelli

[152] http://projectsanctuary.com/the_complete_ferengi_rules_of_acquisition.htm

[153] https://www.sciencemag.org/content/351/6269/aad2622.abstract

[154] André Barbault, *Planetary Cycles Mundane Astrology* (London: Astrological Association, 2016) tr. Kate Johnston from *Les cycles planétaires*, 2014. These Cyclic Index graphs are created by adding the distances between pairs of outer planets from Jupiter outwards, and then drawing a graph to represent the combined mean of waxing and waning degrees.

[155] André Barbault 'sur les Pandémies' in *L'Astrologue*, No. 177, first quarter 2012.

[156] André Barbault 'An Overview of Pandemics' *Astrological Journal* 62.3 May 2020 pp.5-8 (English translation by Kate Johnston).

[157] Voting in some constituencies did not take place until 19 July and the counting and result was not known until 26 July, due to delays receiving the votes of servicemen, who were overseas.

[158] Midnight 17 December 2015, London, UK.

[159] Some would argue that the alienation of many traditional Labour heartland voters was not Corbyn's fault. It had been a long time coming following the adoption of Thatcherite and ill-considered EU expansion policies by New Labour, which Jeremy Corbyn was aiming to correct, if given the support and time. Ironically, it was supporters of New Labour that led the moves to use the EU vote to blame and oust him.

[160] 1 October 1956, Eastbourne, UK, time of birth unknown .

[161] Crowning of William I in Westminster Abbey, Noon, 25 December 1066. The coming into force of the Act of Union between England Wales and Scotland midnight 1 January 1801, Westminster.

[162] The EU came into being on 1 November 1993, when Uranus was within four minutes of arc conjunct Neptune in the nineteenth degree of Capricorn

[163] Gillett, *Reversing the Race to Global Destruction*.

[164] Noon LMT 27 July 1694 OS, London, England.

[165] 23 December 1913 18:02 EST, New York, NY.

[166] Gillett, *Economy Ecology and Kindness*.

[167] Federal Reserve in USA, Bank of England, European Central Bank and The South East Asian Central Banks.

[168] In the UK, QE is distributed to banks and pension funds as purchase government bonds. In the US it is to Primary Broker Dealers. Both groups then invest in various areas of the financial markets. Such investments artificially increase assumed values and do not necessary lead to investment in material industries, home-building and infrastructure projects. Where it does, the employment created is mainly of a temporary, short term nature. The minority, who own or control the financial and service industries, make most of the profit. As a result, the income gap between rich and poor widens, while everyone remains responsible for the consequent national debt.

[169] Polls closed 22:00 BST 11 June 1987 London, UK.

[170] Roy Gillett, 'Working with the Planets', *Astrological Journal* 57.4 (July/August 2015), p.35.

[171] In fact, Article 50 was triggered by Theresa May's six page letter being given to EU officials at 12:25 on 29 March 2017.

[172] Roy Gillett, 'Working with the Planets', *Astrological Journal* 58.6 (November/December 2016).

[173] The danger of medical minds being fixated on the latest drugs and methods was clearly shown in the true story film, starring Meryl Streep, *First Do No Harm* directed by Jim Abrahams (Pebblehut Productions, 1997).

[174] Joe Earle, Cahal Moral and Zach Ward-Perkins, *The Econocracy: The Perils of Leaving Economics to the Experts* (Manchester: Manchester University Press, 2017).

[175] Gillett, *Reversing the Race to Global Destruction*.

[176] For a deeper analysis of the event, see Roy Gillett, 'Working with the Planets', *Astrological Journal* 59.5 (September/October 2017), pp.32-36.

[177] Readers in UK will remember the young Harry Enfield's satire of the excesses of Thatcherite monetarism on *Saturday Night Live* TV.

[178] Words used at the time by Conservative Ex-Prime Minister Harold MacMillan.

[179] The narrative and astrology of the consequences of Reaganomics / Thatcherite free-market monetarist economic policies are explained in detail in Gillett, *Economy Ecology and Kindness*)

[180] Readers living in the Southern Hemisphere may incorporate the Summer Solstice comments in the May / June *Astrological Journal*, while taking account of everything else!

[181] Gillett , *Reversing the Race to Global Destruction* (Abandoning the Politics of Greed) explains in detail how these key areas of our world could be transformed.

[182] A few days after Theresa May's Florence speech.

[183] Roy Gillett, 'Working with the Planets', *Astrological Journal* 59.6 (November/December 2017), p.24.

[184] In the twenty-first century, does this symbolise the Western powers faced with radical restructuring, while the East forges ahead?

[185] The first lead type book printed in 1455 enabled the Reformation. The first computer with RAM was invented five hundred years later in 1955. What is that leading to?

[186] John Stevens and Frederick Perls, *Gestalt Therapy Verbatim* (Moab, Utah: Real People Press, 1969), p.4.

[187] 'Roy Gillett, 'Working with the Planets', *Astrological Journal* 60.1 (January/February 2018), pp.61-65.

[188] To watch the entire sermon visit: https://edition.cnn.com/2018/05/19/europe/michael-curry-royal-wedding-sermon-full-text-intl/index.html. Subsequent events do not make a mockery of his idealism, rather the contrast exposes the cheap cruelty in some elements of the British press and its readers.

[189] Gillett, *Reversing the Race to Global Destruction*.

[190] Mariana Mazzucato, *The Value of Everything* (London: Allen Lane, 2018).

[191] For the True Node, the date is 4 April.

[192] Solar Fire v9 software, Astrolabe Inc.

[193] More commonly known as The Six Realms of Samsara.

[194] When the ultimatum for Germany to leave Belgium expired at midnight on 4 August 1914.

[195] Image credit: National Museum of Health and Medicine. Henry Nicholls, 'Pandemic Influenza: The Inside Story', *PLoS Biol* 4.2 https://doi.org/10.1371/journal.pbio.0040050

[196] For an excellent authoritative account visit: https://en.wikipedia.org/wiki/Spanish_flu

[197] This article draws on in-depth studies presented at the 2018 UAC Conference in Chicago (*The Astrology of a New Vision of Capitalism*) and The Astrological Association's 2018 60th Anniversary Conference (*The Future of Astrology*). Audio recordings with slides of both talks are available at https://www.uacastrology.com/recordings/UAC-2018-c22997087 and https://astrologicalassociation.com/purchase-recordings/

[198] For a full analysis of the reason for this conclusion and the implications of the past and for the present and future, Gillett, *Economy Ecology and Kindness* and Gillett, *Reversing the Race to Global Destruction*.

[199] DJIA Monthly 1929-2022 To see the diagrams on this and next page in clear sharp full colour visit: https://crucialastrotools.co.uk/A_Key_Turning_Point_in_Human_History.pdf or see the original article: Roy Gillett, 'A Key Turning Point in Human History', *Astrological Journal* 61.1 (January/February 2019), pp.48-53.

[200] If the Fagan/Allen ayanamsa is used for the sidereal calculation.

[201] *Goon Show* fans will remember the full implications of this phrase.

[202] Gillett, 'A Key Turning Point in Human History'.

[203] Ibid. This eclipse chart originally included with other key diagrams in that edition.

[204] Attributed to Confucius and the key theme of Gillett, *Reversing the Race to Global Destruction*.

[205] Ibid. Where a full development of this theme and its implications for modern-day institutions is fully explained.

[206] First attributed to Francis Bacon.

[207] Roy Gillett, 'Working with the Planets', *Astrological Journal* 61.6 (November/December 2019), pp.21-25.

[208] Between 17:07 and 21:12 UT.

[209] The eclipse diagram is on page 213, or to see it in clear sharp full colour visit https://crucialastrotools.co.uk/A_Key_Turning_Point_in_Human_History.pdf or see the original article: Roy Gillett, 'A Key Turning Point in Human History', *Astrological Journal* 61.1 (January/February 2019), pp.48-53.

[210] *Tomorrowland* directed by Brad Bird (Walt Disney Studios, 2015).

[211] ' Roy Gillett, 'Working with the Planets', *Astrological Journal* 62.1 (January/February 2020), p.11.

[212] See page 171-72 and Endnote 154 for explanation of Cyclic Index.

[213] André Barbault, *Planetary Cycles Mundane Astrology* (London: Astrological Association, 2016) tr. Kate Johnston from *Les cycles planétaires*, 2014.

[214] Ibid. p. 152.

[215] Roy Gillett, 'Working with the Planets', *Astrological Journal* 60.6 (November/December 2018), pp.33-38.

[216] Roy Gillett, 'Working with the Planets', *Astrological Journal* 61.1 (January/February 2019), pp.26-28.

[217] Roy Gillett, 'Working with the Planets', *Astrological Journal* 62.1 (January/February 2020), pp.9-14.

[218] Details of world weather in April at https://www.ncdc.noaa.gov/sotc/global/202004

[219] Roy Gillett, 'Working with the Planets', *Astrological Journal* 62.3 (May/June 2020), pp.18-22.

[220] Ibid.

[221] Ibid.

[222] At this time Russia announced its vaccine. With Mars retrograde, it seemed dangerously premature.

[223] Earle, Moral and Ward-Perkins, *The Econocracy*.

[224] Mazzucato, *The Value of Everything*.

[225] Kate Raworth, *Doughnut Economics* (London: Random House, 2016).

[226] For diagram see: https://en.wikipedia.org/wiki/Doughnut_(economic_model)

[227] https://en.wikipedia.org/wiki/Red_Scare

[228] Due to Pluto's path moving inside Neptune's, over 10,000 years (4999 BCE to 4999 CE) their conjunctions occur far more frequently in Taurus and especially Gemini. Starting with only twice in Aquarius and Pisces at the beginning of the period, they increase to five in Taurus. The 1891-92 conjunction was the second of eight in Gemini. Could this indicate the considerable expansion of knowledge the planet has embarked upon, since the Renaissance and Reformation?

[229] Bettina Wagner and Marcia Reed (eds), *Early Printed Books as Material Objects: Proceedings of the Conference Organized by the IFLA Rare Books and Manuscripts Section, Munich, 19-21 August 2009* (Berlin: De Gruyter Saur, 2010), p.11.

[230] Campion, *World Horoscopes*, pp.544-552.

[231] Followed by Neil F Michelsen in the 'Phenomena Section Explanation' (c) SVP SYNETIC VERNAL POINT...) introduction to *The American Ephemeris for the 21st Century* (San Diego: ACS Publications Inc., 1988).

[232] The work of many mundane astrologers anticipating events and the mood of society, especially the remarkable André Barbault, has been preparing the ground for this acceptance.

[233] See endnote 11.

[234] Roy Gillett, 'Conservative leader contest' in 'Working with the Planets', *Astrological Journal* 48.1 (January/February 2006), pp.65-66.

[235] Data given to Annabel Herriott in person.

[236] Nicholas Campion, 'What Would Kepler Say?', Astrological Association Annual Conference keynote presentation, 2009. Recording available at https://www.astrologicalassociation.com/purchase-recordings/

[237] Gillett, *Astrology and Compassion the Convenient Truth*, p.227.

[238] What is the difference between investment bankers insisting their expertise in handling our money is the only way, and so it deserves high reward, and a highway robber demanding 'your money or your life'? It will be interesting to see how their bonus intentions survive the mid-November 2009 Saturn squared Pluto and consequent T-square build up.

[239] For full details refer back to Roy Gillett, 'Working with the Planets', *Astrological Journal* 51.6 (November/December 2009), pp.55-59.

[240] Words by Robert Fripp, *In the Court of the Crimson King* (album, 1969).

[241] From Gerome Ragni and James Rado, 'This is the Dawning of the Age of Aquarius', from the musical *Hair* (1967).

[242] It is salutary to consider that, in addition to the massive amounts of energy we use, most artificial fibres and plastics in furniture, general construction, cars, computers and other electronic devices are manufactured as by-products from petroleum. Beings studying our culture from as far away as we are to the dinosaurs, or even as recent to us as Neanderthal Man, might see our 'great modern world' as populated by a deluded species that derived a narcotic-like pleasure from recklessly pouring out and immersing themselves in black, sticky petroleum – like wasps drowning in honey!

[243] Gillett, *Economy Ecology and Kindness*.

[244] *Working with the Planets* 'The Astrological Journal' July 2011 Vol. 53 No. 4

[245] In the original article, Roy Gillett, 'Working with the Planets', *Astrological Journal* 58.6 (November/December 2016), pp.31-35 and Gillett, *Reversing the Race to Global Destruction*, the Bank of England charter chart is mistakenly based on the Gregorian calendar. The error is corrected here, while still considering the mood during the immediate build-up to the signing and its aftermath.

[246] For a full explanation, see Gillett, *Economy Ecology and Kindness*.

[247] The others are 6 January 2019 and 26 December 2019.

[248] An early-day 06:00 time has been chosen. So, the orientation of both charts is uncertain and equal house cusps are used.

[249] Booming financial markets are not necessarily good news, except for carpetbaggers, who sell at the top and buy back at the bottom. Have we learned nothing from the consequences for ordinary people of the 1929 Wall Street Crash, the 2000 dot.com and the 2008 banking collapses?

[250] Gillett, *Astrology and Compassion the Convenient Truth*

[251] https://www.peep.ac.uk/content/1039.0.html

[252] Neil Spencer, *True as the Stars Above* (London: Orion, 2001).

[253] Joan Quigley, *What Does Joan Say? My Seven Years as White House Astrologer to Nancy and Ronald Reagan* (Secaucus, NJ: Birch Lane Press, 1990).

[254] Gary Sloan in his *Walt Whitman: Sins Against Science*. The two Whitman lines are from *Leaves of Grass*. For further information, visit: http://www.liberator.net/articles/SloanGary/WaltWhitman.html

[255] http://royalsociety.org/about-us/history/

Index

Read Roy Gillett's other books

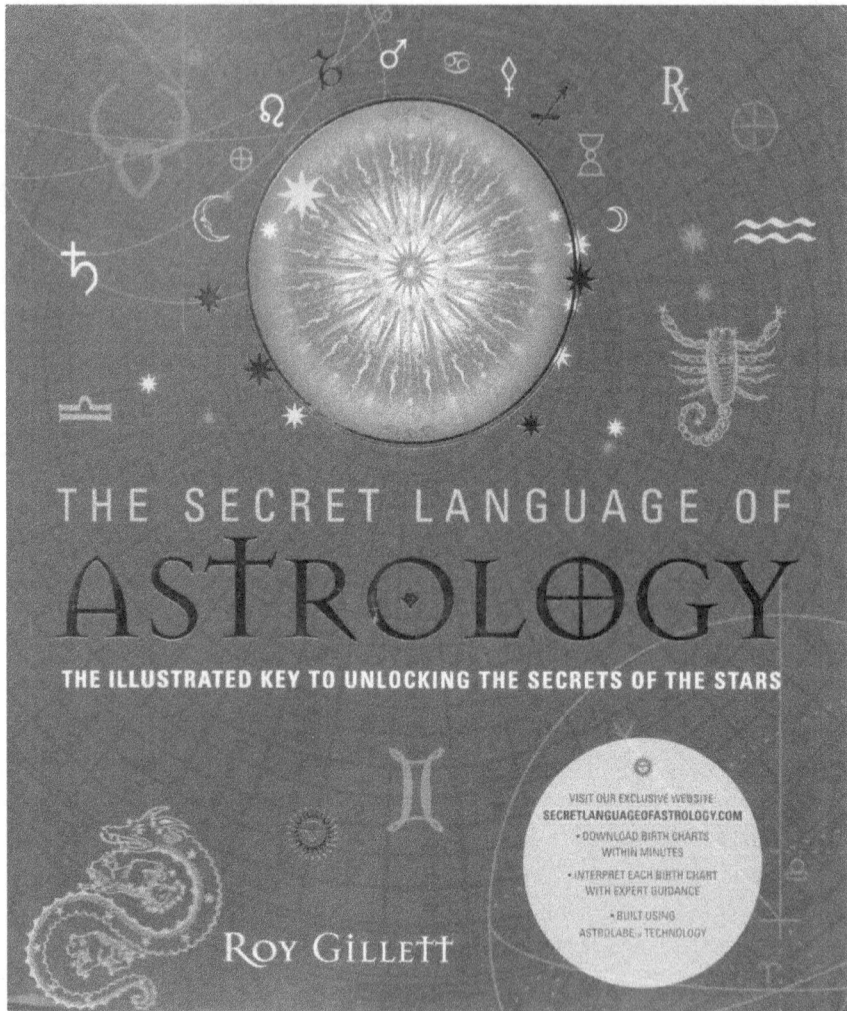

THE SECRET LANGUAGE OF ASTROLOGY

THE ILLUSTRATED KEY TO UNLOCKING THE SECRETS OF THE STARS

VISIT OUR EXCLUSIVE WEBSITE:
SECRETLANGUAGEOFASTROLOGY.COM
• DOWNLOAD BIRTH CHARTS
  WITHIN MINUTES
• INTERPRET EACH BIRTH CHART
  WITH EXPERT GUIDANCE
• BUILT USING
  ASTROLABE™ TECHNOLOGY

ROY GILLETT

Beautifully designed full colour volume, to help you learn astrology from the beginning, or to be a companion to enhance your work and show friends .

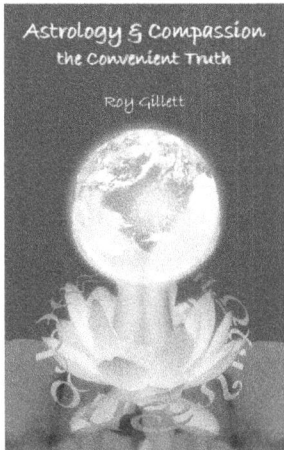

**Astrology & Compassion
the Convenient Truth**
Know the real nature of astrology and its potential to benefit conventional academia and help clarify our legal, financial, social and learning problems.

Economy Ecology and Kindness
This 2009 study describes the astrology underlying the fundamental systemic causes of the two and a half decades that led to the 2008 economic crisis. It then outlines the dangers that laid ahead and the real way to resolve them.

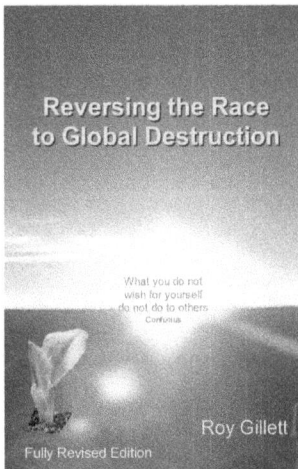

**Reversing the Race to Global Destruction
Abandoning the Politics of Greed**
'Happiness and security do not come from things, but from a world where our actions and our economic, legal, scientific, educational, political and media systems are motivated by principled kindness to each other and the planet.'

Available in hard copy and most E-book formats at all shop and online outlets, or http://crucialbooks.co.uk/

Lightning Source UK Ltd.
Milton Keynes UK
UKHW030615040821
388229UK00005B/161

9 780995 699953